Profitable Top-Line Growth For Industrial Firms

How to Make Any Industrial Firm Grow Profitably

James D. Hlavacek

Co-Author of the Best Selling

Market Driven Management

AMERICAN
BOOK
COMPANY

Printed and Published in the United States of America by
The American Book Company

Managing Editor: Don J. Beville

Book Design: Dennis Michael Stredney

Book Jacket Design: Tuttle Design Studio LTD

Library of Congress Cataloging-in Publication Data

Hlavacek, James D. -1943
Profitable Top-Line Growth For Industrial Firms
With Complete Index

ISBN 0-9710191-0-X   CIP 2001 131670

1. Corporate Growth. 2. Business Strategy. 3. Industrial Marketing.
4. New Business Development. 5. Organizational Change

For information on ordering this book or training workshops please call
The Corporate Development Institute, Inc.
(800) 322-3540 or (704) 366-9024 - Fax: (704) 366-8933
or visit our website at
www.corpdevinst.com

BRIEF CONTENTS

Dedication

Preface

About the Author

Acknowledgements

Contents

Chapters

Index

Order Form

DEDICATION

This book is dedicated to a number of people who have been my mentors and associates. First, Chuck Ames, former chairman and CEO of Reliance Electric, taught me more about industrial marketing than any other person. He was one of the first to appreciate industrial marketing as the general manager's responsibility and to envision that every department and everyone is in marketing. Many of the concepts in this book are Chuck's original notions, and, since we wrote four books together over the past 20 years, I have no idea where his thoughts end and mine begin. Dick Hill, my PhD advisor, was the sole faculty member at the University of Illinois with an understanding of industrial marketing. He focused and inspired me. The late Dr. Bob Adams, senior vice president of research and development at 3M, helped me understand the critical need to couple technology and marketing, and he and other 3Mers, including Desi DeSimone, the CEO, helped make the company my laboratory for many years. For over 20 years I have conducted management development workshops for Parker Hannifin's industrial and aerospace businesses in North America, Europe, South America, and Asia. Pat Parker was the first of many Parker Hannifin CEOs that have been committed to workshops to make marketing the whole company and never just one department. Parker Hannifin's 110+ decentralized divisions and nearly 50,000 employees provided a rich laboratory for experimentation and two-way learning.

Ken Iverson, founder and chairman emeritus of Nucor, taught me the importance of process innovation and the risk of bureaucracy to any business. Dr. Harald Wulff, President and CEO of Henkel KGaA, helped me understand how to organize globally to manage markets, technology, and customers. Ray Corey of the Harvard Business School taught me how to develop and use industrial case studies for management development. The late Phil Hofmann, former chairman of Johnson & Johnson, taught me about good and bad growth and the role of general management in growing a technical business. He also helped me create an annual executive forum on growth, now named for him. The hundreds of CEOs and senior executives who have spoken over the last 30 years at this forum in New York City provided many insights and examples for this book.

Two-way learning occurred in every management development workshop I conducted over three decades. Managers at Cabot Corporation, Henkel, Delphi Systems, Goulds Pumps, Hewlett-Packard, 3M, Loctite, National Starch and Chemical, Parker Hannifin, Sealed Air, and The Timken Company especially stand out for their insights and challenging questions over many years. Finally, thanks to the managers from all over the world, some who are no longer with us, who attended my workshops and taught me so much. All these people contributed to the management practices found throughout this book.

In this preface, I will describe this book's purpose, focus, target audience, and structure.

Purpose:

For every fast-growing new-age company, there are dozens of industrial companies that are desperately searching for more profitable top-line growth. Shareowners expect an attractive return on their investment. In the 1990s, executives could earn big paychecks by merely cutting costs. These days, CEOs and general managers are expected to expand their businesses, or they may lose their jobs. The tenure of corporate chiefs is becoming shorter and shorter. There is no place to hide. Most CEOs are asking how they can create more value. Executives at most slow-growing industrial firms know that they are expected to profitably grow the top line and they are being closely watched.

If you back out the acquisitions made by most industrial companies, you will find little, or no, organic growth. Why have many large industrial companies stopped growing? A study by the Conference Board showed that the major reason companies stop growing is their management practices, not just uncontrollable factors and excuses. Most slow, stagnant, and shrinking situations are caused by management - - - their mindsets, their strategies, their risk-averse cultures, their complacency, and the fact that few industrial companies know how to implement the industrial marketing concept. High value creation is accessible to any company and in any industry. If you pull the right levers, there is no excuse for not growing organically. Every industrial business can be a growth business if it understands and implements the industrial marketing concept across the entire organization.

Any company can cut costs, sell businesses, and make acquisitions. Even after a good-fitting acquisition is made, you still need to grow the acquired business. Great companies don't just buy and sell businesses; they relentlessly build and improve their businesses from within to increase customer and shareowner value over the long term. In short, this book is about organically building and profitably growing any industrial business. This is not a book about short-term balance sheet management, financially driven companies, or a management fad driven by unaccountable consultants. You can make any business in any industry look good for a few years with slash-and-burn tactics and financial engineering. However, long term, you must organically generate profitable top-line growth, or the business will go backward.

The organic growth practices of hallmark industrial companies mentioned throughout this book are what ultimately separate the winners from the losers in any industry and in any part of the world.

Leading industrial companies constantly learn what products and services the market needs and will buy. They don't live in a static world trying to sell only what they can make. Instead, they design and make what they can sell, sometimes moving beyond existing products, raw materials, and process technologies to do so. These same persistent companies accelerate growth in so-called mature markets, while continually making their processes more cost effective. They don't seek sales growth just for growth's sake or simply to become bigger. They know that learning, speed, and adaptability count more than size. And that bureaucracy and size often create a slow-moving, drifting, and declining organization. They seek sales growth and productivity improvements to become and remain the most profitable in their industry and they create a work environment where people are highly motivated, challenged, recognized, and rewarded for good results. They manage very close to their customers and move responsibility and accountability as low as possible in the organization. Empowerment is not a buzzword in high-performance companies, where highly motivated people enjoy coming to work. Employees in these mostly "bottom-up" organizations don't just react or try to predict the future; they are proactive in plotting strategies for businesses in which they think like customers and serve the needs of shareowners.

Focus:

The focus of this book is about making industrial marketing the process by which you transform an industrial enterprise to consistently grow faster and more profitably. This approach to marketing underscores that everyone in every industrial company is in marketing and that it is never just the concern of the marketing department. Industrial marketing must be a way of life that permeates every department and every person in the company. The traditional boundaries between departmental functions are linked by cross-functional business teams that are responsible for weaving marketing into every decision and plan. Cross-functional business teams and business unit managers are the new age industrial marketing "department" that creates increased value for customers and for shareowners.

This is a lot more than a book about industrial marketing and sales. It is a book about how to make marketing the headlights of the business and how to make marketing a vital part of every department, and every person's job. It is also a book about how to focus on attractive opportunities and then align the organization to rapidly and profitably capture them. This book stresses the need for big companies to focus and act like a group of smaller companies, but with the resources of a large company. Small can be beautiful, fast, informal, and very profitable.

Most of the examples in this book are from fast-growing industrial firms. Some of the examples are from slow-growing and shrinking industrial companies in trouble. While numerous books have been written about consumer goods marketing, this book is dedicated to the neglected and different needs of industrial or business-to-business managers. Many of the approaches to developing and marketing consumer goods and retailing techniques are useless to industrial companies.

Over the past 30 years, I have consulted and conducted management development programs with thousands of industrial managers around the world. I have had the privilege of getting inside some of the really great growth companies, and I have been an ongoing part of their in-house management development programs for 10, 15, and in some cases more than 20 years. High-impact management training sessions with the employees and management teams of these industrial companies have uncovered good and bad practices never found in a consulting survey or business school case study. Unlike academics who write about what they think, I have written about what practitioners have tried and lived through. Also, for each of the last 30 years I have had the privilege of conducting an annual forum in New York City on successful internal growth strategies, whose CEOs from well-run companies have shared their practices. More than 400 CEOs have spoken at this annual senior executive program, where they openly share lessons learned from their successes and mistakes. Many of their experiences and guidelines are described in every chapter.

Target Audience:

This book is first intended for CEOs, group presidents, and general managers of industrial companies. If this top management team doesn't understand the industrial marketing concept (and most don't), the concept will not get the commitment and necessary companywide implementation. The mindset of profitable top-line growth starts at the top and then it must permeate the entire organization. Next, this book is obviously intended for those people who have the word marketing in their titles. However, when these people fully understand that marketing should be the entrepreneurial compass of the enterprise, they need a lot of help from those people without marketing titles who are in areas including engineering, manufacturing, technical service, finance, and sales. The people outside of the marketing department are a vital part of the cross-functional teams that must shape and implement the industrial strategies that design, make, communicate, and deliver customer value. When cross-functional business teams and industrial leaders understand and implement the concepts in this book, profitable top-line growth, and shareowner value will accelerate. This book should serve as a handbook for business teams developing winning growth strategies in any industrial manufacturing or service enterprise.

This book exposes a number of growth practices that have succeeded and some that have failed in industrial companies. The purpose of examining failures in this book is not to condemn the companies but to learn from their mistakes. Great companies realize that failure always provides positive information and that learning never occurs without some mistakes. Companies that deny or neglect to learn from failures have a good chance of going backward because they are probably repeating the same mistakes. High performing industrial companies are learning organizations that are driven by a try, fail, learn, and try again mentality.

Structure:

All the chapters provide guidelines of what industrial marketing can do to accelerate profitable top-line growth across the entire enterprise. While there is logic to the sequence of chapters, each chapter was developed as a freestanding module and is informative on its own. This adds a great deal of flexibility to the way the book is read and used. This format also allows the book to serve as a handbook or reference manual. Obviously missing are discrete chapters on globalization, the Internet, and information technology. These subjects have been woven into material where they apply, rather than presented as abstract discussions in separate chapters.

The style of this book is very straightforward and without buzzwords and unproven academic theories. First, the book describes the obstacles that need to be removed from any industrial company if it intends to accelerate profitable top-line growth. Second, the foundations and winning strategies needed to accelerate organic growth are described. The last chapter is a self-evaluation diagnostic to help cross-functional business teams determine the areas for improvement necessary to achieve profitable growth. The diagnostic can be performed by any cross-functional business team as an audit of their business unit's capabilities. In short, this book offers solid guidance for any industrial company that wants to manage itself like a great growth company. It will assist business teams to better manage markets, technology, and customers. The book will help industrial managers throughout the company pull the right growth levers.

Even though I'm an American, I spend much of my time working in companies outside of the United States. A number of the examples in this book are from European and Asian headquartered companies. I have found well run and sleepy industrial companies on every continent, in every country and in every industry. Contrary to the belief of many Americans, we do not have a monopoly on brainpower and common sense, which is what good management is all about. Whether a company is headquartered in Germany, Japan, Taiwan, or the United States is irrelevant. This book is the result of searching for excellence and profitable top-line growth in industrial firms all over the world.

Finally, please remember the saying, "Only diamonds are forever." Fortune magazine every year lists the best-managed and most admired companies in America. The Financial Times newspaper in London does the same for Europe. However, the companies named in these lists change from year to year. Some new company names appear each year, and those that vanish rarely ever reappear. I truly hope that the organic-growth machines mentioned as great industrial companies in this book will remain at the leading edge and become even greater. However, as a realist I must accept the fact that many great companies will lose their edge and will never catch up and regain respected positions. The main lesson of this book is simple: Learn from today's best industrial companies while they are great and then move on to learn from whomever tomorrow's industrial growth machines may be.

ABOUT THE AUTHOR

James D. Hlavacek has more than 30 years of industrial experience and is an internationally recognized executive educator, businessman, and industrial strategy consultant. Jim Hlavacek is an executive counselor to the top and general management of many of the world's largest industrial companies. He has a unique combination of business experience, practical publications, presentation skills, and academic credentials. Jim Hlavacek is the Executive Director of The Corporate Development Institute, Inc., a leading executive development and consulting firm based in Charlotte, North Carolina. His firm has major clients that include Alcoa, AlliedSignal, AMP, Bendix, Borden Chemical, Cabot, Carboloy, Caterpillar, Cincinnati Milacron, Cytec, Delphi Systems, Diebold, Engelhard, H.B. Fuller, General Electric, Goulds Pumps, Henkel, Hewlett-Packard, ICI, ITT Industries, Herman Miller, Kennametal, Morgan Crucible, National Starch and Chemical, Packard Hughes Electronics, Parker Hannifin, Quest, Sun Oil, and The Timken Company.

He is a frequent speaker and workshop leader at national and global company meetings. Dr. Hlavacek is the author of five books including the best-selling book, Market Driven Management, co-authored with B. Charles Ames. He has written more than 40 practical industrial marketing and strategy articles that have appeared in leading publications, including five in the Harvard Business Review.

For 20 years, Dr. Hlavacek was the editor-in-chief of Industrial Marketing Management, the leading international journal of industrial marketing published in New York and Holland. He is a past vice president and director of the American Marketing Association, and was head of the marketing department at Case Western Reserve University for many years. In his earlier career, he was in direct and distributor sales with a chemical manufacturer. Dr. Hlavacek has conducted management development programs at many universities including Columbia, Penn State, Stanford, Wisconsin, The London Business School and Tokyo University. He has received numerous awards from executives for excellence in teaching. He has developed and presented more than 1,000 in-house executive programs to help make marketing the entrepreneurial compass and growth vehicle for industrial firms around the world. About half of his management development programs and consulting assignments are conducted outside of North America.

Jim Hlavacek received a BS from Southern Illinois University; an MBA in industrial management from Louisiana Tech; and a PhD in industrial marketing from the University of Illinois at Urbana-Champaign. Jim Hlavacek is on the Board of Directors of three industrial companies: Nucor Steel, Hargraves Technology, and Xtek. He lives in Charlotte, North Carolina, with his wife, three children, and two golden retrievers.

James D. Hlavacek
Executive Director

The Corporate Development Institute, Inc.
P.O. Box 470188
Charlotte, NC 28247-0188
www.corpdevinst.com

Phone: 704/366-9024
Fax: 704/366-8933
Email: jhlavacek@corpdevinst.com

ACKNOWLEDGMENTS

The research, editing, numerous revisions, and word processing of this book were an enormous undertaking. I am grateful to our staff at Market Driven Management, Inc., a division of The Corporate Development Institute, who contributed to this project while attending to the daily operating tasks of serving our clients around the world. I especially want to acknowledge, Donis Andrews, Nancy Barrett, Nancy Burton, Karen Doran, and Gery Dorazio.

Sue Nodine did an excellent job of editing and proofreading. I would also like to thank our publisher, Don Beville at the American Book Company, who provided many useful guidelines, suggestions, and deadlines. I would like to also thank Peggy Tuttle at Tuttle Design Studio for designing the dust jacket for the book.

Finally, my wife, Ursula, children Jimmy, Annie, and Cindy, and our golden retrievers, Teva and Mandy, were patient over the long period it took to develop this book.

CONTENTS

CONTENTS

CONTENTS

CONTENTS

CONTENTS

CONTENTS

CONTENTS

CONTENTS

Relearning How to Grow

"We are inward looking, complacent, arrogant, and insufficiently entrepreneurial."
Sir John Jennings, Chairman and CEO
Royal Dutch Shell

With all the focus and press coverage about big mergers, consolidations, reengineering, restructuring, and downsizing, followed by round after round of job cuts, it's logical to ask, what's next? In other words, what does a company do after it streamlines its organization, goes on an acquisition-buying spree, and then continues the cycle of job cuts? My answer is simple: Grow the business! You may have cut your way to improved profitability, but you have not, and cannot, achieve profitable top-line growth just through cost savings. The purpose of any business is to continually find and keep profitable customers. Obvious as this answer may seem, I am constantly amazed at the number of companies whose CEOs and management teams, for some reason, don't seem to get it.

I spend about 180 days every year traveling to many of the largest companies in the world to consult and conduct management development programs. A large number of those days are spent outside of North America advising European, Latin American, and Asian companies on how to profitably grow the top line with sound internal growth approaches. Most of these companies generate more than $2 billion in annual sales, and many are in the $10 billion to $30 billion size range. They have between 4,000 and 150,000 employees, and most have operations scattered across many continents. When I arrive at their world headquarters to meet the chief executive officer or the top management team, their common concerns usually go something like this:

> We have had little or insufficient top-line growth in our existing businesses over the past years. Competition is intense, and our markets are mature. We are not as entrepreneurial as we once were, and there is a lack of urgency. Our people don't think out of the box. We had two pricey consulting firms here. They sent in some young MBAs who told us some very similar things – raise prices, cut costs, reorganize, and, if that didn't work, sell the businesses and redeploy our assets. We haven't had a price increase in three years, and with excess capacity and foreign and smaller competitors always cutting prices, we can't pursue a simple cure. Some of our acquisitions over the past years have masked our lack of organic growth. Even after we make an acquisition and reduce the head count and expenses, we see little top-line growth, and then the profit plateaus. A couple of the acquisitions that the consultants and investment bankers advised us to buy were disasters. These acquisitions took a lot of time and resources away from our core businesses. If the stock analysts understood our stagnant situation, our stock price would drop like a boat anchor.

My assignment is essentially the same at each of these multibillion dollar and multinational organizations: to identify the deficiencies and then train their general managers and business teams to profitably grow their businesses. In contrast to most consultants who pretend they know the client's business well enough to plot strategies for them, I train industrial business teams in practical and proven ways to profitably grow, and then I get out of their way so they can accelerate top-line growth.

FOUR MANAGEMENT MIND-SETS

The CEOs of nearly every company where I worked have a sincere desire to accelerate internal or organic growth, but their general managers and department managers often have little practical understanding of how to profitably grow the business. Many managers in large companies have no idea of how a successful startup company or a fast-moving entrepreneurial organization thinks, acts, and profitably grows. Unfortunately, many of today's top and general managers have come from the cost-cutting and deal-making schools of thought, so I call these mind-sets "Cost Cutters," "Deal Makers," and "Milkers." The "Great Builders" are the few managers who can create profitable top-line growth. Let's look closer at each of these four mind-sets.

The Cost Cutters

Over the past several years, most companies have gone through some kind of reengineering, restructuring, or downsizing effort. Some of the "right-sizing" efforts have improved the competitiveness of companies and put them in a stronger position to withstand tougher competition and become a real force in global markets. Whatever the effort was called, the objectives were the same: cut costs, eliminate jobs, improve short-term profit, and, by so doing, hope customer and shareowner value increase.

Cost Cutters have no vision for new business opportunities or for what may be on the horizon. He or she is *totally focused on short-term results*. Cost Cutters are comfortable firing competent employees if it advances their personal financial position or career path. Some of the chain saw cuts have later turned out to be "dumb-sizing." These slash-and-burn executives have too often cut too deep and mortally wounded the culture and the people who do the work to organically grow the company. Understandably, Cost Cutters are lost when it comes to creating an entrepreneurial focus that identifies profitable growth opportunities and then internally develops new products, new services, and new markets.

Great growth companies know they cannot save their way to greatness. Cost reduction and productivity improvements should be an established way of life in every industrial organization. Six Sigma is another cost reduction program that does not address how to profitably grow the top line. However, since Six Sigma is so bottom line focused, it fits the short-term orientation of many companies that have little or no organic growth. The growth approaches in this book are much more robust and enduring than Six Sigma cost reductions.

As I see it, too many companies have taken the necessary steps to become cost competitive only to fail miserably in their efforts to organically build sales. It almost looks as though management teams in many of these companies concluded that their job was done after they laid off a lot of people, cut costs, and watched their paychecks increase. Cutting costs alone doesn't build a business or create long-term shareholder value. You simply cannot be successful over the long term unless you have a solid upward trend in profitable top-line sales from organic sales growth. Job creation (which should mitigate job losses from restructuring and downsizing) depends largely on organic sales growth.

The Deal Makers

In a well-known chemical company, the CEO told me, "We need to make a big acquisition soon because we are experiencing very little real growth in our core businesses." Many of today's "professional managers" say they are growing the business when they have actually been hiding their failure to organically grow by externally acquiring one firm after another. In another industrial equipment company, where they made 26 acquisitions over the preceding seven years, top management was dumbfounded when many general managers said, "Our most urgent need is to develop new products and pursue growth markets in growing countries." The Deal Makers who ran this company didn't have a clue how to stimulate new product development or focus on new markets and business development.

Small acquisitions that involve a product line or a new technology platform can often be very successful. But contrary to popular belief, healthy company growth usually is not created from large acquisitions.[1] More than half of all large acquisitions fail and are later divested (now called "demergers" by the investment bankers, lawyers, and consultants who feed on them), and fewer than 25 percent earn back at least their cost of capital for the investment.[2] Another report by KPMG, a consultancy, concluded that over half of all acquisitions destroyed shareholder value and a further third made no discernable difference.[3] *Large acquisitions inevitably divert a huge amount of time and resources from organic growth.* Acquisitions often create euphoria with no one even thinking about the risk and downside of the deal. Poor integration and unrealistic expectations from so-called synergies are common disappointments for acquirers and their shareowners. The approach of many takeovers is aggressive and with a pirate like mentality that severely upsets morale. When highly dissimilar cultures are forced to marry, culture clashes and collisions are inevitable. The minute a large acquisition is announced, headhunters and competitors try to encourage the best people to leave the targeted organization. Many of the key people leave the acquired company within the first year. And what do you have when the best and most experienced people leave a business you just paid a lot for?

When top-level managers are obsessed with immediate profits, tax carry-forwards, high leverage, P/E ratios, derivatives, asset swaps, leveraged buyouts (LBOs), and junk bonds (now called high-yield instruments), there is little chance for internal growth to have a real effect. Balance sheet managers were the ones who created many of the failed conglomerates and big mergers of the last two decades. The only consistent winners in mergers, acquisitions, and divestitures appear to be the investment bankers, lawyers, and accountants who are paid big fees for their questionable mating recommendations. However, despite those few acquisitions that work out, every company is awakened to the fact that they must still profitably grow the acquisition, which always requires making a product or service that customers need and then selling it at an attractive profit.

The Milkers

If you milk a cow and don't feed it, it will stop giving milk and then die. Some of the cost cutters and dealmakers become "Milkers." A large number of these people don't understand the business enough to make the decisions needed to grow the top line. Many are glorified financial analysts or "bean counters" with no solid operating experience. Some of these Milkers run divisions of good companies into the ground. Many of the Milkers intend to spend a short time in their current job or in the company before they hop to their next-best opportunity. Sometimes they are promoted to group or executive vice presidents, or even CEOs. Their outcomes are identical to the Cost Cutters: Create an improved profit picture over a very short time period. When someone else inherits their job or the business a few years later, the inheritor is blamed for all the downward trends.

Any company can look great in the short term – just reduce the number of people, reduce maintenance expenditures, reduce research and development costs, reduce capital equipment investments, reduce training and development, and reduce marketing. If you basically run a company to maximize cash flow (as is taught in many business schools), you will liquidate the company. If you really want to grow the company organically, patient capital is needed. To grow, you usually need to hire people with particular skills – not just fire every eighth employee every six months and reduce head counts! Creating jobs and capturing markets and growth opportunities for employees are irrelevant to financial engineers; thinking about attractive growth opportunities and the kind of resources and people needed to capture those opportunities are not on their radar screens. The mentality of organic growth is foreign to a financial engineer milking the business.

The Great Builders

These growth-minded managers are driven from within themselves to create more customer value, create employee growth opportunities, and create more shareowner value. They are creators of long-term value for all the stakeholders, not just for some short-term stockholders and a few executives with huge short-term pay schemes. They get excited about growth markets, new products, and growing a business. They see the ride as being as much fun as getting good results. They are innovators who often ignore conventional wisdom and go where others do not. They are often called mavericks because they don't always go with the flock or support the popular notions. While pursuing organic growth, they may also make acquisitions that have a clear strategic fit. These managers buy and then build with smaller acquisitions. They don't buy and then slash and burn and suck cash out of acquired organizations. In public companies, they know they must simultaneously grow the top and bottom lines. The best builders strike a balance between earnings growth and sales growth. They realize that in the long run, profitable top-line growth is the basis for long-term stock appreciation. They know that the right people with the right skills are needed for organic growth. They also know that a well-motivated and smart work force will serve customers and shareowners well. Therefore, recruiting, coaching, development, and training of people are priorities. They are constantly concerned with attracting and keeping the best talent. These leaders are more concerned with leveraging their intellectual capital than with leveraging their balance sheet. These leaders and their managers lead with growth ideas, not by fear or by threats of more downsizing.

The Builders know that growth is imperative for companies in any industry. In the long run, they know it's profitable growth or die. Regardless of the industry or size of the company, research has shown that the most successful companies in the world have continued to grow because they have continued to change. Frequently, these leading companies have either invented totally new industries or completely reinvented existing businesses. These same companies don't live in the past; they create an evolving or changing culture that is always learning and open to changing any past practice if it gets in the way of healthy top-line growth. In short, these builders have the mindset needed to restart and accelerate organic growth.

RESTARTING ORGANIC GROWTH

The challenge is to take a mature company and transform it to more rapidly grow the top line and sustain bottom line profit. In many situations, this process requires the company to learn or relearn how to organically grow.

In a management-training workshop a group of managers voiced real concern about several obstacles to organically growing their businesses. The obstacles they saw were:

- Customers are demanding more product performance, better service, and lower costs.
- New products take too long to develop and are not always demonstrably better.
- Product life cycles are getting shorter.
- Response times of smaller competitors are faster.
- The strength of global competitors is increasing.
- Organic growth has stopped when acquisitions were subtracted out.

Individually, any of these concerns present a serious challenge. Combined, the list was overwhelming and even frightening to this management team. Most industrial companies are faced with similar threats. How should management react? How can management cope with such a broad array of complex problems? They must find viable solutions soon. The emergence of forces and events such as those just mentioned is an inevitable result of our more turbulent world, and it can threaten the very survival of most companies – and even entire industries –

unless they respond faster and more effectively than they have thus far.

After being on a cost reduction crusade for the last decade, Shell's most pressing problem is how to organically grow. Their candid CEO stated:

> Our growing cash hoard of over $12.5 billion is an indictment of our collective failure to bring forward sufficient investment opportunities. Our return on average capital employed has dropped to 7.9 percent, far below our cost of capital and the 9.3 percent average return by the other major oil companies. We are bureaucratic, inward looking, complacent, self-satisfied, arrogant, and insufficiently entrepreneurial. We are struggling to answer the all-important question, "How to grow?" Four different armies of consultants are helping us. We are moving forward briskly into the fog. [4]

Xerox, whose name is synonymous with photocopying all over the world, has faced a host of problems over the past decade. Among them; faster moving competitors, especially Sharp, Minolta and Ricoh from Japan and Canon is now the technological and market share leader; the convergence of copiers and printers with Hewlett-Packard's and Lexmark's printers used for a lot of tasks that Xerox stand-alone machines were used for; and a sales force that has long been organized by geography and large accounts is now trying to be organized by industries or market segments without the proper training and direction[5]. Xerox is playing catch-up on many fronts.

The business world is unquestionably a much tougher place today than it has been in the past. Increasingly volatile changes in the business environment for any firm have greatly increased uncertainty and unpredictability for all industrial companies. Of course, business environments have always been subject to change. What is different today are the frequency and velocity with which changes are occurring and the dramatic effect these changes can have on business results. Some of the harsh realities that face every manager, not just Shell, and Xerox, include the following:

1. Customers are consolidating and becoming smarter and more demanding in terms of response time, product performance, better service, and they resist price increases even if they are flourishing.
2. Global competition is no longer a scattered occurrence. Today, it represents an immediate threat in every market of consequence and in every region of the world.
3. Exploding technology has shortened product and process life cycles and greatly increased the risk of payback on the development investment that must be made simply to keep pace.
4. Lower-cost suppliers and competitors with lower profit goals plague every significant market, and the scramble to remain profitable puts more pressure on managing than ever before.
5. There is excess global capacity in many industries, which, in turn, puts dramatic pressure on prices around the world.
6. Profit margins are flat or declining, and, at the same time, requirements for new product and process improvements are increasing, while the costs of serving markets and key customers are trending upward.

Faced with these conditions, profitable organic growth will only be achieved by companies whose leaders recognize the dramatic differences in today's business environment and have the fortitude to make the wrenching changes necessary to ensure that their organizations adjust to the new rules of every industrial marketplace.

ROADBLOCKS TO ANY TRANSFORMATION

To achieve a transformation such as that faced by Xerox or Shell, the baggage from the past – old habits, practices, attitudes, and behavior – must be shed. Unless such baggage is shed, the required changes cannot or will not be made. There are nine common roadblocks that will inevitably make it difficult for any company to make the kind of transformation that is needed:

1. A company's past success causes it to stay with the same culture and strategy too long.
2. Smarter industrial customers seek more cost-effective solutions that improve their customer and shareowner value.
3. Reluctance on the part of many managers to face the real facts about their markets, costs, and competitive positions.
4. Failure to recognize the crucial importance of being a lower-cost global supplier.
5. Lack of focus on target markets, key accounts, their unique requirements, and their unmet and unarticulated needs.
6. Self-satisfaction with existing products and the company is then vulnerable to shifting customer needs, better competitive products, and new technologies.
7. Lack of focus and speed in the research and development group that has become conditioned to earning a living by working on technically interesting projects.
8. Lack of skill and focus in the sales groups that have become accustomed to simply socializing and taking orders.
9. Excessive management levels, bureaucracy, and too much of an autocratic or top-down approach to managing businesses, product lines, and different market segments.

Let's now examine these nine roadblocks in greater detail and how they are obstacles to transforming any slow-growth industrial company.

Past Success Syndrome

Many successful companies get into trouble because of the 'success syndrome.' They have a proven culture, strategy, and programs that work and then they stay with it all too long. The company gets very good press, much of what is deserved, some of which is not. Many employees believe the company's propaganda. An unhealthy sense of well-being engulfs the company. They do not question what they do or how they do it. These companies try to live off their past success. They talk about how great they are when they are losing market positions, investor confidence, and good people. Any shortcomings are blamed totally on external causes – never management. Xerox's name is synonymous with photocopying because it was the pioneer that created the industry. But as IBM found out and Xerox is now learning, a great name or brand name is never enough to sustain an industrial business. They become internally focused and preoccupied with what's happening inside their organization. They measure themselves against internal measures. They do not continually benchmark with competitors all over the world.

Lucent Technologies' senior executives became blinded by five years of double-digit sales and profit growth and a soaring stock price. Lucent engineers desperately wanted to develop fiber optic products that could move Internet traffic at four times the speed of their current optical networking equipment. Lucent executives were more influenced by their oldest and largest customer and former parent, AT&T, that was considered rigid, slow moving, and not a technological visionary. When Lucent failed to develop the next generation optical networking gear, its main rival, Nortel Networks of Canada, leapfrogged Lucent's old technology. Nortel is now several times Lucent's size in optical networking gear. Lucent got into big trouble by being slow, listening to even slower customers and promising too much to Wall Street.[67]

Few would dispute the claim that Nokia's growth has been Europe's outstanding business success story of the past decade. When asked what is the biggest threat to his company, Nokia's CEO states without hesitation, complacency. Nokia's CEO knows that most successful companies, especially in high technology, have a self-belief that borders on arrogance. But those that stay successful combine it with a restless determination never to underestimate the competition or what Andy Grove, Intel's chairman, calls "healthy paranoia."

Another bittersweet reward of success is that most big companies lose interest in going after emerging markets. With product life cycles getting shorter and shorter, there is a greater need for rapidly entering new markets. These same previously successful companies are no longer driven by an obsession to increase customer value, which, if done properly, will translate into more shareowner value. There is a degree of complacency within each of us. Continued complacency among individuals or an organization is guaranteed to lead to mediocrity or worse. In short, every successful company's greatest competition is its past success.

More Demanding Customers

Industrial customers don't just buy things for their personal use. They buy solutions to needs that will save or make the company money. Finding out what problems industrial users are having is the first step in being market driven. The following two examples show that industrial customers don't just buy things or technology, they buy solutions for specific problems or needs, and they have choices between different types of products to solve each problem:

- Cleveland Twist Drill Company realized that customers didn't want to buy quarter-inch drill bits—they wanted to make quarter-inch holes! In some situations, a punch press was effective to make holes; in other situations a laser beam effectively made holes, and in only certain applications was a quarter-inch drill cost effective.
- Loctite, the well-known adhesives manufacturer, realized that customers weren't just buying an adhesive to bond items together. They were sealing and connecting things together, and they could use adhesives, welding, nuts and bolts, fasteners, or rivets to connect and seal. Many customers evaluated these alternative solutions before choosing one to seal or bond things together.

These examples show that an industrial buyer is always searching for a cost-effective solution to a problem. Market strategies and the accompanying service/product packages must be developed in ways that will attract and keep customers in a cost-effective way. Industrial suppliers must demonstrate and distinguish themselves and their offerings from those of others so users will want, or at least prefer, to do business with them. Industrial marketing is all about differentiating your products and services. Successful differentiation gives current and potential customers compelling reasons to want to do business with a specific supplier. To effectively differentiate a service/product package, a supplier must learn what drives and retains customers. It also requires knowing how groups of customers differ from one another and how the differences can be grouped into commercially viable market segments and served with a better service/product package.

Reluctance to Face Facts

Many companies that have lost profits or market share have managers who are still waiting patiently for their business to "get back to normal." Others are looking for government assistance (e.g., import restrictions or tax subsidies) for their declining market and profit positions. Neither of these approaches is a viable solution. Less wishful dreaming and rhetoric and greater willingness to squarely face the true facts about their markets and competitive positions are what is needed. The changes that have occurred in many markets are structural, not cyclical, and it is unrealistic to expect any kind of dramatic recovery or turnaround that will restore business practices to the "good old days" that increasingly are the "bad old ways."

It is extremely difficult for managers who have built their entire careers around specific products and technologies to accept the fact that their former business base has now leveled out below prior peaks or, worse yet, become obsolete or irretrievably lost to new competitors or technologies. For example, 3M was blindsided by the impact of laptop computers and digital projectors on its overhead projector and transparency businesses. Obviously, many old-line steel managers did not imagine today's world of aluminum cans, plastic auto parts and bodies, and small regional minimills that recycle scrap metal. Nor did managers in the high-flying and glamorous semiconductor business foresee the situation in which their markets not only ceased to gallop ahead but declined dramatically and in which foreign sources, including Brazil, Korea, and Taiwan, captured the bulk of the remaining business. Unfortunately, these are the facts, and an equally discouraging set of forces applies in many other markets.

Being a Lower-Cost Supplier

Increased competition plus the drive for greater efficiency and productivity inevitably lead to excess regional or global capacity. Excess capacity, in turn, makes price an increasingly important factor in the buying decision, and lower prices rapidly cut into profit margins unless total unit costs trend downward. Others make domestic cost comparisons but overlook foreign competitors who are the real long-term threats. A study on manufacturing competitiveness shows that some U.S. and Western European manufacturers still operate at a 20+ percent cost disadvantage to foreign competitors and, more importantly, lose ground on productivity by a margin of two to one. It is not surprising that so many manufacturers are faced with such a disadvantage; they are burdened with:

- Plant, equipment, and manufacturing methods that have not been upgraded to meet global market demands for lower cost, higher quality, and shorter production cycles.
- Labor, engineering and administrative costs and productivity improvements that are noncompetitive by any measurable global standard.
- A balance sheet that is inflated with underutilized or obsolete plants and equipment, antique inventories, and excessive working capital.
- An unrealistically high break-even point with a resulting profit level that does not generate sufficient funds to sustain the business and satisfy shareowners.

Even with all of the reengineering, restructuring, and downsizing that has occurred, a surprisingly high percentage of established companies are still intolerably saddled with many of these items. Also, with more and more companies scouting the world for much lower costs, the situation is unlikely to improve. A business can have the most innovative, brilliant, hard working managers in the world and can pursue the most ingenious marketing and sales strategies, but if it is encumbered with a lot of the baggage just described, there is no way it can be fully competitive, and no amount of hard work or management brilliance can make up for this deficiency.

Lack of Target Market Focus

Most industrial manufacturing companies still try to be everything to everyone. They are product, manufacturing, or sales driven, and they are either pushing products at customers or simply trying to keep their plants full. These same companies don't understand market segmentation or how to target the most attractive markets. They think they understand marketing and yet they equate one customer with a market segment. At the other extreme, they talk about billion-dollar industries as if they were market segments. Market segments are $30 million to $50 million opportunities with similar needs, not billion-dollar industries such as electronics, agriculture, or transportation. These same naïve companies do not understand how to define a market segment (which is a group of customers with common needs), how to select the most attractive segments, or how to develop action programs that enable the organization to capture the target opportunities. Knowing how to segment a marketplace is one of the most important strategic skills, yet it is lacking in a majority of industrial firms around the world. The proper definition and selection of market segments determines your mission, identifies competitors, guides strategy development, and determines what technical and commercial capabilities are needed to profitably serve the target customer groups.

Far too many industrial firms cannot even begin to think about market segments and target markets because they have not realized the strategic value of fact-based market information about end-use customers and competition. Even the largest industrial manufacturers do not have professional marketing research capabilities to define market segments or to determine market needs, market potentials, market share, and profit prospects. In situations where presumably such a capability does exist, it is often staffed with people who do not have the professional skills and technical understanding of the business to do a competent job. Most companies rely on very broad market definitions and "seat of the pants" estimates of market needs and potentials. As a result of their failure to properly define, understand, and select the most attractive target markets, they fly half blind, miss opportunities, get caught by unexpected developments, and remain vulnerable to more focused competition.

Self-Satisfaction with Existing Products and Technology

It is easy to find numerous companies that have suffered or failed as a result of being satisfied with yesterday's products, technologies, and processes. For example, U.S. manufacturers of machine tools have lost most of their markets to Japanese and German companies because they did not respond to clear warning signals that pointed to dramatic changes in technology and concentrated only on cosmetic changes to their products. The increasing use of laser systems to drill and machine parts, and the use of adhesives to avoid the need for making holes, as well as the emergence of new coating technologies that greatly extend the life of cutting tools, were factors that were overlooked until a large chunk of the traditional market had disappeared. Similarly, some manufacturers of hydraulic aircraft landing gear have failed to develop or acquire the electronic and software capabilities necessary to participate in the shift to electronically controlled systems that are now standard design for all new retractable landing gear. These producers may continue to reap handsome profits from repairing systems in the large hydraulic after-market for some time; however, they will ultimately be squeezed out of this business as the hydraulically equipped planes are retrofitted with electronics or removed from service.

Self-satisfaction with existing products occurs for several reasons. First, the competitive and technological changes are often not recognized or accepted as serious threats. Denial is a common problem. Even when threats are recognized, nothing is done because the costs and risks of adopting new technologies and cannibalizing existing products are great and frequently incompatible with all the emphasis on short-term profit. The root cause in most cases, however, is the simple fact that technologists steeped in one discipline are reluctant to accept the advantages or superiority of another competing technology. Why? Technical arrogance? How can anyone have a better idea or technology than us? Another fundamental source of resistance to new technology is the unwillingness of many technologists to admit that they are likely to become less needed or perhaps obsolete if the business moves toward a new technology that requires very different capabilities, which they don't always understand. It's hard to admit personally and publicly that your skills are outdated. The need for retraining in new skills is not limited to factory workers where automation has displaced many people.

Lack of Focus and Speed in Research and Development

Many industrial companies possess a great deal of good technology and manufacturing expertise. But these same companies often have difficulty in rapidly taking a good concept from the laboratory and moving it into the marketplace. New product development is the seed corn of most companies' future. Process development is equally important. Without new product and process development, any industrial company will eventually die from severe price competition and declining sales.

A centralized R&D capability is hard to justify; it tends to be unresponsive, esoteric, and too costly. Unless the business units are based on a common technology, nearly all R&D activities should be directed by and charged to the business units. If marketing or the business units do not give R&D such direction, technology people will understandably take the leadership role in setting their own priorities. If there is a need for R&D that is not business-unit driven, it should be contracted out to universities or government laboratories and appropriately charged to a business unit so that it doesn't become a "sink hole" or "pet project." Individual R&D programs should not be initiated unless they focus on specific applications, market needs, and lead users. Whether a company's strategy is to be a first-to-market or a fast follower, both approaches require being very fast. In terms of product development speed, there are only two kinds of companies – the very fast and the dead.

Many R&D people are disturbed when they are pressured to move rapidly to develop new products. However, the days of R&D as an academic place to "rest and dream" are over. Solid business people, who were once researchers, are increasingly the heads of research and development. New products must be developed and launched as if they were perishable fruit. With shorter life cycles and higher costs of developing new products, firm milestones and the productivity measures applied to other areas of the firm need to be applied to R&D expenditures. The speed or urgency of product development should be measured in terms of the number of months it takes from concept to market introduction. The estimated payback period to justify any R&D commitment should be expressed as a percentage of the expected life cycle of the new product. After an agreement is made about the exact definition of a new product, metrics should be developed that show what percentage of sales and gross profit is derived from new products five years old or less. Next, aggressive new product goals should be set to improve sales and gross profits from new products introduced in the next three to four years.

Lack of Skill and Focus in Sales

"We develop good plans but our results are dismal." "We can't seem to get the strong execution we need at the point of sales contact." These are common complaints of many senior executives in industrial companies. The complaints appear to be more frequent now because the battle for increased sales is so tough. However, the problem has existed for many years; it was obscured by high inflation rates and price increases that allowed many salespeople to look better than they really were in terms of achieving record sales levels. Not much skill was required to dine with customers, take orders, and ride the demand curve upward during this period when a lot of dollar volume was also generated through price increases rather than unit gains.

Now, however, the situation is quite different. Most salespeople are faced with the very difficult task of protecting and growing their positions in mature and declining markets against more intense competition. Products are becoming more complex and life cycles shorter. At the same time, customers are far more demanding, sophisticated, and global in their sourcing practices. Consequently, the sales task is undeniably more difficult today than it was just a few short years ago, and a company's sales capabilities must be much stronger just to keep pace.

The problem is compounded because many salespeople are not properly selected, trained, focused, or motivated to perform this more demanding sales job. Most of these deficiencies result from management's failure to recognize how its customers and products have changed. Management has, thereby, failed to make the necessary adjustments in its sales force's capabilities. A large number of sales forces have not been sufficiently upgraded and are still overpopulated with Willie Loman types, who cannot make a satisfactory transition to the new demands of consultative solution and systems selling. Also, most salespeople are not directed toward priority target markets or armed with sufficient product knowledge, application benefits, or side-by-side competitive comparisons to enable them to demonstrate and document real value to specific customer groups. Some sales forces are overloaded with too many product lines, many of which were clipped on from acquisition after acquisition. With such an information overload, there is no way to know it all. Finally, most sales compensation plans are structured in such a way that there are inadequate rewards or penalties for high or low performers. Complacency and mediocrity have become an accepted way of life in many sales organizations.

Excessive Management

Even after all the downsizing, many companies are still top heavy and are largely still top-down in how they manage. Too many management levels result in an inflexible, unresponsive, and top-down bureaucracy. Questionable management levels tend to interfere, micro-manage, slow down, and reduce risk taking in the organization. Excessive levels slow communication and create filters in the information flow and decision-making process. "What the boss doesn't know won't hurt him" becomes the norm with excessive layers, when the motto should be; "Bad news is good news if it is received early." Excessive levels in any organization lead to expensive vice presidents, redundant staff, too many meetings, and questionable assistants. The rest of the organization is charged for these in terms of overhead or general administrative expenses. People in these excessive management levels are highly paid with no customers or products – just costs that profit centers dislike as an overhead allocation. The effectiveness and efficiency of every management level and every management job should be questioned. In short, many companies still have too many chiefs who are just a high cost and who are of questionable value on the income statement.

The *term middle management* has become synonymous with resistance to change, redundancy, and bureaucracy. In a military like hierarchy, there is a real need for many middle-level managers to pass orders and information down through the organization. More middle-level managers are also needed in a top-down organization as the implementers of strategies developed at the top. Today, electronic networks can move information around to many people very efficiently. However, when there are truly empowered business teams with leaders, there is no need for large numbers of middle managers to pass information up and down a hierarchy and "manage" the self-managed business teams. Furthermore, competent business unit teams prefer to work on their own and be measured by sales and profit results – not by constant oversight, reports, and review meetings. With truly decentralized divisions or business teams that are measured and paid by objective results, who needs all the management?

MANAGEMENT RESPONSES

Overcoming these roadblocks and gearing the business for sales and especially profit growth in a turbulent marketplace requires management skills of the highest order. But it doesn't require a whole new array of sophisticated techniques or complex organizational structures. Rather, it demands a more rigorous application of some proven management fundamentals that are nothing more than common sense. However, as Thomas Paine often stated, "The problem with common sense is that it is not commonly practiced." To thoroughly understand and implement these proven and practical industrial marketing practices requires following six fundamentals.

1. Segmenting markets to a far greater degree than was done in the past.
2. Understanding the true profit economics of each product line, key customer, and market segment.
3. Defining the key issues and priorities in each market segment.
4. Reassessing and adjusting market strategies to meet changing market needs.
5. Realigning the organization to a more demanding marketplace.
6. Pushing decision making down as deep as possible in the organization.

Let's now look at each of these six points more carefully.

Segmenting Markets: All Else Follows

Industrial market segmentation is a "close to the customer" process of splitting industries and specific customers into groups with similar needs. The traditional way of segmenting industrial markets by using standard industrial classification (SIC) codes (the new expanded version is termed NAICS) is often too broad or not relevant. Moreover, such broad cuts of a market may show that intelligent marketing decisions are impossible.

Very few general managers realize that the definition and selection of market segments is the most important strategic decision facing every industrial manufacturer. Everything else follows the selection of target markets. The selection of target markets drives competitive analysis, and it determines the type of technology race you are in and what kind of manufacturing, service, and sales capabilities are needed. The definition and selection of target market segments is the first step in focusing any business unit, and the alignment of the rest of the division to target market segments should follow. R&D, manufacturing, and sales should be aligned horizontally to serve specific customer groups. Industry, market, or business unit managers are the organizational mechanisms to manage market segments.

There are two additional reasons for refining market segmentation to a greater degree. First, it is not unusual to find that, if an overall market that appears to be unattractive is sliced into small enough segments, one or more segments that are very attractive can generally be found. If attention is then focused on the most attractive segments, there is a much better opportunity for increasing sales, and especially profit growth. Second, it is wise to assume that some competitors, particularly smaller ones, will segment the market into smaller pieces, select the faster growing and attractive segments, and then capture market share from the companies that have not geared up to serve the smaller segments. As a rule of thumb, any time a market segment is defined in pieces much larger than $40 to $50 million in annual sales potential, it should probably be segmented again because many smart competitors will look for smaller pieces where they can achieve a unique, competitive advantage. Bigger companies often make the mistake of glossing over these smaller segments, saying they have bigger fish to fry. What they overlook is that such thinking allows smaller competitors to get a toehold that can eventually erode their major markets. Bigger companies also forget that all large markets segments start out as smaller emerging markets. The following statement supports this point:

> IBM did not enter a market unless they could identify it as a $100 million opportunity. That is why they missed both minicomputers and desktop publishing opportunities. IBM and most big companies don't realize that every oak tree started out as an acorn. [8]

Understanding the Profit Economics

Understanding the profit economics of each product, customer, and market segment is also an easy point to agree with, and many will respond to it by saying, "We know all that." In most cases, those responding with these words really don't know all that and, in fact, don't know what understanding the profit economics really means.

Let's examine what is meant by the profit economics of a business and then look at the kind of information needed to ensure the thorough understanding essential for solid business planning. The following information is required to understand the profit economics of a business:

- How many dollars of assets are committed in each stage of the business (e.g., R&D, engineering, materials, plant and equipment, finished stock, post-sale support)?
- What is the fixed-to-variable cost relationship for each product/market business; that is, for each dollar of sales, how many cents are attributable to bedrock fixed costs, how many to structured or discretionary costs, and how many to out-of-pocket costs?
- How do costs and profits change with swings in volume?
- What is the break-even point at the current volume? What actions could be taken to bring that break-even point down should volume potential decline?
- What is the rate of incremental profit on each added increment of volume?
- What are the volume points where new increments of structured cost must be added?
- What are your least profitable product lines? Is additional capacity only added based on the least profitable product lines?
- What does it cost to serve each account? Which customers are the most profitable, marginal, and biggest losers?
- In what market segments are share point gains the most lucrative?

A net profit-and-loss statement (after all allocations) and a balance sheet for each division, business unit, and product line are essential for generating answers to these questions. After gross profit, most companies have no idea what it "costs to serve" each customer. Shared, fixed, and indirect charges often represent the most serious cost problems in business situations where a cost disadvantage exists, and they are impossible to attack in the aggregate. They must be broken down and assigned to discrete business units, product lines, and customers, even if done arbitrarily. A manager with profit responsibility can then – and only then – argue about fairness and whether there is value received for the activity and cost allocations.

Although this may not be a precise exercise, it is effective and essential. Without full-costing and profit-and-loss statements for product lines, customers, and market segments, managers cannot really understand the profit economics of their business.

Defining Issues and Priorities

The third step in implementing these practices is to ensure that the key issues facing each business unit or market segment have been realistically identified and prioritized in light of the current and rapidly changing business environment. An issue is a condition or pressure, either internal or external to the business unit that will have a significant effect on a market segment if it continues. By the time "the numbers" start to decline, it is often very hard or even too late to deal with the underlying causes. Issue management is an early warning system for identifying and responding to market threats and opportunities before it is too late. Issue management, for discreet market segments, replaces the old strength, weakness, opportunity, and threat analysis (SWOT) that too often is a macro exercise for a large division rather than for each market segment.

Very few management teams actually take the time to apply the discipline necessary to objectively define and prioritize the key issues that can make or break them in each market segment. For example, the issues of higher-cost products, lower productivity, a lack of new products, and slow delivery plague most manufacturers. Many large companies around the world in industries including computers, steel, automotive, machine tools, textile chemicals, and construction equipment, suffered badly as a result of not identifying and responding to the early warning signals of change. However, only a few companies identified and addressed these issues in an effective way. Most were unable to clearly identify the key issues, set priorities, and develop the necessary programs to overcome the underlying problems. Companies are often so caught up in carrying out their day-to-day work that they rarely, if ever, stop to think objectively about themselves and the bigger picture for each market segment. Some of my clients go off site every quarter to reflect and think about emerging trends in each market segment, the possible regulatory changes, shifting customer needs, new technology, the customer's customers, and likely competitive moves. A general manager, business unit manager, or facilitator leads the off-site session with the cross-functional team. Everyone is encouraged to "get out of the box" with their thinking about the issues. Each person at the meeting should feel free to challenge any assumption or company tradition. Everyone asks "what if" questions, and a number of likely scenarios are generated, combined, developed, or dropped. Without open reflection from everyone, there is a high chance that the business will be caught off guard when it is too late to effectively respond.

While the specific issues certainly vary for different industries and market segments, the management mind-set should not vary. To deal effectively with an increasingly turbulent marketplace, priorities must be set so that the business can survive unexpected blows, adapt to sudden market changes, and capitalize on windows of opportunity that will develop and close much more quickly than they have in the past.

Reassessing Market Strategies

As a general rule, any business unit pursuing the same market strategy today that it did 24 months ago is probably on the wrong track. Too many changes have occurred in markets, competitors, products, and technologies to allow a market strategy to go unadjusted for this length of time. Therefore, management should set aside a block of time to periodically address four fundamental market strategy questions:

1. What markets and business(es) are we in?
2. What markets are we in today that we would not now enter?
3. What markets and business(es) should we avoid?
4. What new markets and business(es) should we be in?

These are not easy questions to answer any time; they are particularly difficult when so many things change so quickly. Failure to raise and respond to these questions, however, can be fatal.

Market strategies must be designed from outside-in to overcome the product and technology constraints that tend to restrict the strategic thinking and actions of so many companies. This is a crucial point since strategic thinking from outside-in opens a wide variety of options. In being market driven, a company is not limited by its existing raw materials or process technology. For example, consider a manufacturer of industrial drills. Should they simply sell a wide range of standard drills as their traditional manufacturing skills might dictate, or should he move beyond his capabilities into special-purpose drills for specific market applications? Or, going even further, should they conclude that they will help customers make holes in the most efficient way possible and consequently move into laser and/or fluid drilling technologies that are used to drill an increasing number of holes? Perhaps they should move into entirely different technologies and manufacture surface coatings that are used to extend the wear life of tools and many critical parts. While none of these options may actually prove to be strategically desirable, they won't even be raised if historical product, technology, and cultural constraints are not removed.

Obviously, there are a number of points to be considered in evaluating any business strategy, but the following four questions can help avoid wasted time spent arguing about "can't win" strategies:

1. Is the strategy designed to serve specific market segments as opposed to simply selling products to everyone?
2. Do the target markets offer attractive sales and profit growth opportunities?
3. Is the cost/profit structure attractive (e.g., break-even point at 35 to 40 percent of capacity, gross margin of 40+ percent, working capital of 30 to 35 percent of sales, return on assets of 20+ percent, and so on)?
4. Is the plan based on demonstrable advantages over the competition? Does the strategy revolve around distinctive and needed customer benefits that provide superior customer value?

Unless these questions can be answered positively, the strategy has little chance of success. Time shouldn't be wasted talking about what is considered to be a no-win plan. Can't win situations are just too tough to overcome, no matter how effectively they are managed or how hard management works.

Realigning the Organization

Organization or reorganization schemes have been proposed ad nauseam solutions to many business problems. As a general rule, organizational changes, especially those that simply reshuffle the same names into different boxes on the organization chart, don't improve anything. I am not suggesting some new organizational approach that is better suited for these turbulent times. However, many organizations are too top heavy, over structured, and over staffed to be responsive to market needs and too costly to be competitive. The management levels and staffing of any organization must be rigorously challenged to ensure that the organization is really geared to accomplish the fundamental objectives of the business in as cost effective a manner as possible. An honest evaluation of the answers to the following critical questions will provide a good foundation for action:

1. Is the organization structured to serve markets or simply to manage functions and sell products to large customers? Have priority markets been identified? Does someone have primary responsibility for ensuring that the service/product package is tailored to each target market? Do mechanisms exist to ensure

cross-functional coordination on markets, especially for the national and global customers? Is there any kind of a market focus in the selling organization?

2. Are there enough discrete profit centers? Do enough managers and cross-functional teams feel the burden and accountability of full profit responsibility? Is the business unit larger than its most successful smaller competitor? Are there any big cost centers that are not allocated or matched to people who have a profit-and-loss responsibility?

3. Are there corporate, group, or division staff redundancies? Do the same titles exist at different levels (e.g., corporate controller, group controller, division controller, plant controller)? If so, does it make sense? Can staff positions or groups show how they actively contribute to profit results? If so, do profit-center managers (those with products and customers) agree that these functions and allocated cost centers are worth the cost?

4. Are there too many management levels? Are there more than two to three levels between the division manager and first-level workers? Are there managers with assignments limited to managing two, three, or four people? Why? Can any of these activities be combined under one manager or run as self-managed teams? Why not?

These questions are not all new, but the answers are more important now than ever. Traditional or experience-based answers are probably wrong because conditions have changed so dramatically. Moreover, it is doubtful whether existing management can or will ever come up with the right answers because they have vested interests and because the changes needed are simply too tough for them to swallow. These organizational structure questions are not as serious for many young and smaller-sized companies because they are not as likely to be troubled with highly structured, functionally focused organizations lacking a dedicated market orientation. However, even managers in these companies must constantly fight the natural tendency to become more structured, bureaucratic, and complacent.

Push Decision Making Lower

The final or sixth management response requires pushing decision making closer to the customer. Most CEOs and upper-level managers talk about how important their people are and how they want more people to be "accountable" and "empowered." Many of the executives using these buzzwords are centralists at heart, and they really don't want to delegate decision making and power to those closer to the customer. Decentralization involves moving most of the tasks, authority, information, and responsibilities downward. True decentralization and empowerment of business teams require that CEOs, senior executives, and general managers *delegate more decisions to the lowest effective level.*

There are a number of trends that are driving the need to push decision making to the lowest effective level in the organization. These trends include faster, leaner, and smarter customers and competition; shorter product/technology life cycles; lightning-speed information technology; and more knowledgeable and more mobile employees.

Only after the roadblocks to any transformation are identified and overcome by the management, can the enterprise implement the management responses just described. The remaining chapters in this book describe "how to" reduce roadblocks, and "how to" pursue profitable top-line growth.

SUMMARY

Digital Equipment, Hanson, NCR, RCA, Pan Am, Singer, Wang, and Westinghouse were all, at one time, the greatest companies in their industries. These companies unfortunately shared a fatal behavior. They all kept doing what had made them successful for too long. They all failed to change their products, technologies, cost structures, and ways they did business to serve the needs of their ever-changing markets. They clung too long to outdated traditions, values, technologies, products, and cost structures. Unfortunately, there are still many businesses all over the world with outdated management practices that inhibit their ability to have healthy organic growth.

How did the once-great companies get into trouble? Inevitably, a major dosage of complacency and arrogance preceded their decline. These companies were lulled into a false sense of security by their previous success and large size. Their large size left them paralyzed by bureaucracies with too many management levels, too many people, too many outdated practices, and too many antique products and manufacturing processes. They withheld price cuts and new technologies to maximize short-term profit returns when they should have lowered prices or brought new technologies to the market, even at the risk of cannibalizing their existing products with lower-margin new products. For these companies, they simply needed to forget the way things were. They lived in the so-called good old days that became the bad old ways.

Sir Levan Maddock states that it is easier to learn new ideas and approaches than to forget old ones. While there are plenty of schools for learning, there are none for helping you forget. Maddock writes:

> To cherish traditions, old buildings, ancient cultures and graceful lifestyles is a worthy thing—but in the world of technology to cling to outmoded methods of manufacture, old product lines, old markets, or old attitudes among management and workers is a prescription for suicide. A long-established business will have old plant, probably the wrong mix of skills in the workforce, surplus machinery and buildings, and will carry stock no longer relevant to the business. These constraints will be compounded by old-style attitudes towards management methods, a trade union structure inherited from earlier and different times, and an ethos ill-suited to the changing world.[9]

Neither time nor economic recovery can restore the business as we knew it yesterday. We are now playing a new ballgame with a much tougher set of evolving rules and faster and smarter competitors. Every member of a company's organization must understand what the rules of this new game are and the changes necessary to survive and then become a winner. Otherwise, they may not have many more opportunities to achieve profitable top-line growth.

---

[1] Tom Copeland, Tim Roller, and Jack Murrin, *Measuring and Managing the Value of Companies* New York: John Wiley & Sons, (1993).

[2] Ibid.

[3] "How Mergers Go Wrong," The Economist, July 22, 2000, p. 19.

[4] Gunyon, Jant, "How will Shell Grow?" Fortune, August 1999, pp. 119-125.

[5] John Hechinger, "Xerox Faces Mounting Challenges to Copier Business", Wall Street Journal, December 17, 1999, pp. 3-4.

[6] Seth Schiesel, "How Lucent Stumbled: Research Surpasses Marketing," New York Times, October 16, 2000, p. B1.

[7] Deborah Solomon and Shawn Young, "Lucent Pays for Wrong Bet on Fiber-Optic Technology," Wall Street Journal, October 16, 2000, p. B6.

[8] Ray Alvarez Torres, "Niche Market Computer Strategies," *San Jose Mercury News,* February 10, 1999, p. 27.

[9] Sir Levan Maddock, "The Forgetting Curve," *New Scientist,* February 11, 1982, p. 12.

Outside-In Management

"Bureaucracy is the beast that strangles growth."

Ken Iverson, Founder and Chairman Emeritus, Nucor

While conducting management development programs at Caterpillar, I witnessed many of the successful adjustments the company made in an effort to be more proactive to threats and opportunities. After suffering losses of more than $1 billion over a three-year period, which resulted from the aggressive efforts of various global competitors (including Komatsu, Deere, JCB, Hitachi, and Liebherr), the company finally reacted. Cat's management decided to move away from a highly centralized structure dominated by staff groups and created a number of smaller and more focused business units. They added product managers and formed business units around mining, construction, paving, agriculture, and other market segments. The product managers and business units were empowered to make decisions and encouraged to widely share information and listen to customers and dealers. It was by no means an easy transformation. Caterpillar's chairman Don Fites stated to the audience:

> We were too internally focused, too centralized, and too slow to react to opportunities. We had to do something drastic. The viability of the company depended on it. We started by dissecting the competition's products and cost structure. These efforts yielded essential, but unwanted news. We operated at a 30 percent cost premium over Komatsu. That was unacceptable. Target costing helped us climb back to profitability. We pushed decision making down to business teams. We then invested over $1.8 billion in plant modernization around the globe, slashed the number of suppliers and parts, and moved to just-in-time inventory scheduling. We became more market driven.[1]

There is always a risk that a term such as market driven will simply turn out to be a faddish play on words. This risk is very real since so much of the business literature today is overloaded with buzzwords, catchy titles, and simple solutions to complex problems. The term market-driven management could easily fall into any of these categories. However, it does not. I will show that it is a proven and practical approach to accelerate profitable top-line growth. Moreover, market-driven management is based on a time-tested set of management practices that work well at a number of great industrial companies.

THE OUTSIDE-IN PROCESS

Market-driven management is an outside-in process that revolves around what I call the "six Cs of market-driven management." The first two Cs, understanding customer needs and competitive offerings, should be the force that drives and molds the third and fourth, capabilities and costs, to meet the needs of selected target markets. The fifth C, continual improvement in costs and productivity, is a relentless learning process designed to improve customer and shareowner value. The sixth C, cross-functional teams, is the catalyst that ensures all business teams are actively involved in developing focused market strategies and that they are committed to their successful implementation.

While the outside-in concept and six Cs are easy to verbalize and theoretically make sense, they are rarely followed in industrial businesses. Instead, functional managers usually regard its existing capabilities, technologies, products, and costs as "givens" that they must live with as they go to market. Xerox continued to push its large, rapid-copy equipment into the market when many customers needed only a few copies of any document. Xerox's failure to adjust its capabilities, costs, and new products to meet this need opened the door for Japanese competitors to capture a large market share. After dominating the lower- and medium-range copier markets, Canon then developed a high-volume machine that was priced below Xerox's comparable machine. Canon is now the world leader in a business that Xerox pioneered. Xerox ultimately made adjustments to its product design, costs, sales, and distribution capabilities, but the company failed to recover lost ground. Many companies fall into the same kind of trap. They view the business from the inside-out and seek to push their traditional products, services, and costs without learning what customers need and what the best competitors offer.

As Exhibit 2-1 shows, such inside-out management is markedly different from the outside-in approach. A market-driven approach starts outside with an analysis of customers' unmet needs and competitive offerings, and then moves into the business to structure internal capabilities and costs in a way that leads to a superior service/product package that meets the needs of a particular customer group. The market-driven approach is an outward-looking process that first identifies customer needs and competition and then, through an inside-out response, turns market opportunities into attractive profit and increased shareowner value.

Exhibit 2-1

Comparison of Management Approaches

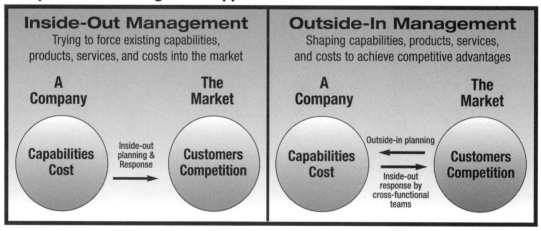

The distinction between *outside-in planning* and *inside-out response* was not as critical when most markets were growing and technology was more stable because competition was less intense and managers could ride with the upward demand curves, price increases, and long product life cycles. However, it now is crucial because many markets are not growing rapidly, customers are more demanding, technology is exploding, and global competition is intensifying from both anticipated and unexpected sources. In short, outside-in industrial companies *make what they can sell rather than try to sell what they can make.*

Many people use the term *market-driven management* mistakenly, relating it only to activities in the marketing department. Pat Parker, chairman of Parker Hannifin, a $6.5 billion manufacturer of motion control components and systems, clarified the term to his business teams. After stating that attendees at the session included managers from engineering, technical service, manufacturing, finance, and sales, he said:

> You might wonder why you are participating in a program about marketing. If any of you think you are not a part of marketing, you are mistaken. Everyone in every func-

tion in our company is a critical part of marketing. Marketing is everything and everyone. If you don't do your job right, our marketing suffers. In other words, marketing at Parker Hannifin isn't one department; the whole company is the marketing department. We are not talking about becoming more marketing oriented. We want to become more market driven. There is a big difference. Being market driven is a much broader concept that must start with the marketplace and then cut across and up and down our entire company.

This attitude is the only sound basis for the intelligent allocation of the company's resources – management's most important responsibility. Failure to think and act this way will lead to mediocre results at best. Pat Parker is right on target. However, it is useful to expand on his statement to ensure understanding and reinforce its importance. Let's first identify some common obstacles to making marketing the whole company with the outside-in approach.

COMMON OBSTACLES

Market-driven management is a cross-functional effort involving all departments and levels of the organization. Properly followed, it ensures that all activities are coordinated to meet the specific needs of target market segments better than any competitors. R&D projects must be focused on developing solutions to common and verified customer problems; manufacturing must be committed to meeting cost targets, quality standards, and delivery cycles; and sales must be focused on identifying and interpreting customer problems and then counseling users on the correct solutions. If you were to ask individual managers within any of these functional areas how they operate, they would most likely answer, "Just as you described." It is unlikely that their counterparts in other functional areas would agree, and it is even more unlikely that there would be a consensus among all managers at all levels. Achieving this market-driven focus with fully agreed-upon objectives and priorities in each functional area requires the complete support of everyone in the organization.

Market-driven management is much easier said than done because it flies in the face of the attitudes and actions of most product-, manufacturing-, or sales-driven companies. This point becomes clear when the common management and operating practices of most industrial companies are examined:

- Most manufacturers tend to view their markets too broadly, classifying them by raw material or product type (e.g., large versus small motors; truck versus passenger tires; wide industry categories such as agriculture, construction, retail, and manufacturing) rather than by user requirements, trends, and unmet needs.
- Most manufacturers are not close enough to customers to understand their problems and how they operate and, therefore, cannot develop a service/product package that offers superior value to customer groups with similar unmet needs or problems.
- Most manufacturers' thought processes and actions tend to be dominated by existing technology and product features that they blindly or arrogantly assume provide unquestionable customer value.
- Most manufacturers often make sweeping generalizations about competitors but don't have the facts to make accurate side-by-side comparisons of competitors features, benefits, costs, or market positions.
- Most functional areas of the business tend to operate independently as territorial fiefdoms without any cohesive cooperation to ensure that all functions are geared to meet the requirements and unmet needs of target markets.

- Most marketing and sales programs revolve around aggressive efforts to get large purchase orders rather than identifying and solving customer problems with cost-effective solutions that create attractive supplier profits.

These practices eventually cause market positions and especially profit margins to erode, and they increasingly threaten a company's independence and survival.

INSIDE-OUT EXAMPLES

Making the transformation from an inside-out to an outside-in approach is never easy. To clearly see what is required, two examples, one at Texas Instruments and one at Siemens, help us see what every inside-out company faces.

Texas Instruments

A situation at Texas Instruments, the global electronics giant that pioneered the mass production of semiconductors, illustrates what can happen when management follows an insular inside-out approach and fails to recognize the dynamic nature of the marketplace. Long the worldwide sales leader in semiconductors, Texas Instruments slipped to fourth place - behind Intel, Japan's Fujitsu, and Nippon Electric. With semiconductor sales of $2 billion, Texas Instruments had a long way to go just to get back to where it was four years ago, when its chip business earned $516 million before taxes on sales of $2.7 billion.

For decades, Texas Instruments dominated the world semiconductor industry because of its overwhelming strength in technology and manufacturing. Its success caused the company's leaders to believe that TI could do no wrong, according to long-time employees. But that attitude of technical arrogance created an insularity that left Texas Instruments out of touch with its rapidly changing markets. That inside-out isolation, in turn, caused marketing blunders and big losses in such consumer products as digital watches and home computers. "We got too damn arrogant," said the president of the semiconductor division.[2]

In the mid-1990s, TI had been dabbling in everything from military electronics and notebook computers to memory chips and printers. It spread its resources, especially R&D, across too many fronts and was vulnerable to more focused companies. They first withdrew from market segments that they could not defend. TI sold off some of its businesses and concentrated on digital signal processors (DSPs) and analog chips, two of the semiconductor industry's fastest-growing segments. The demand for DSPs and analog chips is growing by more than 25 percent a year. In the era of digital communications, Texas Instruments now knows exactly where it wants to go. In four years, Tom Engibous, TI's CEO, lead the market capitalization from $10 billion to more than $70 billion.

Siemens

Siemens, the $65 billion German giant based in Munich, is typical of many European manufacturers. Siemens was an inside-out engineering powerhouse, selling everything from railroad locomotives and nuclear power stations to telephone exchanges and memory chips. For decades the company was highly centralized to capture the so-called synergies between its diverse businesses. R&D was centralized and put at the heart of its organization. Sales and customer service were "pooled" around large families of products, not around customers or market segments. Many products were over-engineered, late, or not demonstrably better than competitive products.

For years the centralized and inside-out approach worked for Siemens. But in the 1990s, response time, flexibility, and a sense of urgency became big issues. Japanese product development cycles were typically half the length of their German counterparts. Moreover, it cost Japanese and U.S. firms less to develop and manufacture finished products. The German cost base became a burden.

Siemens' CEO, Heinrich von Pierer, responded by confronting the firm's traditions, centralization, and bureaucracy. With its previous inside-out approach, Siemens rarely looked outside for better practices and different ways of doing things. Suddenly, the company began to compare or benchmark itself against its various competitors around the world. Siemens then created some 250 decentralized business units, and more emphasis was put on marketing and profitability. Conscious that cost cutting without internally generated top-line growth wouldn't work in the long run, they introduced a companywide program to accelerate innovation. In the old days, such a new program would have been organized centrally and pushed down through the bureaucracy. Each business unit was made responsible for its own innovation and for bringing about its own cultural change. Employees are now paid by results rather than by rank, and senior management jobs are open only to those with international experience. Mr. von Pierer has taken a surgical knife to the company's culture of complacency and concentrated on financial performance. Some 60 percent of top and general managers' pay has been linked to targets for return on capital, a radical move in a company used to predictable paychecks. These initiatives stood Siemens on its head, and the organization is now doing a lot of things right. These changes are just the beginning for Siemens' long journey to become market driven. More major changes are likely.

Managers in most industrial businesses are too internally focused. They need to begin with a deep understanding of customer experiences; then develop and manufacture a better service/product package that provides attractive profit for shareowners. Companies that begin with its imagined advantage or so called "core competency," and then develop products that they try to make customers want, are inside-out companies. Companies that are internally focused are significantly different than those that are outside-in oriented to identifying, developing, and delivering superior customer and shareowner value.

THE SIX Cs OF A MARKET-DRIVEN COMPANY

There is nothing magical about how a market-driven industrial company operates, but the contrasts between a market-driven company and an inside-out approach are dramatic:

1. *Customer groups.* In a market-driven industrial company, all thinking and actions begins with a complete understanding of a customer group or market segment; its requirements; and its unmet, unarticulated, and emerging needs.
2. *Competition:* Market-driven industrial companies study and document side-by-side the product and service performance of the best competitors, and from this analysis they determine their relative strengths and weaknesses in each market segment.
3. *Capabilities.* Market-driven industrial companies objectively compare their existing technologies and capabilities with changing market requirements and are willing to make the changes necessary in their technologies and capabilities to serve attractive market segments with the right service/product package.
4. *Costs:* Market-driven industrial companies are always striving to improve their costs and efficiency so that they can provide their target customers with greater value while improving their company's productivity, profits, and shareowner value.
5. *Continual improvements.* Market-driven industrial companies continually improve customer value, response and cycle time, productivity, costs, and profit by constantly learning and working smarter in every area of the organization.
6. *Cross-functional teams:* Market-driven industrial companies utilize cross-functional

business teams with profit responsibility and business plans to ensure that all key activities, priorities, and decisions are synchronized to serve target market needs.

As shown in Exhibit 2-2, these six Cs build on each other to form a powerful framework for any business to accelerate profitable top-line growth. In high-performance industrial companies, prominent positions have been built by following these concepts in all areas of their organizations. These successful companies are learning organizations where leaders and cross-functional teams continually seek out better ways of doing things.

Exhibit 2-2
The Six Cs of Market Driven Management

HOW MARKET-DRIVEN MANAGEMENT BEGINS AND ENDS

Many focused smaller companies have achieved enviable results because of the way they got their start. They concentrated on a market segment and provided a demonstrably superior service/product package at an attractive profit. Many larger companies that were market driven lost their competitive edge because they lost sight of the factors that made them market driven in the first place. Exhibit 2-3 shows the natural evolution of many companies as they grow, enjoy success, plateau, become bureaucratic, lose ground, and fail to catch up.

During its entrepreneurial or startup period, a company has all the vital characteristics of a market-driven business. The organization is highly focused and responsive. It operates informally around teams in an open-minded environment of change. The egalitarian culture is a place where every employee is encouraged to have ideas and to challenge the other people to the limits of their abilities. A heightened sense of urgency exists throughout the organization. As the business grows and succeeds, more products, structure, and management levels are added.

Exhibit 2-3

How Market-Driven Management Begins and Ends

Most companies evolve from left to right:
Market-driven management moves companies to the left.

Market Driven Stage	Plateau Stage	Bureaucratic Stage
Cross-functional teams focus on the most attractive segments and accounts prioritized as attack, counterattack, study, de-emphasize, or withdraw.	New products, capacity, and new customers added; new markets and countries entered; larger families of products result.	Volume objectives take a priority to cover fixed costs and to utilize plant capacity; throughput and volume are emphasized over profit and customer value.
Everyone is sensitive to competitive advantages and disadvantages by market segment and key account.	More investment in plant, equipment, people, and overhead; more meetings, management levels, and reports.	Smaller but attractive market opportunities are overlooked, disregarded, or pursued too late.
Decentralized decision making and informal, cross-functional team spirit dominates; nothing is sacred, new ideas and criticisms flow freely in these fast learning and agile organizations.	More people and structure added; staffs and management levels added; more forms, procedures, ISO 9000+, and approvals needed; learning and internal and external benchmarking slows or stops.	Past success, size, arrogance, and complacency cause a decline in margins and profits; market positions begin to drop; the company is in denial, it drifts; learning and global benchmarking stop.
Information is widely shared; everyone acts to improve costs and productivity; people are empowered to share practices and make many decisions.	Increases in fixed costs, shared costs, total unit costs, and higher break-even points; productivity improvements level out or stop.	Department isolation; more form filling and bureaucracy sets in; CYA; no sharing of practices; cycle times are slower than best competitors.
Everyone thinks and acts with a relentless sense of urgency of a start up to profitably serve customer needs, increase customer value, reduce threats and profitably capture opportunities.	Effective customer solutions and prompt service take a backseat to meeting sales quotas, getting products shipped, and keeping plants filled; quality, speed, and lead times begin to slip.	Aggressive self-starters become disenchanted, leave, or develop other interests; mediocrity permeates the business unit and productivity declines; severe learning disabilities prevail.
Examples: Any company or business unit that is focused, open, fast, accountable, and stresses results.	Examples: Any company or business obsessed with volume or just being bigger.	Examples: Companies and business units that are trying to live in the past and need to be transformed.

Larger families of products are added, multiple facilities are built, and bigger business units result. More investments are made in plant and equipment, and volume becomes increasingly important to absorb higher fixed costs. As procedures, forms, and policies are added, management levels increase, which slows decision making and response time. The enterprise plateaus.

When a business moves into the bureaucratic stage, it often faces very serious problems that can easily go undetected. Profits may initially be high even though margins and market positions have slipped as the organization coasts on its past momentum. An overemphasis on traditions, ceremonies, folklore, and past successes inhibit an objective self-examination that could lead to appropriate corrective actions. Bureaucracy, complacency, arrogance, and internal politics take over. Decision-making processes become constipated, while the outside world moves increasingly faster. New ideas or different approaches are regarded with contempt or disregard. As a result, good people tend to become disenchanted and plateau, seek outside outlets, leave or decline to join the organization; mediocrity prevails and productivity declines. The top and upper management are in denial and most top executives have severe learning disabilities.

Ken Iverson, chairman emeritus of Nucor Corporation, terms the tendency to become more bureaucratic as "the drift" that can quickly paralyze any company and add costs if it is not constantly on the lookout for the early warning signs of bureaucracy. This bureaucratic drift explains why most rapid-growth companies grow rapidly for a period of time, then grow slowly, plateau, and decline. The centralization of decision making is one of the worst forms of bureaucracy. Centralization works well for many consumer goods manufacturers and retailers such as Wal-Mart and for most banks that sell standard products to millions of customers. In centralized organizations, no problem is too mundane to refer to regional or corporate headquarters. However, industrial businesses serve diverse markets and often must tailor products, services, and manufacturing processes to the special needs of business customers all around the world. This requires flexibility, innovation and problem-solving capabilities, and decision making as close to the customer as possible.

Most companies fail to interpret the signals of impending trouble in the plateau and bureaucratic stages and thus fail to make corrections. A rapid decline in sales and/or profits often serves as a management wakeup call more than a gradual decline in performance. Many companies wait too long for evidence of failing performance, only to find that it's too late to even catch-up to the better-run competitors.

There are *leading and lagging indicators of a declining business* unit or company. The lagging indicators are the traditional measures of decline including return on equity, return on assets, return on sales, a stagnant or downward stock price, and loss of market share. The leading indicators serve as earlier warning signals of problems. Leading indicators include complacency, customer deflections, few or no new products, flat or declining sales revenue, slow response and cycle times, management arrogance, and denial.

In most large and especially older companies, the signs of decline go unrecognized too long. The top management and the board of directors act as though it's "business as usual" as the company is mired in sub-par performance and their stock value lags behind the market. One cannot review the histories of once great companies without wondering what role members of the board of directors played in the drift of the firms they were supposedly "directing." In every underperforming case, one wonders why top management and the board of directors did not press for earlier action when these once high performing companies showed clear signs of decline.

CULTURE IS A DOUBLE-EDGED SWORD

Culture and values, by definition, require substantial continuity over time. Doing things a certain way constitutes an organization's identity and makes it unique. A firm's culture is embodied in its various practices and many traditions that require a taken-for-granted behavior. Challenges to doing things counter to the culture, can constitute an attack on the very identity and values of the firm. When I conduct workshops and present approaches that are different than the client's organization is currently practicing, I often hear the following comments:

"This is the way things are done here."

"This is how we have always done it."
"We have a lot of sacred cows here."

Trapped By The Past

Precedent, when universally applied, can interfere with both the process of learning and applying knowledge to improve organizational performance. The most serious problem with precedent is that if it is used automatically, without thought, mindless behavior results. When people in an organization engage in mindless acts, they rarely even consider whether the current practices need to be reexamined.

People in organizations that use a strong culture as a substitute for thinking, do so even when a new problem confronts the organization. The mindless silence on how things have been done in the past means that acquiring new knowledge and translating it into actionable improvements is difficult. Since it is easier to rely on precedent than to learn and implement something new, many organizations avoid accepting new practices even when some managers realize they are doing the wrong things. Doing the wrong things well is worse than doing the right things inadequately.

Relying strictly on what was done in the past can get people and organizations into big trouble if the environment changes or if the past actions have produced declining results. Even when people know that the existing ways of doing things are flawed, they are often afraid to raise objections or even suggest different ways of working. And even when people are courageous enough to question the old ways of doing things, and provide good reasons why these practices should be discarded and replaced, they are often ignored or rebutted by their peers and supervisors.

A strong culture and history can stall an organization's ability to learn, let alone to actually implement new knowledge into visions, actions, and decisions. This problem is often magnified in companies that most need to break from their pasts. Unfortunately, the threat of change in these firms cause people to cling even more tightly to their old ways of doing things. At the same time, if they do try new approaches, fear and anxiety makes it difficult for them to learn. External threats and fear cause many people in under performing firms to increasingly do what they have done in the past, and therefore, to engage in even more mindless behavior than usual. Hunkering down and concentrating on what the firm has done in the past is wise when the organization has done the right things, makes good profit, and the present is much like the past. But the human tendency is to react to all problems, at least at first, by using the old and engrained practices.

Drive Out Fear and Bad Practices

In company after company that failed to improve performance, I have observed a pervasive atmosphere of fear and distrust. I have come to appreciate the wisdom of quality guru W.E. Dening's prescription for success: drive out fear. Fear and distrust undermine organizational performance and inhibit the ability to learn and turn knowledge into sound actions. People must believe they will not be punished for taking calculated risks. When people fear for their jobs, futures or even for self-esteem, it is unlikely that they will feel secure enough to do anything but what the organization has done in the past. Andy Grove, chairman of Intel, recognized the dysfunctional consequence of workplace fear when he said:

> Fear that keeps employees from voicing their real thoughts is poison to any company. Almost nothing could be more detrimental to the well being of the company. Once an environment of fear takes over, it will lead to paralysis throughout the organization and cut off the needed flow of bad news, which is good news when it is received early.

A small number of progressive companies has developed intentional practices to drive out fear and the bully managers who humiliate others. These leading companies actively practice some of the following approaches.

1. Constantly encourage open communication.
2. Don't punish people for trying new things.
3. Give people second and third chances.
4. Encourage leaders to talk about their mistakes.
5. Learn from mistakes and even celebrate them.
6. Praise, pay, and promote people who deliver bad news.

Unfortunately fear-inducing managers are still prevalent in many industrial organizations. I have never met anyone who likes to work for these people. A boss who is feared or even distrusted because of this intimidating or bully style should be counseled, changed, or if necessary, removed from the organization. This applies to autocratic department managers, general managers, group presidents, and even CEOs who are increasingly being removed by their board of directors for this serious character flaw.

Not all companies are trapped in the past and doomed to repeat the same errors simply because they were done before, or constrained by their history from learning new things or applying what they know. Companies that constructively question all their existing practices will use precedent wisely and won't be trapped by memories of how things used to be. Every company must decide when the experience of the past is more of a burden than a blessing. This requires constant vigilance, but it has tremendous payoff. The payoff comes from the willingness to forego mindless behavior and avoid the problem of blind inertia and traps that comes with every company's previous success.

SMALLER COMPANY ROLE MODEL

To avoid the natural tendency for any successful company to drift from entrepreneurial to bureaucratic, we need to look at how smaller and faster well-run companies operate. Every day the business press glorifies big companies with stories about their size, global reach, and number of employees. Being bigger is assumed by many journalists and businesspeople to be better. Nothing could be further from reality. In the management workshops I've facilitated, some of the very best questions, solutions, and strategies come from people who previously worked in smaller companies. The real heroes of organic growth are often the smaller and medium-sized companies, not the Fortune 500.

The competitive disadvantages of being large have been recognized by some big companies that have moved to create smallness within their largeness. They have "reinvented" smallness by creating smaller divisions or small business units within divisions. In other words, any large organization that desires to survive and thrive from steady organic growth must create divisions or business units that have the characteristics of a smaller entrepreneurial company, while having the resources of a large organization.

Let's now describe how people work in smaller, informal, flexible, fast-moving, and entrepreneurial business units:

1. *People speak-up in simple and straightforward language.* They prefer direct communication in the form of informal face-to-face discussions rather than writing buzzword-filled memos with many copies to a perceived powerbase. Everyone comes forth with ideas and passionate arguments, and people are not afraid to speak up in this open-book culture.

2. *People move fast in everything they do.* They act as if they were about to lose every customer, and they see opportunities as a window that will close rapidly. Most threats are seen as opportunities that urgently need a strategy and action plan. Informal cross-functional teams brainstorm the issues, gather necessary upfront facts, develop what-if options, weigh the pluses and minuses of each option; and then implement the most valuable course of action.

3. *People see connections between their job and the entire organization.* They do what is important to serve customers and make money. They realize that if profitable and growing customers are lost, everyone, including the president or general manager, can lose their job. People don't hide behind narrow job descriptions. They think of the big picture and determine how their work relates to it and the other departments.

4. *People are responsible, accountable and prefer to be evaluated by results.* People just do what is right for the customer and the organization and then later ask for forgiveness. The real leaders are people with followers, not just titles. Because they are paid by business performance, low performers are obvious; they are helped and, if necessary, removed from the organization.

Not many large organizations have these characteristics within their divisions or business units. However, within Johnson & Johnson, HP, ITW, Morgan Crucible and ABB, you find that most of these businesses exhibit the characteristics of a smaller company. These few large and well-managed companies have what I call a small company entrepreneurial mentality surrounded by a large company's resources and management sophistication. And while realizing the benefits of decentralization and operating on a largely independent basis, they collaborate and leverage their strengths in many areas.

Case Study: A Big "Little" Company at HP

One of the few large companies I've worked with that consistently behaves as if it is a smaller startup is Hewlett-Packard. The "HP way," started by founders Bill Hewlett and David Packard, is rooted in decentralization, egalitarianism, individual freedom, and pragmatism. Many companies talk decentralization or strategic business units while they micromanage and rely on too many levels of management that then interfere and constantly check up on and harass people. When an HP division grows beyond $100 million in sales, it routinely breaks it up or creates another new division. The company has never had a layoff in its 60 years of existence, and it now employs more than 100,000 people around the globe. Bill Hewlett and David Packard were running a boundaryless company decades before General Electric's Jack Welch began preaching about "boundaryless GE" as he slashed more than 110,000 jobs and auctioned off their highly competitive consumer electronics, semiconductor, and small appliance businesses. HP has largely grown organically and achieved steady productivity improvements without using the common slash-and-burn approaches. HP has plateaued a few times, but it has been able to transform itself and rejuvenate organic growth.

In 1990, an often-fatal disease called "bureaucracy" threatened to cripple HP's perpetual growth machine and regulate it to the status of just another big, slow-growth company. Its decades of success, no layoffs, and favorable publicity helped create complacency. With the decision to develop a new computer workstation, the company drew upon many divisions and laboratories for their resources. Following other large computer companies, many of which have become dinosaurs, HP's CEO, John Young, thought the central control of the workstation development project was the way to go. Centralized R&D, marketing, and sales took control of functions that were previously performed within each division. Product and market development managers, who once made all decisions in their divisions, had to obtain approvals from several levels of management and various "steering committees." Finance people at headquarters gained power and determined pricing and payment policies. Profits between 1990 and 1992 dropped like a rock. Major development projects lagged. Many employees were frustrated and demoralized, and some joined faster-moving companies.

In 1992, the founders, Bill Hewlett and especially David Packard, stepped in to return the company to its decentralized values and smaller company practices. Lew Platt replaced John Young as CEO. Dozens of questionable committees were abolished, most corporate centers or staffs were ended, many group executive positions were cut out, and two levels of "management" were eliminated over a weekend. Within 18 months, the time-to-market for new products dramatically improved, sales surged, and profits again accelerated. Centralization was a stranger to the small-company autonomy that the founders had begun and in which each business controlled its own engineering, production, marketing, and sales.

Hewlett-Packard's revenue growth throughout the mid-1990s regularly hit 20 percent per year, but was flat in 1998 and early 1999. CEO Lew Platt had to do something. He responded by splitting HP into two totally separate companies: a $40 billion company selling computers, printers, software, and services and an $8 billion company selling test and measurement equipment and medical diagnostic instruments now called Agilent. Ned Barnholt, the former president of the test and measurement group at HP, heads Agilent. HP's original business, test and measurement equipment, was not getting the attention and resources the much larger and glamorous computer business was receiving. The test and measurement business now has more focused resources, and accountability with its own company name, own stock, and dedicated management. Broken loose, Agilent grew at a faster rate than its parent, HP.

Top-Down and Bottom-Up Companies

Most companies can be categorized as largely top-down or bottom-up organizations. The top-down approach features more centralized organizations in which upper management creates strategies, policies, and orders that are passed down the organization. When any level of management closely holds authority and power, business teams won't be very empowered. In every top-down organization, I have found many people with great ideas who are frustrated and buried in the organization. They too often report to a questionable level of management or maybe a supervisor who is incompetent but can hide forever in a top-down bureaucracy. A top-down organization is a very natural environment for managers who are "control freaks" and autocratic.

A bottom-up organization is basically the opposite of a top-down company. Instead of a hierarchy and narrowly defined jobs, there is autonomy and knowledge created and implemented by bottom-up business teams. The bottom-up management styles that I have observed first-hand at Hewlett-Packard, Johnson & Johnson, ITW, and 3M are lacking in many large manufacturing companies. These great organic growth companies are mostly bottom-up organizations with some top-down goals. In truly decentralized organizations, every single employee is expected to think like a business owner and not like a robot in a narrowly defined bureaucracy. Front-line employees are considered the innovators with the great ideas. In a bottom-up company, all employees are encouraged to challenge current practices, traditions, and procedures. Top management, in a bottom-up company, simply trusts all their employees and expects them to take risks. At 3M, new employees take a class in risk taking. They come with their managers and are taught, among other things, to be willing to defy their supervisors and speak up. How many top-down executives would be comfortable with their people attending such a training session?

A bottom-up and decentralized approach to management is entrenched in every large multi-business industrial organization that is a perpetual organic growth machine. The values and management style of these innovative growth companies demand a bottom-up approach. The following quotation from the late William McKnight, chairman of 3M, is typical of the importance placed on tolerant management styles in bottom-up companies:

> As our business grows, it becomes increasingly necessary for those in managerial positions to delegate responsibility and to encourage people to whom responsibility is delegated to exercise their own initiative. This requires considerable tolerance. Those people, to whom we delegate authority and responsibility, if they are good people, are going to have ideas of their own and are gong to want to do their jobs in their own way. It seems to me these are characteristics we want in people and they should be encouraged as long as their way conforms to our business policies and our general pattern of operation. Mistakes will be made, but if the person is essentially right, I think the mistakes are not so serious in the long run as the mistakes management makes if it is dictatorial and undertakes to tell people under its authority to whom responsibility is delegated, exactly how they must do their job. If management is intolerant and destructively critical when mistakes are made I think it kills initiative and it is essential that we have many people with initiative if we are to continue to grow.[3]

Too Much Management

A top-down company stems from the reluctance of CEOs, group presidents, and general managers to push decision making responsibilities deep within the organization, relying instead on centralized organizations with too many management levels and 'top heavy' staff people. Too many layers insulate, slow the decision making process, stifle innovation, and raise costs. Even after downsizing, many companies still have too many management levels. The real contributions of many vice presidents and their highly-paid staffs cannot be demonstrated to many people's satisfaction. Some corporate and group activities are redundant, allow management responsibilities to interfere with decision making, or are too costly to justify. Excessive levels and top-heavy positions create unnecessary reports, memos, procedures, nonstop meetings and unneeded sign-offs. Where three to four levels of sign-off signatures are required, in many cases one or two would be sufficient. In some cases, no signatures are really necessary.

In addition to the unavoidable cost penalties, overstructuring and excessive layering have more serious consequences for the long term. I doubt that senior managers actually know what is going on when they are several levels removed from where the action takes place-with customers in the field, in the plants, and in the laboratories. All they know is what they are told, and this information, whether verbal or written, has all the deficiencies of any message that has been filtered through multiple layers. As a result, the decision making process is almost certain to be slow and unresponsive and is usually not based on the current facts of the situation. An expert in market research once told me how, at her company, every layer of management between her and the CEO watered down her fact-based research. Bad news rarely reached upper management, and it never got to the CEO. That company has gone from greatness to tough times.

Give a laptop computer to everyone, network them, trust them, and you don't need as many managers. Truly empowered and electronically wired cross-functional business teams can be highly effective with cross-continent counterparts in other areas of the world. Dow Chemical, a 100-year-old basic chemical company with sales of $21 billion, made the transformation. There are now only five management layers between the CEO and the global business teams. Before Dow's delayering, business team empowerment, and advanced information technology, there were twelve layers. In short, the goal is to be run like a small and flat organization and not like a large and tall one where people "pass the buck" and are not accountable for results.

THE NEEDED TRANSFORMATION

The huge success of the cartoon character Dilbert and the best-selling book, *The Dilbert Principle*,[4] is a sign of bankrupt corporate life in many companies. Too many companies are still trying to manage their businesses around big chunks of business, generally defined by historical product groupings and a centralized top-down approach that stifles people, slows decision making, and adds huge costs. The expression "small is beautiful" really makes sense in today's more turbulent business climate. An industrial business is better off if it is broken down and managed decentrally around a number of discrete profit centers. There are several distinct advantages: the planning and decision making process is streamlined and fast; the bureaucratic "drag" that is inevitably found in big organizations is avoided; a much better basis for planning and accountability is provided because people with clear-cut profit and decision making responsibility are on top of everyday problems, and finally, more strategic options are uncovered because people close to customers are thinking strategically about what they can do to accelerate sales and profit growth in their particular business.

Case Study: ITW - A Big, Flat Organization

Why would a $7 billion company choose to divide itself into more than 400 business units? Better still, how can such a seemingly splintered organization not only succeed but also thrive in this fashion? These questions are more than adequately answered by Illinois Tool Works (ITW), the Chicago-area based industrial manufacturer of self-described dull products (welding machines and electrodes, nails, spray guns, adhesives, and molded parts) that parlays smallness into big and brilliant profit numbers. Like microorganisms undergoing cell division, ITW's businesses grow to a certain size and then are split apart. Acquired businesses, likewise, are divided into more focused parts or business units. In each case, the objective of the business unit is to focus on its market segment as a niche market with laserlike intensity. It costs ITW money up front to split the businesses, but each grows so fast afterward that it eclipses the small amount of premium it pays to separate them.

Although the decentralization strategy has driven a healthy 12 percent compounded annual revenue growth for many years, the yardstick of performance at ITW is earnings. The company has consistently delivered double-digit earnings growth during the last decade when average compounded earnings was 17 percent, and the stock grew more than 700 percent during the same ten-year period. Return on equity averaged 22 percent for the last ten years. ITW loves competing against large and less focused competitors. ITW often divides a business unit when it hits $50 million in annual sales because they feel it will begin to lose its focus. It might take a $50 million business and split it into three $15 million to $18 million businesses, each narrowly focused. It gives them their own engineering and manufacturing areas. They might share accounting, sales, and distribution. As some business units have grown, they have been split out three or four times.

In addition to the business benefits of ITW's extreme decentralization, this grow-and-divide approach rapidly develops department managers and general managers. If people in their twenties run a $5 to $8 million business, they learn rapidly. If they worked for another company, they might be buried and trapped in some large silo. Acquisitions to fill product lines or a market segment are identified by ITW business unit managers or their general managers. ITW has some 35 general managers responsible for more than 400 business units led by BUMs (business unit managers). Smaller acquisitions are favored because of the ability to rapidly integrate them at the business-unit or general-manager levels. Small acquisitions that can be pumped up are also less risky if they fail. As with any existing ITW business, the first scrutiny of a potential or newly acquired company is industrial market segmentation (described in Chapter 4). Orgapack GmbH, a $50 million Swiss packing equipment company, was acquired and split into four business units. Sales have increased in all four units, and, more importantly, margins on average have doubled as a result of the ITW focus principles. Business-unit executive compensation strongly reinforces the emphasis on earnings growth with 50 percent of each annual bonus opportunity directly tied to the unit's net profit.

Reward and Recognize Team Results

In spite of all that has been written about the importance and need to work well in cross-functional business teams, I hear the following common complaints at nearly every workshop:

"We are too departmentalized, in silos."
"Our business plans are not cross-functionally developed."
"We have poor implementation."
"Our product development has too many hand-offs."

These same companies still work too much in sequence and not enough in parallel processes. Product development and business plans are two big clues to see how much or how little cross-functional teamwork is occurring. Few large organizations do enough up-front work with teams in their product development and business planning process. These very same companies have even greater difficulty working across continents on either product development or business planning. However, I often find well working cross-functional business teams in small businesses or divisions that are a fair distance from corporate headquarters. National Starch's Alcoa Standard adhesives unit in Chattanooga, Tennessee, and its Mexican operations work well in cross-functional business teams. Timken's South American and South African divisions have the spirit and speed of honeybees at work. Such pockets of high-performing business teams should serve as models for the rest of the organization.

Another critical dimension in creating and sustaining high-performing business teams is incentives that reward and recognize business teams and their leaders for good results. Without the proper incentives, a complacent and low-performing country club environment will set in. In high-performing organizations, job titles, job descriptions (if they exist), and job levels are less important than individual contributions to results. These few, great firms are meritocracies. If groups of people are made accountable for their own results, they should be given a financial incentive for the results. When people turn to each other to solve problems or hatch opportunities rather than wait for a hierarchy, pay should be based on objective results, not a lot of "touchy-feely" and subjective criteria. Rewards have to be tied to the business unit's results as well as to the overall company results. In many progressive companies, 60 to 70 percent of the variable pay is related to the person's profit center, and the remainder is based on the corporation's overall success.

A sound pay system should recognize outstanding team and individual performances. It is encouraging to see a growing number of companies putting more of an employee's pay at risk, calling it "variable" pay because the variable part is beyond a person's base salary. If the variable part of the pay is only a small percentage of the base pay, say, 5 to 7 percent, the variable pay won't be much of an incentive. The variable pay should be based on measurable and predetermined goals and should strive to balance shorter- and longer-term profit results of the business unit. Group efforts and cross-functional teamwork will eventually be reduced if the paycheck isn't significantly linked to group and individual performance. However, at many of the companies I work with, the methods are outdated and far too subjective, and they are not tied to group and individual results. Teamwork and cooperation will decrease if the pay systems do not encourage high-performance group and individual results. Too many pay systems encourage mediocrity—and this penalizes high-performing business teams and individuals. Top management must ensure that the reward and recognition systems encourage profitable growth to flourish.

Keep It Informal

Constant management attention is required to fight the natural evolutionary tendency to become more formal and more bureaucratic. Unless formality and all of its bureaucratic clues are constantly fought, it will grow and take over like crab grass, leading to all the negative consequences the term suggests. Managers must constantly be on the prowl for signs of too much formality. Unnecessary meetings, too many committees, extensive reports, excessive management levels, too many procedures, and approvals are common warning signals that formality and bureaucracy are taking over. There are two quick tests of how formal and bureaucratic a company is. First, is the size of the corporate, group, and country staffs; the minimum possible number is best. Second, is whether communications are through strict hierarchical channels as opposed to boundaryless communications where anyone can communicate directly with anybody to address business issues. Being informal gives you speed in sharing ideas, brainstorming, and making fast decisions.

I don't think many people realize the value of making and keeping a large organization informal. The benefits of an informal company culture are enormous. Being informal gives you speed. It allows for fast information flow. It allows you to make quick decisions by fax, phone, e-mail, and in the hallways. As the opportunities arise, you can attack new market segments and/or add the needed capabilities. To make informality work, the CEO, group presidents, general managers, and department managers must embrace it and practice a "walk the talk." They must all be serious about informality as a daily way of life, e.g. with fewer and shorter memos, fewer and shorter formal meetings, and accept ideas regardless of one's title, pay level, seniority, or dress.

The trend to business casual dress is a strong sign that employees cherish informality over a strict dress code. However, when visiting customers, it is best to follow their dress code. High tech companies in California's Silicon Valley started the dress-down trend twenty years ago, which spread throughout California to both operating business units and corporate headquarters. The Eastern half of the U.S. was much slower to embrace the trend. Dress codes were first relaxed for offsite meetings and management training programs. Then Friday became a companywide dress down day, and some firms in the South allowed it during the entire summer months. Finally, even the most stodgy and formal organizations (blue-chip investment banks and Wall Street law firms such as J.P. Morgan, Goldman Sachs, and Morgan Stanley) went business casual to attract employees and to appear as much in the new economy as possible. Employees love business casual for economic and morale reasons. Meetings are more informal, open, and productive. However, some senior executives, typically over fifty-five years of age, still believe they must dress for success or they will reduce their credibility and authority. Most of these executives are from the old school and just don't get the whole importance of keeping it informal.

The Internet and electronic networks are creating a truly boundryless and informal organization where knowledge is far more important than one's title, years of service, or organizational level. A wired world results in global sharing, collaboration, and learning at unprecedented speeds. E-business puts another nail in the coffin for bureaucracy. It helps keep organizations flat by creating a boundaryless company and networks with other organizations around the world. Since everyone in the wired company has access to everything worth knowing, a very transparent company is created. Bureaucrats should be ridiculed, converted, or eventually removed from the organization. With filters, gatekeepers, and bullies removed, people are more productive and have more fun. Informality and the resulting spontaneity create contagious excitement so important to growing a company.

ASSESSING YOUR BUSINESS UNIT

It is important to determine how market driven a business unit is and, more importantly, where it falls short of achieving profitable top-line growth. Corrective actions or improvement programs are needed where deficiencies exist. Determining the areas for improvement, however, is not a simple task. As I said at the outset, market-driven management is too often a buzzword statement that everyone espouses without really knowing what he or she are talking about. Because it has not been defined in operational terms, there are many conflicting views on what the term means, and there is little evidence that it has a substantive meaning, even in companies where it is commonly used.

To overcome this problem, I developed a rating scale for the operational factors that determine whether a business unit is market driven in key areas of the business (see Exhibit 2-4.) The scale has two sets of extremes. The left side describes the worst-case situations that would represent growth liabilities to any company or business unit. The right side describes the ideal situations that would be advantageous for any company or business unit for accelerating profitable top-line growth. My experience suggests that rarely is the ideal +5 ever plotted for any of these factors. I have never encountered a case where the majority of these factors were rated higher than 3 or 4 on the positive side. Rather, most ratings tend to be on the negative side, which demonstrates the difficulties of becoming a market-driven growth business.

Exhibit 2-4

Market Driven Growth Diagnostic

Liabilities	-5	0	+5	Advantages	Consensus
1. Market facts about customer needs, trends and competition are nonexistent, unverified, or underutilized in planning and decision making.		| | | | | || | | | | |			1. The value of market facts about customers' unmet needs, market trends, and competition is widely recognized as the foundation for all planning and decision making.	____
2. Market segment definitions are too broad or based on an industry, products, technology, manufacturing, or customer sizes in each country and region.		| | | | | || | | | | |			2. Market segments and key accounts are defined by common needs and prioritized as attack, counterattack, deemphasize, and withdraw in each country and region of the world.	____
3. Side-by-side competitive comparisons are nonexistent, unverified, too broad, internal, or underutilized in decision making.		| | | | | || | | | | |			3. Competitor analysis is done by segment, country, and region of the world and is used to develop product/market strategies.	
					4. Net profitability is reported, shared, and reviewed regularly for each ____	
4. Accounting systems driven by GAAP and upward reporting rather than for management decision making.		| | | | | || | | | | |			product line, customer, market segment, and distributor.	
					5. Documented side-by-side comparisons show that all costs and ____	
5. Lower cost and productivity gains are unsupported, but competitor actions and results imply otherwise.		| | | | | || | | | | |			productivity gains are in line with or lower than the best competitor's.	
						____

Liabilities	-5	0	+5	Advantages	Consensus
6. Quality goals, product performance, and customer satisfaction measurements are nonexistent or talked about without programs for continual improvements.		I I I I II I I I I I		6. Superior quality is consistently demonstrated through global side-by-side comparisons of yield rates, product performance, delivery, services, and customer satisfaction.	_____
7. Machine efficiency and capacity utilization considerations dominate product line and customer mix decisions.		I I I I I I I I I I I		7. Manufacturing achieves continuous productivity gains that lower costs and they seek a richer product and customer mix.	_____
8. Response and cycle times in many departments are lagging, and programs are not in place to improve response times and create a sense of urgency.		I I I I I II I I I I		8. Response and cycle times are equal or superior to the best competitors, and the organization relentlessly searches for more speed.	
9. Existing raw materials, know-how, and current technology suppress thinking about emerging market needs and new opportunities.		I I I I I II I I I I		9. People are willing to think beyond existing materials and technologies to serve current customer needs and new market segments.	
10. New products and services are too late, too costly, or not demonstrably better for target customer groups and are not a major source of sales and profits.		I I I I I II I I I I		10. New products and services are a major source of sales and profits and are developed by cross-functional teams focused on verified user needs and benefits.	_____
11. Sales training is mostly product and feature driven, at odds with target market priorities, company profit goals, customer benefits, and competitive offerings.		I I I I I II I I I I		11. All direct and distributor sales training activities are focused to solve customer problems and communicate customer value to target markets and accounts	
12. The organization is too structured around functions, wide families of products, large accounts, with too much bureaucracy and insufficient accountability.		I I I I I II I I I I		12. The organization is relatively flat, informal, and focused on small families of products or markets, and net profit responsibility is assigned for each major product, market, and key account.	_____
13. Planning is done sequentially by individuals and functions, and without necessary market focus, cross-functional integration, or team commitments.		I I I I I II I I I I		13. Cross-functional teams develop and implement business plans for each product, market, and key account to achieve sales and profit goals.	_____
14. Recognition and reward programs are not aligned to market priorities, short- and long-term goals and individuals, business teams, and business unit performance.		I I I I I II I I I I		14. Recognition and reward programs honor both short- and long-term results and are aligned with market priorities that recognize individuals, business teams, and business unit performance.	_____

The advantages of using this scale to assess any business unit should be clear. The mystique is taken out of the concept of market-driven management, and a base is provided for discussing it in operational terms. Individual or composite ratings that can be used as a basis for gaining agreement on the problem areas can also be obtained. Once problem areas are defined, the foundation has been laid for meaningful corrective action. Properly used, the rating scale provides a solid base for building real substance into profitable top-line growth. Without an operational definition and an objective evaluation of the current situation, market-driven management is not a useful description of anything. I have worked with hundreds of managers who know that market-driven management is absolutely essential for profitable growth. However, they are often at a loss to articulate it and make it a reality across all functions of their business.

I have used the market-driven growth diagnostic with managers from numerous companies in a wide range of industries and countries. The results have invariably been very useful. They have shown that some units within these companies are more market driven than others. They have enabled senior management to zero in on problems and then suggest corrective actions or solutions that worked for one business unit and may work for another. Most importantly, they established a reference point that can be tracked to determine where progress has been made and where more work is needed.

I suggest you *first read this entire book before making an initial evaluation* of your situation because all chapters of the book further explain how to accelerate profitable top-line growth by being more market driven. Chapter 14, "Correcting Your Weaknesses," describes how to conduct the ratings with a cross-functional business team and put the corrective actions to work.

SUMMARY

Astute managers recognize that a business is defined by an outside-in approach to the needs and requirements of customer groups and competitive offerings, not by existing products, technologies, or management experience. The advantages to this outside-in and close-to-the-customer growth approach are enormous:

- The employees closest to the customers, laboratories, and factories develop and execute bottom-up plans to meet or exceed company goals. More innovative options for improving sales and profit growth are uncovered by those close to the marketplace.
- Strategic thinking and planning is no longer simply a bureaucratic form-filling exercise with no real meaning for those actually doing the work. Substance is provided in planning by cross-functional business teams agreeing on the attractive market segments, the issues, setting priorities, and developing winning strategies and action programs.
- Market focuses that demand the early assessment of threats and opportunities and much quicker responses are provided. Resources are allocated to the most attractive market segment opportunities to attack and counterattack, while resources are reduced or withdrawn from unattractive situations.
- Fast-changing product and process technology is applied appropriately, and the payback odds are increased, despite shorter life cycles and pricing pressures. Everyone has a sense of urgency and accountability to improve results. Pay and recognition systems recognize individual and group performance.

This chapter addressed the cultural underpinnings needed to allow outside-in thinking and actions to flourish throughout the enterprise. If the organization is largely inside-out, fairly bureaucratic, and top-down, it will have difficulty to profitably grow. In a fairly flat and open learning organization, profitable growth will become the entrepreneurial compass it should be in every business unit. The result will be a market-driven enterprise with consistently attractive sales and profit growth.

[1] "Adding Focus and Speed To A Company" *Industry Week,* June 9, 1997, p. 16.
[2] Thomas C. Hayes, "Texas Instruments versus Japan," *The New York Times,* July 1, 1988, p. 2.
[3] Jones Huck, "A History of the 3M Company", 3M Company. St. Paul: 1995. p. 239
[4] Scott Adams, The Dilbert Principle (New York City: Harper Business, 1997).

Everyone Is in Marketing

"Industrial marketing is too important to be left to only the marketing department."

David Packard, Co-Founder
Hewlett Packard

Many of the shortcomings described in the first two chapters can be traced to deficiencies in understanding industrial marketing, particularly at the top and general management levels. Unfortunately, most CEOs, and general managers in industrial manufacturing companies have the wrong idea of the role marketing should play in their companies. They typically see marketing as simply advertising or marketing communication. At best they see marketing as a subset of sales or as a support staff. Few industrial CEOs and general managers understand that *marketing should be the headlights of the business unit and that it should engage the whole business unit, never just one department.*

The edge has been dulled, and the effects—losses—are there: loss of productivity improvements, loss of world share, loss of entire markets, and, what's worse, loss of thousands of jobs. Today, Japan—not the United States—is producing the greatest numbers of automobiles, machine tools, televisions, motorcycles, photocopiers, and so on. Business is booming in some markets while it is stagnant in others. Why? There are many explanations: too much emphasis on short-term profits, balance sheet management, too few new products, too many "me-too" products, bureaucratic organizations, high cost structures, and work ethics, just to name a few. There is also the cultural explanation: Americans—and their work ethic—differ from Europeans, Latin Americans, and Asians. There are also many reasons companies are uncompetitive. I can subscribe to all of them as elements of the picture. But that's all they are—pieces of the picture or piecemeal causes that don't frame the central issue.

I suggest that a case can be made for another cause, perhaps even more comprehensive, for which there has been little public debate. I believe we can argue that our *most significant miss has been in industrial marketing,* something we in America pioneered as a management concept nearly 30 years ago for consumer goods companies but haven't practiced it well in industrial businesses. Few industrial managers know how to profitably grow the top line around the industrial marketing concept. If any industrial business unit is to thrive, and not just survive, it must align every employee around the industrial marketing concept, which is much more difficult to achieve in an industrial business than it is in a consumer goods company.

Why INDUSTRIAL Marketing Is Difficult

Where is industrial marketing now that we really need it? The answer is less clear because, in this day and age, one rarely quarrels with the importance of marketing. In fact, it would be difficult to find someone willing to argue against the idea that gearing all the activities of a business to be responsive to user needs (a simple but meaningful description of what industrial marketing is all about) is not only sensible but the only way to run the business. Executives and managers that I've met all around the world agree that increased marketing effectiveness is the key to being more competitive and to accelerating sales and profit growth. Despite agreement on this point, many of these industrial executives are disappointed with their companies' marketing capabilities. To quote one company president in Wilmington, Delaware:

Our marketing effort is simply too narrow. We concentrate way too much on selling more of today's product, and we think far too little about what our customers and competitors are doing or where new technology could lead us. Our engineering and sales activities do not look to marketing for leadership, and I know a lot of the things they do would be done differently if we were a stronger marketing company. There is no doubt in my mind that marketing is very important, but how do we make it work the way it should?

In only a very few industrial companies can executives honestly say they are happy with what marketing has done for them. More important, even fewer can state they support this belief with concrete evidence of improved results. The majority of executives in these companies talk about the concept, but it's hard to find examples where strong marketing has actually produced positive results. In many companies, executives are downright discouraged with the results of their efforts. Very few of these executives have written the concept off; it is fundamentally too sound. But many of them are perplexed about what they need to do to get the results they want.

Too many industrial executives regard marketing solely as an isolated function and reason that if they pay enough money or hire enough people, the company's marketing should improve. This approach might work in a retail goods company, but it won't work in an industrial company. *Most industrial companies have too narrow a view of marketing;* even fewer executives see marketing as something that begins before you design a product and ends long after a customer buys the product. Simply pouring more money or people into this function in no way ensures a stronger company. To be a significant force in a company, marketing—like quality—must start at the top. Top and general management must provide the leadership and direction to ensure that marketing considerations are woven into the very fabric of every function or discipline involved in the business. At the beginning of each management workshop conducted for Hewlett Packard employees all over the world, David Packard opened each session with the following statement:

> Marketing should be the headlights of every division and business unit. Even though most of you do not have marketing job titles, you are all in marketing. Industrial marketing is too important to be left to only the marketing department.

This chapter is designed to identify the obstacles that have prevented industrial companies from getting the payoff they should from marketing. Then some proven approaches on how to clear these obstacles out of the way are presented. This chapter also shows how to work closely with customers to develop products and services that provide superior customer value. Finally this chapter describes how to face up to your marketing deficiencies.

Where INDUSTRIAL Marketing Fails

Marketing has not measured up to expectations in many industrial companies because management has concentrated on the trappings and quick fixes rather than the substance. When most executives' talk about what their companies have done to become more marketing oriented, they usually point to such actions as the following:

- Declarations of support from top management in the form of speeches, annual report hype, and public relations talks to the investment community.
- Creation of a marketing organization, including appointment of a marketing head and product or market managers.
- Establishment of a market research function and reassignment of some salespeople to large customers.
- Increased expenditures for customer surveys, advertising, and trade shows.
- Hiring of MBAs with "marketing" backgrounds from the better-known business schools.

• Hiring of managers from consumer and retailing companies known for their marketing.

These actions by themselves are no guarantee of marketing success. In fact, many of them are a waste. Effective industrial marketing requires *a fundamental shift in attitude and behavior throughout the company* so that everyone in every functional area places paramount importance on being responsive to market needs. The steps taken in most industrial companies are not very helpful because they fail to accomplish the crucial shifts in attitude and behavior throughout the organization. The most highly developed marketing departments cannot, by themselves, produce the needed changes.

Why have so few industrial companies gone beyond the trappings to achieve the change in attitude and behavior that ensures substantive marketing? My 30 years of business experience and management training suggests that frequently one or more of these situations exist:

1. Top and general management have no idea how the industrial marketing concept should be applied in an their company.
2. Management understands the industrial marketing concept but has not committed itself to the actions and decisions needed to reinforce it throughout the organization.
3. The company does not know how to segment industrial markets, and it lacks market facts and cost-profit information to select target markets, technologies, and customers for emphasis.
4. Management has failed to install a cross-functional business planning process necessary for effective implementation of the industrial marketing concept, especially across the nonsales and marketing functions.

The INDUSTRIAL Marketing Concept

When I say that in most cases top management does not understand how the marketing concept applies to their industrial situation, you may wonder how highly paid, presumably intelligent industrial executives can fail to understand a concept that is discussed so extensively. But time and time again, I find evidence that although most top management are quick to say they understand and believe in the marketing concept, most of their actions and decisions show otherwise.

Industrial marketing is not simply a departmental operation set up to handle advertising, promotion, merchandising, and selling, as might be the case in a consumer goods company, nor does it necessarily mean striving for the greatest short-term profit contribution, going all-out for volume and large accounts, or seeking to serve everyone in the market with the best possible service. *Industrial marketing should be defined as a companywide business philosophy that first identifies requirements and unmet needs of each customer group. It then designs and makes a superior service/product package that enables the supplier to serve the needs of target market segments more effectively than its competition and at an attractive profit.*

In the above definition of industrial marketing, the supplier draws on the base of knowledge and experience that exists throughout its company. Knowledge and experience define the capabilities of industrial firms that adapt their services and products to fit their customer's needs and strategies. Progressive industrial firms use everyone's experience to interact, create, and develop products and services with customers. This definition of industrial marketing requires a dialog, not monologue, with customers. Two-way learning occurs and it enables the industrial supplier to adapt or alter its capabilities to fit the customer's needs. As the customer and the supplier learn and work together to define what is needed and possible, mutually dependent learning occurs by jointly defining the problem and the potential solutions. This often leads to a new capability or service/product package for both parties.

Marketing in industrial companies is much more a general management responsibility than it is in the consumer products field. In a consumer goods company, major changes in marketing strategy can be made and carried out within the marketing department through changes in advertising emphasis, types of promotion, package design, and positioning brands. But there are no brand managers in industrial companies! In an industrial company, changes in marketing strategy are more likely to involve commitments for new equipment, shifts in product development priorities, or departures from traditional engineering and sales approaches, any one of which would have companywide implications. Marketing may identify the need for such departures, but general management must make the strategic decision of what course the company will take to respond to the market. More importantly, general management must see that the focus is implemented in every functional area of the business unit.

Following through on the Commitment

Understanding the industrial marketing concept is one thing; following through with the commitment to make tough implementation decisions is quite another. Most companies stumble badly here. On the other hand, companies with a superior marketing effort, repeatedly demonstrate their commitment to follow the industrial marketing concept by their willingness to require cooperation from all functions; to invest for long-term goals; and to face up to deficiencies in product, price, or service or in any department or division.

Once again, Parker Hannifin is an example of a company that is truly committed to industrial marketing. For each of the past 20 years, top management in this hydraulic, pneumatic, and electronic controls company has invested the time and funds to make marketing a dominant force in the company. To begin with, Parker annually trains many people in how to gather and use market facts and cost-profit information, and how to develop strategies and cross-functional business plans. This is not an easy task because many of the company's products are sold through distribution, and a special effort was required to develop information on their end-use customers who are serviced by distributors. Parker Hannifin also requires monthly feedback from its distributors on its end users: who they are, what they've spent, and the application for which they used the part or system. Parker's divisions also regularly do an analysis of the strengths and weaknesses of their service/product package versus the largest and fastest growing competitors in what Parker's COO, Don Washkewicz, calls "competitive war rooms."

To avoid the bureaucracy that often interferes with strategic marketing, Parker Hannifin made the decision to keep all divisions small, lean, and focused. Today, the company has more than 100 such decentralized business units with average sales of $60 million each. Each functions as a "PT boat" rather than as an "aircraft carrier." More importantly, the company continues to make investments in management training programs every year to help all management functions understand what industrial marketing is all about. Even in slow economic periods, the company invests in strategic marketing training so that it is ready for the next up-turn to counterattack existing positions and attack the more attractive new opportunities all over the globe.

Cross-Functional Cooperation

The next commitment that top and general management must make is a willingness to require and, if necessary, force all functions to make the changes necessary to be responsive to market needs. In many cases this is more difficult than one might expect because management in most industrial companies must overcome a long-standing preoccupation with business objectives that cripple the marketing effort. For example, objectives such as "get more feet on the street," "keep the plant loaded," "get business at any price or cost," or "more volume" are common watchwords in too many industrial companies—and are often the death knell for profit-making marketing. These attitudes are extremely difficult to overcome, especially when the product is the origin and chief reason for the past success of the enterprise. People are naturally reluctant to abandon a concept that has proved itself in the past.

Remember too that marketing recommendations lack the precision of technical data. Typically, top management is confronted with hard numbers from manufacturing and engineering about material costs, product costs, product performance, and so on. Marketing must make its case on the basis of early warning signals, subjective forecasts, competitive intelligence, judgments from working with lead customers, and from intuition. Of course these forecasts are quantified, but they can never be stated with as much precision as the data submitted by manufacturing and engineering. Finally, many general managers have a technical background themselves and frequently tend to assess their products from a technical rather than a user point of view.

The difficulties with committing to a cross-functional approach are well illustrated by the case of a large industrial pump manufacturer that historically focused on selling the largest, highest powered, most maintenance-free units possible, with the thought that this approach favored its manufacturing economics. User needs, however, shifted toward smaller, less costly units without the rugged engineering characteristics required for maintenance-free operation. Because this trend was clear with the progressive users, the supplier was losing its market position, and marketing recommended a major redesign of the product line. The company's manufacturing and engineering executives, who were acknowledged industry experts, argued convincingly that the current product design was still superior to any competitor product and that the company just needed to "sell harder" and "put more pressure on those damned distributors."

Faced with these conflicting points of view, top management decided to stick with the original product, and they put pressure on the marketing group for a more aggressive selling effort. It was not until the company lost substantial market share and its entire business was threatened that the general manager could bring himself to change the product-driven opinions of his engineering and manufacturing executives and force the requested redesign.

As this company discovered, the task of shifting any company that has historically been dominated by products, engineering, manufacturing, or sales considerations to one that is truly market oriented and driven by the needs of customer groups is always enormous. It takes a tremendous effort on the part of top and general management to ensure that all proposals are carefully thought out, are solidly documented with verified customer needs and economic facts, and demonstrate an understanding of the effect on the other operating departments in the company. It also requires top management's understanding, as well as active support with both words and actions, to make the transition successfully. This usually takes training to achieve, and then it must be implanted in new employees and continually reinforced throughout the enterprise.

Four Basic Steps

A sound understanding of industrial marketing can be viewed in four basic steps: (1) identify customer requirements and unmet needs; (2) select customer groups or market segments for which the company can develop a competitive edge; (3) design and make the right service/product packages; and (4) aim for improved cost, profit, and productivity. Let's amplify each point.

> **1.** *Identify customers' requirements and unmet needs.* There are many manufacturers who know all there is to know about their own technology and virtually nothing about customer's problems, how they really operate, make money, or lose money. Most industrial suppliers are not close enough to their customers to learn about their unmet, emerging, and unarticulated needs—these same suppliers are even further from the needs of their customers' customer. Many of these suppliers spend millions of dollars developing labor-saving parts for the least costly aspects of their customers' operation, or they design

costly features into the product without considering the benefit of each feature to groups of customers with similar needs. They then wonder why their sales personnel are not able to sell the "differentiated" new products. These companies try to sell what they can make rather than make what they can sell.

2. *Select customer groups for emphasis.* We all know companies that strive to be all things to all customers. Such companies inevitably end up with a warehouse full of marginal products and a long list of unproductive customers who generate a small fraction of profits. It is not surprising that the more selective and focused companies earn better profits; they concentrate their limited resources on filling specialized needs for customers who will pay for value. These same disciplined suppliers also know when to walk away from and deemphasize some market segments and customers. While there are always attractive market segment opportunities even in the most mature industries, it is easier to profitably grow in growing markets. They use cross-functional teams to select attractive market segments and key customers for emphasis.

3. *Design and make the right service/product package.* We have all heard horror stories about companies that failed in the marketplace because they tried to sell a Mercedes or Range Rover when the customer group wanted a Ford or a Jeep Cherokee. Actually, a company does not have to be this far off the mark with its product or service package to be a marketing flop. Most industrial buying decisions hinge on minor differences, and a company is in trouble whenever the competition has a service/product package that meets the customer's needs just a little better. Smart companies know that marketing starts before you begin designing a service or product, and they use cross-functional teams from the very beginning to develop, make, and deliver a service/product package that is demonstrably better than competitive offerings.

4. *Aim for improved cost, profit, and productivity.* Too many companies talk a lot about a marketing and profit orientation, but a close look at how they make decisions reveals that sales volume is still the main consideration. Many of these companies would actually have a better profit picture if they gave a lower priority to volume, even if it meant scaling back the business and de-emphasizing or firing some customers. Most companies have insufficient cost-profit information about their product lines and customers to soundly make such decisions. Even fewer companies know the total cost to serve even their largest customers. Those who have cost-profit information that they have confidence in must share the information widely in the organization. Furthermore, a supplier's total costs must constantly decline, or the marketing effort will fail. To put it simply, you must improve productivity by continually achieving more with less.

Now that we have defined marketing as a total business philosophy that encompasses every aspect of the business, it should be easier to distinguish those executives who understand the concept from those who do not. The general manager who consciously targets market segments and has cross-functional teams develop business plans in response to each market's needs shows that he or she understands the indistrial marketing concept. The general manager who creates or merely enlarges the marketing department, who continually pushes salespeople to find new customers of any sort, or who indiscriminately adds more products or capacity, does not understand the concept and has no chance of leading a market-driven business unit.

The general or business unit manager must lead the market orientation. Very few top managers realize that industrial marketing should be the primary responsibility of a general manager or business unit manager. Even fewer realize that industrial marketing must be woven into the fabric of a business plan developed by the appropriate people in multiple disciplines. A marketing plan will never be sufficient in an industrial company that wants to make marketing a stronger force in every department. *A cross-functionally developed business plan is needed to implement the industrial marketing concept.*

The Entrepreneurial Compass

Marketing should be the entrepreneurial compass of the organization. Marketing should be constantly scanning the environment for new opportunities and threats to your existing business. It should help people define and assess the opportunities and point each business unit in directions that profitably capture the most attractive opportunities. Marketing should be every division's navigator. Without this entrepreneurial orientation from marketing, a business will likely be mostly reactive rather than a fast-moving entrepreneurial one. Entrepreneurial organizations have a different perception of the world than reactive ones. They think and act outside the box of conventional thinking and practices. They see the unmet needs, the better mousetrap, and big growth opportunities. They see the bigger picture of how things fit together or what some people now call "vision."

High-growth companies attract and keep imaginative and energetic risk takers who have an ability to turn early warning signals into successful business opportunities. Entrepreneurs or intrapreneurs basically converge market opportunities with the needed companies capabilities; in short, they create new business combinations. Intrapreneurs need the freedom to act or try things and the freedom to fail. Most companies filter these people out in the hiring process, and others cause them to leave the organization to either start their own company or to join a more adventuresome enterprise. Then many companies wonder why their people don't "think out of the box," while they keep people in narrowly defined job descriptions. The downsizing and top-down management styles of many companies have caused many intrapreneurs to hibernate or leave the organization.

The entrepreneur or intrapreneur needs a secure and supportive environment that encourages and supports experimentation and failures. You can't stumble if you're not moving. If top and general management does not encourage, expect, and tolerate failures, employees will not come forth with growth ideas. The great organic growth companies have guts and tolerance. Their people (not just top management) are willing to take bold risks, stick to their convictions, and bet on cross-functional teams with a new concept and sound business plan.

Market Maturity is a Mind-Set

I nearly always hear executives say, "Our industry is mature." These same managers typically blame the lack of profitable top-line growth on the industry, not on their company. These managers believe that outside forces totally control their destiny. Most so-called mature markets can be revived with better products and services. Technological change doesn't stop in slow-growth industries; in fact, it intensifies. Enthusiastic people in "mature" businesses dream and experiment to find new uses, develop improved products and lower costs. After more than 20 years in the market, Monsanto's Round-Up brand of herbicide is growing sales at 20 percent per year and is still able to maintain profit margins of more than 40 percent. Much of the sales growth for Round-Up has come from new applications and geographic expansion to emerging markets in Brazil, Indonesia, and other countries. Continuous process innovation and higher productivity have enabled Monsanto to profitably reduce its selling prices on Round-Up by more than 50 percent over the past twelve years. Sales of Monsanto's Round-Up today are more than $3 billion, and profit is still very attractive.

Many managers inaccurately equate a slow-growth or mature market with one that doesn't need more cost-effective solutions. Nothing could be farther from reality. In slow-growth markets technology doesn't stagnate, in fact, *new technology can create rapid growth in a mature market.* For years, many people predicted the decline of U.S. railroads; however, they still move more than 40 percent of the nation's cargo. Far from being a relic chugging toward extinction, railroads now haul three times as many ton-miles of freight as they did in 1950. This freight includes millions of new motor vehicles and a growing number of "intermodal" trailers and containers, which over long distances move more cost-effectively when piggybacked on trains than on the highway. Manufacturers now use railcars as rolling warehouses for their inventory. While railroad freight trains look pretty much as they did 30 years ago, new technology is transforming this huge industry and making the railroads more powerful, lighter, and less susceptible to wear and tear. Some of the new technology from industrial suppliers to the railroad shows how innovation can accelerate growth in a "mature" industry:

- *New materials.* Most freight cars are no longer made of just steel. Aluminum is now a widely used material, and some cars are being built out of space-age composites. The lighter materials allow today's freight cars to carry 10 to 20 percent more payloads, the empty cars put less wear on the tracks, and maintenance cost is reduced. Improved efficiency, higher productivity, and lower maintenance costs drive the new technologies.
- *Power generation.* Alternating current is replacing locomotives running on direct current. The new and retrofitted brushless AC locomotives selling for about $2 million a piece, have 50 percent more power, are more fuel efficient, and are less likely to break down because they have fewer parts than the older DC locomotives. Electronic fuel injection systems lower the exhaust emissions. In the past it took six DC locomotives to pull 140 loaded cars; three AC locomotives now do the same job.
- *Wheels and brakes.* When the brakes are applied, the wheel rims heat up and expand, which can cause the wheels to crack. As the bearings lose lubrication, they create a "hot-box" hazard. New bearing designs have reduced the problem, and advanced brake systems apply brakes on every car at the same time, reducing the friction, distance, and amount of time it takes to stop a train. Dispensers that apply traction-enhancing sand to the rails, once manually operated by the engineer, are now triggered automatically when a computer chip senses wheel slippage.
- *Computers and satellites.* As cars with identification marks pass transponders, they are read and relayed to a computer so that every car and locomotive can be located at any time. Sophisticated solar-powered tracking systems allow dispatchers to locate trains and adjust their schedules. An onboard computer system alerts the train crew and railyard people whenever a part needs maintenance. Computer chips coordinate the self-diagnostic functions that display the train's entire health on computer screens at the engineer's stand.

This is just a sample of the new technologies that help reduce the costs and improve the profits for the "mature" railroad industry all over the world. Industrial suppliers are increasingly trotting out technologies that can add speed, reliability, freight-hauling capacity, and other cost savings to their so-called mature railroad customers and, in turn, make them more competitive with other railroads and trucking and shipping companies.

WORK CLOSER WITH CUSTOMERS

Effective industrial marketing requires some new ways to think about customers needs. The era of the pure industrial product is over. The distinction between industrial products and services has eroded. The service component of any service/product package is as critical as the product. What once appeared to be a rigid polarity between products and services has become a hybrid. Since products and services have merged, it is critical for industrial marketers to learn about a customer's service as well as product needs.

As everything technological becomes connected, the value of a product lies increasingly with its links to other products and services. Every industrial supplier must no longer think of itself as a maker of stand-alone products, but as a provider of applications knowledge, systems, solutions, maintenance, and wrap-around services. Companies that primarily see themselves as inside-out pushers of products to customers will never be as successful as those that take an outside-in view of customers by first uncovering their known needs, expectations, and unarticulated needs. To begin, ask customers about their current and emerging business problems, not just about their needs for a given product.

All customers are living with problems or needs. In some cases, industrial customers challenge suppliers to solve a particular problem and in so doing, force the supplier to come up with an innovative solution. Often the solution to one customer's problem can be generalized to solve similar problems with other customers in the same segment all over the world. There are ten basic areas to learn about customer problems and ultimately provide them with more value:

1. Learn about how customers operate from procurement through after sales service.
2. Learn about customer problems, bottlenecks, and hassles, and how much it costs per day, month, or year to remedy the situations.
3. Learn about customer service needs and do R&D on their service requirements.
4. Learn about customer safety and environmental needs, and pending legislation.
5. Learn about customer maintenance needs, periodic repairs and downtime costs.
6. Learn about the customer system needs, not just the components.
7. Learn about customers' total costs, not just unit price.
8. Learn how to make or save customers money, help reduce costs, avoid a cost, reduce their hassles, and/or improve their sales revenue.
9. Learn how to follow customers overseas by building on your domestic relationships.
10. Apply 1-9 above to your customers' customers, and provide more value to your immediate customers, customers' customers, or both.

Each of these ways of thinking and working with customers will uncover unmet needs, help develop better service/product packages, enlarge your opportunities, and accelerate growth. Your company's sales, tech service, customer service, and engineers must all have antennae out to hear, observe, and learn about these needs. Formal customer consultations conducted by marketing and R&D teams are usually needed. Forums, including technical seminars and user councils, are additional ways of bringing vital customer need information into your organization. Customer need information is the foundation from which a supplier develops and delivers more customer value.

Provide Superior Value

Increasingly, industrial companies all over the world are struggling under the pressure to add more value to the products and services they sell. The pressure is coming from ever-improving competition, new technologies, and more demanding customers. In order to just maintain the current levels of sales and profit, smart industrial companies are continually driven to add more customer value year after year. If a supplier doesn't provide customers more value, a competitor will figure out how to do it. Since improved customer value is such a vital marketing concept, it is helpful to distinguish between customer value for retail and industrial customers.

Retail and Industrial Customer Value

The most brilliant and targeted retail brand advertising campaign cannot create or deliver superior customer value for an industrial firm. Value to industrial customers is a lot more than brand management or a slick corporate identity program that claims your product or company is great. In retail goods companies, brands and emotional appeals are the focus and heart of the value adding process, more commonly known as brand equity. In contrast, industrial managers must relentlessly present their products and services with documented and verifiable benefits to users before the brand is valued by customers.

Many consumer goods value statements (typically called Unique Selling Propositions) are a lot of emotional and social psychological reasons why people should buy the product. The Marlboro man takes refuge in its image of American masculinity. These huge advertising campaigns try to have people recall one message, image, or slogan. When the unique selling proposition is remembered, the consumer goods retailer distinguishes their brand from competitors'. Instead of the brand becoming a permanent icon of value, industrial customers are constantly looking for ways to make or save money with their purchases. Industrial customers are constantly searching for more value, not just image advertising with unsupported customer claims.

Industrial products cannot command premium prices by only the virtue of advertising-generated awareness. Performance must justify the price. In the industrial world, a product cannot succeed only because of a good brand name. Established industrial brand leaders cannot maintain premium prices with me-too products and services. IBM's name was one of the best-known names in the world, yet the company was in a free fall for years before it was turned around. Digital Equipment had a strong brand name and, after two years of loses, was acquired. Newer, lower-cost and more innovative PC builders such as Dell and Gateway grew to dominate markets that IBM and Digital pioneered. As much as 80 percent of the total cost of owning a business computer is in customer training, upgrading, and troubleshooting. EDS, Anderson Consulting, and hundreds of other firms give IBM intense competition for this service business. Poor sales support and customer service is the surest way to spoil an industrial manufacturer's corporate and brand name.

Industrial companies also create value by helping customers decide what solution is best and then by producing to order at agreed times and with fast post-sales service. As industrial products become more sophisticated and customer demands on performance and service grow, suppliers must increasingly offer a total solution to user problems. Packaging unconnected products as a system or kit is a growing way to provide value. Linking the supplier and buyer's business processes with electronics increasingly generates customer value for industrial products and services. These linkages start with face-to-face technical exchanges and then electronically network the supplying and buying organizations.

In order to provide superior customer value, it is helpful to think about a customer's system needs and total cost, not just in terms of one component and its unit cost. When you are able to reduce a customer's total cost or life cycle cost, you are providing tangible economic value. Life cycle cost is the total lifetime cost to purchase, install, operate, maintain, and dispose of equipment or material. Goulds Pumps developed a new pump, PumpSmart™ that significantly reduces a customer's life cycle cost. Goulds put together the customer's total costs with the framework shown in Exhibit 3-1.

Compared to the conventional pump system, the higher unit price of PumpSmart™ resulted in lower total costs. When marketing PumpSmart™, Goulds had to educate plant managers, maintenance engineers, designers, and other buying influences on the economic benefits of the new product. A number of tools were used to communicate superior customer value. The tools included educational workshops on pump energy usage, energy costs, maintenance and life cycle costs. Goulds developed documented case studies of the PumpSmart™ life cycle cost savings in

Exhibit 3-1
Life Cycle Cost Comparison

Customers Cost Components (Identify these costs and make assumptions)	Conventional[1] System	PumpSmart™[1]	Savings
1. Unit Purchase Price (initial capital cost)	$20,660[2]	$30,800[3]	(-$10,140)
2. Installation Costs	$83,000	$53,750	$29,250
3. Operating Costs (energy)	$606,644	$377,371	$229,273
4. Maintenance Costs (includes seals, bearings, impeeler and labor)	$31,000 (10 repairs)	$14,877 (6 repairs)	$16,123
5. Downtime Costs	$1,500	$1,000	$500
6. Switching Costs	-0-	-0-	-0-
7. Trade-In, Salvage, Resale or Scrap Value	$500	$500	-0-
Total Life Cycle Costs and Savings	$743,304	$478,298	$265,006

[1] Assumes a 15 year equipment life for both pumps.
[2] Includes pump and motor, flow control valve, flowmeter, and starter
[3] Includes only pump and motor, and PumpSmart™ system. (flow control valve, flowmeter, and starter are not required)

many market segments. The target market segments included chemicals, petro-chemical, pharmaceutical, municipal water works, irrigation, pulp and paper, and snow making. Press kits, trade show exhibits, direct mail literature, on-site demonstrations, field trials, and technical articles in market-specific publications were employed to communicate the value. All the communication tools helped change the customers' reference point from unit price to total life cycle costs.

A superior customer value statement (SCVS) must meet three criteria: (1) customers must find it superior to competitive alternatives; (2) the supplier must be able to document the stated value in total cost savings and customer satisfaction, and (3) and the customer value should translate into attractive profit for the supplier. A SCVS should state the amount of something saved over a specific time period. Customer value must be presented in the customer's language, metrics, annual usage, cost savings and satisfaction.

Differentiate Your Capabilities

Directing the efforts of the entire business unit to the supply needs of the buying organization creates value for industrial products and services. As compared to consumer goods psychological positioning, industrial firms provide value with their know-how, experience, and capabilities. No retail brand can provide the necessary companywide commitment required by an industrial supplier. Cross-functional business teams, led by product, market, business unit, or general managers, create industrial customer value. *Industrial corporate and brand reputations are the by-product of supplier performance.* The capabilities that drive supplier performance include consultation, design, manufacturing, on-time delivery, and product support. Industrial buyers measure and benchmark these capabilities against the competitive suppliers. If any of these capabilities fail, the supplier fails. In order to differentiate their organization's capabilities, some companies organize divisions, business units, or management teams around specific market segments and the needs of these markets. They simply align their organization to provide value to discrete market segments and key customers. If customers are global, these value-creating capabilities must be in place around the world.

A business plan for the market segment and for individual customers is the mechanism for developing and delivering value across the industrial supplier's various departments. The cross-functional business team that develops the business plan is the same people committed to delivering the value. A marketing plan is never sufficient in an industrial company because many departments and people outside of the marketing department provide value to customers.

Winning industrial companies are those that have the right mix of company capabilities in place that directly translates into serving customers in a superior way. Capabilities are more dynamic and interactive than the static notion of "core competencies" or a company's strengths. For example, Canon's wide range of technical capabilities in optics, imaging, and microprocessor controls have enabled it to enter markets as seemingly diverse as copiers, laser printers, cameras, and image scanners. Capabilities also consist of technical knowledge, application know-how, problem solving skills, and strong distributors. Great companies realize when they lack a certain capability that needs to be added to serve customers.

Many businesses try to grow sales with products and services that are already available to the market. Today, marketplaces are crowded. Industrial customers are well informed and more sophisticated. When the services and/or product are generic, it is difficult to accelerate sales and profit growth. If your service/product package is not perceived as different and better, why would anyone buy from your company? However, when your service/product package is both different and better (in the eyes of users) than competitive offerings, take advantage of it. Which of your products and services are different and *better* than the competitive offerings? What documented benefits do you provide to each market segment *better* than the competition?

The Value Package

The term value added is used so loosely that the meaning has become a vague buzzword. Historically, value added referred to the materials, features, and services added to a product at any given stage of production. A vaguely stated value added strategy is supposed to lead to a higher price for the supplier. In marketing terms, developing customer value does not necessarily require adding anything to the product—in fact, a company might deliver more customer value by taking away materials, features or services from a service/product package. In marketing terms, value is in the customer's total costs and experiences. If you are not creating more customer value in the form of customer profit improvement, you may not be adding any value. Added value must come from the customer's positive return and total experiences from their purchase and use of the service/product package.

When many industrial managers think about customer value, they think only in terms of tangible product benefits. Their mind set of value is usually limited to the product's physical performance. The product performance benefits are important but are often only the tip of the iceberg relative to the total value that customers need or receive from suppliers. The intangible service benefits of every service/product package sometimes outweigh the importance of tangible product benefits. Technically proud manufacturers often forget that service benefits such as a service manual, customer counseling, an efficient order fulfillment process, and a strong distributor network all help provide superior customer value. Supplier's should identify both the service and performance needs that are important to each market segment. The Customer Value Iceberg with product and service benefits is shown as Exhibit 3-2. Most industrial user value is quantifiable. All physical product benefits can be measured. Many of the benefits from the services shown in Exhibit 3-2 can also be measured. Because industrial customers buy products and services to make or save money, they want documented economic value—not vague claims that cannot be supported. Cost-justified procurement managers will not accept exaggerations and unverified selling propositions that are so common in retailing. Industrial

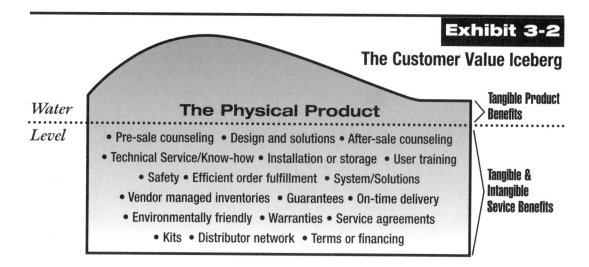

Exhibit 3-2

The Customer Value Iceberg

Water ···········

Level

The Physical Product

> Tangible Product Benefits

• Pre-sale counseling • Design and solutions • After-sale counseling
• Technical Service/Know-how • Installation or storage • User training
• Safety • Efficient order fulfillment • System/Solutions
• Vendor managed inventories • Guarantees • On-time delivery
• Environmentally friendly • Warranties • Service agreements
• Kits • Distributor network • Terms or financing

> Tangible & Intangible Sevice Benefits

users need to know the number of something saved per day, per shift, per month, or per year.

After a supplier has learned how customers make or save customer's money, they need to present the value to be received in the form of a documented sales proposal, or value statement. The value customers are to receive must be based upon the customer's normal usage and costs. Any assumptions about costs, usage, throughput, or savings must be clearly stated in a value statement. *Customer value always consists of a combination of product performance, service, and price.*

Customer Value Statements

A good value statement should provide superior customer value. A value statement that just provides "equal or equivalent value" is not a strong position to be in. Who needs another me-too product in an era of supplier reduction and inventory rationalization? Me-too value increases the likelihood of getting or losing business based on lower unit price. Competing on unit price alone can create a price war in which all suppliers may suffer. However, if several suppliers offer identical value and if one supplier has a significantly lower cost structure and lower price, it can earn attractive profits before competitors learn and catch up.

If a supplier wants to provide superior customer value, it is necessary to ask, "Superior value relative to what?" Side-by-side comparisons and field trials conducted by the supplier, or done jointly with a customer are usually needed to support a superior customer value claim. Many industrial suppliers equate a superior customer value statement with broad claims about their "world-class manufacturing" or "core competencies" as if no other competitor can match or exceed claims that "we're better at doing so and so." A superior customer value statement (SCVS), first and foremost, *describes the customers' benefits from using your value package.* A SCVS does not just describe your capabilities, core competencies, or strengths. The supplier's ability to do something well does not necessarily translate into superior value for any customer. Remember the old adage, "The operation was a great success but the patient died."

The definition of superior value means it must be perceived better than all other solutions. Many steel companies have failed to compare their products to other materials such as aluminum and wood. If some steel manufacturers do consider the substitution effect of other materials, many only think in terms of the unit or per-pound price, not the customer's total cost or total value received in each end-use market segment. When evaluating alternative customer value statements, it is important to think like the respective customer in terms of needs, usage, and total costs. The entire process of providing superior value is based on understanding the customers' operations as much as they do and the economic value of alternative technologies in their operation. A teardown-and-failure analysis of customers' products and their competitors' products can help identify opportunities to substitute your product for another product. Product development people need to think about product benefits from the customers' perspective before they freeze the design for a new product. Every product development proposal and new product launch should have a clearly stated superior customer value statement. The supplier who genuinely learns how the customer operates and what these costs are will be more likely to develop superior customer value statements. A salesperson who is trained to identify, measure, and communicate the value received will execute a value selling approach more readily than the sales rep who only employs hard selling, price haggling, or social relationships to keep or get new business.

Formulating a market strategy and business plan does not start with competition; it starts with customers and compares the current or potential value package with competitive alternatives. Managers with a match, meet, or commodity mentality start and stop the value process by studying the competition, but the competition does not buy much from its competitors. After learning what customers need, suppliers should be concerned with creating more value for customers by comparing what they offer to the competitive offerings as show in Exhibit 3-3. This comparison should be done with your best, not worst, competitors and for like, as well as unlike, solutions. The side-by-side competitive value comparison should start with the tangible product benefits, but it must always include the intangible service benefits that are important to the customer. A competitive customer value comparison identifies where you are weak and strong. Such competitive match-ups, based on customer needs, especially non-price needs, give clear clues as to what strategy, and improvement programs are needed. In short, before developing strategies that deliver superior customer value, suppliers should learn what type and amount of value competitors are providing, and then they determine how they can provide customers with more value.

Exhibit 3-3
Side-by-Side Competitive Value Comparisons

With current, former, and potential customers, complete the following:

Identified and Verified Customer Needs	Benefits We Offer	Best Competitor Offers
1.		
2.		
3.		
4.		
5.		

Superior customer value is the difference between the total customer value received (from tangible and intangible benefits) to perform the same function(s) with like or functional substitutes. When a customer's total value exceeds their total cost and experiences, customer value occurs. When a customer's total value received is less than expected, customer dissatisfaction occurs. In the industrial world, it is usually far better to under promise and over deliver rather than do the opposite and create customer dissatisfaction.

Customer Dissatisfaction

Every company should investigate many of their lost or former customers. Few companies do an objective analysis of lost customers—especially for the ones that everyone didn't want to lose. Some companies create and distribute a monthly or quarterly "lost business report" of former customers who are still in business. Most industrial firms do not measure customer defection rates, and they fail to use customer defectors as guide to improving their business. By searching for the root causes of each customer departure, companies with a desire to learn can identify business practices that need fixing.

Some progressive industrial companies have tightened the definition of lost business to include the loss of any portion of a customer's business, not just the total loss of a customer. National Starch refers to any loss of a customer's business as "the leaky bucket" effect. If your business is flat with a customer and that customer is growing rapidly, you may be losing market share at the account and never know it. The same customer may have opened new facilities elsewhere in the country or in another region of the world where you have little or none of the business. Customers who are giving you a decreasing "share of their wallet" are just as important to analyze as those who may have totally defected to another supplier.

Deere, the farm and equipment manufacturer, uses retired managers to interview defectors and those "good" customers now buying less. Many people at Deere listen to taped interviews with former customers, which help search for root causes of why a customer switched or bought less. Deere realizes that the key to organizational learning is to grasp the value of customer failures so they can turn customer dissatisfaction into customer satisfaction.

There are many other useful ways to learn about customer dissatisfaction and turn it into better customer value. Warranty claims from product registration are a valuable source of learning about product design needs. Deere carefully catalogs equipment-caused injuries and analyzes global insurance records for injuries by type of farm products, crops, and regions of the world. Deere knows that safety sells. Aggressive distributors are another excellent source of "complaints" that are really suggestions on how to improve customer value. Toll-free hot lines make it easier for customers to report complaints. Every web site should have an area for suggestions. The information that a supplier uses to track and measure customer dissatisfaction can ultimately help develop cures that will improve customer value and the supplier's profit.

Before a company can provide superior value to customers, two necessary conditions must exist. First, the company must take a longer-term view of the business, and then they must face up to their deficiencies. Let's now amplify these final considerations.

TAKE A LONGER-TERM VIEW

The idea of investing to build and strengthen market position is accepted and practiced every day in consumer goods companies. In fact, *investment spending* is a consumer goods term often used when describing commitments required to achieve longer-term objectives. This longer-term notion is not acceptable or even considered in many industrial companies, perhaps due to Wall Street's pressure for improved quarterly performance. I argue that a longer time frame is more critical in industrial companies than in consumer packaged goods companies because of the longer cycle times needed for the design, manufacture, and selling of any new product. Designing performance or cost improvements for an established product is a long, hard job; developing the field test or performance data to prove these advantages takes even more time. Many industrial users rigorously evaluate the cost effectiveness of each product offering for months and sometimes years before they buy.

It is difficult to get an industrial customer to try a new or different piece of equipment that may cost thousands or even hundreds of thousands of dollars and, more importantly, that may affect an entire production process. It can take months or years to gain full customer acceptance and build a solid market base for a product in the industrial world. And that, in turn, bespeaks the necessity of a longer-term view. At General Electric, former CEOs Ralph Cordiner, Fred Borch, and Reginald Jones nurtured the aircraft engine, gas turbine, and plastics businesses when they were small and money-losing operations. What chance of survival would embryonic businesses have under GE's current management who mandates that an operation must be number 1 or 2 in its field, with minimum returns, or else it must be either quickly fixed or sold. Such short-term decisions caused GE to exit many manufacturing businesses in favor of quicker cash crops from financial services, broadcasting, and entertainment services. Whenever there is an obsession with the short term, effective industrial marketing will be difficult to implement. There are no quick fixes to build, improve, or turnaround a declining industrial market position. Unfortunately, many companies pay closer attention to security analysts than they do to customers' needs or employees that serve those customers.

Despite these realities of industrial marketing, many executives are loath to consider spending more money to build a stronger market position if the outlays cut into short-term profits. Ironically, the same people are often willing to spend much more on a capital proposal for a new plant or equipment. A sound outside-in marketing approach might have discouraged the capital expense or it could have suggested an investment in making better new products with needed benefits and focused on the faster-growing customer groups and regions of the world.

Consider the case of a chemical manufacturer that committed several million dollars for the development of new products to make its line more competitive. It had also invested heavily in manufacturing equipment to get the new products ready for market. When plans for market introduction were being made, the marketing director requested a budget increase to set up a small special sales group that would focus exclusively on the new products. He pointed out that although the added costs of a special sales group would not be recovered during the first two years, by the end of the second year the added volume at that time would more than cover the cost of the new group. The division general manager initially balked at the budget increase, claiming it would slash short-term profits. It took a lot of effort, but the marketing director finally convinced him this was shortsighted by saying, "If we don't get these products established this year, we will lose the slim lead time we have in the market—and the $7 million we sank into development and equipment will be down the drain."

Unfortunately, marketing people rarely score such wins. Usually, the overriding emphasis on the short term prevents new products from either being developed or effectively launched even when they are clearly needed. Division managers are generally reluctant to weed out marginal products or customers so that the mix can be upgraded because they've never been trained to distinguish winners from losers when they look at products, customers, or market segments. Until more CEOs and general managers start thinking in those terms and adopt a longer-term perspective in industrial firms, marketing's effectiveness and top-line growth will be limited.

Face Up to Your Deficiencies

Even when top management does make a commitment to longer-term thinking, it must also be willing to face up to the company's critical deficiencies in product performance, cost, price, or service. While almost all industrial managers acknowledge that quality and service are lethal weapons in today's competitive environment, many display the natural tendency to view their own products through rose-colored glasses. They conclude that any advantages claimed for competitors' products are exaggerated or insignificant, that the competition is giving the business away, or that it has a cheaply engineered or shoddily manufactured line that explains its ability to sell at a lower price.

One maker of electronic test equipment lost considerable business because the division's executives would not face up to the fact that its product was inferior to that of its competitors in terms of price and user performance. The division's major product line was losing market share, and margins had eroded several points, despite the fact that two different product managers had made the point that competitor changes in product and price had made it impossible to compete with the company's line as currently designed and priced. Both product managers recommended a redesigned program to take cost out of the line and to incorporate desperately needed product features. At the same time, they proposed a lower price schedule to make the line more competitive.

Top executives, including the vice president of sales, reacted negatively. They simply could not accept that their product line, which had once been the top-quality product, was now out of synch with the marketplace. Instead, they blamed the product managers for not having a good grasp of the business and for not being imaginative in their recommendations to rebuild market share with more sales volume. But they had a problem that they couldn't "just sell their way out of."

It wasn't until a new division general manager came on the scene that the company reversed its position. He took a fresh, unbiased look at his company's product as compared with the competition and concluded that the two product managers had been right and that no amount of aggressive selling, creative merchandising, or any other so-called marketing activity could overcome the product's basic competitive disadvantages.

Admittedly, facing up to a critical deficiency is difficult. However, management cannot allow emotional ties to what has been done in the past to overrule current market considerations of what customers need and competitors are doing. Otherwise, as a CEO in one major chemical company told me, "Management does a lot of talking about following the industrial marketing concept, but in reality it's often a joke. We're too often driven by existing products, folklore, and inflated perceptions about the value of our products and our company name."

When implementing the industrial marketing concept, I repeatedly find deficiencies in three areas:

1. Insufficient industrial marketing competence and experience in the business.
2. Insufficient market facts and cost/profit information.
3. Insufficient market focuses and market management.

Many executives who are vitally interested in making marketing the core thrust of the business are often thwarted because of deficiencies in these areas. Let's examine each deficiency to see where the difficulties lie and how improvements can occur.

Competent and Experienced People

It takes superior knowledge of customers' needs, competition, and the cost-profit economics of the business, along with a working knowledge of the technology and a healthy dose of good business judgment, to be an effective general, product, market, or business unit manager in an industrial business. A general manager cannot be a general manager for any industrial business; a competent general manager must learn the details of the particular industrial business, which usually occurs from the bottom up, not by parachuting in from a very different business. *And it takes years, not a few months, to learn any industrial business.* Without critical knowledge of the technology, costs, customers, and competitive solutions, the business unit manager can never command the respect of the other managers and get them to follow marketing's lead. Effective cross-functional leadership is always based on knowledge, expertise and professional respect from colleagues who work in that same business. It is usually far more effective to teach proven industrial marketing practices to people who intimately know an industrial business than it is to have someone come from outside a business who must first learn the business (which takes years) before he or she can even think about developing sound market strategies for the business.

Many companies have staffed key marketing positions (marketing director, product manager, market manager) with people who clearly have none of these qualities or experience in the specific business. Where does management go wrong? In some cases, the problem stems from a tendency to equate marketing with aggressive selling or promotion; thus, management looks no further than the sales department for people to move into these positions. In fact, we often see senior executives wrongly use the words "sales" and "marketing" interchangeably. Many have titles of "sales and marketing" rather than "marketing and sales"—a sure sign that they do not understand industrial marketing. The problem is that many salespeople simply do not understand the costs and operating dynamics of the business, and their sales or volume orientation too often dominates their recommendations and decisions. As you would expect, they quickly lose the respect of other functional and top management executives and have no chance to influence major decisions.

In other cases, management turns outside the company, searching for candidates to make the company market driven overnight. But, except in rare cases, these people perform well below expectations because their skills are not all applicable. There is no general group of skills for industrial marketing that is readily transferable from one industrial business to another as there is in consumer goods marketing, where basic advertising and promotion skills are applicable to a wide range of product and market situations. One company equipment supplier to the telecommunications field learned this lesson after the fact. Top management decided that the company needed a stronger marketing effort and recruited a successful sales manager from a chemical company whose background included three years as a product-line marketing manager and an MBA from an Ivy League school. On the surface, he appeared to be very well qualified for the job. His performance, however, was abysmal. He did not understand the underlying technology and was unable to shepherd the company's new product program against very stiff competition, particularly from abroad. He also failed to understand the intricacies of designing and selling complex communications systems and was frequently caught off base with proposals that did not meet customer requirements. Moreover, he suffered from an insufficient understanding of how customers bought and used the product. After one year, both top management and the individual agreed that the fit wasn't good. He quietly resigned and joined a large management-consulting firm where he didn't have to live with any of his recommendations.

A number of well-run industrial companies hire marketing managers from target markets and customers' operations. Some companies also train their technical people in customer applications and overall business economics before they become profit-center managers. None of the high-performing industrial companies I know takes newly minted MBAs or people with no hands-on industry-specific experience and expects them to take a lead role in developing the industrial marketing concept. Furthermore, because nearly all marketing taught at business schools is focused on consumer goods and retailing approaches, smart companies know people from these institutions usually have no understanding of sound industrial marketing. Therefore, to have competent people implementing marketing throughout the organization, training in practical, proven, and cutting-edge industrial marketing concepts is usually needed for the entire cross-functional business team and the general or business unit managers.

Accurate Market and Cost Information

Companies generally lack the following four types of information:

1. What existing products and customers make or lose money?
2. What markets are growing and/or are underserved?
3. Who are the fastest growing competitors in each segment, and why?

4. How to develop winning strategies and business plans by bringing cost-profit, market, competitive, and technical information together?

I have conducted management training workshops for industrial business teams around the world for many years and continue to be amazed at how many companies, especially some of the largest ones, have little confidence in their cost-profit and market information. After gathering and sharing this vital information, a motion control business unit learned the following: 35 percent of their customer relationships were unprofitable; 40 percent of their accounts were marginally profitable; the remaining 25 percent of their customers generated the bulk of profits. Having good cost-profit and market segment information about customers and competition is the first step; then it must be widely shared throughout the organization. The wide sharing of this information—especially deep into the organization with those close to the customers, plants, and laboratories—helps energize people and generate many what-if solutions. The wide sharing of all information must take place, or empowerment and managing close to the customer will only be buzzwords. Unfortunately, too many companies around the world still do not have an open culture, and the close-to-the-vest style of many managers is often an obstacle. In these situations, the need to know mentality should be changed to "Who doesn't need to know?"

Correct Market Focuses

Armed with the necessary information, cross-functional business teams, led by a product, market, business, or general manager, are ready to develop a focused business plan. To do this, marketing has to be the lead activity and must see that everyone understands the lead role. This means that marketing people have the responsibility for identifying the changing needs of the market and the opportunities these represent for the company. *Marketing people, with the cooperation and assistance of a cross-functional team, are expected to translate market requirements and trends into the actions that must be taken by the other principal functions of the company (engineering, manufacturing, sales, and finance) to capitalize on opportunities.*

When David Packard referred to industrial marketing, at the beginning of this chapter, as the headlights of the company, he did not mean that marketing is organizationally superior to the other functions. Marketing's role is to point the way toward better opportunities in the marketplace. The role of the other functions is to follow this and ensure that they perform in a way that is consistent with market requirements. In effect, the cross-functional business team must act as if they were a small startup business and determine where they want to attack and build strong market positions and develop a business plan. Top and general management must decide in which market segment(s) they want to add, deemphasize, or withdraw resources.

The final step in generating the correct focuses is to set quantitative growth goals for the next three to five years. Starting with existing market segments, sales and profit goals must be clearly stated in the business plan. Then goals should be set for entering new segments or countries each year and for the desired sales and profit results. Finally, annual goals for new products as a percentage of sales and gross profits should be set for each business unit. It is against these goals and results that resource allocation decisions should be made across the organization.

SUMMARY

There's nothing particularly mystical about what it takes to build substance into industrial marketing as opposed to simply having the trappings of a marketing orientation. In an industrial company, however, marketing requires an in-depth understanding and strong leadership from the top to make marketing work because marketing must be a total business philosophy from the boardroom to the boiler room. Marketing must be the entrepreneurial compass of the enterprise. At the same time, saying there is nothing particularly sophisticated about the concept of industrial marketing that doesn't minimize the huge cultural change required to make a product-, manufacturing-, or sales-oriented company into a market-driven one. You must work closely with customers to identify unmet needs and develop better new products and services. To be better, the products and services should be able to demonstrate and document how customers will make or save money. Superior customer value statements are the foundation for developing winning business strategies. In order to provide more customer value, industrial suppliers need to move from a product-driven business model of "make and sell" to a market driven business model of "listen and serve."

Developing sound industrial marketing capabilities is a very difficult job that takes company-wide commitment and a significant investment in the training of people throughout the organization. The effort will be under constant fire from those with a short-term or mature market mentality and those threatened by change. But those companies that deflect the spears and persist will reap enormous rewards in the form of a newfound responsiveness to market opportunities and competitive advantages. When everyone in an industrial company realizes they are in marketing, the enterprise will accelerate profitable top-line growth.

Segmenting Industrial Markets

"We have segmented our businesses so we can better understand and respond to customer needs."

Jim Griffith, President and COO
The Timken Company

From the 1970s through the 1990s, business diversification was the rage. The theory was that the greater number of different businesses a company was in, the better it was insulated from business cycles. These companies believed that a manager in one business could successfully transfer that knowledge to a totally different business in which he or she had no experience. Many companies eventually realized that without either some technical or market similarities among their businesses, they had no operating fit. In short, these companies needed to have *more focused businesses* that concentrated on a narrower field of business and specific market segments. Wall Street applauded the moves of the more focused companies. Parallel to the strategic development of more focused companies have been the escalation of demergers, which narrow the focus of companies by breaking them up with divestitures and spin-offs.

Corning Incorporated was an old-line manufacturer that reinvented itself as a nimble and more focused company. Once known for its glass casserole dishes and Corning dinnerware, the company has shifted focus in recent years to industrial products including optical fiber and liquid crystal display screens for the closely linked telecommunications and computer industries. The company has jettisoned operations representing half of its sales since 1996, including the division that made the casserole dishes and dinner plates. Roger Ackerman, the CEO who led the transformation stated:

> We've clearly moved from being a very diversified company to a much more focused one. Corning still works mostly in glass, but often in forms most people would barely recognize. Beyond getting more focused, Corning has managed to move into markets and businesses that are growing much faster and offer higher margins. With this focus, we're able to invest more heavily in fewer areas and have been able to develop more breakthrough products and do less line extensions and product tweaking. Three times a year, we now hold "growth days" meetings where we review markets and product areas that we might want to grow.

A successful small company usually starts out highly focused on one or a narrow range of products, services, and markets. Over time, the business unit offers too many products and services for too many markets and, with less focus, the company and its resources get spread too thin. It then loses its sense of direction by pursuing growth for growth's sake. Competitiveness and the ability to effectively manage a diverse collection of unrelated products, services, and markets are lost. These companies have to narrow their focus like a laser does. In the long run, winning companies, divisions, or business units are the most focused, while losing companies are the least focused. From a strategic point of view, companies are learning that they simply have to be more selective when choosing where to concentrate their resources.

This chapter describes how to define market segments and focus a company on a logical combination of products and markets that will accelerate sales and profit growth. When industrial market segmentation is performed well, it can be one of the most powerful factors behind growing sales and profits. Industrial managers usually experience difficulty with the definition and selection of market segments because they lack any kind of road map to guide their strategic thinking. In the absence of such a map, it is not surprising that market segment definitions often tend to be naïve with respect to sharply focused strategies, and implementation programs are little different from those used by their competitors.

Why Segmentation is Important

Companies lack the resources to effectively compete in every product/market segment. A business unit should focus on the requirements and unmet needs in market segments in which it can compete effectively and generate the needed sales and profit growth. Strategies should be focused on discreet market segments where they can profitably grow and defend themselves against competitors. Defining market segments can help identify customer needs that no other suppliers have addressed or even thought of. New products, services, and superior customer-value statements can then be developed around the unmet needs of clearly defined market segments.

Over the past years, a number of successful companies rediscovered Demosthenes' idea: "Small opportunities are the beginning of great enterprises." Unable to compete broadly against entrenched competitors, they adopted a successful divide-and-conquer strategy of identifying unmet market needs and then focusing resources and energies on meeting those product and service needs better than anyone else. This seemingly simple, yet highly effective approach has led to a number of individual success stories in a wide range of industries.

Nalco Chemical is a $2 billion global manufacturer of water treatment chemicals for a wide range of industries including steel, paper, shipping, electronics, and mining. For years, Nalco has had divisions dedicated to each of these industries and sub-industries. As the environmental standards became stricter on pulp and paper mills and the needed water treatment chemistry became increasingly different between these two types of mills, Nalco formed one business unit to focus on paper mills and another to serve pulp mills. Nalco's market penetration improved with both pulp and paper mills because its sharper focus helped each of these customers improve operations and exceed the environmental regulations.

The Timken Company is one of the largest and best-known manufacturers of tapered roller bearings and specialty alloy steel bars. The roller bearing industry is fiercely competitive with many European and Asian companies competing with Timken all over the world. After we conducted workshops around the world for The Timken Company, its president Jim Griffith stated:

> We have segmented our bearing businesses into market segments so we better understand and respond to customer needs. Our major market segments for tapered roller bearings include the automotive, truck, railroad, steel, construction, and farm equipment industries. Our superprecision bearing business has segmented the market into aerospace, instrumentation, computer disk drives, and medical and dental equipment. This approach has worked well to focus our engineering , manufacturing, sales, services and distribution. Not only will we continue to have market segments, you can expect to see more of them and to see them more precisely defined.

The secret behind General Electric's sales, profit, and stock market value growth is not its refrigerator, light bulb, or industrial equipment businesses. People close to GE know that many of its manufacturing businesses have been growing at only about 4 percent per year over the last ten years, while GE Capital services grew at more than 10 percent per year and with a much smaller asset base. GE Capital now generates more than half of GE's total earnings. Why is GE Capital so successful? GE Capital is a $40 billion empire run as a string of market-segment-focused business units. Each business unit operates as a separate and independent business with no shared resources or shared overhead expenses. GE Capital has a lean and flat headquarters in a nondescript building about an hour from corporate headquarters. Its twenty-seven business segment leaders are totally dedicated to discreet market segments. This narrow focus of each business unit, with profit and loss statements and balance sheets, enables each unit to operate with a clear idea of where it wants to profitably grow. The most important key to GE Capital's success is the very specific market focus of each business unit. For example, equipment leasing represents about 25 percent of GE Capital's revenues. Equipment leasing has seven totally dedicated business units organized around clearly defined industrial market segments as follows:

1. *Aviation*. This business unit manages the leasing of more than 1,00 large jet aircrafts. The leader of this business unit came from GE's aircraft manufacturing business.
2. *Vehicle fleets*. This dedicated jet engine manufacturing business unit is the world's largest corporate fleet management company.
3. *Containers*. This dedicated unit owns and leases shipping containers that travel on ships, trains, and trucks.
4. *Railcars*. This dedicated unit leases railcars to North American and European railroads. It also repairs and refurbishes railcars. The business segment leader came from GE's locomotive manufacturing business.
5. *Information services*. This dedicated business unit leases mainframes and sells information time-sharing.
6. *Satellites*. This dedicated unit owns, operates, and leases commercial satellites in North America and Australia.
7. *Modular housing*. This business unit owns and leases modular structures from portable toilets to relocatable house trailers used as offices and school classrooms.

After GE Capital analyzes and selects market segments, it typically creates another dedicated business unit to develop the defined market. To keep each business unit from getting into each other's markets, every business unit has a charter that defines its market boundaries.

FAILURE TO SEGMENT AND FOCUS

We have all been warned of the risk of trying to be all things to all customers. The failure to segment a marketplace and concentrate resources on one or a few customer groups is at the heart of many industrial business failures. The following examples show how market leaders and pioneers became market followers.

For decades, Xerox has emphasized large "national accounts" without any sound segmentation in place. Xerox failed to properly segment the marketplace and allowed aggressive Japanese competitors to do it for them. Japanese competitors were the first to identify unmet market needs for low-speed and small-volume applications, and they then developed a desktop plain paper copier for these business needs. Furthermore, Xerox's lack of a strong distribution network helped competitors focus on underserved market segments with a fined tuned distributor organization.

IBM did not enter a marketplace unless it could identify at least a $200 million business opportunity, which explains why it missed the minicomputer and desktop publishing booms and other business opportunities that have grown dramatically. IBM's "bigness mentality" was the penalty of its past success. IBM's bigness resulted in a slowness and aversion to risk taking. IBM chose to play it safe and was a late follower in the fast-moving electronics industry. EMC, the leading mainframe storage supplier, increased sales and profits 100-fold since 1990. In this same period, sales went from $40 million to more than $2 billion, and its market share of 50 percent was all taken out of IBM's hide. The only way a company can avoid the reality of bigness is to create more small entrepreneurial divisions or business units that focus on one or a few market segments. The "small is beautiful" phrase applies to market segments as well as to how firms organize to capture opportunities.

Sales engineers from a major manufacturer of seals and gaskets identified an opportunity with the railroad maintenance departments. As the number of diesel engines and railroad cars grew, the seal maintenance and repair aftermarket also grew. The maintenance service provider decided which gaskets, seals, bearings, and lubricants to use. The aftermarket was much larger, less cyclical and had higher margins than the original equipment (OE) market. The seal manufacturer initially ignored the vast aftermarket potential and continued to concentrate on the slow growth and price sensitive railroad OE market segment. The seal company's vice president of marketing said: "We saw the railroad aftermarket as an afterthought because we liked the technically more challenging OE business with engineers working with engineers." Taking advantage of a neglected segment, the seal manufacturer's sales engineers left the company and formed a new enterprise to repair locomotives and railroad cars. They bought bearings and lubricants from other suppliers and supplied a kit of bearings, seals and lubricants to the railroad repair yards. Without any real direct competition, their sales and service business flourished and reached annual sales of over $50 million in just a few years.

To emerge as a winner in today's dynamic and highly competitive market arena, every business unit must be quick to identify new windows of opportunity and then rapidly develop a unique service/product package based on some demonstrable competitive advantage. Today, windows of opportunity are opening and closing with increasing speed. Smaller firms and smaller business units are often more successful than large ones in pursuing "strategic windows." Frequently, it is the very reason for the smaller companies' existence; that is, someone with entrepreneurial instincts (now more popularly termed a "visionary") spotted an opportunity and established the business specifically to provide some combination of better product, service, and price. With few exceptions, larger and older companies find it difficult to develop and implement these focused strategies. Why? *The vast number of industrial CEOs, group presidents, and general managers do not realize that the definition and selection of attractive market segment opportunities are the strategic foundation for developing and implementing high-growth strategies.*

THE FOUNDATION FOR STRATEGY

The identification and selection of market segments is the most important strategic decision facing industrial or business-to-business firms. The choice of which market segment(s) to pursue is the key starting block for developing focused strategies, business plans, and cross-functional implementation programs. Only after the industrial firm defines market segments can it identify common customer requirements, unarticulated needs, and relevant competitive suppliers. The identified market segment serves as a mirror to appraise a firm's strengths and weaknesses in meeting the segment's current and future needs.

Most strategic planners and academics who simply conduct macroanalysis have ignored the strategic importance of industrial market segmentation. Strategic planning formats that do not demand specific market segments when analyzing situations and developing strategies can easily become form-filling exercises. A strengths-and-weaknesses analysis that is not conducted objectively against competitors' offerings and the requirements of an identified market segment is usually a waste of time. Similarly, if strategic thinking and strategy development are not based on key market segments and without considering what is necessary to serve the identified market segment, the result will most likely be a broad-brush strategy that ineffectively tries to be everything to everyone.

A well-thought-out division or business unit charter should define its business mission first in terms of key market segments served and then in terms of technologies. Too many division or business unit charters simply describe products manufactured and some broad industry groups to which they are marketed. A clearly stated mission, in terms of market segments, focuses the entire business unit on customer groups with common requirements. *Markets are more enduring than a product or a technology.* Market segmentation is a powerful tool for staying on top of any fast-changing environment.

Simply stated, *the definition and then selection of market segments drives everything!* The selection of market segments spearheads competitive analysis, guides strategy development to secure competitive advantages, and determines what action programs are needed to achieve sales and profit goals in the segment. The selection of market segments determines what type of technology, manufacturing, sales skills, and other capabilities are needed. The final selection of market segments is a long-term strategic decision that cannot be easily reversed without severe penalties. Reactive, tactical, and short-term-oriented business units need to first determine their longer-term direction by focusing on the most attractive strategic market segments.

The decision to focus on certain market segments is always a strategic decision. Many managers incorrectly think of market segmentation as a tactical decision that only involves changing the promotional messages and the company's literature. Industrial market segmentation has long term and far reaching effects across the entire business unit or division. Implementing the industrial marketing concept with market segmentation choices always has impact on the technical, manufacturing, and sales areas of the enterprise.

A business strategy that does not build on market segmentation choices has a lower chance of being a winner. After choosing target market segments, management must decide how to position itself in each attractive segment. Superior customer value statements should be developed for each chosen market segment and guide the product/market positioning. Following the decisions on target market selection and positioning strategies for each segment, consistent decisions about product design, technical support, service, market channels, and pricing must be made and implemented with an integrated business plan.

COMMON ERRORS AND MISTAKES

If market segmentation is so important, why is it so rarely practiced or not performed well by industrial or business-to-business firms? Market segmentation as a business practice has long been recognized and well practiced in the consumer packaged goods sector. There has been no corresponding level of interest or rigor in industrial companies. Most industrial executives have no idea that to be market driven is an outside-in process that begins with customer groups or market segments and then works back into the entire company. In fact, market segmentation should be one of the major preoccupations of every general manager and his or her management team because the importance of segmentation goes far beyond marketing—affecting literally every aspect of the industrial firm's activities. However, few subjects have produced as much confusion for industrial managers as segmenting markets. Many of the following common segmentation mistakes are made in industrial companies.

Sales Segmentation

In sales-driven companies, salespeople do the segmenting based on the size of their existing customers, which they categorize as A, B, and C accounts and national or global accounts. Their largest existing customers are called key accounts regardless of growth and profitability. These companies think of each customer as a market segment and too often develop one product for just one customer without considering other customers in the market segment. The sales department determines how the rest of the organization selects and serves customers. These sales-driven companies see segmentation as simply adding more volume, providing additional customer service, and improving customer satisfaction for everyone. Large accounts and volume dominate their thinking. These same companies think that all business is good business, especially from the largest customers. Marketing is seen as something that adds costs and slows the organization. In these sales-driven companies, marketing is, at best, seen as a subset of sales and consists of flashy brochures, multicolor trade advertising, toll-free numbers, extravagant trade shows, free monogrammed hats, and golf balls with the company logo.

Misusing Consumer Retailing Approaches

The segmentation approaches for consumer and industrial markets are as different as potato chips and integrated circuit chips. Household markets are segmented on the basis of personality, lifestyle, income, sex, image, social status, ethnic group, age, and personal wants. Industrial markets are segmented on the basis of performance needs, emerging requirements, needed services, manufacturing processes, cost-effective solutions, and the customer's customer needs.

In industrial markets, the benefits sought depend less on psychological or socioeconomic needs of the buyer and are based more on the actual use of the product/service package. For these reasons, it is far more relevant to segment industrial markets by product use needs and service benefits than by social and psychological personal wants. Naive academics, inexperienced consultants, and superficial advertising agencies eloquently tout retail segmentation approaches for industrial markets that are often pure nonsense for industrial businesses. Any industrial manager who believes that consumer goods segmentation approaches equally apply to industrial markets is simply wasting time and money and may ultimately jeopardize his or her career. Industrial suppliers typically face more astute buying organizations. For example, one user group of engineered plastics, lacking development capability, may be more interested in obtaining technical support from the supplier than another customer group that has competent technical support in-house. A third customer group may be more interested in lower-grade plastics because of different requirements and their strategy in selected markets.

Lack of Market Facts

Most industrial firms do not have the vital facts required to define, evaluate, and select the most attractive market segments. Up-front market segment facts are also needed to guide product development, make better capital decisions, and ensure that the entire resource allocation process is not based only on intuition. Few major industrial firms have in-house marketing research capabilities to obtain these facts. When an in-house marketing research staff does exist, it is typically one of the most underpaid and under appreciated units in the firm. It is sometimes staffed with people who do not have the requisite professional skills to do sound market assessments.

General management in industrial companies rarely appreciates the value of professional market assessment and relies instead on trade or seat-of-the-pants estimates. General and business unit managers are too often unwilling to commit the time and money necessary to perform the segmentation job. In most industrial companies, it is far easier to get approval for a large capital expenditure than to invest in a market study or hire a competent market researcher. As a result, the company flies half-blind, misses opportunities, gets caught off base by unexpected product or market developments, and becomes increasingly vulnerable to competitors with better market information. These same companies have little information about how their products are used and how they compare with competitors in each market segment. A sound market fact base has information about the usage, growth rates, and trends in each segment and an understanding of the largest and fastest growing competitors in each segment including their advantages, disadvantages, costs, pricing strategies, and likely next moves. The cost and risk of not having this market information far outweighs the needed investment. Not until upper and general management realize that market facts are a necessary small investment and not an unnecessary cost will the definition, evaluation, and selection of the more attractive market segments get started properly and result in better strategic decisions across the entire organization. (the next chapter, "Assessing Industrial Markets," describes how to gather and organize the necessary market facts.)

Confusing Markets with Products

Product- and manufacturing-driven companies have great difficulty thinking in terms of market segments. After thinking for many years first in terms of product composition, manufacturing methods, product forms, and technical features, these managers have difficulty thinking about market segments, customer benefits, and the unarticulated and unmet needs of discreet market segments. They need to first think of the requirements and emerging needs in a market segment, and then fit, or tailor, their service/product package to the segment. Not until they dispel the foolish notion of product "segments" that do not exist will they make the transition to a market-driven company.

An example of a product-driven company was the tantalum capacitor division of the Cabot Corporation. Cabot at first compared itself only with other tantalum capacitor manufacturers, while its customers in various segments were conducting side-by-side comparisons with tantalum, ceramics, and aluminum as alternative capacitor materials. Cabot also gained many insights into market segmentation by determining how its immediate customers segmented their markets, which segments they emphasized, and why. When a company relies too heavily on the physical properties of the product in defining product/market segments as Cabot originally did, it will also miss important nonproduct service needs in market segments. These same firms vaguely speak about supplying the "high quality," "high performance," or "specialty end" of the market. Such statements often reflect a manager's hope, but not concrete plans, to achieve higher margins by serving specific market segments.

Segmenting Too Broad Or Too Narrow

One of the most common mistakes in segmenting industrial markets is defining segments either too broadly or too narrowly. How broad or narrow to segment depends on many factors, including the type of service/product package offered to a specific marketplace. For example, Emerson Electric Company does a good job of defining market segments they call an end-industry focus. Emerson has targeted seven industries: power generation, natural gas, telecommunications, semiconductor, chemical, pharmaceutical, and food and beverage. Emerson "packages" a wide-range of its process controls, electric motors, and industrial automation products and services to its seven target segments. A manufacturer of phenolic resins would probably find Emerson's market definitions too broad. Therefore, what is sufficient segmentation to a manufacturer of one product/service package may be too broad or too narrow to a supplier of a different product/service package. Let's look closer at what is meant by segmenting too broadly or too narrowly.

Thinking Too Broad

An industry is a group of manufacturers producing and selling similar or related products, whereas a market is a much more distinct group of customers or users who have similar requirements. Confusing industries with market segments is dangerous. *Companies must learn to distinguish between an industry and a market segment.* Product- or sales-driven industrial firms usually do not attempt to make a distinction between the two. One component manufacturer told me, "We serve the computer market with solid-state connectors." This kind of statement is useless because there are many distinct market segments within the computer industry, and each segment has specific requirements, unmet customer needs, growth rates, and trends.

As another example, an industrial firm's division charter states, "The division is a supplier of hydraulic pumps and hoses to machinery markets." Again, a general industry (machinery) is being defined, not market segments. Further analysis revealed that the division was primarily supplying farm equipment manufacturers, three kinds of construction machinery producers, and heavy-duty truck makers. To avoid this kind of thinking, the president of one company told his business team that they were not segmenting properly if its total market was more than $50 million. Defining themselves this way forced them away from industry definitions, which typically report sales by the billions of dollars, not millions.

Thinking Too Narrow

At the other extreme, some sales-focused firms do not think beyond the needs of the one or a few customers who dominate their business. One manufacturer of flexible machining systems developed a $150 million business with the three major auto manufacturers in Detroit. This total involvement with just three firms in one industry led to myopic thinking, which prevented the manufacturer from even considering other situations or groups of customers (e.g. farm equipment, the truck industry, and oil field equipment) with similar manufacturing requirements.

Other manufacturers think too restrictively about their markets because they are constrained by their existing products, technologies, and manufacturing methods. They think of expansion only in terms of extending their product lines. They do not consider how new products or services, beyond their existing capabilities, could help them strengthen their position or develop more attractive new markets. For example, an electronic sensor producer sold chiefly to nuclear plants, where its line had been qualified and approved by the appropriate government agencies. This narrow focus on a slow-growth market with a narrow customer base greatly limited sales potential. Management ultimately redefined its business to include semiconductor manufacturing and the packaging equipment segment and, by acquisition and internal development, introduced several products that filled the needs of these specific market segments.

One can see that there is an art to segmenting industrial markets. If you are going to err by either segmenting too broadly or too narrowly, it is better to define segments too narrowly because they can usually be regrouped into larger segments with similar requirements. However, if you define segments too broadly, it is more difficult to "break them down" into smaller customer groups with common needs. Generally, specialty chemical and material suppliers have to define narrower market segments because of their ability to adapt or tailor the chemistry of their end-products to more specific market segments. Equipment, mechanical, electrical, or electronic parts manufacturers usually need to define broader market segments. Of course, there are always exceptions to any generalization.

Too Few or Too Many Segments

After conducting a segmentation analysis, some firms experience one of two extreme situations. First, they may not have identified a large enough number of market segments. If too few segments have been defined, a competitor may zero in on a segment and gain a major part of the business. Large corporations frequently segment the market into segments that are too few and too broad. What is small to a $1 billion company may be large to a $40 million to $100 million company or division. However, if large companies do not segment small enough, competition will often do it for them. Smaller industrial firms (or smaller business units) are usually more able to think and act in terms of small or emerging segments and then position themselves within those segments to gain real competitive advantages.

At the other extreme, some companies carry the idea of segmenting beyond the point of practical value. After investing in a seven-month segmentation study that produced mountains of data, a division general manager told me:

They have divided our business into twelve market segments. I think this is about double the amount we can reasonably and profitably focus on. Even if it isn't, there is no way we can develop a competitive strategy for twelve segments without spending all of our time in planning meetings. I believe we could combine some of the smaller segments where the requirements are similar. I sent the team back to work and said I wanted their top three segments to counterattack and their top two new segments to attack. Finally, I asked them to tell me how we should evaluate their results in each market segment they select.

Profitable top-line growth starts with breaking down industries into market segments and subsegments. A look at the broad aggregation of demand usually reveals a "mature market" growing at only 1 to 3 percent per year. However, every industrial market is the sum of many market segments with various growth rates. After breaking an industry into segments and then learning about their needs, numerous options are uncovered for growing faster than the aggregate marketplace. The methodology of market segmentation has transformed many industrial businesses and helped sustain profitable top-line growth in slow, no-growth, and even shrinking markets. Sound industrial market segmentation and market selection enable top and general management to allocate resources on a prospective basis and not on a historical basis. Industrial market segmentation helps liberate resources for the most attractive future opportunities.

SEGMENT BY OEMs, END-USERS, AND AFTERMARKET NEEDS

A beginning approach to industrial market segmentation is to first classify customers as original equipment manufacturers (OEMs), end users, or aftermarket customers. The aftermarket is sometimes called the maintenance, repair, and operating (MRO) supplies. For farm tractors, Deere would be the OEM and the individual farmer would be the end user. The repair parts bought by the farm equipment dealer and farmer would constitute the aftermarket.

All industrial products can be classified into one of three categories.
1. *Components or subassemblies.* These are parts, systems, and kits used to build and repair machinery and equipment, which includes items such as switches, integrated circuits, machine tool parts, connectors, and pistons, and are often required for both the OEM and aftermarkets.
2. *Machinery and equipment.* These are end products used by the industrial users, such as machine tools, bulldozers, computers, laboratory instruments, and trucks. They require repair parts (components) as aftermarket items.
3. *Materials.* Materials that are consumed in the user's production process and include such items as chemicals, coolants, metals, herbicides, and adhesives. They do not usually have an aftermarket.

OEM, end-user, and aftermarket segmentation generally cannot be done from existing sales records, as sales records do not usually show any information about the product beyond the customer or distributor name. Sales personnel can be helpful in developing some of the necessary information, but are often limited in their knowledge of end-user and aftermarket customers, especially when distributors are involved. In some cases, the problem of who the customers are is further complicated by distributors or subdistributors that are integral links in the customers' supply chain to end-users. Unfortunately, the broad OEM-aftermarket classification is far too often the beginning and end of segmentation in many industrial firms. Such companies are still flying blind. Finer segmentation is usually needed.

Another approach to segmentation involves the use of Standard Industrial Classification (SIC) or the newer and expanded NAICS codes, which are published by the U.S. government.

This publication classifies all business firms by the main product or service provided. It then classifies all like manufacturers under broad industry groups and assigns a numerical code that indicates the basic industry and the type of product and service. Once this extensive list is available, it is then possible to determine what manufacturers make what products by going to many industrial and trade associations and compilers like Dun and Bradstreet. The next chapter on "Assessing Industrial Markets" describes how to use the SIC/NAICS codes for defining market segments, determining market segment usage, and estimating market segment potentials.

SEGMENT BY SERVICE NEEDS

Segmenting by the type or amount of service a group of customers needs is often an overlooked way to retain customers, attract new ones, and generate more sales revenue from existing customers. All industrial customers have unmet needs for product support, maintenance, systems management, and the efficient management of various procurement and manufacturing processes. Segmenting by needed services will create higher profit margins and help a company stay very close to customers, especially existing ones. An existing customer base equals instant credibility and leverage that competitors cannot duplicate. Such service-based top-line growth is usually profitable and sustainable through the later stages of the product life cycle when service and price become the two most important buying criteria. Customers who demand a low price can be offered a "no frills" or "bare bones" product with minimal service, and customers who value service and will pay for it should be offered a full menu of services. The key is to know what type and amount of services each market segment needs.

Bendix is a major supplier of truck braking systems to the heavy-duty truck market. The traditional approaches to market segmentation in this industry were by truck size or weight, OEMs and the aftermarket. After studying the service needs of users over the product life cycle of heavy-duty trucks, a segmentation approach based on first-, second-, and third-owner needs emerged. Jeff Sinclair, president of Bendix and an advocate of industrial market segmentation, described the first-, second-, and third-owner segmentation approach as follows:

> **First Owner.** New truck and fleet owners were primarily interested in low maintenance and little downtime. For long distance hauling needs, Bendix promoted its premium products, a three-year or 350,000-mile full labor and parts warranty and a premium price. Buyers of new trucks were encouraged to specify the Bendix three year or 350,000-mile warranty to OEM truck builders that included Freightliner, Mercedes, Navistar, Volvo and Kenworth.
>
> **Second Owner.** Primarily for trucks four to eight years old. They were primarily owner/operators with one to three trucks. These owners typically bought trucks from the large fleet owners who usually owned a new truck for only three to four years. The second-owner segment was targeted with genuine Bendix replacement parts and offered a one-year or 100,000-mile warranty at a premium price. Truck dealers and independent heavy equipment repair shops usually did this work.
>
> **Third Owner.** For trucks that were nine or more years old, the owners typically wanted to fix trucks for the lowest unit cost. Since these trucks were primarily used for local hauling, downtime was less critical. Lower-priced remanufactured or rebuilt parts with or without the Bendix brand were targeted to this segment with a 30-day parts warranty. These small and local owners sometimes did their own maintenance and repair work.

In companies where a service is the product, there is usually great sensitivity to the different needs of customer groups. Consider the Wireline division of Schlumberger, a major player in the petroleum services industry. Wireline helps owners of oil properties assess the configuration of the oil reservoirs on its properties. Simply stated, Wireline helps owners maximize the yield from their petroleum assets by combining geological, mechanical, and electronic engineering skills. The company drills holes several thousand feet into the ground, lowers electronic sensors underground, and interprets the signals it receives. In the mid-1990s, Wireline's general manager realized that its overall market share was slipping. They started their analysis by visiting their largest customers, including Exxon, Mobil, and Shell, which usually commissioned large, deep-well, and complex applications. By and large, these companies valued Wireline's professionalism and in-depth technological leadership. Through this analysis, Wireline's managers uncovered some different needs in another market segment. Close to 40 percent of Wireline's market was in shallow wells and smaller property owned by cattle ranchers and small businesses. This group of customers did not need Wireline's full range of technological skills or the high cost for the unnecessary expertise if they could get someone else to do the job for less. Competitors had identified the different needs of this segment and targeted it, causing Wireline to lose market share in this segment. Wireline responded by creating a new division focused on the needs of shallow-well and smaller property owners. They designed a simpler and smaller downsized service truck with less sophisticated electronic capabilities. In the business plan for the new division, Wireline established a different pricing approach and scheduled smaller wells with these service trucks. Within a year, its market share and profits in this segment began to improve.

A service orientation causes suppliers to think in terms of the customer's entire system—bottlenecks, labor, material costs, and downtime—from the customer's procurement through after-sales service to the customer's customers. If you improve the customer's processes and can get higher selling prices while retaining and attracting more customers, the added service should significantly increase your net profit. Documented customer savings, cost avoidance, added throughput, and increased revenue for customers help justify and maintain higher selling prices.

Outsourcing trends are driving the need for industrial customers to buy more outside services. Services can provide additional revenue and force suppliers to stay close to customers and anticipate, rather than react, to their needs. Industrial services typically require less capital investment than a manufacturing business. Finally, a service orientation helps guide suppliers on how to bundle or unbundle service/product packages to more closely fit the needs of customer groups or market segments.

ADJACENT MARKET SEGMENTS

Before finalizing your choice of market segments to counterattack or attack, it is always beneficial to identify and evaluate the attractiveness of adjacent market segments. An adjacent market segment has many similarities with the segments you are currently serving. Adjacent segments are those in which many of your existing capabilities (technology, manufacturing know-how, costs, sales force expertise, or distributors) can be used to develop a winning competitive advantage, and can often be served with less additional investment.

Every business unit should consider ways to use its existing capabilities and cost base to attack adjacent market segments, which is normally a more sensible step than going after more remote segments. The following examples explain the logic of identifying and capturing adjacent market segments for profitable top-line growth.

John Deere moved from its existing agricultural equipment segments to the adjacent construction equipment crawler segment for earth moving. It chose to make only small earth-moving machines because they were a closer fit to its farm equipment technologies, manufacturing capabilities, dealer network, and cost structure. Caterpillar, who had emphasized the large earth-moving equipment, was caught off guard by Deere's attack on the underserved, small earth-moving machine segment. Caterpillar was put on the defensive and had to counterattack and engineer new and smaller earth-moving machines to compete with Deere. Caterpillar then retaliated by developing a rubber-track-type farm tractor that competed against Deere's largest farm tractors. Caterpillar's large earth-moving capabilities were adjacent or close to Deere's very large farm tractor segment.

Henkel served the adhesive needs of the corrugated boxboard market segment for years. Some of the corrugated box manufacturers also had bookbinding plants. The adhesive needs for the bookbinding segment were an adjacent segment for Henkel, so it created a business unit dedicated to bookbinding. Henkel also had a business unit dedicated to the adhesive needs for regular business envelopes. Some of these same envelope manufacturers began making overnight mailing envelopes for FedEx, DHL, UPS, and the U.S. Postal Service. Henkel then attacked and profitably penetrated the rapidly growing adjacent segment of overnight mailing envelopes with a dedicated market manager.

Great organic-growth companies are always thinking about new uses for their existing products and current technology platforms. These companies consistently achieve top-line growth by identifying, evaluating, and selecting new market segments that are underserved—but they first examine the most adjacent new market segments. At Sealed Air, a maker of protective industrial packaging products and systems, top management requires every business unit to enter one new market segment each year. This corporate goal helps create healthy stress and a sense of urgency across the organization for profitable top-line growth. Without this corporate goal, Sealed Air is aptly concerned that people would become complacent and cozy with their existing markets and customers. If every top and general management doesn't stress the need to develop or enter new markets, especially adjacent ones, people might focus on increasing market share with yesterday's markets. Unfortunately, most divisional and business-unit organizational structures and incentives reinforce serving only existing markets—not developing new ones.

The concept of adjacent segments shows the need for segment-by-segment invasion plans. A company is wise to enter one new segment at a time without revealing its long-term growth plans to outsiders. Every company needs a planned sequence of new segment invasion plans. Unfortunately, many companies fail to develop any long-term attack plans. When a company has a well thought out segment-by-segment invasion plan, it has a long-term strategy in place.

Pursuing new or adjacent market segments requires time, market development skills, dedicated resources, and is risky. Short-term sales and profit pressures typically do not provide the time and resources to define, evaluate, and capture new market segments. In more bureaucratic and "silo" management companies, people don't readily share technology, know-how, customers, or leads across divisions or business units. Short tenure in job positions inevitably discourages new business or market development in even the most adjacent segments. Furthermore, people may lack the management skills to define, evaluate, and pursue the most attractive new market segments. A small commercial development department may be needed to gather market facts and leverage technology to new market segments. Finally, in a risk-averse culture, few people think about new market segments, and even fewer will incur the perceived career risk from any market development failure. For these reasons, top and general management must create a safe culture to experiment, set new market segment goals, provide the needed training and dedicated resources, and have the appropriate recognition and rewards for pursuing new or adjacent market segments. If top management does not provide these critical ingredients, very little market development and top-line growth will occur in adjacent or new market segments.

SEGMENT AND RESEGMENT

Industrial market segments are dynamic. Competitive activity, technological advances, swings in the business cycle, and changing customer needs can dramatically change the boundaries and attractiveness of segments. With market segmentation, you don't pick your markets and then sit back for years. It is necessary to periodically evaluate existing segmentation and consider new or different approaches. Today segmentation is not a once and for all activity; it is an on-going state of mind and a dynamic process where one is always thinking about new and different ways to segment a marketplace. Business history is replete with cases in which an existing competitor saw market segment boundaries as static or did not identify new, emerging segments and so lost out. Xerox failed to resegment the photocopier marketplace and, by not doing so, allowed Japanese competitors to do it for them. Digital technology has blurred the line between copiers and printers, and has made it possible to plug printer-copiers into computer networks. This has moved responsibility for buying the computer printer out of the purchasing department (once a Xerox stronghold) and into a buying realm of information system specialists who are more familiar and comfortable with computer companies.

The x-ray film market provides an example of just how dynamic a market segment can be. Although Kodak is the broadest supplier of photographic film to the most market segments, DuPont has concentrated on the hospital x-ray film segment and achieved a large market share. The hospital x-ray market formerly consisted of five market segments: government owned, private, university, specialty, and community hospitals. With the emergence and increasing importance of hospital chains, health maintenance organizations, more specialty hospitals, extended care facilities, and clinical groups, DuPont had to resegment the marketplace. Furthermore, developments in nuclear magnetic resonance imaging (MRI) technology promise to replace x-rays in some large hospitals with a process that develops the "picture" electronically and displays it on a monitor. As segments of the hospital x-ray market shrink, DuPont has to determine what technologies and capabilities it needs if it is to hold onto its positions in various medical market segments.

GE Capital, mentioned earlier in this chapter, has resegmented its marketplace as much as any business-to-business company I have known. Each of GE Capital's major businesses are continually studying industries and markets and resegmenting them into subsegments. GE's resegmenting process identifies new market needs and sources of double-digit top line growth that were previously unrecognized opportunities. Market resegmentation throughout GE Capital stimulates everyone in the business unit to think in terms of an endless series of market segments with discreet needs. As many of the resegmented markets grew, they became full-fledged business units with a dedicated general manager and cross-functional business team. Gary Wendt, the CEO of GE Capital, described this process:

> Our approach to segment and then resegment is one of the key secrets to GE Capital's explosive growth for the last decade. Resegmentation helps us apply the small business approach of narrowing in on the needs of specific niches, understanding them better than the customers, and then focusing on them. You break the entire business equation down to segmentation and gearing in on the customer group. Growth becomes a systematic process instead of just making broad generalizations of why you need to grow and how much growth you need to meet your aggressive goals.

Sales managers are accustomed to grouping customers by geography for planning purposes, but until recently few top managers had thought to try developing niche strategies on the basis of geography. Yet the opportunity often exists. An example of ingenious geographic segmentation is the case of a midwestern construction materials firm that found itself faced with overcapacity and unable to take share away from its competition in its 200-mile trading area without starting a price war. Industry folklore maintained that because of high transportation, no producer could ship more than 300 miles from plant to customer and make money. This was true on an all-in cost basis; as this company discovered, the fixed costs included in its all-in costs were so high that sales to customers as much as 700 miles away would still contribute to overhead. The result of its analysis was three strategic market segments: core markets (up to 200 miles distant); secondary markets (200 to 400 miles); and fringe markets (400 to 700 miles). For each of these segments, the firm developed different pricing strategies. In the core market, the strategy was business as usual; in the secondary markets, prices were cut to take a few selected bids away from competitors, but not enough to provoke retaliation; in the fringe market, prices were reduced in order to fill the plants—but again, not frequently enough or severely enough to provoke retaliation. With this strategy, the company doubled its volume in the first year. Although much of the added volume was from marginal business, its profits doubled—and the industry price structure remained intact.

Segmenting industrial markets is an intuitive, analytical, and creative process. Management should not allow ties to previously segmented markets to strangle new ways to segment. In markets with rapid technological change, more frequent resegmentation is needed because new technologies blur segment boundaries. Solid market facts, competitive intelligence, and early warning signals help identify new or emerging segments.

SET RESOURCE PRIORITIES

To set priorities intelligently, it is essential to weigh all the attractiveness variables (size, growth rates, profitability, competition, trends, unmet needs and the operating fit) along with your current share position and any proprietary advantages. One useful approach is to calculate the current and potential profit value of a share point of each segment. This helps determine which segments are most attractive from a future profit point of view instead of just sales potential. Bandag, the retread rubber and tire equipment manufacturer, religiously determines the present and future profit value of all market segments before setting priorities. Its CEO, Marty Carver, told me at our annual senior executive workshop:

> The approach that works well for us is selective profit-based market segmentation. We spend a great deal of time and effort studying market segments or niches and categorizing them by end-user type or applications, performance need, market potential, and the present and future profit potential. We then impute a present and future ROI [return on investment] for each segment before we set any product/market priorities. It brings home the point that some of the larger segments your salespeople lust after or which your engineers find technically interesting may not be worth a candle. Quite frankly, we have walked away from a number of larger volume or technically interesting segments that were low ROIs and had limited profit prospects.

Dell Computer's founder Michael Dell also described how they analyze the cost-profit attractiveness of market segments before setting resource priorities:

> We really look closely at gross margins and net profit by customer segment—and we focus on segments we can profitably serve. When you're trying to target profitable segments, averages obscure a lot, and aggregate financial statements are pretty meaningless. Our approach to segmentation is to take really big numbers and "de-average" them. Until you look inside and understand what's going on by segment, and by customers within a segment, you don't know anything. We let our competitors have segments with insufficient profit. We don't actively pursue market segments that don't reach our profit objectives.

Too many companies look at the most attractive market segments through a rearview mirror when they should be looking ahead to the future. The mind-set of profitable top-line growth should be built on the definition and selection of today and tomorrow's most attractive market segment opportunities in counties and regions around the world.

Many business units fail to refocus and set segment priorities because they are preoccupied with the past. These same business units have no formal procedure for reallocating resources to the more profitable opportunities. I often hear gung-ho managers enthusiastically talk about seizing new markets, developing and launching new products, and landing new customers. Soon their enthusiasm diminishes because there is no time or too few resources to pursue the most attractive high-growth opportunities. What a shame, because when resources, especially people, are wasted on yesterday's markets, customers, products and services, how can a business unit become more entrepreneurial and experience great sales and profit growth? Strategic market segmentation requires a disciplined approach to allocate and reallocate resources to the most attractive future opportunities with the full support of top and general management.

FOUR SEGMENT CATEGORIES

A useful way to finalize the prioritizing of market segments within each country and region of the world is to assign them to one of the following four categories:

1. *Counterattack.* This is the most important category and deserves top priority. It includes segments that are currently a major source of sales and profit and that must be defended and fortified. If after assessing your current sales and profit performance in these segments, the prospects for profitable growth are attractive, then these segments should be counterattacked. Cash is often best used to defend and invest, not just milk and starve these cash cows. If investment is needed in a new technology or plant, it usually should be made in these counterattack situations. Sales and especially profit growth should occur in this category. These segments typically receive more services, new technology, new products, and acquisitions.

2. *Attack.* This category includes segments that offer attractive long-term growth and profit potential but where current market positions and profits are low or nonexistent. What would be a counterattack segment in one country or region of the world could be an attack segment in another geographic area. Adjacent market segments, described earlier in this chapter, would be included in this category because they are close to your existing capabilities and the costs to serve your current segments. These segments usually receive more services, new technology, new products, and acquisitions.

3. *Deemphasize.* Little or no additional investment is made in these segments. The near-term sales and profit growth prospects are not attractive. Prices might be significantly increased. This may be a "take-order" or retreat situation or the first "up or out" step before withdrawing from a segment in a region of the world. These situations receive fewer products and services and may be assigned to inside sales or distributors.

4. *Withdraw.* This category includes markets that do not offer attractive short- or long-term profit prospects. A plan is needed to withdraw or exit from these segments or possibly assign them to distributors. If you are not currently serving these segments, a no-go decision should be made unless you have a significant advantage over competitors that can be used to profitably grow these segments.

It is very important to decide which segments you want to deemphasize or withdraw from because those decisions help conserve resources for the more attractive counterattack and attack opportunities. If market segmentation does not help a company reallocate resources, the full value of market segmentation has not been realized.

At an annual business planning meeting at Unilever Chemicals in England, Dr. Iain Anderson, the chairman, was concerned that business teams around the world were not disciplined when selecting which segments to counterattack, attack, deemphasize, and withdraw. The following statement made Dr. Anderson's selection process clear to everyone:

> Our global business planning process has identified over 80 market segments to pursue and that are supposedly all fantastic opportunities. However, I have a hunch that a good number of those will do very little for our bottom line in the short or long term. We simply must become more selective and disciplined in determining which opportunities to invest in with our limited resources. Some of our companies have been using a one-gallon watering can to feed an acre of plants. With that approach, some will die, some will be marginal, and very few will rapidly grow.

> Therefore, I have asked all company presidents, general managers, and SBU managers to rethink and to group every segment into one of four categories—counterattack, attack, deemphasize, and withdraw. I would like the people to prioritize every segment within each of the four categories and to arrive at a balance of short- and longer-term attractive market segments for us to invest in, deemphasize, and withdraw from.

A word of caution about categorizing segments is needed. As a result of insufficient market, cost, and/or technology information, there is often uncertainty of whether to categorize a market segment as attractive or unattractive. Many companies place segments in the attractive category with only intuition or seat-of-their pants information. Better market segment definitions and accurate estimates of market size, growth rates, trends, emerging needs, market shares, and the present and future profit prospects are needed before categorizing a segment as either attractive or unattractive. Furthermore, customer needs and trends need to be validated and assumptions about costs, pricing, and competitive response need to be researched. Only after additional study and sufficient facts are obtained, should a company categorize market segments as counterattack, attack, deemphasize, or withdraw. Any attempts to categorize segments with insufficient factual information should be stopped by general and top management.

(In the following Chapter 5, "Assessing Industrial Markets", there is a section at the end of the chapter titled, "Market Segment Attractiveness." That section should be read and understood before any final choices or categories for market segments are finalized.)

RESPONSIBILITY FOR SEGMENTATION

Many general managers believe that market segmentation is the responsibility of marketing or a market research staff. The importance and responsibility for market segmentation goes far beyond marketing—it requires the involvement of the entire division or business unit and full support of a general manager. While an increasing number of general managers and business-unit managers are aware of the need to do a better job of segmenting the market, their enthusiasm or ability to do so is often limited by short-term sales and profit pressures. Far too many general and business-unit managers still regard volume gains and relationships with large accounts as the most important factors in their business.

Market segmentation is frequently regarded as some kind of theoretical exercise that is not worth much time and money, especially if it interferes with bringing in or running the business. Segmentation requires a good deal of careful thought and information, and it is the primary responsibility of general management to make the money and resources available to ensure that it is accomplished. Segmentation is not a theoretical exercise, and any general manager or business unit manager who ignores or shortchanges the need to define and select discrete markets to be served is making a serious mistake. To ensure that the business is properly segmented, every profit center and general manager should be satisfied with the answers to the following ten questions:

1. How do we now segment the business?
2. Have we defined the segments in the best way possible?
3. Are we segmenting too broadly or too narrowly?
4. Is there any evidence that competitors, especially small ones or the fastest growing ones, have achieved an advantage by segmenting differently?
5. How do our customers segment their business and which segments are they emphasizing?
6. What customer benefits and competitive advantages do we have (or can we achieve) in each defined segment?
7. Which segments offer the greatest profit potential two to three years out?
8. In which segments do we have an attractive position(s) that we should continue to defend, grow, and counterattack?
9. Which adjacent segments are the most attractive to enter, attack, or build a position?
10. Which unattractive segments should we deemphasize or withdraw resource from?

If these ten questions are difficult to answer or cannot be answered at all, the chances are that the marketplace has not been properly segmented and evaluated.

RAPIDLY CAPTURE SEGMENTS

Even when larger firms clearly understand segmentation and identify new opportunities, they sometimes do not respond fast enough to capture them. To pursue small but attractive growth markets, most large corporations break down their organizations into smaller business units, each with a profit center responsibility. This doesn't necessarily mean setting up a number of full-fledged operating divisions, although this is certainly an alternative to consider. A matrix approach involving product, market, or business unit managers can also be used to assign profit responsibility when the business unit is small and cannot afford to carry the costs of full divisionalization. Small and dedicated profit centers can stay close to changing market requirements, are quicker to identify and pursue new market opportunities, and can help create entrepreneurial enthusiasm. Mistakes and fundamental waste are more likely to surface in small and focused profit centers, and corrective actions can be taken more quickly.

Market segmentation with small business units, allows companies the flexibility to leap from one attractive market opportunity to another. These smaller business units are less apt to take on the large fixed investments in production facilities and develop the lengthy product development cycles so common to most large and centralized business units. Although small companies have traditionally exploited niche markets most effectively, successful examples clearly demonstrate that larger companies can play the same game if they really want to. To attack or counterattack increasingly turbulent markets, companies need to pursue fast-moving market segment opportunities with small and very focused business unit teams. If they don't, they will miss many attractive windows of sales and profit growth.

ALIGNING TO TARGET SEGMENTS

Implementing a strategy should begin with a business unit mission statement that defines your target market segments. *Programs in all functional areas should then be structured and focused to effectively serve these target markets.* If marketing has the final say on R&D project funding, product development projects will be aligned to market segment priorities. Likewise, manufacturing, sales, and technical service must be informed of the requirements of the target segments so that action programs to gear operations toward successfully serving each segment can be developed. Acquisition programs should be linked to target markets. If the specific technology, manufacturing process, or expertise does not currently exist to serve the emphasized market segments, new capabilities must be developed and/or acquired and must be shown as action programs in the business plan. All R&D or engineering programs should be directed by market segment priorities and not by the technical whims of engineering or research directors. The technical, sales, and manufacturing people should be aligned to the target markets with some fairly straightforward programs. Sometimes, these programs must be accompanied by organizational changes. Let's now describe some of the other implementation programs to achieve market focuses.

Technical and trade association involvement should correspond to your counterattack and attack market segments. There are trade and technical associations for virtually every defined market segment. These segment-specific trade associations don't just gather shipment data and project the overall market size. They usually identify subsegments, have technical committees where industry standards are determined, and have membership directories with the current titles, addresses, and phone numbers of the key buying influences. For example, the Institute of Electrical and Electronics Engineers (IEEE) has a subcommittee on power transformers. Engelhard Chemical is an active member of that subcommittee because it manufactures epoxies and coatings for the wire and cable in power transformers. Being an active trade association member in your target markets is a vital part of up-front marketing that helps you learn about trends and influence the technical standards. Your market and technical people should jointly participate in the technical and trade societies in your target markets all over the world. Sound target marketing often starts at these associations and with information from the most progressive members.

Marketing communications must be developed around the important benefits (not features) that the service/product package provides for each target segment. Advertising copy, trade show participation, media selection, application seminars, and sales letters must all be developed specifically in the language of the target market segments. DuPont developed the manmade Kevlar fiber that *Fortune* magazine described as "a miracle material in search of a viable market." Pound for pound, Kevlar is four to five times stronger than steel, lighter, and does not rust or corrode. Market research identified several end-use markets with different needs and economic values for Kevlar. The many potential end-use market segments or applications included commercial fishing boats, underwater cables, aircraft "skins," and bulletproof helmets and vests. The product benefits of Kevlar varied significantly across these three market segments. Kevlar provided commercial fishing boat owners the benefits of a hull that saved fuel, traveled faster, and allowed owners to carry more fish. For commercial aircraft builders who used Kevlar, a Boeing 777 or Airbus 320 was stronger, safer, and more than 5,000 pounds lighter. Finally, when military people and police wore Kevlar vests and helmets, they received the benefits of increased safety, maneuverability, and less weight. Application stories for sales promotion should be developed for each chosen market segment and written in the language, benefits, and economics of the respective segment. Most marketing communications should be oriented to the needs of each respective market segment.

Direct and distributor sales representatives must be provided with the *appropriate training and selling aids* for each target market. The sales force must be thoroughly trained to emphasize benefits as they apply to each respective market segment. The training of technical service people, field sales, and distributors in market segment needs and the benefits of your products is often done poorly, if at all. Traditional product training, which does not concentrate on target market applications, will not help implement a segmentation strategy. Good in-depth application success stories are frequently the central focus of market segment training sessions. Sealed Air has developed follow-on application seminars for its product training programs. Its application seminars feature company specialists in each segment with extensive use of successful case histories that it develops for each target market. The Swagelok Company developed videocassette and audiocassette job stories for salespeople to review before calling on accounts in various segments. Competent product and market managers and application engineers are the logical people to develop the materials and conduct the training seminars for direct and distributor salespeople. As Sealed Air has found, a short quiz given after market segment or application-specific training accelerates the learning process.

Sales incentives or changes in compensation are often necessary to direct salespeople and distributors to the chosen market segments. Sales forces that are exclusively compensated on a sales volume basis are usually difficult to direct to new market applications that require more time to learn about customers' requirements, run trials and build new relationships. New commission structures, bonuses, or incentive programs tied to accounts to counterattack or attack in the target segments are usually necessary to ensure that segmentation priorities are pursued throughout the existing salesforce. In some situations, a specialized or dedicated salesforce must be created for key segments. The trade-offs for these situations are explained in Chapter 7, "The Consultative Sales Force". Frequently, a different network of distributors must be recruited to penetrate any new segments being emphasized. Distributor agreements should emphasize primary market segments, not just a geographic area. In some cities, you might need distributors that focus on different market segments. For example, Ingersoll-Rand had two pump distributors with the same product lines one mile from each other in Bakersfield, California. One distributor focused on the oil field market for pumps and the other nearby distributor served the water irrigation pump market for farmers.

SHIFTING ATTITUDES AND BEHAVIORS

One of the most difficult issues facing most industrial companies is overcoming the serious lack of thinking strategically about market segments. For years, and often for generations, the management of these companies has looked for ways to strengthen R&D, sales, and/or production activities without a clear focus on defined market needs. Now these same managers must reorient their thinking first to define specific segments and then determine what it takes to serve these segments more effectively than the competition. This attitude shift is much more difficult to achieve than it may appear. Many executives who have talked a good game of marketing without actually doing things differently must now provide the leadership to ensure that R&D, production, and sales activities are aligned to the requirements and unmet needs of target market segments.

No group of customers has all its needs filled. Even fewer customer groups have articulated all their product and service needs. Astute suppliers identify unmet and unarticulated needs in discreet market segments and then develop a service/product package to fill these needs better than any competitor and at an attractive profit.

The requirements of each segment should include providing services that "go around" your product and for which the customer will pay. Customers are increasingly seeking turnkey solutions and sole-source-supplier agreements as they outsource or shed activities they previously did in-house. The right services can help pull through demand for your products, upgrade customers, and, in many cases, generate good cash flows with minimal new investment.

When general managers have advanced through sales, engineering, or manufacturing, a sound understanding of strategic market segmentation is even more necessary. These managers must learn that market segmentation and market selection are the starting points for all strategic decisions and action programs. They simply must understand that *everything follows the definition and selection of target market segments*. They must also realize that strategic market segmentation is quite different from the traditional "ABC" analysis and market segmentation done by a marketing staff group. To change any company's mind-set to strategic market segmentation, intensive management development programs are required to move the organization's attitude and behavior through three phases of the learning curve shown in Exhibit 4-1. To become market-driven, companies must evolve from "sales segmentation" to "market segmentation" and finally to a "strategic market segmentation." There are no short cuts.

Exhibit 4-1

The Evolution of Industrial Segmentation

Phase 1 ⟶ Sales Segmentation	Phase 2 ⟶ Market Segmentation	Phase 3 Strategic Market Segmentation
Business units that are sales driven	Business units that recently discovered marketing	Business units that are market driven
• Sales department determines who the business unit will serve • "Segmentation" is based on customer size, A, B, C accounts, and geography • Undifferentiated features are promoted broadly • Insufficient market facts, market attractiveness, and company "fit" information • Sales volume and account relationships dominate decisions • All business is considered good business	• The need for market facts is realized • Some market needs, and trends are identified • Some product/market combinations are defined • Differentiation and benefit segmentation is done for some defined markets • Segmentation is done by marketing, without much input from technical, sales, finance, or manufacturing • Segmentation doesn't drive other functional activities or set business unit priorities	• Global market definitions and market segment management • Regional cross-functional teams evaluate and select attractive segment opportunities • Cross-functional teams develop business plans for target markets and key customers • SBUs are established for key markets and account coordination • Resources are allocated to the most attractive market segments and accounts around the world

There are no quick fixes to change old ways of thinking and behavior. Without this shift in attitude and behavior across the whole business unit and without the full support from the general manager, the change will be short lived or will never get started. Marketing people are the starting point to lead the cultural change, but without the understanding and commitment from the general manager and each respective functional manager, it will be an uphill battle every day. Because general mangers have the power to make marketing the guiding force across all departments, they must lead the process of thinking more strategically about market segments and then developing the needed service/product packages for target markets. Finally, general managers must fully support the training and learning process that will trigger the shift in culture, behavior, and resource allocation across the enterprise.

Strategic market segmentation always brings a common language, methodology, and resource allocation discipline to every business unit and person in the organization. The precise definition of a target market's needs can lead to innovative product, service, price, sales, and distribution strategies. These same progressive companies think about customer needs beyond their existing products, technical capabilities, sales skills, or manufacturing know-how when they define and select segments. Everyone starts to think about how he or she can bring more product and service value to each target customer group's needs. Such strategic thinking significantly broadens the opportunities, improves profit, and ties suppliers closer to customers. Strategic market segmentation allows a company to marshal its engineering, manufacturing, sales, and service efforts toward specific areas rather than spread a little of each across a wide range of vulnerable marketplaces. At the same time, market segmentation and the selection of strategic segments provides direction to the entire business unit, which enables it to develop the necessary capabilities to serve each market segment effectively. Many of top management's criticisms about the failure to execute or poor implementation stem from inadequate market segmentation and cross-functional programs that have few links or none at all to target market segments.

SUMMARY

Many industrial companies pay lip service to the definition and selection of the most attractive market segments to focus on. However, most companies lack the resources, technologies, or capabilities to compete in all market segments. We've all heard horror stories about business units that try to be all things to all customers. Business units are a lot like people; neither can be good at everything. Not all prospects were created equal. When unable to compete broadly in any industry against entrenched competitors, or when desiring to enter new markets or capture emerging opportunities, progressive suppliers have learned to adopt a divide-and-conquer or market-segmentation-driven approach. Industrial market segmentation gives managers one of the most powerful competitive tools of all: a strategic focus. A growth strategy based on sound market segment priorities has a much greater chance of being successful than one that is not.

Learning how to segment a marketplace and select the most attractive segments are important strategic skills an industrial firm must possess in each region of the world. Segmentation defines what business(es) the firm is in, identifies the competition, guides strategy development and the technology race, and determines which capabilities and cross-functional programs are needed in the business unit. Industrial market selection is clearly a longer-term strategic decision that cannot be easily reversed without severe penalties. Therefore, it is important that the general marketplace first be segmented into viable targets before any market selection and investment decisions are made. Market segmentation is also the basic building block for developing a global outside-in information system. Market segmentation creates a global business language around common market segment definitions and common customer needs.

The single-minded focus of market segmentation creates a powerful lens through which to view and interpret customers' current and emerging needs. Acting on a clearly defined opportunity, as well as identifying it, is to some extent easier when you're committed to specific industries and market segments. Without market segmentation, decisions and programs tend to be unfocused and lack the effect they could have if aligned to specific markets. Once a business unit loses focus, it is usually only a short time before sales and profits begin to erode. When market positions are lost, it is extremely difficult to regain them, and when most companies fall behind, they never catch up. A well-defined business focus results in growth. Industrial companies that narrow their scope have a better chance of achieving profitable top-line growth.

Assessing Industrial Markets

*"Market facts are a strategic investment,
not an unnecessary cost."*

Pat Parker, Chairman
Parker Hannifin Corporation

Mention the word marketing to most people and images of consumer goods and their manufacturers emerge—General Mills, Colgate Palmolive, Wal-Mart, and Nestle. Then mention the term marketing research and consumer examples are again mentioned—Procter & Gamble, Gillette, Pepsi-Cola, and Budweiser. Most marketing research books and college courses reinforce this perception of the emphasis on consumer-goods retailing. However, only a small percentage of the annual output of goods and services goes to consumers. *More than two-thirds of the U.S. sales and jobs reside with industrial or business-to-business firms making and selling products and services to other organizations—not to households.* Industrial firms are impatient with marketing research examples based on selling detergent to households and cosmetics to customers buying hope. Complex industrial products, their technical performance and service requirements, specialized niche markets, and dynamic technologies create market information needs quite different from those of the mass merchandisers of consumer-packaged goods.

At minimum, industrial marketers need to know the current size, market needs, growth rate, profit prospects, and competitive market shares for any market segment of interest. This includes markets the company is currently serving as well as those it is considering entering. Every industrial company needs this basic information to help select and then gear its operations to the most attractive market segments. *Market information helps companies decide which products, markets, and individual customers to emphasize, deemphasize or move away from.* The approach for evaluating both current and potential markets is essentially the same. The difference, of course, is that more historical sales and first hand knowledge of the marketplace are available for the markets currently served. However, many of the market facts needed to assess current and potential business markets are sometimes unavailable from existing information sources. Therefore, special market studies are often needed to assess customer needs, market potentials, market shares, profit prospects, and competitive advantages and disadvantages in each market segment.

This chapter examines ways to assess the outlook for markets in which the company has a presence; it then goes on to describe how to estimate sales and profit potential for any market of interest. Finally, the chapter outlines specific approaches to conducting market studies that will help determine the attractiveness of various market segments and individual customers.

CONSUMER AND INDUSTRIAL MARKET RESEARCH

While some of the basic objectives of market research apply to both consumer and industrial markets, there are significant differences between industrial and consumer market research because of the structure of industrial markets and the technical needs of industrial users. Four of the major differences are:

1. *Industrial markets are concentrated.* It is not unusual to have a small handful of OEM customers account for the bulk of the total market for any given product or service. When there are after-markets, there are of course a larger number of users, but many of them depend on first being specified with a small number of OEMs. In most industrial markets, a handful of customers have huge purchasing power

over suppliers and can cause big shifts in market shares. A small number of progressive customers result in concentrated sources of information about trends, consumption, and technical needs. Statistical sampling, the lifeblood of consumer research, is not needed in many industrial markets. In-depth customer consultations and discussions about annual usage, requirements, and trends are a common form of industrial market research.

2. *Industrial products and services are more complex.* The technical complexity of most industrial products requires an understanding of how the products work and, equally importantly, how they work in the customer's operation. Even if the supplier's product is not complex, the customer's operation is becoming more complex. This technical complexity requires interaction among engineers, production, maintenance, and procurement people in collecting any information from the immediate customer and customer's customer. Therefore, the interview team of people visiting customers must be technically proficient in the products and the customer's operation. If they are not, they will gather less useful and less accurate information for decision making.

3. *Industrial purchases are driven by the need to solve business problems.* Few industrial users buy a product or service just because it looks or smells good. They have real problems to solve, and they are looking for cost-effective solutions. They tend to conduct side-by-side competitive comparisons before they make a buy decision, and they formally rate and review all suppliers throughout the relationship. Furthermore, with rapidly changing technologies and more frequently changing customer requirements, industrial users are relentlessly searching for more value from the products and services they purchase.

4. *Industrial technical and trade associations provide vital market facts.* Secondary data from trade associations, government publications, technical societies, industrial directories, trade magazines, and buyer guides help determine trends, define markets, estimate market potentials, design sales territories, and set quotas. Much of the secondary data are collected and classified by SIC or NAICS and are available electronically and, increasingly, from trade organizations all over the world. Trade shows, technical seminars, technical papers, and technical standards committees are all important sources of industrial market facts.

Mainstream packaged goods companies participate widely in market research with internal professional staffs and armies of outside consultants doing the field research. In contrast, top and general management in most industrial companies do not understand the need for market facts about customers and competitive offerings. *Far too few industrial firms have realized the strategic value of fact-based market information.* Many large industrial firms do not even have one market research professional. When a competent, in-house marketing research staff does exist, it is typically one of the most underpaid and under appreciated units in the firm. These situations occur because industrial managers do not understand the strategic value of professional market assessment and rely instead on secondary information, or seat-of-the-pants hunches. As a result, industrial companies tend to fly half blind, missing opportunities and getting caught off-base by unexpected product or market developments; they are continuously vulnerable to competitors with a better base of market information. These same industrial executives do not realize the cost and risk of not doing market research to guide their decision making.

In many industrial marketing companies, especially in some sales and engineering circles, market research is regarded with suspicion and as waste of time and money. Some common excuses for not doing market research include not having the time, funds, or people qualified to do the work. The two or three weeks needed for desk research and one to two months required for in-depth customer consultations can be a small investment that saves or makes the company millions of dollars. I am often asked about the difficulty to justify the cost and time to conduct a specialized market study. I respond; what is the cost of being wrong when making decisions? What if there is no market need for your new product or service? What if critical product benefits are missing? What if the economics are not favorable for the customer or the supplier? What if you end up targeting no customer group or the wrong target market? And so on. How expensive would the mistake be? Rather than think market research in terms of cost, think of the sales and profit lost or gained. Many venture capital firms think about market research as an investment in gross profit or a return on the investment. Most venture capital firms are far more sophisticated about the need and importance of market facts than most large publicly owned industrial manufacturers. If more top managers in industrial companies understood the importance of investing in market research and feasibility studies, they would not waste millions of dollars of shareowner money on shaky projects year after year. Would these same managers demand more market facts if some of their own after-tax money were invested in the venture? Yet as trustees of other people's money, they should be even more prudent than if it were their own funds.

The consistently more successful companies I work with have a sound fact base about their industry, market segments, customer needs, profitability, and competition. *Market facts about customers and competition are their starting point for the outside-in process of being market driven.* Good decisions always involve a degree of luck and risk. However, gathering relevant information about customers and competition can significantly reduce the ever-present risk.

A few progressive industrial companies see industrial market research as a *necessary investment* and not as a wasted cost. These same companies see industrial market research as a much broader activity than consumer goods market research. Consumer market research is heavily concerned with sociopsychological attitudes and demographic data to position a retail brand. A consumer goods marketing plan is then created from the sociopsychological and demographic data, often with the help of an advertising agency. Most industrial executives have too narrow a view of marketing research. Few general managers see industrial market research as much broader commercial research that drives strategic planning, product/market selection, and the market strategy development process.

The few leading industrial firms that see the need for this broader role of "market research" call it *commercial research*. In these more advanced companies, the activity correctly guides the strategic planning process by helping to define markets, determine the needed product/service packages, recommend strategies for market segments and outline what capabilities are needed. In this broad concept of marketing research, these people are correctly referred to as business or commercial research professionals. In short, industrial commercial research is more cross functional than consumer-goods attitude research, and it requires professionals with a broad understanding of the business.

COMMERCIAL RESEARCH PROFESSIONALS

Commercial research refers to any effort to gather information about markets, customers, products, technology, profitability, and competition. Because of the broad commercial and technical nature of most industrial products and markets, the kinds of people who conduct sound industrial commercial research are quite different from those involved with consumer-packaged-goods companies. A technical degree in a relevant area is often a must, and hands-on experience in the industry and knowledge of the technologies is necessary (beyond being able to pronounce some of the technical terms). For example, most of the full- and part-time commercial research people at Hewlett-Packard's instrumentation group (now called Agilent) have degrees in electrical engineering, and many have advanced technical degrees. A minimum of five years of business experience in the industry is also common before managing a marketing research project. Whereas advertising agency experience is very desirable for consumer-goods market research, it doesn't mean much in an industrial business.

Industrial commercial research requires interfacing with the customer's design and development engineers, manufacturing engineers, application specialists, and the customer's marketing and sales people. Because the customer interface people are largely technical, a good commercial researcher has to have a sufficient background in the relevant technologies to enable him or her to ask the right questions, aggressively listen, then ask even more probing questions about their needs and what the supplier can do. *It is a lot easier to teach an engineer how to do commercial research than it is to teach engineering to a nonengineer.*

Finding people with the needed technical background, aptitude, industry knowledge, and business research skills are difficult for every industrial firm that is committed to the strategic use of commercial research. Some industrial managers see marketing research as little more than a clerical activity, and they staff and reward it as such. Less competent people are hired for business research; the results are too often unimpressive, while low salaries perpetuate the problem. Many younger people lack business experience, especially in your company's products, technologies, and industry to lead market research projects. The difficulty in locating, hiring, and keeping good commercial research people is a major challenge faced by every industrial company in the world. Semiretired people and telecommuters with the relevant technical backgrounds and industry experience often make great commercial researchers.

What are some other advantages of hiring semi-retired and part-time people for commercial research, sales support, and new product development studies? Patrick Daly, director of marketing services, at Parker Hannifin supplied the following five advantages:

1. They have analytical backgrounds well suited for training in market research.
2. They are usually easily trained in your products and technologies.
3. They are stable people with a good work ethic.
4. They have low turnover and are long-term workers.
5. They can be employed on a project-by-project basis and during peak periods.

Parker Hannifin's corporate market research unit serves as an internal resource for the company's more than 100 decentralized divisions. Mike Marvin, Parker's vice president who heads the unit, reports to the company's executive vice president. Parker is one of the few industrial firms that understands the strategic role of business research. This appreciation starts with the top management and it is shown by chairman Pat Parker's statement, *Market facts are a strategic investment, not an unneccesary cost.*

Mothers who have technical backgrounds are another excellent source of part-time business researchers. Parker gives all their part-time engineers the titled of "commercial research engineer". With computers, some work at home or do telecommuting. Parker's part-time commercial research engineers perform a number of tasks including:

- Locating secondary information from the Internet, trade associations, technical societies, trade journals, state and federal governments, and universities and institutes all over the world.
- Qualifying sales leads that come in on 800 numbers. These prospects are entered or updated on a global database with global SIC/NAICS and Parker specific codes.
- For sales leads, they find out the kind of technical system the customer has, what products they are currently buying, who they are buying from, and their annual usage.This information also goes into Parker's global marketing databank.
- Telephone qualification of new customers. Literature is then sent with a cover

letter from the commercial research engineer; above a certain minimum sales potential a Parker direct sales rep follows up with a personal sales call.

- Visit trade shows to interview customers and competitors, make contacts for follow-up calls, and learn about customer needs. Conduct focus group interviews or customer plant visits to uncover needs of current, deflected, and new customers.
- Develop literature for specific target markets and conduct training for direct and distributor salespeople. This task often includes doing side-by-side competitive comparisons and developing competitive product information and product interchange information.

Full-time commercial research people should hire, train, and supervise the part-timers. If an outside interviewer or market research firm is considered, it should be competent in your relevant technologies, know your company's capabilities, and be able to have an in-depth discussion with customers. External researchers without these qualifications will be, at most, facilitators at a customer visit. Once a company has a competent commercial research staff, they can begin to assess your markets and provide information that will help grow the top line. One of the first and ongoing assignments of a commercial research staff is to define and assess your current market positions.

ASSESSING MARKET POSITIONS

The first step in any market assessment is to define market segments and then assign accounts to the defined segments. The next step is to determine the market size, market share, growth rate, trends, and profitability in each defined segment.

Define Market Segments

As we saw in the last chapter, there are many different ways to define a market segment. As a result, confusion often abounds in discussions of market potential because those involved have not reached common agreement on the definition of the market in question. Potential estimates are often discussed in terms of total industry sales. Other times they are discussed in terms of certain classes of accounts. However, these estimates of market potential are of little value to anyone trying to evaluate target markets for strategic market planning. To be useful, any discussion of market potential should address a defined customer group as outlined in the last chapter's discussion of segmenting industrial markets.

To develop more meaningful market information on U.S. businesses, the federal government has segmented all businesses into fairly homogeneous categories. The government coding system classifies all business firms by the main product or service provided at the location. Formerly called Standard Industrial Classification (SIC) codes, they were changed in 1999 to the new North American Industrial Classification System (NAICS), which is pronounced nakes. The United States, Canada, and Mexico developed the new NAICS. The new classification scheme includes 350 new businesses and it uses twenty, instead of the SIC's ten broad sectors of the economy, reflecting how the economy has changed and added many new technology and service areas.

The finer detailed NAICS is even more valuable than the SIC system to segment, analyze, select, and target markets. If a supplier understands the requirements of leading firms within a classification, projections can be made for all firms in the category. The number, size and geographic dispersions of firms can also be identified. This information can be converted to estimates of market potentials, market shares, and sales forecasts, and it can help develop sales territories and goals. Equally important, this information can be used to identify new customers for a supplier's products and services. These codes also help to eliminate industries and companies that are not likely prospects for your product or service. Because so many government agencies, trade associations, and private companies collect data on the basis of these codes, they are the starting point for defining and analyzing markets segments and building and maintaining a global market database.

Convert Accounts to Market Segments

Classifying your existing customers into market segments is one of the most important activities for an industrial company if it wants to become market driven. It requires identifying your current customers' primary line(s) of business and use(s) of your product or service at their ship-to location—which is not necessarily the billing location. If there are multiple lines of business at each ship to customer location, multiple segmentation codes have to be assigned to the customer. In these situations, the salesperson is requested to identify what percentage of the annual purchased volume is used for each segment. Sometimes it is also useful to identify and record the type of manufacturing process or system being used at each customer's location at which the product is used. *All market segment information from customers should be uniformly captured on all purchase orders and for all quotations with a global market segmentation classification system.*

When converting customers to market segments, top management must adopt a uniform global classification methodology. There will often be resistance, especially from those business units located on continents far from headquarters. Most of this book prescribes a bottom-up or decentralized approach to managing businesses. However, when it comes to marketing information systems and multinational target marketing, a global market definition system must be in place even if the CEO has to force it on the entire organization. The SIC/NAICS codes are a common beginning for classifying customers into uniform global market segments. Some companies may find it necessary to add one or two digits to the NAICS codes to account for the more specific application needs in their industry. It is important that all regions of the world adopt the same market coding system so that the same markets and customers can be analyzed, selected, and targeted in various regions and countries of the world. Exhibit 5-1 shows how one company reclassified its accounts into market segments, which was a much more meaningful basis for developing product/market strategies than the previous "ABC" listing of accounts by their annual purchases.

When current and potential customers are uniformly captured by a globally-agreed upon segmentation method, database marketing can become a reality. Because this information is continually updated, shared, and used for decision making, the organization will reap the long term benefits of this investment. Business teams in each country and region of the world should have access to the global marketing database and share market segment knowledge with their colleagues around the world. To not share and use this information after it has been uniformly gathered is worse than not having the information at all.

Exhibit 5-1

Classify Each Account Into Market Segments
(Moving from "ABC" Sales to Market Segments)

ABC Sales Orientation	Sales Revenue (millions)	Global Market Segmentation Codes
A. Caterpillar—construction	$ 14,100	**1.** All accounts were reclassified into market segments including:
Caterpillar—mining	4,000	
Detroit Diesel—mining	16,120	
John Deere—construction	14,900	**A.** Mining (SIC or NAICS code)
J.I. Case—agriculture	14,500	
B. J.I. Case—mining	2,000	**B.** Agriculture (SIC or NAICS code)
Massey Ferguson—agriculture		
Rockford Clutch—agriculture and mining	1,575	**C.** Construction (SIC or NAICS code)
Twin Disc	1,400	
Ford Tractor	1,063	**D.** Lift trucks (SIC or NAICS code)
Saab Scania	1,000	
New Holland	975	
Clark Equipment	970	**2.** The following information was then obtained and shared for each market segment, country, and region of the world.
Hyster Company	908	
Warner Gear—agriculture	800	
Warner Gear—mining	588	
	550	
C. Toyota—lift truck		**A.** List of all segment accounts
Caterpillar—lift truck	540	
Fiat Allis—construction	531	**B.** Market segment potentials
Jeffrey Mining—mining	430	
Raymond—lift truck	410	
Marathon—construction	201	**C.** Segment growth rates
LeTourneau—construction	390	**D.** Functional substitutes
Franklin Equipment—agriculture	389	
U.S. Industries—agriculture	170	**E.** Competitive shares
Funk Manufacturing	140	
Joy Manufacturing—mining	119	**F.** Trends
Mine Machinery—agriculture and mining	12	**G.** Unmet needs
Perkins—engines	10	**H.** Existing and/or future profit prospects
	8	

Annual total sales = $77,799

ESTIMATING SEGMENT POTENTIALS

In addition to assessing the company's current market positions and converting customers to market segments, management is next faced with the task of estimating market potentials for both existing and new market segments. There are a number of ways market potentials can be estimated, and how it is done depends chiefly on the sources and availability of data.

Trade and Technical Associations

Many trade and technical associations forecast total industry demand for their member companies. These forecasts usually show the annual total market size and sometimes indicate competitor shares. A massive amount of trade association data is available on the Internet. Some trade association data are already connected to SIC/NAICS codes for possible segmentation. But most trade association data do not show future demand by market segment. Each market segment has different growth rates, different needs, different trends, a different set of competitors, and different factors driving demand. In short, industry associations can serve as a useful beginning for aggregate and historical industry data and trends, but further refinements are often required before the data can be used to estimate specific product/market potentials. Active membership and involvement in the trade associations and technical committees of your target markets are an excellent upfront marketing investment that usually pays big long-term dividends in the form of identifying information about market segment sizes, growth rates, new technologies, and various trends.

Usage Factors

When estimating the potentials for a specific product or service, the consumption for a given product or service must be determined for each market segment. The actual consumption by market segment is termed a *usage factor*. Usage factors need to be developed for every segment currently served or that might be served in the future. Usage factors are sometimes called *conversion factors* because one must *convert* aggregate customer production figures into the usage of your present or proposed products. The calculation of usage is based on some unit of the customer's economic activity and specific to the industry and market segment. The following examples help explain how to calculate usage factors by market segment:

- A Honda automotive assembly plant had an economic output on average of about 800 cars per day. The level of output consumed or used was about $60,000 (USD) in welding rods for each day they produced 800 cars. That equates to a usage factor of about $75 per car produced ($60,000 ÷ 800). Furthermore, two different welding technologies were used. About 80 percent of the usage ($51,000) was done with a robotic laser welding process and the remaining 15 percent ($9,000) was done with a metal-arc welding process.
- A Nike athletic shoe plant in Korea used about $4.00 U.S. of an anaerobic adhesive for each pair of shoes. A Bally leather shoe plant in Europe used an average of about 70 U.S. cents of the same adhesive per pair of shoes. When the average daily and yearly production rates were estimated, usage factors for these two different market segments were determined in each country.

The usage factors for purchases like Nike adhesives or for large OEMs such as Honda are easier to calculate than they are for fragmented markets where usage is just a few dollars per year for each end-user. For example, the OEM usage for heavy-duty truck bearings in the United Kingdom was based on interviews with each of the four truck builders and their estimated production rates over the next two years. These estimated OEM production rates by customer and plant locations were simply multiplied times $305, the average cost of bearings per new truck produced.

The fragmented after-market potential is always more complicated to estimate than the concentrated OEM market. First, from government truck registration data, the bearing supplier learned that there were 430,700 heavy-duty trucks registered in the United Kingdom. From personal interviews with fleet personnel and owner/operators, the percentage of U.K. trucks replacing wheel bearings each year were estimated. Finally, from the same personal interviews, they learned that the average wheel bearing after-market repair kit was purchased for about $395. From the secondary government registration information, an estimate of the current and future market potentials for the heavy-duty truck after-market was developed for the United Kingdom. The U.K. after-market was about five times larger than the OEM market, was less cyclical, and had larger profit margins for bearing replacement kits.

The usage of complementary products can sometimes help predict the market potentials for another product. For example, where bearings are used there are usually complementary seals and lubricants used. By knowing the OEM or aftermarket usage rate of truck seals, the usage of bearings, and lubricants can be estimated. Sister divisions making complementary products in the same market segments are another source of usage information.

Extreme care must be used in selecting a usage factor. With accurate usage information, market segments can be prioritized as heavy, medium, and light users when determing their attractiveness. If the wrong usage factor is chosen, major strategic errors can result. A major strategic error would be to select target markets that consume considerably less than the usage factor indicated. Errors could also result in capital expansions, the wrong alignment of sales or distributor territories, location of distribution centers, or sales quotas.

Buildup and Breakdown Methods

Sales forcasts are a vital beginning in the development of a business plan. Everyone in the company works from estimates of how much will be sold in a given time period. Production schedules, raw materials sourcing, capital equipment needs, staffing, and budgets all flow from a sales forecast. Sales forcasts should be developed with the buildup and breakdown methods or by combinating these two forecasting approaches.

The Buildup Method

This method starts with the collection of usage data from individual accounts in the market segment. A list of all customers in the segment along with their usage based on past and planned usage rates are needed. Because direct sales are such a dominant influence in most industrial markets, this method widely uses salespeople's' estimates. This approach also works well when sales are limited to a well-defined market with relatively few customers. The jet manufacturers that make 80- to 110-seat aircraft are a good example. There are a small number of these jet OEMs for which the usage for gaskets can be accurately predicted for the next three years based on order backlogs and long delivery cycles. Each sales rep knows exactly how many gaskets will be needed and the backlogs and needed lead-time at each OEM in their region. The aftermarket for aircraft gaskets was estimated from the small number of airlines in each country flying regional jets and was based on usage estimates from the airline maintenance departments. For wide customer bases, survey sampling and extrapolation should be done.

There are, however, some drawbacks to be considered with the buildup method. There is sometimes a lack of uniformity among salespeople in both ability and willingness to participate. Some salespeople may purposely underestimate potentials to protect themselves against receiving higher sales quotas—commonly known as sandbagging. When a manufacturer markets its products through distributors, the distributor may not have the time or interest to develop these estimates for each account. Some distributors are helpful with this method, but it is the responsibility of the manufacturer's territory manager to work with the local distributor and a divisional or corporate market research person to perform an annual account analysis of the potentials in each distributor's territory.

The Breakdown Method

This method starts with aggregate government or industry trade data that usually must be "broken down" into usage data for your defined market segment and each product/technology. Current and expected country gross domestic product (GDP) might be the starting point. In some industries, more specific indexes exist, such as new construction starts, miles flown per year by type of aircraft, number of oil rigs pumping per year, or government health care spending.

A drawback of the breakdown method is the gross level at which the forecasts are made. Basic economic data is often too broad for managers to use and such data are typically not segment specific. However, some trade association data are more specific than the data provided by aggregate economic sources.

Rarely are either the buildup or breakdown methods used exclusively to determine the potential for one market or to develop the sales forecast. The most common approach is to use both methods to develop and verify estimates of market potential. For example, Loctite, a maker of industrial adhesives, develops a sales forecast by polling its territory salespeople in order to estimate sales for the coming year by segments and accounts with over $5,000 potential. These forecasts are received by each division. The final sales forecast is developed by adjusting the buildup sales force estimates with broader trade and economic data for the region or country.

Leading-Edge Customers

Leading-edge customers are most helpful for sales forecasting, for predicting the substitution rate of one technology for another, for identifying early warnings signals and trends, and for articulating and verifying customer needs. A lead user is someone who sees the need in the marketplace or in their operations months or years before the rest of the market. These people are able to determine the direction and speed by which a particular technology or market segment is moving. These individuals and their companies are early to see how they can gain an advantage by making a change. Lead users are not always the largest customers in a market segment. They are often the medium sized and less bureaucratic companies.

Leading-edge customers are those who make the most advanced use of a supplier's products. In product development, lead customers are not only a source of new product ideas, they may have actually experimented with your product and made modifications and improvements to meet their current or emerging needs. Typically, in every market segment then are such innovators, who are first to perceive the advantage, trend or need to change. They are the first to try a new product and are usually good technologists with a marketing imagination. These people are sometimes able to envision needs and market opportunities that may not yet exist. Traditional market research targets the "average customer" to see what they like and dislike with their current products. By contrast, lead user commercial research identifies the most progressive customers and ask many probing questions such as; "What trends do you see?" "What needs do you see coming around the corner?" and "When do you think they will occur?" Lead users help you spend more time looking at the horizon than at your feet. Companies that spend too much time looking at their feet will find themselves stumbling in the footsteps of their smartest and fastest competitors. In every target market, you should have one to two lead users identified for your research needs.

CONDUCTING MARKET STUDIES

The complete range of information required to assess any business market is seldom available from internal sales records or trade association data. To obtain the more precise information required, it is usually necessary to conduct some kind of a market study that involves existing customers, prospective customers, and possibly distributors. Market studies of this type can provide firsthand information about:

- Market size and growth rates
- Buying influences
- Annual purchases
- Technical requirements
- Service needs
- Supplier performance requirements
- Side-by-side competitive comparisons
- Product line gaps
- New technologies
- Environmental and safety trends

Specify the Information Needed

The most important step before embarking on a search for market information is to define the problem and specify what specific information is needed. A clearly and accurately stated business problem is often well on its way to being solved. The definition provides the direction and control for the entire information-gathering process. If the problem is not properly defined, time, effort, and money will be wasted, no matter how well the project is carried out. Who needs the right answer to the wrong question?

Defining marketing and business problems is frequently a complex process. To locate and define problems, a written list of all the pertinent areas to be considered should be prepared. Secondary research (research done and published by others) may help to define and develop a more specific checklist of information required before primary research is undertaken. The results of an internal sales analysis, also usually help focus market research on more specific objectives.

Secondary Information and the Internet

Secondary research is the search for previously published material that can provide more background information and a closer focus on the problem. Sometimes called "desk or library research," secondary research utilizes internal data, including sales records, salespersons' call reports, a reanalysis of previously conducted studies, and identification of industry-wide studies that are available. Sales analysis is a form of secondary research.

External sources of market information include trade associations, technical journals, government agencies, and industrial directories. The names, locations, and major activities performed by more than 35,000 national and international trade and technical associations are contained in the *Encyclopedia of Associations,* a reference book that is available in most libraries and should be available in every industrial firm. Any desk research should start with identifying the relevant trade associations and determining what information they provide. An increasing number of associations are global and if they are not, their respective counterpart organizations in other regions of the world are shown in the *Encyclopedia of Associations.* The *Census of Manufacturers* and *County Business Patterns* are other secondary sources that show production output by SIC/NAICS. Another source, *Thomas's Register of American Manufacturers,* classifies all manufacturers by products produced, assets, state, and city. It is used by many purchasing departments to identify suppliers and producers. Each industry or profession usually has at least one trade association. A few trade associations are little more than public relations offices; others keep close track of industry sales and trends. Some of the larger trade associations have their own full-time market assessment staff.

The Internet is a major source of secondary information about products, customers, markets, and competition. The Internet competes with several professional online services. The Internet is very broad in scope and is a comparably low-cost source of secondary information. The Internet is also a prime tool for gathering competitive intelligence in a timely and cost-effective way. Because many corporations, especially the larger ones, display product and financial information on their websites, this competitive information is easy to track. If a company is actively selling over the Internet, list pricing information is usually available to track. If a company does not sell on its website, it usually does not display product prices. Information about products can be obtained by using search engines on the web. There are providers of custom search services on the web who search for information for a fee. The Internet allows you to gather a large amount of secondary information rapidly without going to libraries or contacting other sources. Even more impressive, the secondary information can be gathered without even leaving your office or your desk at home. The Internet has leveled the playing field for smaller companies in need of secondary information.

As a general rule, no market study should be undertaken before a search of secondary sources has been completed. Secondary sources can sometimes solve the problem without any primary research. The cost is much less than a primary investigation, and at the least, such a search will establish a higher plateau from which a primary study can be launched. Secondary research is not as exciting as primary research for both the analyst and user, but because of its exploratory nature, it can establish patterns of careful, thoughtful analysis that will carry over to any subsequent primary market assessment study.

PRIMARY MARKET STUDIES

The quality of the data obtained from a primary market study depends on asking the right questions to the right buying influences, employing qualified interviewers, and verifying the quality and validity of the responses. Let's now address each of these areas.

Asking the Right Questions

Once the needed information is specified and agreed to by management, the next task is to ask the right questions. The poor wording of questions can result in misleading and inaccurate information. Questions that ask for ways to improve a product—or "What would you like improved?" will get more in-depth responses than questions that simply ask what the user likes and dislikes about an existing or new product. Showing a customer a prototype elicits specific responses. Following are ten guidelines to consider when constructing a interview script or questionnaire and selecting the precise wording:

1. All questions should relate directly to the research objectives that management has agreed to.
2. Avoid examples—they may divert the response from the research objectives.
3. If you wish to extract many thoughts on the topic, add a probing question that goes deeper into the topic.
4. Use as few and as simple words as possible in each question.
5. Make questions specific without being elaborate.
6. Avoid wording that causes ambiguous responses.
7. Use trade jargon only if all the respondents know and use it.
8. Even if it is an open-ended question, consider providing categories or precoded check boxes for the answers. This is especially helpful when asking for annual usage amounts, downtime, and cost information.

9. Instead of asking "how much?" indicate the units for which you desire answers—pounds, dollars, gallons, pressures, temperatures, throughput, yards, parts per million, etc.
10. Provide for "don't know" responses rather than force a guess.

Selecting the Right Interviewers

Accurate business interviews depend on asking the right questions of the appropriate people and then listening with educated ears and astute observations. Because person-to-person and telephone interviews are vital for most industrial market assessment projects, the person asking the questions and receiving the verbal responses plays a key role. The interviewer must know the industry, how the product is used and bought, and your technical capabilities. Without such background knowledge, the interviewer cannot ask probing questions and will probably miss key words from the respondent. It usually takes extensive briefing and indoctrination to the industry, the technology, substitute products, and the competition to get less knowledgeable interviewers up to an acceptable level. The vice president of marketing in a major industrial firm evaluates market studies by outside suppliers by the kind and depth of briefing they do of their field interviewers. Often he personally interviews one of the field interviewers to see how well he or she was briefed and made aware of the problem and concerns of the study.

The need to have expert interviewers knowledgeable in the technical language and about users' needs is usually best addressed by full-time or part-time in-house commercial research personnel. They need less timely and costly indoctrination. In a larger firm, an in-house marketing research staff is a necessary and usually cost-effective alternative to having outside firms plan market studies and conduct personal interviews.

The business respondent's time is important. Therefore, the interviewer must gain as much useful information as possible within a limited time. As a consequence, industrial market research field interviewers must state questions clearly, attempt to trigger the memory, and listen very carefully. One manufacturer of electronic testing equipment always sends a team of R&D and marketing people to conduct person-to-person interviews for product development. The team method allows for better questioning, customer interaction, notetaking, and richer insights to later couple product design to customer requirements. R&D/marketing team interviews can also help in creative market analysis immediately following the interviews. The use of annual customer reviews, with R&D and marketing present, reinforces the use of technical/commercial interview teams.

Selecting the Sample

Samples for industrial marketing studies are nearly always much smaller than those used for consumer goods marketing studies because of the concentrated nature of most industrial markets. For example, a manufacturer of specialty chemicals identified a total of twenty potential users for a new high-performance chemical. The producer was able to personally visit eight users and to conduct telephone interviews with the remaining twelve in the total market. Because a total market might consist of a handful of customers, one hundred percent "sampling" of the entire universe is not uncommon in some industrial market segments. If larger customer bases are involved, it is often best to stratify the sample by size or type of customer and/or by country or geographic areas. Furthermore, in-depth interviewing of multiple buying influences at leading-edge customer locations is more important than superficially interviewing a large number of customer locations. *The quality of each industrial interview is far more important than the quantity of interviews.*

Industrial market research sampling is largely judgmental, meaning that researchers and management use their own judgment to decide who would be knowledgeable sources for the specified information. Customers who are open, accessible, and considered progressive are prime candidates. If you interview ten customers and continue to find the same information, you might end the "sampling" because the time and cost do not justify the value of the additional information. When a larger number of customers must be sampled, the samples are usually generated from industrial directories, trade association lists, and annual buying guides. Internal customer lists are also used, but they can be partial and biased.

Survey information can be obtained from sales forces, from experts, by mail or telephone, and with person-to-person customer visits. All of these approaches to conducting primary assessment studies should be considered when a problem is to be studied. Each of these approaches is a compromise of some form. The manager or user of the market information must weigh the cost, time, and value of the project when choosing one or a combination of these survey approaches.

We will now describe each survey approach and place special emphasis on person-to-person customer consultations because they are the most useful method of conducting primary studies in industrial markets.

Sales Force Opinions

The industrial sales force is sometimes considered a biased and poor source of market information. This is sometimes true, but an industrial sales representative can also be a prime source of market information. The intelligence the industrial sales representative develops about end users' needs, buying patterns, and competition can serve as the foundation for future product and market plans and tactics. Salespeople typically have well-developed interpersonal skills, are familiar with customers' operations, speak the customers' language, and know which customers are progressive. Sales professionals know most of the customers' rational needs and emotional buying factors. Joint customer visits with salespeople can also be an excellent beginning for an exploratory study before the full study is finalized. Some of the best sites to visit for a pilot study may be at the customer locations at which your salespeople have developed the most open and trusting relationships. Salespeople with the appropriate technical background are a big plus.

It is impractical for most industrial companies to structure market tests as consumer goods companies do to evaluate the needs, likes, and dislikes of market segments. The industrial marketer must gear the sales force to provide this information or, in many cases, do without it. One major part of the market planning and research function of any company should be to develop and provide intelligent, continual feedback from the marketplace. Industrial firms should spend considerable effort and emphasize the importance of developing ongoing market assessment information from the field sales force. Call reports and competitive intelligence are two vital sources of ongoing feedback from a sales force.

Seeking Expert Opinions

Sometimes the opinions of experts on a subject are far more important than the results of any other kind of study. For example, a manufacturer of surgical hip joints wanted to determine whether hip implants made of ceramics would eventually be selected by physicians over the current implants made of titanium. Expert opinions from leading orthopedic surgeons were obtained at a national orthopedic surgeons convention. After obtaining a preregistration list of physicians, the supplier was able to schedule interviews with 25 surgeons by offering $500 to each for participation. The supplier was able to gauge the physicians' initial reactions to the use of ceramics and identify sources of resistance to the new material. The expert opinion interviews were a very efficient and rapid way to obtain information for product development, market entry strategy, and development of promotional materials.

Expert opinions are frequently sought in high-technology industries such as medicine, pharmaceuticals, and aerospace. Interviewers visit key people at universities and corporations who are recognized as the innovators or leaders in the profession. The whole approach depends on knowing how to identify the real experts. Colleagues and peers recognize true experts as nationally and internationally knowledgeable about the topic. Good interviews with true experts usually reduce the need for additional interviews with more people. It is a mistake to think that expert opinion is inferior to more scientific approaches to gathering market information. In some industrial market situations, expert opinions can be far superior to large sample information. However, a small sample of experts is usually better than a single expert. Since an expert opinion person can sometimes also be a lead user, I suggest you refer to the earlier section of this chapter titled "Leading-Edge Customers."

Mail or Telephone Interviews

In situations in which the cost of person-to-person interviews–either individual or group–is too high, the marketer can choose the mail or telephone approach. It is also not uncommon to first conduct a few person-to-person interviews and then complete the study with the mail or telephone approach. Telephone interviews, like the person-to-person approach to gathering market assessment information, allow industrial marketers to reach the appropriate people and ask probing questions. A telephone interview of up to a half hour is a relatively low-cost approach. Like person-to-person interviews, telephone interviews require people trained in the product or technology. Of course, complex technical questions that require seeing the customer's operation or using visual aids are not feasible with the telephone approach. Telephone market assessment is limited to rather simple questions about annual usage, current supply sources, and image perceptions.

Mail interviews are usually low in cost and do not require the training and supervision of interviewers. They are especially good when surveying a wide customer base with many segments about relatively few items. For example, a manufacturer of agricultural chemicals periodically surveys about 1,000 farmers to learn of different trends and purchase preferences for different chemicals. The producer supplements the periodic survey with person-to-person interviews at agricultural cooperatives and county fairs. The shorter the mail questionnaire, the better. Low response rates may create a strong response bias, and there is often little control over when the response is returned and who provides the information. When $1 or $5 bills are inserted with each questionnaire, the response rate will improve.

Customer Consultations

Customer consultations (sometimes called person-to-person interviews) allow the interviewer to see a customer's operation and ask more specific questions. For example, one manufacturer developed a new insulating material for greenhouses that would reduce energy costs. There was no substitute for conducting person-to-person interviews at a cross section of greenhouses. The field interviews helped the producer make a cost/benefit analysis of the energy-saving material in large, medium, and small greenhouses in each climate zone. Energy costs and technical requirements were also obtained from each greenhouse. The person-to-person interviews also revealed some potential application problems. In other cases, a small number of interviews with customers can stop a supplier from providing an expensive function the customer does not need or want. For example, a major farm tractor manufacturer learned from farmers that a side power unit to raise and lower implements was not needed. The final engineering and manufacturing costs for the unit would have been nearly $1 million, and it would have added an unnecessary 5 to 6 percent to the purchase price of the tractor. *The probing nature of consultative interviews is excellent for two-way learning between suppliers and customers.*

Each personal interview can last one to three hours, considerably longer than is practical for telephone or mail interviews. Person-to-person interviews are costly, especially if extensive travel is required, and may be ineffective if interviewers are not properly trained or indoctrinated. Using focus groups can reduce the cost of person-to-person interviews. An industrial focus group consists of a small number of individuals with a common occupation. One machine tool manufacturer usually discusses a new product and a prototype with focus groups of machinists to obtain their reactions. A hospital equipment manufacturer conducts group interviews with nurses to obtain responses to its and competitors' machines. In still another situation, an electrical producer sometimes conducts group interviews with distributors at regional meetings to obtain competitive intelligence.

Focus group interviews are a relatively inexpensive and quick way to gather market information. The combined group effect often produces a wide range of information and insights, but the results are sometimes hard to interpret and quantify. The stronger personalities in the group can influence the more passive members. The tendency to seek consensus may also dampen the responses of some members. But if resources are limited, the focus group may be the best alternative to no person-to-person interviews at all.

SPECIAL STUDIES

Researching international markets and conducting new product studies are common areas for conducting special studies. Electronic databases and the Internet are shrinking the time and cost to research international markets. New product studies are most effective when coupled to the technique of observing users in their workplaces. Let's now address some proven approaches to researching international markets and conducting new product and new service studies.

Researching International Markets

With the globalization of many industrial markets, there is a need to enter new countries and regions of the world in which you have less experience and fewer facts about customers and competition. It can be disastrous to parachute into any new country or region without these facts. Trade and government usage information taken for granted in the United States, Western Europe, and Japan is often sketchy or totally lacking in the less developed countries of the world. Sister trade associations in the respective countries are often valuable sources of secondary information. However, if there are secondary data in some of these countries, it may be old, erratically collected, and not reliable. If any import, export, local production, or usage data are collected, it sometimes is not comparable to data available in the more developed countries.

Language and cultural differences among countries makes it difficult to gather firsthand information from customer visits. It is also often difficult to identify the buying organization and key buying influences in some countries. For all of these reasons, it is usually necessary to use a local consultant and/or an interpreter in each country. Employees from your companies who are nationals from the target country can sometimes help with interviews and with gathering local trade, technical, and government association information. Parker Hannifin had a Japanese national and a Chinese engineer working for the company in the United States assist with market research projects in their native countries. Sister business units selling complementary products or services to the companies in other countries might also provide some guidance. Joint venture partners can also be a great help in gathering market facts. Caterpillar's joint venture partner in Japan, Schin Mitsubishi, provides cost and competitive information about Komatsu and other competitors in Japan and throughout Asia. Unfortunately, sister divisions and joint venture partners are often overlooked as a domestic and foreign information resource.

The Internet, as a global medium, tremendously increases the scope of generating and gathering information across borders quickly and at a low cost. The collection of intelligence from international sources is rapidly increasing across the world as more computers and countries are hooking up to the network.

Interpreting market information is always a challenge and even more so in another culture where words have different meanings and where buying roles and ethics can vary greatly. Therefore, a competent local consultant is nearly always needed in the new country. The person should be technically proficient and have good competency in English, which has become the business language of the world.

New Product Studies

The need for market facts is especially evident when developing new or improved products. The number one cause of new product failures is frequently cited as the lack of up-front market research on the vitally important "fuzzy front end" of the product development process. Market research is an especially important means of identifying unmet and unarticulated customer needs. Successful new products tend to be those backed by early and in-depth user market research. For market pull new product innovations, market research verifies the need and determines the market and profit potential for the opportunity. For technology-push new products, which are often high risk and high reward, even more commercial research is needed to uncover and verify unarticulated needs. New product and service concepts require more extensive market research than product-line extensions or me-too products. For breakthrough new products, the big question is; "How do you identify the latent and unexpressed needs of customers?"

In new product research, marketing and engineering people should work together very closely. It does not work if only marketers or engineers visit customers because they have to design and conduct the program together. In some companies, engineers only get memos from marketing people. By working together with customers, marketing and engineering can facilitate the transfer of complex, ambiguous, and novel information. The following statements are frequently heard from marketing and engineering new product teams at Hewlett-Packard:

> Get as much customer contact as possible.
> Go see the customers to prove or disprove the point.
> Take the project team out to customers.
> Let's go visit some former customers.

Marketing managers should encourage engineering and scientific people to accompany them on new product customer visits. Marketing should no longer toss user information "over the wall" to engineering and and then wait for engineering to toss back a new product design. Marketing executives should encourage technical employees to get out and spend quality time with customers. This process could eliminate a lot of the suspicion and shouting matches between marketing and R&D. Instead, marketing and engineering must collaborate and work together from the very beginning to understand the needs of customers.

New product market studies, like new product development, are difficult and risky. Usually the newer the industrial product or service, the less accurate or reliable will be the prospect's responses. If the product or service is fairly revolutionary or requires a different way of using the product, evaluations tend to be more negative. In cases where the product is radically different or performs the same function but in a different way, it is often difficult for customers to visualize the value-in-use. Revolutionary products also tend to be rejected as "crazy" or strange, especially from small or less known companies. New product concepts often have more credibility and understandability if they come from a well-known producer. But because many innovations come from small companies that are not well known, new product research for these suppliers is even more difficult.

Observe Unarticulated Needs

For new product studies, there is no substitute for observing users in their workplace. Observations of users are helpful to uncover or verify new product concepts. New product commercial research must carefully examine the existing production systems of leading-edge customers and then document their problems or needs. Videotaping the entire process often helps.

Observing the customers' process, from procurement through after sales service, can *reveal many unarticulated needs*. Crown Equipment, which invented the narrow-aisle lift truck, observes operators using their equipment in a variety of material handling situations. Crown's designers also spend a lot of time watching videotape of how the trucks are used and maintained. New ergonomic controls, safety features, maintenance signals, and faster serviceability were the result of numerous firsthand and video observations. Many of the things learned in observation cannot be obtained from conversations or any other means. Seeing your product in use helps you see things and ask questions that otherwise may never surface. Sealed Air, the packaging company, spends a lot of time at the end of production lines around the world watching customers pack and protect their products for shipping. Many ideas about materials management, stacking of materials and packaging needs are uncovered by observing packing and shipping employees working with an array of products. The observation of gestures and body language in different countries can be more revealing than a word open to multiple translations from cultural differences. The artificial setting of a focus group or meeting in a conference room will not uncover many unarticulated needs that are observed on a production floor or in the field, with leading-edge users.

In another situation, Weyerhaeuser won an important advantage in the market for particleboard after identifying an unarticulated need during a visit to a customer's plant. The customer, a major furniture maker, created table legs by laminating together narrow boards produced by some of Weyerhaeuser's competitors. Unable either to match the competitors' prices or to convince the customer to pay higher prices for superior quality, Weyerhaeuser instead came up with a new way to make table legs–a new, much thicker particleboard that did not have to be laminated. The consequent savings to customers in tooling and labor costs put Weyerhaeuser back in the competitive running with a superior value product.

When using the on-site observational setting to generate or test new product concepts, it is important to clarify who should be observed, who should do the observing, and what the observer should be watching and reporting on. Those interviewed may be customers, noncustomers, the customers' customers, or others in the user's organization. For example, maintenance people or technicians at work may be as or more useful to observe than an engineer at the same organization. A small cross-functional team of two to three people from different disciplines should conduct the observations. If outside interviewers are used, some of the team members should be employees who understand the company's existing capabilities. A good observer/interviewer is able to defer judgment, build on the ideas of others, stay focused on the topic, and encourage so-called wild new ideas. Well-chosen observers with a deep knowledge of the supplier's capabilities, especially the technical know-how, should observe customers in their workplace.

Steelecase is the largest manufacturer of office furniture in the world. Jim Hacket, the CEO, described the importance of observing customers in the workplace during a presentation at our annual senior executive seminar:

> When we design new office furniture and modular units, we nearly always learn more by watching how people actually do work and then asking them questions. Sometimes it is better to temper or ignore what customers say they need or don't like about a new product. It is often far better to observe and pay more attention to what customers do than what they say.

(Chapter 6, "Successful New Products," further describes the use of the observation approach for generating new product ideas in the section titled, "Identify Unarticulated Needs.")

Qualitative and Quantitative Research

The old idea of market research being divided into *hard* (quantitative) or *soft* (qualitative) is outdated for industrial market research. Both methods are used, but open-ended qualitative market research questions are very important in industrial marketing because you are often dealing with a small universe or sample size, and the opinions of experts in a few buying organizations can provide extremely insightful information about competition, new product needs, and buying trends. Verbatim quotations about needs from leading-edge customers are wonderful.

Academics and consultants have promoted a wide range of multivariate statistical techniques, which include regression, cluster, and conjoint analyses. Most of these sophisticated techniques have limited value to industrial marketers because they usually require large sample sizes, are costly to conduct, and too often are overkill techniques that some computer jockey or statistician is in love with. Because most good commercial research is based on in-depth customer consultations with multiple buying influences at a small number of leading-edge users, this book will not bore you with limited value and esoteric statistical techniques. Basic mathematics, frequency distributions, cross tabulations, attribute ratings, and rank ordering are usually sufficient quantitative measures for analyzing most industrial market data.

Rating and Ranking Factors

Rating and rank-order scales are commonly used industrial marketing research tools. Market research needs to first identify the important product and/or service attributes to measure. The relative importance of each customer need must then be determined by interviewing each buying influence. A quantitative rating scale should be used to translate verbally stated needs and attributes into numerical values. Customers should be asked to rate and/or rank the importance of a given product attribute or service: Exhibit 5-2 shows a sample rating scale. Each buying influence was asked to rank-order the importance of predetermined factors.

Exhibit 5-2

Sample Rating Scale

Rating Guide

4	=	Critical or a "must"
3	=	Very important
2	=	Somewhat important
1	=	Of little importance
0	=	Of no importance

Attribute Rating

Heat resistance	❏
Ease of preparation	❏
Longevity	❏
Technical service	❏
Reuseable	❏
Disposability	❏
Just-in-time delivery	❏
Vendor-managed inventory	❏

Respondent's title (buying influence)
Phone, fax, and email
Company and market segment
Date and location

The raw data obtained from questionnaires must undergo some preliminary preparation before it can be prepared. The data have to be edited, coded, and statistically adjusted (when necessary). The role of editing by the interviewer is to identify omissions and errors in the responses. If critical information such as usage and cost information is missing, the interviewer might again contact the respondent. Coding the closed-ended questions is fairly straightforward. Coding for open-ended questions is much more difficult. Usually, a list of possible responses is generated, and then each response is put into one of the categories. Finally, when analyzing the data, responses from some people may have to be weighed more than responses from other people. For example, a design or maintenance engineer's response might be weighted more than a response from a purchasing agent at the same company.

Analysis and Visual Presentations

Most analysis of business research consists of drawing conclusions from statements made by knowledgeable people about their operations, applications, requirements, purchase plans, and buying considerations. When the results of the research are quantitative, graphs should be used to show trends and changing relationships. Graphs are generally limited to showing the relationship between two variables. The graph should show if there is any relationship and also whether the relationship is up (direct) or down (inverse) or whether some type of curve best shows the relationship. Graphs show relationships that do not appear in various kinds of statistical analyses. They help managers make generalizations and predictions by looking beyond the data. Graphical excellence is that which gives the viewer the greatest number of ideas in the shortest time and in the smallest space. The adage, "A picture is worth a thousand words," applies to both written and oral effective presentations. A mass of data can usually be communicated clearly with graphs. A wide variety is available, such as bar graphs, line graphs, and pie charts. Color can be employed to add interest, to highlight findings, and to help deal with complexity. Also, use short, crisp titles as opposed to longer titles. There is limited need for the presentation of detailed statistical tables in the presentation of findings. Management should challenge any study that hinges on just the presentation of tables of data, which should be included in appendixes. There is a high probability that studies of this type are made by people who are more interested in some rigorous statistical technique than in providing useful information to decision makers. Any data that slow down the flow of presenting the findings should be put into a graph or placed in appendixes.

MARKET SEGMENT ATTRACTIVENESS

Not all market segments are equally attractive. The end result of the strategic market management process is to be able to select the most attractive market segment(s) and account(s) to attack, counterattack, deemphasize, withdraw from, or avoid. The following six guidelines should be considered before determining the final attractiveness of any market segment:

1. There are always multiple external and internal factors that determine the overall attractiveness and fit of any market. Because precise estimates of any factor are often subjective and sometimes elusive, any rating methodology with too many factors and elaborate weightings should be questioned.
2. In some markets, a few factors have such a high level of importance that the other factors are nice to have, but not necessary. Start with the dominant non-price factors and get agreement from industry experts and lead customers on their relative importance.
3. You should be able to supply documented superior customer value to the segment.

Attractive market segments should have relatively good sales growth and especially good profit prospects. An attractive market should provide a return on investment that is well above the firm's cost of capital.

4. When there is a good match of goals, skills, and resources of a firm with those of the needs of the segment, it should be chosen to attack or counterattack. If the necessary capabilities are not in place to pursue an attractive segment, consider acquiring or building them. A company's goals and resources dictate how many segments it can attack and counterattack.

5. Just because a segment is attractive to one company does not mean it will be suitable to another firm. Companies have different sales and profit goals, different cost structures, different capabilities, and differences in the fact base from which they make decisions.

6. Industrial market segments are complex moving targets for strategists. What is an attractive market today for given capabilities may be unattractive later. The adage that change is the only constant is increasingly valid in today's more turbulent environments. You must periodically rethink market segment definitions and evaluate every segment's attractiveness.

Because so much information is involved in selecting the most attractive segments, the commercial researcher must organize information in a meaningful way. The framework to help organize information about each market segment is shown in Exhibit 5-3. This framework depends on first defining market segments for each of your businesses. If the definition of segments is wrong, the entire process will generate different information. After defining segments, the next steps provide a basis for presenting historical size and growth patterns as well as the estimated size, growth, and profit potential. It also provides for listing the major competitors and their market share positions along with major customers and their annual purchases. Obviously, simply filling out this framework is not an end in itself. It is designed to help managers evaluate and cross check a variety of data for defined market segments into trade-offs that must be considered before deciding which segments are the most attractive.

Before the selection of target segments is made, it is always important to weigh the profit potential into the choice of market segments, as shown in Column 7 of Exhibit 5-3. I am consistently surprised at how many bright managers naively equate the size of a market segment with attractive profit prospects. *Most of these same managers never consider the profitability of each market segment before selecting the most attractive segments.* Even fewer managers consider the profit value of one share point in each market segment before selecting the most attractive segments. In markets where a company does not have a presence, the profit potential is generally not readily available. Nevertheless, profit estimates can be developed through published financial data and interviews with suppliers and investment analysts who follow particular industries and companies. Considering the changes in three key variables—size, growth rate, and the earnings before tax percentage over a three- to four-year period—can lead to different conclusions than market data alone might suggest. If more managers considered the profit potential when they access various market segments, the relative attractiveness of market alternatives would change many of their final choices.

Exhibit 5-3

Analyzing Market Segments (To Be Done For Each Country and Region of the World)

Industry Groups	1 Defined Market Segments	2 Segment Size Today (units & money)	3 Annual Growth rates (% for last 3 years)	4 Forecasted Market Size (units/money) 1 Yr 2 Yr 3 Yr	5 Current Competitors & Market Shares	6 Major Accounts' Annual Purchases and Needs	7 Profit Potential Today and for the Next 3 Years
Chemicals:	Adhesives				1. ___ 2. ___ 3. ___ 4. ___ 5. ___		
	Bonded abrasives						
	Coated abrasives						
Industrial Controls:	Hydraulic						
	Pneumatic						
	Electronics						

When determining the attractiveness of each market segment, there are many facts that must be considered before a firm finally classifies each segment as either attack, counterattack, deemphasize, withdraw, or avoid. Determining the attractiveness of any one market segment can be done with a short list of six questions:

1. What is the size of the segment today in units and money?
2. What is your current market share?
3. What is the annual growth rate of the segment today and three years out?
4. What are the current and emerging needs of the segment?
5. Does the segment fit with your goals and current capabilities? Are any new capabilities needed to improve a currently poor match or fit?
6. What are the future sales and profit prospects in the segment for the next three years?
   A. For yourself?
   B. For competition?
   C. Profit value of a share point today and three years out?

If any company can answer these six questions with a high level of confidence, the firm will be close to making their final choices. Before prioritizing the final group of market segments, it is often helpful to group market segments with similar requirements. How to group segments is more of a matter of experienced judgment than any precise summary. For example, if the requirements are similar for aircraft engine parts, the customers might be grouped with companies making steam, hydraulic, and gas turbines into a segment redefined as "aircraft engines and turbine parts."

A cross-functional team should make the final decision in determing market segment attractiveness. Overly elaborate attractiveness rating methods should be avoided because precision can quickly become confused with accuracy. The give-and-take decisions of an experienced cross-functional team that knows the market needs and your present or needed capabilities are superior to one or two people creating elaborate "attractiveness ratings."

Not all customers within an attractive segment are equally attractive accounts. The logic and process of selecting the most attractive market segments also apply to the selection of specific accounts within an attractive segment. Furthermore, you generally would not pursue an attractive account within an unattractive market segment. However, as an opportunist, if an attractive account is within an unattractive segment, you might still "check it out" with this disciplined process.

SUMMARY

The day-to-day pressures of business tend to focus attention on the immediate situation. But a more systematic study and fact gathering of market trends, market potentials, market growth rates, and market profitability information will result in more proactive management and less defensive and catchup reactions. Accurate usage factors and market segment potentials are vital beginnings for this process.

The time and cost required to conduct most market studies that result in better decisions should be considered a necessary investment. The cost and strategic risks of not having the necessary market facts can be huge. Top and general management must support the value of having professional people assess the attractiveness of any given market segment. The commercial research function must be led by highly respected and well-compensated, in-house people. Having highly skilled in-house professionals gather the market facts is preferable over having outsiders who often do not know your company, technologies, or customers. If outsiders are used, they should work closely with your own people. Semiretired and part-time engineers can be a cost-effective resource to enhance any company's commercial research capabilities.

With slow- or no-growth market situations and rapid technical changes occurring in many business markets, sound market facts are even more important. When developing new products, entering new markets or new countries, sound market information should guide the key decisions. The relative attractiveness of any given market segment cannot be determined without good market, competitive, technical, and cost-profit facts.

Only when market assessment is a key input in all strategic thinking and strategy development will the industrial firm have the appropriate foundation for fact-based decision making to focus and profitably grow the top line. Market strategy and commercial research have an interdependent relationship. When commercial research is conducted before a market strategy is developed, the firm embarks on a study of markets and customers and alternative ways to develop a winning strategy. Industrial firms that are market driven place great importance on commercial research for discovering and developing winning strategies and business plans.

Successful New Products

*"We need to identify customers' unarticulated needs,
and then develop new products that are
demonstrably better than other solutions."*

L.D. DeSimone, 3M
Chairman and CEO

Developing new products that perform better or cost less has always been crucial for any industrial company. New product development is the seed corn for the future. Without new products, a business will eventually die from declining sales. Many big and previously successful companies are being beat by upstarts and smaller companies with more innovative solutions. In our increasingly turbulent business environment, developing the expertise and speed to keep pace with, or even ahead of, technological developments and competitors' moves is more important than ever for several reasons:

- Exploding technology is spawning new products and processes at an accelerating rate that threatens almost every product and process in place. The fast rules of play that originated with the electronic industry have spread to chemicals, materials, machinery, and even to the traditionally slow-moving steel and paper industries. Industrial companies accustomed to 20- to 30-year life cycles are getting zapped. Smaller companies that usually move much faster than big companies know the penalties for indecisiveness or moving too slow with a new technology.
- Competition continues to intensify from different industries, new competitors, and countries all over the world, generating a plethora of new entrants and substitute technologies that encroach on established products and processes. As increasingly smarter customers constantly consider more cost-effective solutions, technological substitution and the displacement of incumbent suppliers occur faster than ever.
- Product innovations that result in superior performance or cost advantages are the best means of protecting or building market position without sacrificing profit margins. This is especially true today when many industrial markets are flat or where slow growth and excess capacity are commonplace. Most industrial companies experience the greatest profitable market share growth when they introduce demonstratively better new products.

History is replete with examples of companies that lost their competitive advantage and perhaps even their business because a competitor entered the market with a superior product that had performance and/or cost benefits. These examples are not limited to small or weak companies; even industrial giants such as Siemens, IBM, and AT&T have seen many of their markets eroded by competitors who surprised them with a distinctly superior product. IBM, despite its formerly dominant position in the computer market, lost position to several smaller companies that were the first to develop powerful minicomputers to replace the larger mainframe computers that were the cornerstone of IBM's business.

Nearly everyone in every industry acknowledges that product life cycles are getting shorter. Patents are important but they do not give the length of protection they used to. Cost-justified procurement pressure and competitive substitutes have significantly shortened the effective life of every patent.

WHAT IS A NEW PRODUCT OR NEW SERVICE?

Each company usually has its own definition of what is a new product or new service. Some companies include "product tweaking" line extensions, reformulations, and cost reductions as new products. If a company doesn't have an operational definition of what a new product is, it should develop one that everyone is aware of. There are six categories of new products—in terms of newness to the company and to the marketplace—that will help guide people's thinking[1]:

1. *New to the world*. Products that are breakthroughs; they create a new basis of competition and are the first to fill an unmet need.
2. *New to your company*. Products that allow a company to enter an established market for the first time.
3. *Additions to existing products*. Products that supplement a company's established lines.
4. *Improvements and revisions to existing products*. Products that are usually replacements or tweaks to a company's existing lines.
5. *Repositions*. Existing products that are targeted to new market segments or new countries with or without any adaptations.
6. *Cost reductions*. Products that replace existing products with similar performance benefits but at a lower unit cost. (Some companies exclude this category from the definition of a new product.)

3M, which has rigorous criteria for new products, only considers the previous first two categories as new products. This chapter is concerned with new products in all six categories. Please keep in mind that most companies maintain a mix or portfolio of these new product categories within their organization. Any product can be pushed from the growth phase of its life cycle to a mature or obsolescent position very quickly by a new product that offers the customer significant performance or cost advantages.

BETTER MOUSETRAPS

No matter how superior a product may appear or how dynamic its growth, its market position is always tenuous. Modern technology is a powerful force and full of surprises, and it is a serious mistake to assume that any product has a lock on any market or that any supplier "owns a market." When a successful product enjoys a strong commercial position in an attractive market, management is foolish to be complacent. In fact, the larger a company's market share, the more vulnerable it is. Not a day goes by that someone else is not working to invent a "better mousetrap" that will weaken or possibly destroy the existing product's competitive advantage. The chance of such a better product appearing in the marketplace has increased, and the effect can be devastating to the arrogant, unwary, unresponsive, or slow-moving company.

Most consumer and industrial executives around the world refer to Procter & Gamble when they talk about excellence in new product development. However, for the last two decades, the opposite has been true. P&G's CEO admitted that they had not invented a new product category for the last twenty years! He said the company strategy for the last two decades was to tweak products and introduce existing products to emerging countries around the world—often at the expense of product innovation. P&G's centralized organization, ultraconservative, and risk-averse culture may need to dramatically change if new product development is to flourish. Al Zeien, the CEO of Gillette's new product machine, spoke at our annual senior executive program and was critical of the "me too'ism" and brand extensions of most consumer goods companies. He scorns phony consumer product innovations as "putting blue dots in the same soap powder." Gillette, unlike most consumer and industrial companies goes for breakthrough global new products that create new product categories and redefine the rules for competition. Furthermore, Gillette encourages all business units to cannibalize their current products with new products before competition does it for them.

PRODUCT/MARKET INNOVATION

It is widely believed that most innovation begins with either the discovery of technology or the discovery of an unmet market need. The underlying distinctions are termed technology-push or market-pull innovation and are shown in Exhibit 6-1:A and B. There are passionate advocates of these two approaches to innovation.

Exhibit 6-1
Approaches To Innovation

A. Technology-Push

| R&D defines the technical solution | → | Manufacturing | → | Sales | → | Market need? |

B. Market-Pull

| Marketing defines the needs | → | R&D Fit? | → | Manufacturing | → | Sales |

C. Product/Markets (Hybrid of A & B)

| Marketing and R&D define the needs, fit, and solutions | → | R&D | → | Manufacturing | → | Sales |

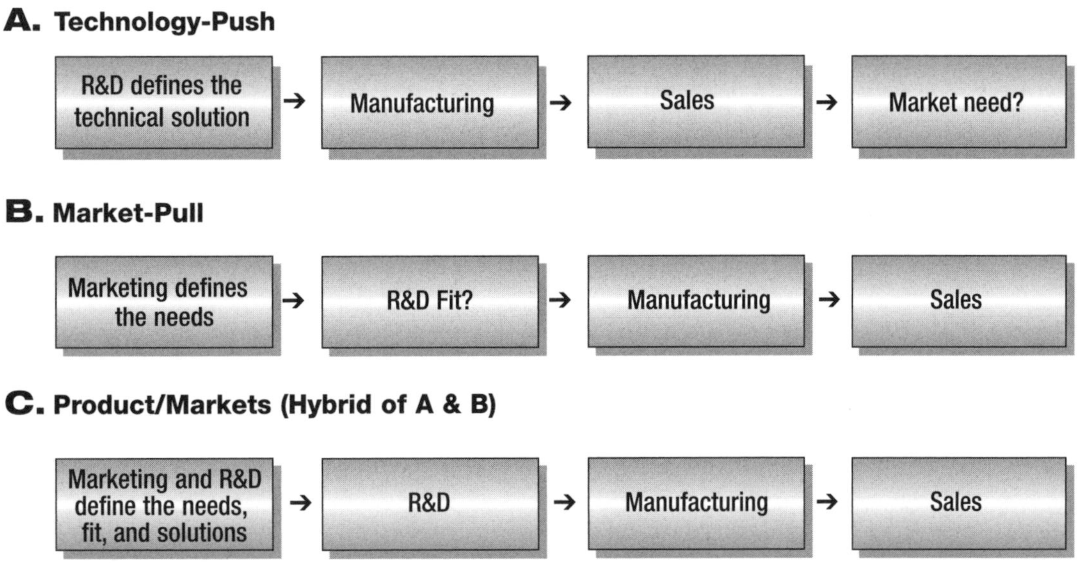

The technology-push approach in Exhibit 6-1A implies that a new invention is pushed through manufacturing, and sales departments into the marketplace without proper up-front considerations of whether it actually satisfies an unmet market need. Technology-push new product ideas are believed to be generated by R&D, are often the result of serendipitous discoveries, and represent radical innovations or breakthrough products. Hunches and intuition play a big role in technology-push innovation. Technology-push innovation is controlled by the R&D function. These innovations are often criticized as elegant solutions without a market need or as solutions in search of problems. Solutions may come before problems because a researcher cannot foresee the range of possible applications for the new technology. Technology-push innovations assume that industrial customers have unarticulated needs or unstated problems.

In contrast to technology-push innovation, the marketing department controls innovation based on the market-pull model shown in Exhibit 6-1B. Market research is first done to uncover and verify needs before development begins. The market-pull approach assumes that customers are able to articulate needs and that problems should be identified before solutions are developed.

Industrial manufacturers that take this approach to innovation typically first survey customers' needs and then develop new products. These innovations are sometimes criticized as line extensions or improvements to existing products that do not redefine the competitive playing field.

The two traditional views to innovation claim that a firm must be either technology driven or market need driven. But in reality, neither technology nor markets can create successful innovation by themselves; *they need each other to be successful innovations*. With the product/markets approach to innovation shown in Exhibit 6-1C, *every successful new industrial product is the result of carefully matching, fitting, and shaping technical capabilities to verified market needs*. The concept of product/market, as mentioned throughout this book, is an operational definition of this interactive product development process. Most technology has value to multiple market segments. This approach to new product development results in a product/markets matrix or technology/applications matrix of opportunities for strategic thinking, analysis, and making choices. A company can stay with any current product/market combinations or it may enter new product/market combinations with existing or new technology. If a technology, capability, or product is not currently owned, the firm can develop, license, or acquire it.

With the product/markets approach, the firm can start with either a technology or a market need, but commercial new product success requires a good fit or match within each product/market combination. Marketing, and R&D teams should be conditioned to look for both articulated and unarticulated needs. *In the product/market approach to innovation, it doesn't matter so much whether the solution arrives before the problem or vice versa, as long as they link up to provide customer value*. Don Hargraves, the founder of Pneutronics, says this well:

> Half of my mind is focused on finding customer needs and the other side is always aware of our technical capabilities. I use a parallel mental process that connects customer needs with technical solutions. The sooner we can find the connections and fit, the better.

Companies with a consistently high new product success rate do not choose between technology-push and market-pull. They combine both of these into the product/markets innovation approach before more advanced development proceeds. The product/markets approach requires full cross-functional team input from the beginning. The cross-functional team fits existing or new technology to a verified market need and then develops a business plan for the most attractive market segments or applications.

The historical technology-push or market-pull dichotomy exists because departments have not worked well between functions, specifically between R&D and marketing. In progressive companies, marketing and R&D work very closely together and in a small but increasing number of industrial firms the marketing and R&D departments have been merged. When market-need research, market potentials, and technical feasibility studies are conducted early in the up-front process, the distinction between technology-push and market-pull innovation will continue to diminish. *Close R&D and marketing coupling is vital*. The product/markets approach is a parallel R&D and marketing process that seeks a fit or match between a technology and a market need. The hybrid product/markets approach to innovation helps reduce the development of me-too products or new products that customers don't need or want. The product/markets approach to innovation also recognizes that a existing technology might be old to one market segment but new to another segment. The product/markets approach helps to leverage a firm's technology platforms and capabilities to multiple market segments. Finally, this approach also recognizes that a new technology may be needed to defend or counterattack an existing market position. In such situations, the decision must be made to acquire, build, license, or form an alliance with a partner.

THINKING SMALL TO WIN BIG

In Chapter 2, I suggest that the thinking of a smaller company needs to be implanted in most large companies. In Chapter 4, I stress the importance of thinking in terms of smaller niche market segments. Furthermore, when it comes to innovation and successful product development, big firms should also think and act like smaller organizations.

Most big firms have trouble thinking small. Because they are a big business, doing things in big and lavish ways often traps them. 3M does a better job at thinking small with product innovation than any other giant firm I have worked with. No project is too small for 3M to consider, despite its $17 billion size. 3M methodically identifies and analyzes product/market combinations and then determines which combinations to pursue. Still another characteristic of smaller companies that should be followed by big firms is making small acquisitions. Many acquired small technology platforms can be pumped up to become huge enterprises. The giant Johnson & Johnson has long favored buying small firms or toehold acquisitions, pumping them up, and then growing them globally. If the small acquisition fails, the big company does not suffer.

Another big company mindset that impedes innovation is spending too much money. A well-funded project can lose its sense of urgency and pressure to innovate. The heavily-funded project becomes too elaborate, and failures are met with even more funding. Big projects can lose their focus and have an endless life. They often have no application or market segment focus. Heavily-funded projects are too often driven by a technology champion with minimal customer involvement and commercial input. In contrast, small and focused R&D projects with firm milestones and good cross-functional team input have a focus, a sense of urgency, frequent customer testing for feedback, and everyone thinks about customer value, margins, and time to market.

With customer requirements changing frequently and users constantly searching for more value from suppliers, many market segments are shifting rapidly from one technology to another. In an increasing number of situations, suppliers must ask if their existing capabilities and product/service package are competitive for each discreet market segment. The market timing and suitability of a supplier's given technology raise the concept of "strategic windows" for each market segment.

STRATEGIC WINDOWS OF OPPORTUNITY

The term *strategic window* is used to focus attention on the fact that there is frequently a limited time period or market opening during which there is a "fit" between the requirements of a market segment and the existing technology offered by the supplier. The investment in a product line, new technology, or market area should be timed to coincide with the time period that a strategic window is open. Conversely, in areas that were once a good technology/market fit, withdrawal of funding or minimal new investment should be made if what was once a good opportunity has eroded. Furthermore, the new requirements of the market segment may require capabilities that the supplier does not have nor does it wish to develop or acquire. However, if the supplier chooses to either build or acquire the needed technology and capabilities, it must adapt its organization to the industry's shifting requirements.

Managers in rapidly changing industries face the challenge of deciding which technology to invest in as well as when to invest. By investing too early in a new technology, the firm faces the risk of entry before the market is ready. By investing too late in a new technology, a company may fall behind its competitors and lose a market position that is tough to recapture once a competitor establishes a new technology position. By failing to invest in a new technology, a company runs the very real risk of seeing its existing products become obsolete in a relatively short period of time.

The medical electronics field demonstrates how quickly companies must move in rapidly advancing technologies. When the CAT scanner was introduced, it was immediately recognized as the most significant breakthrough since the discovery of x-rays. Technicare, the first U.S. CAT scanner company, saw sales grow from $20 million to more than $200 million in five years. The number of employees grew from 200 to more than 3,000 in the same period. The CAT scanning market then went through several technology life cycles, each of which made products obsolete in less than eighteen months. The rapid obsolescence of technology, coupled with the swift growth of sales, fueled Technicare's need for cash, which nearly caused disaster for the startup company. Johnson & Johnson (J&J) then acquired Technicare. Without J&J's acquisition and cash infusion, most believe Technicare would have soon declared bankruptcy. Reflecting on the rapid developments in this industry, Richard Grimm, founder and former chairman of Technicare, made this comment:

> The way this technology moved was unbelievable. There were four major developments in three years that basically obsoleted all prior CAT scanning devices. We were smaller than some of the other competitors and if we were not quick on our feet in terms of product development, we could have been out of the picture overnight.

Deep pockets and the willingness of J&J to spend a lot of money on CAT scanning was not the answer. After five years and millions of dollars of additional investment in people and technology, J&J threw in the towel. They sold the remains of the business to General Electric. J&J's former CEO, Phil Hofmann, said to me:

> CAT scanning was a glamorous and rapid-growth business that attracted us. But the rest of J&J had little experience designing, making, selling, and servicing large capital electronic equipment. We mostly sell consumables that have little or no after-sales service requirements. I doubt if GE, Siemens, or Toshiba, the CAT scanning competitors, would have entered our pharmaceutical, suture, or bandage businesses.

The dynamic and interactive concept of strategic windows requires industrial executives to anticipate and respond to rapid technology advances. Product life cycles or, more appropriately, technology life cycles in faster moving industries, should be evaluated in the dynamic context of a strategic window in each market segment.

The strategic window concept does not preclude adaptation by the incumbent, but some suppliers are more suited to compete in certain technologies than others. With the emergence of a new technology, strategic decisions have to be made by incumbent competitors to invest resources, fight to protect and fortify their existing market segment positions, cannibalize their past success, or pursue opportunities elsewhere. National Cash Register (NCR), the pioneer of mechanical cash machines, successfully made the technology transition to the window of opportunity created by electronic cash registers that were later connected to computers and networks. The dynamic nature of fast moving technology and strategic windows presents *four basic strategic choices for the incumbent suppliers to the industry:*

1. The incumbent company may attempt to assemble the new skills internally or acquire the new technology to close the gap between the strategic window requirements and the firm's existing capabilities, as Parker Hannifin did for the transition from hydraulic to pneumatic and then to electronic motion control technology.

2. The incumbent company may shift its resources to selected market segments where the "fit" between market requirements and the firm's existing capabilities are still acceptable, as Bendix did for pneumatic truck aftermarket brakes when it lacked the new electronic technology for the truck original equipment manufacturers (OEMs.)

3. The incumbent manufacturer may shift to severely limiting further capital and deliberately milk the business for short-term profit, as Toledo Scale did when measuring, weighing, and packaging systems largely replaced stand alone component weighing scales.

4. The incumbent may liquidate or sell the business, as Johnson & Johnson did when it fell behind in the fast-moving medical CAT scanning business they sold to GE Medical Systems-who primarily wanted J&J's installed customer base.

Of the four basic strategic window concepts, the first requires the highest level of resource commitment. If there is enough time to develop new technology, without forfeiting a major share of the market, this may be a very viable approach. Acquiring the new technology and running it as a separate business unit away from the exiting business is still another way to achieve option number one.

The strategic window concept requires distinctly different types of thinking and response by incumbent suppliers. First, they must think in broader terms about customers' unmet needs, system solutions, and capabilities beyond their companies's existing know-how or "core competencies." Secondly, incumbent suppliers must make an objective audit of their firms' strengths and weaknesses against customers' needs and new technologies. Finally, the strategic window concept reinforces the idea that the life of a product or technology is more limited than the longevity of a market. *Timing is the critical dimension related to strategic windows.*

Every industrial manufacturer should choose between two basic technology timing strategies to pursue—either be first-to-market or a fast-follower. Very different company cultures, mind-sets, and capabilities are needed if you choose to be either a first-to-market or fast follower.

FIRST-TO-MARKET OR FAST-FOLLOWER

In deciding what kind of product development capabilities any company needs, it should first decide whether it wants to pursue primarily a first-to-market or fast-follower company strategy for new products. Let's look at these timing based product development strategies.

First-to-Market Strategy

This approach requires a company philosophy of "being first with the most." The first-to-market approach that is usually followed by companies such as Hewlett-Packard, 3M, Pall, Sony, FedEx, Sealed Air, Toshiba, and Festo. First-to-market companies must encourage risk-taking and expect and tolerate failures. The first company to a market has a temporary monopoly. This approach requires an ability to identify unarticulated needs, spend a lot on R&D and market development with trial and error testing, learning, and patience associated with the costs. The first-to-market with the new technology usually wins, but how much it wins depends on how long it takes everyone else to catch up.

Being first-to-market is glamorous but doesn't always guarantee success. In the early 1980s VisiCalc dominated the market for computerized spreadsheets. After developing the first spreadsheet product in 1980 in Cambridge, Massachusetts, the technical founder did not do enough marketing and did not protect his intellectual property. Meanwhile, a young VisiCalc product manager who had overseen the development of VisiCalc formed Lotus Development down the street in Cambridge. The Lotus Development product was named Lotus 1-2-3, and it quickly swept into first place for spreadsheet programs after VisiCalc declared bankruptcy. VisiCalc was an idea whose time had come. The idea was sound, the technology was strong, but marketing and intellectual property protection were lacking. New industries and strong competitors often emerge over the dead bodies of the pioneers or, as Lee Morgan, CEO of Caterpillar, stated at one of my workshops, "Pioneers are sometimes people with arrows in their backside."

Fast-Follower Strategy

This delayed approach requires a company philosophy of "taking the second bite of the apple," or as they say at Panasonic Industrial in Japan, "The second mouse gets the cheese." This strategy requires superior global intelligence, a reverse engineering mentality, and strong patent infringement skills. The term fast follower is used to emphasize the difference between a slow company and the fast company that waits like a snake in the grass, poised to jump into a market when the timing is right. The fast follower strategy is pursued by firms including UPS, Emerson Electric, Panasonic, Caterpillar, and Cooper Tires.

Cooper Tire and Rubber Company has historically been a successful fast-follower. While Goodyear and Michelin battle it out to be number one in world volume or production, Cooper Tire is pleased to be the world's eighth largest tire maker, and it consistently leads the top ten tire companies in profit margins. Marketing tires to the replacement or aftermarket has proven to be one of the company's quiet strengths. The OEM automakers around the world have forced suppliers to trim prices, and profitability has suffered for tire makers who produce tires mainly for new cars. The pricing for replacement tires has held up somewhat better. Similarly, Cooper has benefited from not having to spend huge amounts of their profit margins on the research and development necessary to support the OEM car makers. Cooper typically takes up the innovations introduced by other tire makers. The company makes no secret about its intentions to not spearhead product innovations. The little it spends on innovation is for process or manufacturing improvements. Besides not having to spend much on research and development, Cooper spends less on advertising. Its advertising is largely cooperative with independent dealers in smaller cities and rural areas. The company states that it has always been a fast-follower, and now they are attempting to *be an even faster follower.*

A company can go from pioneer to follower across the product life cycle. Every company has nightmares after it develops a new product and profits start flowing in, and then a well-financed industry Goliath may swoop in and snatch away most of the market. That's what happened to U.S. Surgical when J&J's Ethicon division targeted its market for minimally invasive surgical instruments. U.S. Surgical invented the industry by being the first to develop and introduce endoscopic surgery instruments that only required a small incision. Sales at U.S. Surgical went from $291 million to $1.2 billion in three years. After three years, J&J entered the market with a lower-priced product and sold it through surgical distributors while U.S. Surgical continued to sell directly to surgeons at higher prices. J&J also negotiated hefty three-way volume discounts with large centralized hospital purchasing groups. A price war resulted, and U.S. Surgical's earnings of $138 million in the third year fell to a loss of $136 million in year four. J&J became the market and profit leader. The conglomerate, Tyco Industries, then acquired the wounded U.S. Surgical Company.

Neither the first-to-market nor fast-follower is better than the other. The choice depends on company culture, existing capabilities, and the rate of technical change in the industry. In the fast-moving electronics industry, it is difficult to be a successful fast-follower, whereas in the slower-moving tire, steel, and paper industries it is easier to be a profitable fast follower. Furthermore, for a few product lines you might choose to be a fast-follower, and for the rest of your products your company might pursue a first-to-market strategy. However, because of the different capabilities and mind-set requirements, you must choose to become primarily either a first-to-market or a fast-follower business unit. *Both the first-to-market and fast-follower strategies require a fast product development process.* In both cases, the advantages of being the fastest are greater than those of being first or a follower. An inferior and slow product development process will hinder either strategy.

COMMON NEW PRODUCT COMPLAINTS

Despite widespread agreement that new products and technology developments are the lifeblood of most technically based companies, very few managers are satisfied with the results of their company's new product activities. Every manager I have worked with has a different way of expressing dissatisfaction with his or her product development efforts. For the most part, however, these complaints represent effects or symptoms rather than root causes of the problems. As I see it, these complaints, and others like them, stem from fundamental problems in two areas of management. One set of problems occurs during the product development cycle; another set occurs during various stages of the product life cycle beginning with the launch.

Exhibit 6-2 highlights the common problems in both the development and life cycles that are frequently the basis for managers' complaints. The four major problems are:

1. Lack of top management involvement.
2. The wrong market segment focus or none at all.
3. Insufficient cross-functional linkages.
4. Slow response and cycle times.

These problems are made more acute by the increasing velocity of change that compresses the time frame. Let's look now at each of these common problems in the product development cycle, why they occur, and how they can be improved.

Exhibit 6-2

Problems In Product Development and the Life Cycle

Time-to-Market	From Launch to Payback and Profit Returns	
Product Development	**Product Life Cycle**	
Top Management Involvement ♦ Stress the importance and urgency of new products ♦ Encourage risk taking and new product champions ♦ Serve as project sponsors **Market Segment Focus** ♦ Good product ideas ♦ Verified customer needs ♦ Important benefits ♦ Good up-front work ♦ Leading-edge users **Cross-Functional Linkages** ♦ First-to-market or fast-follower ♦ Focused business plan ♦ Cross-functional programs **Fast Response and Cycle Times** ♦ Shorter strategic windows ♦ Shorter time-to-market ♦ Shorter payback periods	**Introduction** ♦ Target markets are not well defined ♦ Leading-edge customers are not well selected ♦ Field trials are not well managed ♦ Launches are penalized by lack of market focus, market development, specification work, and approvals ♦ Time to gain new product approvals and new sales are underestimated ♦ Fail to do post-launch reviews on all successful and unsuccessful projects	**Growth Maturity Decline** ┌ *Apply to All Phases* ┐ • Failure to manage projects, programs, and products from concept to postlaunch • Cost reductions are not started soon enough • Enhancements to extend the life cycle are started too late • Next generation products are not begun early enough • Failure to cannibalize one's own products • Failure to learn from post-launch reviews

Top Management Involvement

The first problem rests clearly with top management. Top management should see product development as an agent of change for the entire organization, and aggressive new product goals should create healthy tension and a sense of urgency throughout the organization. If top management doesn't stress the importance and urgency of new and improved products, product development will not receive the necessary resources. Top management must give each new venture team great freedom to carry out a project, but, at the same time, very challenging and firm milestones should be set.

Top management must also encourage and tolerate new product risk taking. Top management should serve as sponsors for product champions who are willing to stick out their necks. The company culture at Johnson & Johnson exemplifies the proper role of top management to encourage risk taking in product and process development.

Years ago, when Jim Burke, a young product manager at Johnson & Johnson, was summoned to CEO Mr. Johnson's office, Burke thought he was going to be fired. His first new product had failed miserably. Instead, Mr. Johnson said:

> Are you the one that cost us all that money? Well, I just wanted to congratulate you. If you're making mistakes, that means you're making decisions and taking risks. And we will never grow the top line if you don't take some new product risks. You also saved us a lot of money by suggesting that we pull the plug early and shelve the project.

To continue this risk-taking culture, when Jim Burke became CEO of Johnson & Johnson, he frequently reminded employees of their multimillion-dollar new product failures in CAT scanning equipment, baby diapers, and adhesives—not to admonish anyone but rather to emphasize the lessons learned from mistakes. Great companies realize they can often learn more from a new product failure than they can from a success.

Upper management must also be physically involved (not just verbally committed) to new product development as sponsors and reviewers. At Sealed Air, president and CEO Bill Hickey and all group and general managers are members of at least one new product team. At the Fluke Corporation and Hewlett-Packard, upper management receives a one-page monthly summary of every R&D project. Top and general management must also realize that new product ideas are fragile and, like a lighted match, can easily be blown out by the strong winds of rigid management. Without the support and encouragement to overcome the fear and shame usually associated with making errors, people will generally not stick their necks out to champion a new idea. Companies need norms that legitimatize innovative thinking and the making of errors. To have breakthrough product development, people have to feel safe and have an opportunity to experiment and try out new things without any fear of punishment. Second and third chances should exist for competent and aggressive people.

Market Segment Focus

The lack of market focus is one of the major reasons so many new products miss the mark and so many product development dollars are wasted. Achieving market focus is unquestionably difficult because it requires both a deep understanding of stated and unarticulated customer needs as well as knowledge of how the technology can fulfill those needs. Selecting a market(s) for emphasis requires sufficient up-front work and knowledge of the customer's operation and the economic benefits they would incur from using the new product or service. Generally, this customer and technical knowledge does not exist in any one buying influence but is scattered among the buying organization. Pulling these scattered information fragments together is a difficult but essential step to selecting the proper market focus. 3M makes available Genesis grants of up to $50,000 to anyone who wants to develop a new concept idea at this stage. The up-front funding to uncover and verify a market need and do an initial feasibility study is usually a very good investment.

Once the target market segment(s) is(are) selected for the new product, confidentiality or secrecy agreements should be employed with any lead users or progressive customers who guide the product through all the stages. Any new product project that does not keep a lead customer involved in each target market and each important region of the world has a significantly higher chance of failing. Some of the best lead customers to guide product development are smaller to medium-sized customers who are often more open, more aggressive, and faster to make decisions than many large customers. (See the section on "Leading-Edge Customers" in the previous chapter, "Assessing Industrial Markets.")

Cross-Functional Linkages

Weak or missing cross-functional linkages, the third problem, are a frequent source of complaints and frustration. It occurs because the activities of many product development groups are not linked as closely as they should be to the priorities and commercial strengths of the operating units. Achieving this linkage is not as easy as it might sound. Product development personnel are likely to have advanced degrees and a knowledge of technology that no one else can match. Moreover, their interests are frequently focused more on professional associations and advancing the technology than on meeting customer needs or financial goals. Getting this group to subjugate their natural interests to those of the business unit's and customers' needs, without limiting their ability to stay at the forefront of technology, is a crucially important responsibility of general management. R&D people must get very close to customers in their workplace. They must listen to and observe what progressive customers need and help them define their perceived and unarticulated needs. In a small but increasing number of companies, there is very little distinction between marketing and R&D. Marketing and R&D must work side-by-side from the very beginning. In a few leading new product companies such as Henkel Surface Technologies, most R&D projects are funded, guided, and evaluated by marketing to achieve the needed technical and commercial coupling. Marketing and R&D are increasingly becoming one department. Technical service, manufacturing, finance, and key salespeople should also be part of the cross-functional product development team from the very beginning.

Time-to-Market

The fourth problem, cycle times and costs misaligned with reality, occurs because management and product development personnel have not adjusted their sense of urgency and pace to the accelerating rate of technological change. Today, market windows of opportunity open and close quicker, and acceptable payback periods have decreased, in many cases, from years to months. This means that time-to-market must be quicker and time periods for all product development activities must be compressed. Firm milestones must be agreed to and enforced—not just pushed back time after time. Some companies have reduced their time-to-market but then fail to reduce the launch time and payback period. Yesterday's standards for developing new products and achieving a payback simply no longer apply. My rule of thumb for an acceptable payback period in today's world is that it should be no longer than one-half the anticipated life cycle. This allows a payback that will support continued investment in new product and new-process technology. In many cases more resources are needed for a product launch, which includes missionary work, running trials, making presentations, getting specified, and approved at key accounts.

PROBLEMS IN THE LIFE CYCLE PHASES

Most companies today concentrate on reducing the time-to-market or the period from the product concept through and up to the launch phase. Many of these same companies would be better off if they dedicated more resources to the launch and other activities in the introduction phase. A new product can be developed in record time and still be a commercial flop. Time-to-market is only one milestone. Other milestones must be met in order to have a commercial success and achieve a favorable payback on the investment. Let's examine the problems that occur in the introductory, growth, maturity, and decline phases of the product life cycle.

Introduction Phase

In the introduction or launch phase, problems inevitably result in disappointing sales and profit shortfalls. Most industrial companies do not do an inadequate job of training the sales force and distributors on the product's benefits and in directing salespeople to the high-potential applications. My experience suggests that many new product sales forecasts can be cut in half and still be too ambitious. Most managers inevitably overestimate the value of their new products to their customers and underestimate the time their customers will take to evaluate the product and finally place a significant order. *Many companies need to have a manager guide the product through the launch.* Some of the resources to reduce time-to-market might be better employed in the launch. Since you never have a commercial success until after a successful launch, the payback time and profit-return time should be as urgent as the time-to-market part of the process.

The concept of leading edge users, described in Chapter 5, is a progressive customer that helps launch new products. For example, when Airbus launched its more than $200 million jumbo airliner to compete against Boeing's 747, it carefully selected the launch customer or lead user. Of the world's major airlines, Singapore Airlines is acknowledged as the world's best carrier in terms of service and profitability. East Asia, where air travel is concentrated in a few big hubs including Singapore, is the world's fastest growing aviation market. Singapore Airlines proved to be a progressive high-profile launch customer. British Airways, United, Qantas, and Virgin Atlantic rapidly followed Singapore's initial orders for the 550-seat long haul machine.

Few companies launch new industrial products as if they were perishable fruit. Even fewer do any kind of postlaunch review. Sealed Air does both. For every new product Sealed Air launches, salespeople are required to take a proficiency test on the new product's customer benefits and how they compare with competitive substitutes. The salesperson must retake the proficiency exam until a predetermined score is achieved. Our experience has found that many industrial salespeople and sales managers resist such proficiency training. Pharmaceutical companies have required new product proficiency training and testing of their salespeople for decades. Industrial firms should employ the pharmaceutical industry's longtime approach of requiring salespeople to have new product proficiency. (This point is further emphasized in the next chapter, "The Consultative Sales Force.")

After every new product launch, CertainTeed, the fiberglass unit of the French-based Saint-Gobain, always conducts a post-launch review. The post-review process is regarded as a learning process, not as a finger-pointing exercise. Knowledge and experiences are gleaned from the commercial process of bringing a product innovation to the market place so the lessons can be incorporated into future projects. Postlaunch reviews are scheduled and conducted at CertainTeed within a twelve-month period after the launch date. CertainTeed conducts a "no blame" review of all successful and unsuccessful new products. This and other knowledge-driven practices help make CertainTeed a learning organization. Unfortunately very few organizations are open and candid enough to do constructive post-launch reviews and learn from their past. These companies repeat the same product development and launching errors because they do not learn from their own mistakes as a learning organization does.

Growth and Maturity Phases

It is in the growth and maturity phases of a product's life cycle that products are often allowed to drift into a noncompetitive position. In today's world of accelerating and competing technologies, this can happen very quickly unless management keeps abreast of changing customer needs, stays a step ahead of competitive moves, and pursues the right technologies. Cost-reduction programs, product enhancement, and even next-generation products must be defined much earlier in the cycle than ever before. As product life cycles shrink, second-generation products must be started well before the first generation is launched. Most new industrial products are not limited to one customer or one market segment. In the growth and maturity phases, new countries, new applications, or new market segments should be identified for the products. Products that are mature to one market segment might be new to another market segment or different country. New market segments and new countries are common ways to extend the product life cycle for an existing technology and thus add significant top-line growth.

Decline Phase

The decline phase is where huge amounts of money are wasted. It is not uncommon to find 80 percent of the effort going to defend products that are more important for what they have contributed in the past than for what they are going to contribute in the future. The dollars lost or wasted in inventory write-offs and customer returns are also critical because management often overlooks the importance of following an orchestrated plan to phase out old products. Most companies have too many existing products that need to be rationalized to free up resources. Again, these problems are made more acute by the increasing number of new products and technologies and the rapid obsolescence of old ones. A cluttered product line is costly for any manufacturer and distributor. Companies need to regularly rationalize and cannibalize their old products with new products or competition will do it for them with dire consequences.

There is no magic formula for overcoming these problems. Successful new product companies, however, generally follow several practices that improve their chances of breaking through the roadblocks to achieve a bigger payoff from their new product development activities. These best practices have been distilled into twelve guidelines.

IMPROVING THE ODDS: TWELVE GUIDELINES

Although few companies are completely satisfied with their new product efforts, it is clear that some companies do a much better job than others, as shown in their internal or organic growth rate, market share, and profit picture. Just look at multibillion-dollar industry leaders such as Intel, 3M, Sony, and Hewlett-Packard. A number of newer or less well-known companies such as Pall and Applied Materials have achieved phenomenal success through new product leadership. All of these companies have a record of new product introduction that has contributed much to their success. Why are they able to achieve better results with new products than their competitors? How do they work around, or at least minimize, the risks and pitfalls in new product development that plague most companies? Each of these companies has its own development priorities and needs, but they all follow twelve fundamental principles:

1. They strike the right balance between investing in future products and generating current and future sales and profits.
2. They face up to fundamental cost and performance deficiencies and develop

demonstrably better products, not just "differentiated" ones.

3. They ensure that product development efforts are directly supported by a business unit and they use their market segment strategies to set product development priorities.
4. They learn and understand the customer's operation and the customer's customer's requirements from procurement through after-sales' service.
5. They identify stated and unarticulated needs in the user's workplace.
6. They think through their product/service package and focus to provide the maximum commercial opportunity.
7. They do sufficient upfront work on the opportunity before making a "go" or "no-go" decision, and they develop a business plan for every new product.
8. They utilize cross-functional teams to guide new product and market planning from the very beginning.
9. They are willing to go outside for new technology, expertise, or specialized marketing or sales skills in the target market.
10. They rationalize, shelve, and cannibalize their own product lines.
11. They develop global-base products that are later customized to meet local requirements.
12. They protect their proprietary positions and respond quickly to any encroachments on intellectual property.

Let's look more closely at each of these principles to see what they involve.

Match Future Products with Sales and Profits

In companies known for new product success, management has mastered the ability to strike the right balance between investing in future products and generating current profits. This raises some obvious questions. How much should be invested? How much is too little? How much is too much? New product leaders are now answering a number of questions to better measure, evaluate, and plan their new product development and organic growth efforts. After earlier agreeing to an operational definition of a new product, the following questions should be answered:

- What percentage of companywide sales came from external acquisitions and internally developed new products over the last five years? (For some companies this answer is a shocking blow to their new product development efforts.)
- What is this percentage for each business unit?
- What percentage of each business unit's gross profit comes from products introduced in the last five years?
- What has the overall success rate been with new products?
- What percentage of planned organic sales and profit growth can be expected from new products introduced in the next three or four years?

The penalties are severe if a mistake is made either way. A company can get by and may even prosper in the short term by spending too little because money not spent obviously increases short-term profits. It is not uncommon for managers, under pressure to meet certain profit goals, to take this path in an effort to make their results look good. However, such an approach is shortsighted and foolish. If the market is attractive, enlightened competitors will introduce new and improved products that will quickly erode the company's market position and cut into its future earnings stream. At the other extreme, some managers overspend for new products without sufficient regard for achieving satisfactory short-term profits. These managers are so enamored with the promise of tomorrow that they spend a disproportionate amount of money on new product efforts that can ultimately undermine the financial health of the company. More importantly it is not how much you spend on new products, but how effective your spending is for generating new product sales and profits.

Face Up to Deficiencies

Many companies fail to objectively evaluate their existing and new products against competitive offerings in rigorous side-by-side comparisons. If they do go through an evaluation process, it is often superficial or biased, leading to a continuation of business as usual rather than dramatic cost or performance improvements. Management is not always presented with the real facts because it is easier not to rock the boat. In other cases, management may see the facts but not accept or face them squarely because it is not easy to admit that a product is not competitive. As a result, a surprising number of companies continually try to get by with products that are not competitive and not significantly better in the eyes of customers. For example, a major manufacturer of tapered roller bearings failed to compare their products with spherical, needle, and ceramic bearings in each application. In many applications, their tapered bearings were overengineered, too costly, or had a shorter user life. Not until they developed other types of bearings were they competitive in certain applications.

There are many product development lessons to be learned from smaller and often very focused manufacturers. The major electric motor manufacturers such as Emerson Electric, General Electric, and Reliance saw this clearly when Baldor Electric, a much smaller company, designed a narrow range of energy-efficient motor products with a focused manufacturing process that gave it cost and lead-time delivery superiority. Baldor was able to capture market share because its larger competitors were slow to recognize and react to its strategy, which was based on unmet customer needs. The management teams of these large companies spent too much time rationalizing their loss of position by claiming Baldor was losing money, selling inferior products, and buying the business away when they should of spent more time getting a factual picture of what was really happening.

These examples highlight three important points that successful new product companies follow. First, it is often more useful to scout and learn from the smaller or mid-sized competitors rather than just the largest one. Second, it is essential to ensure that products are designed for efficient manufacturing and assembly. Finally, me-too parity is never a solid basis for gaining or regaining position. Even if a company is not first-to-market, it can learn from its competitors' mistakes and develop a better product from the customer's perspective. Engineering programs should be designed to leapfrog the competition rather than play catch up or be just a me-too match-up against competitors.

Align to Target Markets

Companies with excellent records of successful new product introductions are likely to ensure that new product programs flow from and are controlled by agreed-upon market priorities. While this sounds obvious, we can cite several multimillion-dollar product development programs that resulted in the following products:

- An over-engineered anaerobic adhesive that was two times as expensive as any competitive offering and far exceeded the requirements of any identified market segment.
- A twelve-axis, high-speed machine tool that could only be used by a small handful of machine operators with the requisite skills in the shrinking military aerospace market.
- An expensive robot designed to assemble computer printers was a technology

overkill because humans in even high-cost countries could assemble printers faster and at lower cost.

Many other ludicrous examples could also be cited, but these are sufficient to make the point. Unless product development efforts are linked to a verified market segment need, technical management will often assign the wrong priorities to development efforts or be led to products and markets that have no real commercial value. Literally hundreds of millions of dollars are wasted each year because technical efforts are poured into products that are out of touch with market needs. This is the chief reason the success ratio of new product development efforts is so low in many companies. R&D programs should focus on market segments, verified needs, and progressive customers that can guide the development process. The plain truth is that, left on their own, product development people will spend a lot of money developing products that interest them or what they think is right for all markets. Technical people will not just sit still waiting for direction. General management and marketing's responsibility is to provide sufficient direction by ensuring that development activities and priorities are defined by cross-functional business teams and focused on defined market segment(s) and verified customer needs.

Many executives argue that the idea of linking every new development project to a commercial need or plan is impractical and too restrictive. I remain adamant that this is not so. The only rare exception is when senior management makes a conscious decision to spend money on basic or exploratory research. This is an expensive process, however, and a company that follows this route must have plenty of money to support "interesting" research that may lead nowhere. My point of view is supported by Roy Vagelos, Merck's longtime chairman and CEO, who was formerly head of Merck's R&D department. At our annual new product workshop he stated:

> We have many scientists, but they have work objectives about some specific diseases or disorders that we have targeted. We challenge these people with the clear objective of making a drug for a specific unmet need and not to just discover interesting facts and publish articles in journals. Since cost-justified procurement pressure and competitive substitutes have significantly shortened the effective life of every patent, we can't afford a lot of unfocused R&D.

Understand the Customers' Operation

Remember, no one in the industrial world buys products or services because they want them for themselves. Business products or services are purchased to perform a specific function or fill a need that directly or indirectly makes or saves the customer money. Therefore, it is essential to understand the economic and functional needs of the user and to keep these needs foremost in mind so that competitive substitutes cannot erode the supplier's market without its knowledge and thus without an opportunity for counteraction.

The outside-in approach I described in Chapter 2 is the foundation for any market-driven company. Examples of companies that have succeeded with this approach are legendary. Chomerics, a successful electronics company that is part of the complex of high-tech companies near Boston and now a division of Parker Hannifin, attributes much of its success to understanding the magnitude of the electronic contamination problem in both commercial and military communications. Chomerics developed this in-depth knowledge by conducting a series of educational seminars (80 in one year) for design engineers working on these problems. These seminars enabled them to see the range of problems much more clearly. Chomerics' response was to design and market lines of electronic shielding products that reduced radio interference and enhanced the quality of both voice and data communication. Their design engineers had to get very close to customers before they made recommendations and developed solutions. Two-way learning always occurred at the seminars between the customer and Chomerics' people. The technical seminars were the vehicle for initiating technical-to-technical dialog, which eventually led to collaborative co-design solutions.

Identify Unarticulated Needs

Companies that have chosen a first-to-market new product strategy need to get very close to customers, observe and listen very carefully, and then ask customers "what if" questions. Of the twelve guidelines for improving product development, this is one of the most neglected, most complex, and most fruitful approaches for developing new products. Desi DeSimone, 3M's CEO, said it well at our annual senior executive seminar in New York City when he stated:

> We need to identify customers unmet needs and then develop new products that are demonstrably better than other solutions.

An example of identifying unarticulated needs is the invention of Post-it Notes®, one of the most successful entries ever in the office supplies field. Art Fry, a research director in the commercial paper division of 3M, first recognized the possible need for the product when he was directing the choir in his church. He saw how difficult it was for choir members to locate hymns. He noticed a similar problem throughout 3M's offices where paperclips, cards, and rubber bands were used to separate and identify pages and paragraphs. He linked these customer problems to 3M's adhesive capabilities and came up with the Post-it Note® product as a possible solution. The adhesive technology that enabled Post-it Notes® to be a success had been shelved for ten years because no one had connected the new technology to a market need. Obviously, additional research and refinements to the product and manufacturing technology were necessary before the product was actually ready for the market. The key point, however, is that it all started with the recognition of a need or a problem users were having in their church, office, or workplace.

The customer may have already invented your new product! Users often reconfigure or redesign a product to better fit their operating environment. Sometimes, users combine several existing products to solve a problem, not only revealing new uses for traditional products but also highlighting their shortcomings. Unconventional market research methods, including observing customers' operations and videotaping users, can uncover unarticulated needs.

The observation of current or potential customers encountering problems with existing products can identify unacknowledged needs. For example, a product development engineer from Hewlett-Packard sat in an operating room with his marketing manager observing a surgeon at work. The surgeon was guiding his scalpel by watching the patient's body and his own hands displayed on a television screen. As nurses walked around the room, they would periodically obscure the surgeon's view of the screen and the operation for a few critical seconds. No one complained. But this unacknowledged problem caused the astute developer to ponder the possibility of creating a lightweight helmet that could suspend the images a few inches in front of the surgeon's eyes. Hewlett-Packard had the technology to create such a product. The surgeon would never have thought to ask for it, even though its potential to improve productivity, increase accuracy, and make the work easier was substantial. (Also see chapter 5, "Assessing Industrial Markets," the section on new product studies and observations.)

Define the Right Product/Market Focus

In most technically based companies, a market can be defined in different ways, and there are vast differences in the size and potential of any market, depending on how it is defined. It can be defined as a component, a finished product, or a system based on the integration of several products. It can be defined to include various stages of production and distribution. It can be defined to meet specific customer needs in specific market segments in a way that goes well beyond the existing capabilities. If a company only defines its business and focus around existing products or technologies (an inside-out approach), it is bound to be caught off guard time and time again. If a company takes a "circle the customer" approach to providing a broader package of needed products and services as Ecolab, the great specialty chemical company does, they will inevitably enlarge the size of the market opportunity and sales revenue at each account.

A company's business strategy and the scope and flow of new product activities are greatly influenced by how the opportunity is defined. Consider the case of an industrial company that is a market leader in industrial drilling and cutting tools. Its management and engineers have traditionally seen themselves as being in the business of simply making and selling more and better drilling and cutting tools. It is obvious, however, that no one really wants to simply buy drilling or cutting tools. What the customer or user wants to buy is the ability to make holes or fabricate parts in the most efficient way possible. In fact, from the user's point of view, drills or cutting tools are far from the final answer. They are costly, they break, they wear out, and, in that sense, they actually interfere with the manufacturing process. If the company had defined its business objective as helping its customers or users make holes or fabricate certain parts more effectively, instead of as making and selling more and better tools, it would have been on much sounder strategic footing. Instead of confining itself solely to improving or expanding its line of drilling and cutting tools, its engineers would be looking for different methods of drilling holes or cutting materials, including such new approaches as the use of lasers, electron beams, and ultrasonic waves. It would also be aware of the increasing use of materials that are easier to cut and drill with these new and unconventional methods. If the company had pursued this broader business objective, it would have been better able to respond to the equipment manufacturers that introduced laser, electron beam, and ultrasonic machines to "drill" holes or cut material far more efficiently in many situations.

Perform Sufficient Up-Front Work

Many technical people get so excited about a new product that they forget that there must be favorable economics for the customer and their own company. The challenge is to have bright and creative people turn good new product ideas into profitable new products. The cost of doing upfront work, before deciding to go ahead with or shelve a project, is an insignificant part of the entire new product development cost. However, it is ironic that this step is frequently not done or is done poorly. Good up-front work should begin with customer consultations with people who are the kind of customers a supplier would want to have. Such in-depth customer visits help develop an understanding of the customer's operation, their usage, and how the proposed or prototype new product will make or save the customer money. Visits to multiple customers, done by a team of two to three people (usually a technical and marketing person and maybe a salesperson), help uncover and verify any assumptions about customer needs and the customer economics for your product or services.

After the needs and economic benefits are determined for the customer and possibly the customer's customer, the small technical/commercial feasibility team should develop a business plan or new venture proposal—an R&D brief or marketing plan is never sufficient. The business case for the new product should include an assessment of the market opportunity, the technology, and a financial assessment. The financial assessment should include estimates of the size of the opportunity, pricing possibilities, the investment required, the break-even points, and the pay-back period. Optimistic, pessimistic, and most likely estimate of sales and profit should be developed with pro-forma income statements. If upper management approves the business case, further development would proceed with project timelines and fixed milestones. Chapter 5, "Assessing Industrial Markets", address upfront commercial research approaches in more detail.

Utilize Cross-Functional Business Teams

Peter Drucker, the well-known management visionary, stated, "Successful innovations in all fields are now being turned out by cross-functional teams with people from marketing, manufacturing, and finance participating in research work from the very beginning." What he is saying is that leader companies recognize the fallacy of relying on any one individual or department to mastermind their new product activities. They know how important it is to have inputs from all areas of the business as market opportunities are identified and product solutions are developed. *They know that the best hand-off is no hand-off.* The use of cross-functional teams from the beginning creates a sound product/market applications approach to product development and reduces the simplistic technology-push or market-pull approach to innovation discussed earlier in this chapter. Leader companies put together cross-functional teams to accomplish the following:

- Identify and verify customer needs, cost-effective solutions, and market potentials by market segments, major accounts, countries, and key regions of the world.
- Develop an integrated business plan (never just an R&D brief or a marketing plan) for taking the product to market and for achieving sales and profit objectives in the launching.
- Agree to firm technical, sales, and financial milestones in the business plan, and use project management techniques to keep concurrent activities on time.
- Define product, performance, customer benefits, costs, and designs globally by maintaining commonality as long as possible in the manufacturing process.

I must emphasize that we are not talking about a loosely formed committee that is not accountable for results. We are talking about a carefully selected cross-functional business team with the combined knowledge to define market needs and technical solutions; with the authority to set priorities, budgets, and deadlines; and, most importantly, that is accountable for business results. Cross-functional teams should always include one or two key lead customers for guidance and feedback throughout the entire process. Leading new product companies also include purchasing and key suppliers on the cross-functional team before any design is frozen.

Speeding to the market with a new product requires a multidisciplinary team approach, which is called the "parallel method" in Japan. Masters of the team approach to speeding new ideas to the Japanese market include Canon, NEC, and Toshiba. Cross-functional teams in Japan stay with the project from start to finish in a manner that resembles a rugby match, where the ball is passed back and forth down the playing field, rather than the more traditional relay-race approach, in which responsibility is passed sequentially from department to department. Designers start to work before feasibility testing is over, and manufacturing and marketing are deeply involved long before the final design is set. One of the best examples of the parallel or cross-functional team approach is seen in action at Toshiba Corporation.

Toshiba is fast-to-market because it is slow to lock itself into a final design. In Japanese terms, this is called "working slow upfront so that you can work faster in implementation." A product definition team of managers from engineering, manufacturing, marketing, sales, and finance must reach a consensus on features, performance, and costs before development engineers get the green light. This team approach enabled Toshiba to develop and introduce a successful LCD projector in just eight months. Toshiba starts its normal nine-month development cycle with a one-page product description. As soon as top management approves the concept, Toshiba organizes teams in engineering, manufacturing, and marketing. The teams work together under a project manager. When team members hit snags, they are required to return to their departments to resolve issues instead of thrashing them out in a cumbersome and slow-moving committee. The central virtue of this approach was described by Tadashi Okamura, president and CEO of Toshiba:

> Our process minimizes formal communications, and the common nonstop meetings, turf battles, and people claiming ownership to some idea. At Toshiba, this cross-functional management approach is simply called "the process," and it involves informal team meetings. Every department involved gives its view. Then the group attempts to separate facts from instinct, examines the trade-offs, and arrives at a decision. At a recent new product meeting, managers from Toshiba's international group argued against the date the domestic division had chosen for a new product launch. Furthermore, the sales department staffers worried about the product's effect on dealers' inventories. As a result, the date was set back. It is rare that a single member or group will dominate at Toshiba.

Go Outside for Help

Few industrial companies can today do it all alone. Most technically based companies, particularly if their products are developed around different disciplines (electronic, mechanical, chemistry) find it impossible to stay abreast of all the technological developments that can affect the business. Recognizing this, enlightened management continually monitors and searches for ways to capitalize on technological achievements outside the company as a means of sustaining or improving their market positions. *They realize that they must have tentacles around the world.* While this seems logical, many companies do not do this, usually because their management has the self-centered or arrogant attitude of believing that anything "not invented here" (often called the NIH factor) can't be very good. Such an attitude doesn't have much virtue in any situation, and in today's constantly changing world, it can easily lead a company into a position in which its products and/or technology are suddenly and unexpectedly obsolete.

There is no mystery to keeping up with outside developments. One way is to develop a relationship with the appropriate university engineering professors and people at government laboratories. University engineering departments and government labs throughout the world are involved in a variety of advanced research programs. As a general rule, they welcome and actively seek arrangements with companies that will support their efforts; in turn, they provide the company with a window into their developments and engineering students. More companies should follow the lead of many biomedical companies; such companies have built entire new businesses around their close relationships with leading scientists in medical and engineering schools and government labs working on a mutually beneficial area. DuPont has a five-year biotech research program with three universities around the world and it employs many Russian chemists in Moscow and St. Petersburg. However, before plunging into such outside relationships, it is necessary to avoid sticky patent situations by agreeing up front who owns the intellectual property.

Another way to stay abreast of new technology is to participate either as a sub- or prime contractor in government or military projects that focus on or require advanced technological development. Many companies have successfully used this approach to capture technology for their own later commercial use. Harris, Raytheon, and Motorola are good examples of companies that have concentrated on military-funded contracts that later provided technological advances for the commercial side of their businesses. Personnel in these companies are routinely transferred from government or military projects to commercial business units to ensure the effective transfer of technology.

In-licensing is yet another way to gain new technology. Companies that fail to license the "Rembrandts in the attic" from their patent portfolio will not get higher returns from their R&D. Intellectual property licensing and electronic trading exchanges for patent licenses have increased. Many inventors and companies do not have the financial resources or interest to commercialize all their developments. They can realize an attractive return without risk by entering into a licensing agreement with another manufacturer. University research laboratories offer opportunities in which researchers are more interested in advancing the state of the art than in commercial accomplishments. The key is to follow an organized and focused approach that covers all the sources in which new ideas are likely to develop and that ensures early identification of developments with promising commercial potential.

Suppliers are increasingly being looked to for technological advances. Key suppliers should be involved very early in the concept stage before a design is frozen or prototypes are made. A great deal of two-way trust, cooperation, and sharing of information with these suppliers must exist as it does with the long-term keiretsu relationships many Japanese firms forge with suppliers. The supplier and customer usually sign secrecy agreements in these "co-design" type of arrangements.

Finally, new product technology can be gained through outright acquisition or the formation of an informal or formal alliance with another company. Sometimes acquiring a product platform or piece of new technology is the best approach. However, the company with the technology may not want to be acquired, it may be too big or too expensive, or the needed technology may be such a small part of the whole that an acquisition doesn't make sense. Whatever the reason, an alliance that provides the basis for coupling new technology to a commercial need is a very feasible alternative.

The most successful companies pursue some combination of these avenues to achieve technological superiority and build market positions. They recognize that no company or country has a monopoly on new technology, and they constantly search the world market for new technologies and vital technical people to strengthen their ability to serve their target markets and key customers.

Rationalize, Shelve, and Cannibalize

Most older companies have too many product lines. Before adding more new products to cluttered families of products, most companies should rationalize or prune their existing product lines. Some older product lines or the "antiques" should be priced much higher, phased out, sold as specials, or completely eliminated. This frees up resources for new product development.

Many companies have too many active R&D projects that move slowly if at all. These same companies wonder why they are slow to market new products and why they haven't had many true new product successes. These companies need fewer R&D programs and should stop reprioritizing or reordering the same long list of projects. Projects that will have little effect on sales and profits should be shelved. Business units need a mix of product improvements and big breakthrough programs, sometimes called "high impact" projects, with dedicated people. Most companies waste money on tweaking lines and developing line extensions that do very little for profitable top-line growth.

A surprising number of top and general management people have difficulty shelving or saying no to a team that continually misses milestones in their business plans. Management simply must shelve a project that has little chance of technical and commercial success. Furthermore, even if a lagging program is a "pet" project of an influential executive, it should face the same project review scrutiny as every other new venture.

When a manufacturer introduces a product improvement that is interchangeable and better or lower priced than their existing product, cannibalization occurs. The new product might help one business unit while it takes sales and profit from another business unit in the same company. When the new product will replace an existing product at a lesser profit, there is even more internal resistance to developing or launching the new product. Sometimes timing and different pricing to specific market segments and individual customers can control the rate of cannibalization. However, planned cannibalization must become a more common strategy before competitors do it to you.

Whether choosing a first-to-market or fast-follower strategy, industrial companies around the world are learning that they must increasingly and more rapidly obsolete or cannibalize their existing products. If eating your own sounds like a horrid thing to do, it is. It's counter-instinctual. It often means embracing technologies that will destroy the value of past investments. It sometime means purposely depressing profitability. It means, in short, doing things that every good manager is trained not to do. The old metrics for making investment decisions will almost certainly not lead you to cannibalize. Forget the ROI spreadsheets and the traditional discounted cash flow (DCF) and internal rate of return (IRR) calculations. You have to trust your competitive instincts and the power of rapidly moving technology that causes customers to buy the more cost-effective product/service package.

Lew Platt, CEO of Hewlett-Packard, explained why they intentionally obsolete, cannibalize, and then bury their own products:

> We've developed a philosophy at HP of killing off our products and rendering them obsolete with new technology. We have learned the hard way that it's better that we do it than have a competitor do it. We aggressively pursue strategies to kill the very revenue streams our company has grown with. We sometimes call it survival by suicide. Yes it hurts at first, but it sure beats extinction. To make sure we have killed the technology, some business units conduct formal funerals to signal to everyone the technology is obsolete or dead because it is usually hard to kill an old product!

In another approach, Denny Sullivan, executive vice president at Parker Hannifin, explains why the company makes multiple technologies available to the same customers:

> Some people wonder why we make products that overlap some applications. In some situations you can control motion with hydraulic, pneumatic, or electromechanical technologies. We have full-fledged divisions for each of these technologies that compete for the customer's business. The different divisions sometimes end up competing with one another. But that's okay. Our group salesforces and distributors offer the customer all three technologies. We then help the customer decide which of our technologies or solutions are best for their application.

Develop Global Products

With the increasingly high costs of developing new products, duplication of R&D efforts around the world cannot be tolerated. The large sunk cost of development needs to be leveraged or spread across much larger worldwide market opportunities—the result is a more favorable risk/reward. Furthermore, global companies including ABB, BASF, Caterpillar, Daimler Chrysler, GE, and Unilever, are demanding that their suppliers become global and have resources to support them all over the world.

The historical export strategy of developing a product for the home market and then export-ing and trying to force fit the product into foreign markets is more difficult, limits sales growth, and sometimes, due to trade laws, is not feasible. Far too many U.S.- and European-headquar-tered companies try to force many of their existing products into the different needs of regional markets, when they should develop a base global product and then adapt them to the regional or local county market.

Most larger U.S.- and European-headquartered corporations have sister divisions and labo-ratories on both sides of the Atlantic Ocean. These are the more multinational industrial organ-izations. When some companies including 3M, Loctite and National Starch have full develop-ment labs in the United States, Europe, and Asia, they are more truly global organizations with the capabilities to independently take a new product from concept to launch. However, no com-pany can afford the duplication effort in two or even three different regional laboratories. The economics of building global products far outweigh the redundant efforts of each laboratory "doing its own thing." With the economics of globalization, global customers, and increasingly global technical standards, the need to globalize product development will only increase. However, what are some of the common obstacles that inhibit the development of global-base products? In my management development sessions around the world, I hear the same follow-ing complaints about the obstacles to global product development:

1. There is insufficient communication between sister divisions and laboratories in various regions of the world.
2. R&D, engineering and marketing people develop products for just their country or regional needs.
3. There is little or no global coordination of R&D programs around the world—duplication of efforts then occurs across regions of the world.
4. Regional divisions try to push their products on sister divisions in other areas of the world without considering regional differences.
5. Cultural differences, territorial fiefdoms, regional vice president's power needs, and egos can get out of hand far from headquarters.
6. There are few or no incentives (sometimes penalties) to working with your counter-parts in other regions of the world.
7. Strained relationships result when professional colleagues in the same corporation act more like competitors between regions of the world.

Divisions and individuals that don't work well in cross-functional business teams will have more difficulty coordinating global product development. Top management must make sure that people communicate and cooperate between regions and that they don't "circle the wagons" around their regional turf. Short-term or temporary cross-continent transfers of technical and marketing people are usually necessary to transfer technology and marketing know-how between regions of the world. Global market segment definitions, global customer databases and global product launches to common target markets help improve this process.

After the launch of every new product, leading companies conduct a post-launch review to learn where they succeeded and erred in product and market development. Post-launch reviews should be conducted within six to twelve months after every launch. Lessons are always learned from post-launch reviews, and they in turn help improve the company's product and market development processes.

Protect Intellectual Property

Many companies make the mistake of developing first-class products that provide significant competitive advantages and then fail to protect their positions or react quickly enough to competitors' copying. Successful, first-to-market companies aggressively protect their proprietary positions, reacting quickly and with real force when competitors threaten. Companies such as 3M, National Starch, and Abbott Laboratories are almost paranoid about information leaks that might get into the hands of competitors. Jim Kennedy, chairman and CEO of National Starch states, "Intellectual property is not an afterthought—it is a proactive process and always a part of the upfront product development and overall business strategy." These same companies routinely seek the strongest possible patents, get international trademark protection for brand names, limit the access (even to some employees) to many restricted areas, and make noncompete agreements a condition of employment. They usually also develop and sign secrecy agreements with key suppliers and customers. Individually, none of these activities is particularly unique. Taken together and coupled with a constant watchdog attitude that is part of the culture, those companies are a formidable force.

These companies also take a number of other actions to reduce the possibility of competitors hurting their positions with some kind of a surprise blow. They continuously gather intelligence about their competitors all over the world. Because a new technology always starts in one country of the world and in certain market applications, employees scout trade shows around the world. In addition, they keep competitors off base by starting work on product enhancements and even next-generation products while the growth of existing products is still healthy or before the first product has been launched. They sometimes keep these improvements in reserve and wait for the most appropriate time to introduce them. An executive from a highly successful medical equipment company told me:

> We always try to keep well ahead of our competitors with new products or enhancements. When they come at us with something that threatens our existing product, we then jump out of the grass and kill them with something they didn't know we already had on the shelf.

Marketing intellectual property has become a new corporate strategy. In addition to protecting their intellectual property, a growing number of companies, including IBM, 3M, Boeing, Dupont, Dow, TRW, and Honeywell, are aggressively marketing their own intellectual property. The stakes are high, sometimes billions of dollars, for companies that successfully mine and maximize the value of their patent portfolio. For example, in one year, IBM added over one billion dollars to its bottom line with revenue from out-licensing or marketing their patents. This was about one-tenth of IBM's annual revenue. After management buys into the economic value of marketing some of their patents, companies can move form a strict no licensing approach to one that sees the limited time benefit of many technologies and the substantial income that can be generated from out-licensing.

SUMMARY

No for-profit industrial company can manage new product development as an isolated department in a bucolic academic setting. They are increasingly making new product development a vital part of the business. The risk of new products being too slow, too late, too costly, or not demonstrably better to customers is great. Industrial companies can pursue either a first-to-market or fast-follower new product strategy. Whenever the external rate of change by customers and competition is faster than any supplier is able to profitably respond with new products, the supplier is in trouble.

Keeping pace with demonstrably better new products is a risky, difficult process under the best of circumstances, but it is vital to the long-term success of every enterprise, especially in a time of rapidly changing technology and intense global competition. There are some proven steps firms can take to better the chances for their products: They should understand customers' operations and observe unarticulated needs. They should carefully think through their market focus to zero in on significant value-added opportunities. They should do sufficient upfront work, assessing the opportunity and its economic feasibility and learn from postlaunch reviews. They should face up to cost and performance deficiencies in their product line. They should prune marginal products from the existing line. They should ensure that all development efforts are linked to strategies to counterattack or attack a market segment, and lead users should always guide the development process from the very beginning and up through a successful launch. They should ensure that cross-functional teams play an important role in the entire development process. Cross-functional and cross-continent teams should guide the global development of new products. Furthermore, companies should increasingly cannibalize their existing products before the competition does it for them.

Finally, top management should see product development as an agent of change for the entire organization. New product sales and profit goals can reduce complacency and create healthy tension and a sense of urgency throughout the organization. Top management must encourage and tolerate risk-taking in product and process development. Without top management support and involvement in the innovation process, very little will be ventured and little will be gained. By following the approaches in this chapter, successful new products will create a strong foundation for profitable top-line growth in any industrial company.

---

[1] New Products for the 1980s (New York: Booz, Allen & Hamilton, 1982).

The Consultative Sales Force

"Sales professionals should have a doctor-patient attitude and aptitude."

T. J. Dermot Dunphy, Sealed Air Corporation
Chairman and CEO

Sales force performance has always been an important contributor to the success of industrial companies. Other elements of the marketing mix—that is, advertising, promotion, and merchandising-simply do not have the same effect for industrial companies as they do for consumer goods manufacturers. Unlike consumer products, there are very few situations in industry in which the buying decision is made because of some especially creative advertising campaign. In contrast, industrial selling is usually accomplished by a credible salesperson demonstrating the value of the manufacturer's product and services to many influences within the buying organization. Industrial salespeople must often go through many lengthy steps in a consultative process that ultimately may lead to a purchase order. It often takes several calls to secure an initial order, and, given the high cost of the average sales call (estimates of $600 to $1,000 are not unusual), the minimum cost to close a new sale can be several thousand dollars. This lengthy, costly, and often very technical buyer-seller interchange is dramatically different from many arms-length and often impulsive retail goods transactions.

The task of selling industrial products ranges from one extreme of being an order taker and expediter to the other extreme of being a creative consulting engineer. As I see it, the order taker/expediter type of salesperson is an endangered species. Selling jobs that are at the order taker extreme can be accomplished with telemarketing, electronic ordering (EDI), e-commerce, the web, email, and faxes and are better handled by inside sales, customer service, or distributors. Direct sales are too costly to serve these transactional customers.

At the other extreme, many industrial products have become more complex and most customers' operations and procurement have also become more sophisticated. In these situations, industrial salespeople must have more technical knowledge about their products and an aptitude to understand the customers' operations. Today's industrial salesperson must be a creative consultant to the client, suggesting a cost-effective solution with a value statement that puts money in customer's pocket. Sales and support people should be perceived as counselors who improve a customer's costs, performance, and productivity. According to Dermot Dunphy, chairman and CEO of Sealed Air Corporation, the industrial selling process should be like a physician who questions, listens, and diagnoses a patient's symptoms and then prescribes a cost-effective remedy. Chas Eggert, the vice president of marketing at Engelhard Corporation, thinks similarly to the CEO of Sealed Air. After the completion of a four-day in-house workshop for business teams, Chas Eggert presented framed certificates to each participant proclaiming that they were "doctors" of market-driven management. The message from Engelhard and Sealed Air is identical: Sales professionals should have a doctor-patient attitude and an industrial engineering aptitude. This chapter focuses on today's and tomorrow's industrial salesperson, who must be a trusted and respected consultative problem solver to the customer, not simply an order taker, expediter, or someone that just schmooses with customers.

COMPLEX PRODUCTS AND CUSTOMERS

Industrial sourcing decisions are becoming more sophisticated. The quality movement, vendor ratings, supplier reductions, sharper customers, and various types of buyer-supplier alliances have permanently changed the role of industrial buying and selling. Customers don't care about the supplier's problems. As Larry Combs, vice president of marketing at Parker Hannifin said: "Customers today aren't interested in only the feeds and speeds of your products; they have less time to baby-sit salespeople, play a round of golf, or take long lunches, and they don't care how wide your product line is—they simply want help with their problems." Customers are asking suppliers to help them in many areas. They are increasingly choosing only those suppliers who can help streamline their operations, reduce their costs, and put speed in their new product development efforts.

All this requires a sales force with a different aptitude, mind-set, and skills than the stereotypical image of the high-pressure, fast-talking salesperson who can't be trusted and who is just pushing hard for an order. Consultative selling takes a lot of time, it demands intimate application and product knowledge, and it requires making sophisticated presentations to many different audiences in the buying organization. The quantity or number of sales calls a person makes each day or week is less important than the quality of each sales call.

Unfortunately, many industrial suppliers are still selling the old-fashioned way. A 33-year retired IBM salesperson described the old ways that still persist at many industrial firms:

> I sold products that people didn't want, didn't need, and couldn't afford. We were so articulate that we could persuade people to act against their own interests. Pushing metal or selling boxes and meeting product volume quotas set by our regional sales managers was our mission. We were a legendary army of well-paid generalists selling hundreds of different products to dozens of different types of customers while some of our more successful competitors had more specialized sales forces that helped solve customers' problems. As competitors like Hewlett-Packard helped customers develop solutions to capture, move, and share information, some IBM salespeople lost the confidence of many customers.

Some major customers were equally critical of IBM's former sales approaches. The senior vice president of GTE, one of IBM's former top ten customers, stated:

> When we needed to move from just buying mainframes to information management systems with many networks, IBM reps tried to talk us out of these approaches. IBM's well-scrubbed and white shirt salespeople made flashy presentations, smiled often, used a lot of buzzwords, but had little substance. Many of IBM's salespeople were a mile wide and an inch deep. Hewlett-Packard's salespeople were different. First of all, they listened a lot, asked probing questions, and took a lot of notes. They found out our information needs at all levels of the organization and forged strong ties with top, middle, and lower management and with the people that actually operated our computers. HP's telephone support people were often more helpful than many of IBM's direct salespeople. We now use HP for most of our information technology needs. Fortunately for IBM, they have changed and are now a lot better.

COMMON MANAGEMENT CONCERNS

In the many training sessions I conduct every year across the globe, I hear many of the same concerns about industrial sales forces. The common uneasiness about each sales force is expressed in the following statements:

- Our salespeople spend too much time on paperwork and expediting and too little time in front of customers.
- Our sales force is evaluated and rewarded on tonnage or sales volume, while the rest of the organization is measured and rewarded on profit results.
- We have had productivity improvements in all areas of the organization except in our selling organization, where we spend a lot of money with questionable returns.
- As we add more product lines to our sales force, I'm afraid our salespeople know less and less about each product line . . . our best competitors are much more specialized and focused.
- After some product training and a basic selling course, we don't do much to make our salespeople more professional and aware of how we stack up against competitors.
- We talk a lot about value-added or consultative selling, but many of our sales people lack the aptitude and have no training, no tools, and no incentive to invest the time required to do value selling.
- We sell a lot of our products through distributors, but our salespeople don't know how a distributor makes or loses money, and we don't develop action plans with distributors to help them sell our products to target accounts.

SUCCESS DEPENDS ON THE SALES FORCE

A focused, well-trained, trusted, and motivated sales force is always a powerful competitive advantage for an industrial supplier. Looking ahead, several factors are certain to make the role of the sales force even more important to business success:

1. Buying practices all over the world are becoming sharper and more sophisticated because companies have more supplier choices and recognize the tremendous profit potential of building more analysis into all buying decisions.
2. The technical complexity and sophistication of products, systems, and services continue to increase and require more in-depth industry, application, and technical knowledge.
3. Competition from substitute technologies and foreign suppliers is increasing and making the selling task both more complex and important.
4. First-hand market intelligence from customers and about competitors is increasingly important to develop superior product/service offerings and presentations that help keep customers and attract new ones.

The first two previous considerations place a much greater premium on intelligent selling to help customers articulate their needs and then to demonstrate the tangible and intangible benefits from a product/service package in meeting those needs. The third consideration means that many companies will become far more dependent on value-added selling presentations to overcome unit cost or price objections. Finally, the need for more and better intelligence about market requirements and competitive actions means sales personnel will have to be more resourceful and better trained on how to draw this information together and rapidly share it within their organizations; they must also learn how to develop cost-effective presentations based on the customer benefits from their recommended solutions.

Most senior executives are quick to agree with the importance of having an outstanding selling force. However, only a few are fully satisfied with the effectiveness and productivity of their selling organizations. Most see their selling arm falling short of the performance they want in many ways:

1. They (the sales force) do not have a clear view of the important market segments in the various sales regions and do not understand the unique needs of each market segment.
2. They do not effectively identify and demonstrate the total value of their products and services to customers for existing and (especially) new products in a way that takes pressure off unit price as the key buying consideration.
3. They do not prospect for new customers or to new segments to build a broader customer sales base; they mostly try to sell more products to their existing customers.
4. They do not provide a useful flow of market intelligence about customers and competitors to aid planning strategies and to develop new product offerings.
5. They do not improve their productivity at a pace sufficient to keep abreast of constantly increasing selling costs.
6. Where relevant, they do not understand how distributors make money or how to evaluate and improve a distributor's sales of your company's product lines.

The sales force in many industrial manufacturing companies functions more as a collection of independent sales agents than as an extension of the marketing arm. The problem can be traced back to the failure to follow one or more of ten essential sales principles of a market-driven industrial company. The balance of this chapter discusses each of these ten principles in detail: (1) focus on customer problems and needs; (2) understand your customers' operations and the competition; (3) determine cost-effective solutions; (4) select the appropriate organizational approach; (5) organize ongoing training; (6) take advantage of electronic advances; (7) link compensation to business-unit goals; (8) develop a sales career ladder; (9) provide first-line supervision; and (10) determine their business planning role.

PRINCIPLE 1: FOCUS ON CUSTOMER PROBLEMS AND NEEDS

I don't know of any customer in the industrial world who gets really excited about any supplier's product. In fact, no matter how well designed or low priced a supplier's product is, the prospective buyer would rather avoid the purchase entirely. The product usually has no personal appeal to anyone in the user's organization. *Its main purpose is to reduce costs, improve production, or increase sales revenues.* Thus, the buying decision is more analytical, rational, and economic, with personal considerations playing a less significant role. The following example illustrates this point:

> A few years ago, a sales team from the Toledo Scale Division of Reliance Electric met with a manufacturing team from Frito-Lay, the world's largest supplier of chips and other snack foods. The meeting was set up to discuss a manufacturing cost problem that was very significant to Frito-Lay. The problem centered around the need to ensure that customers were never "shortchanged" on the stated net weight of the package. To eliminate this possibility, the bag-filling operation was set up to overfill by as much as 10 percent. When considered against the tremendous volume, the overfill costs represented millions of dollars each year. The question was how to minimize the overfill cost and still ensure that no customer would ever be shortchanged.

Shortly after the problem was described, a Toledo Scale sales representative said, "What Frito-Lay needs is our check weighing system that automatically kicks out any package that doesn't fall within a prescribed weight band." The product idea may have had merit. But the comment rubbed the Frito-Lay procurement team the wrong way. The team leader responded, "We don't want to buy your product. We want a solution to our problem and you don't know enough about our business to recommend anything yet."

The Toledo Scale sales team had lost credibility, which was then very difficult to regain because they were not sufficiently sensitive to the customer's stated needs.

PRINCIPLE 2: UNDERSTAND YOUR CUSTOMERS' OPERATIONS AND THE COMPETITION

Achieving an understanding of a user's operations, requirements, future needs, and competitive information is the most important activity that industrial sales representatives perform. Salespeople are the primary source of competitive intelligence and a helpful source for segmenting markets, identifying customer problems, and designing new product/service packages. To achieve the degree of understanding necessary, the salesperson must become intimately involved with and really learn about the customer's business, and often this includes learning where costs are incurred, what bottlenecks are worrisome, and where operating problems occur. Achieving this level of understanding inevitably requires more time than some salespeople care to spend asking questions and listening to the people responsible for running the business. Even fewer salespeople have an inclination to learn about the customer's customers' needs. Despite the salesperson's natural aversion to this activity, it is an absolute must for any high growth industrial company because it is the way to identify customer problems and come up with the best solutions to lower costs, enhance productivity, or provide some other important benefits to customers.

The right sales force must be recruited, trained, and given incentives to provide solutions and organized feedback on such questions as these:

- How does the product or service fit into the customers' operations, fill an economic need, and compare with competitive offerings?
- What benefits from the product's or service (e.g., initial cost, life-cycle cost, failure rate, support service, total system cost) are really key in the immediate customer's and end user's minds?
- What current or potential developments in the customers business could change cost or design requirements, and how can these needs be met?
- How do your customer's products fit into the current and future needs of their customer's operation?
- What changes in the user's operation or the competitive environment could affect the customer's business, and how could these changes, in turn, affect the requirements and demand for your product or services?

Management must do more than simply tell the sales force to provide such information; it must take three important steps to ensure this information is properly developed:

1. Sales assignments must be made in a way that gives each salesperson a fair chance of achieving an understanding of what is going on at the immediate customer and end-user levels. In effect, the professional sales assignment should be structured to encourage the salesperson to become, to some degree, a market specialist with in-depth knowledge of specific applications. However, it is unlikely that any salesperson can develop the kind of detailed product and application knowledge required if he or she is expected to sell a broad line of products to all customers in all markets. A salesperson in such a situation will naturally gravitate to the less complex environment and devote a lot of time to negotiating unit price instead of identifying and communicating customer value. As a result of insufficient product and application knowledge, any salesperson will be more of an order taker and expediter.

2. A formal system for distilling and interpreting the account information received from the sales force must be installed. This sounds like a very basic point–and it is. However, time after time we have heard a salesperson say, "I send market or competitive information into headquarters or the regional office, but nobody ever listens to me or believes what I say." Before long the sales representative will not bother. Call reports that are cut and dried or that list only the company visited and product sold are of little value. Unfortunately, many of the end-of-the-week call reports or activity reports are instruments of torture for sales reps and tell his or her manager and others in the organization next to nothing. In contrast, the Warner Electric division of the Dana Corporation requires every salesperson to list on each monthly sales report the two or three best ideas that he or she learned from customers. The divisions top management group reads every idea.

3. The company's value system must reflect the high priority management places on a clear understanding of user needs. If not recruited carefully, some salespeople may not have the technical background or aptitude to understand a supplier's products or the technical complexity of the customer's operations. This priority must be reflected in recruiting the right people and in an ongoing commitment to training. Unless every industrial salesperson receives at least one to two weeks of training annually, they are probably not current. This priority must be reflected in an ongoing commitment to product, application, market segment, distributor management, and personal skills training, including using laptops, listening, and making effective technical and business presentations. This emphasis on training and keeping current may be manifested in a recognition and compensation structure that pays a premium for developing business in certain end-user groups or for certain applications. Then, again, it may simply be reflected in the way management compliments those who do a good job or, more importantly, chastises those who do not. Training and continuous improvement of the sales force must be nonstop and must occur in both good and slow economic times.

PRINCIPLE 3: DETERMINE COST-EFFECTIVE SOLUTIONS

After hearing from many customers that their sales force was "just raining new product features on them,"[1] Hewlett-Packard set out to upgrade their sales force over a three-year period. First, it structured the sales force so that it paralleled the company's business strategy by aligning the sales force by industry rather than organizing it by geography. In the previous geographical sales organization, a salesperson called on anyone in a defined territory. Industry or market concentration allowed for more in-depth customer contact, and with more knowledgeable salespeople, in Hewlett-Packard jargon, they became "trusted advisors." HP salespeople calling on just the financial services sector are required to take an average of at least two weeks of classroom training every year to understand everything from the basics of banking to what happens in each phase on the trading floor. Dick Justice, Hewlett-Packard's head of American sales, explained:

Customers want to solve business problems, not just buy analytical instruments or technology. Our reps can now go to a customer and say, "I understand your business, and my job is to apply technology to improve your competitiveness or reduce your cost." We realize that customers' careers are at risk today if they buy the wrong technology. Customers are looking for suppliers to work with them and help in their total operation. We had to become industry experts. In the old days we sold just the sizzle to customers with fancy presentations. Today we must sell documented cost and performance improvements to many horizontal and vertical buying influences.

The approach taken by AMP, the world's largest electronic connector company, is another example of what today's professional industrial salesperson should do. To focus on customer problems and the fastest growing customers, AMP has mostly electrical engineers on its sales staff. AMP's vice president for U.S. sales stated:

> We want to have more cerebral discussions with customers who are in the planning and product development mode. All of our reps have laptops so they can tap into their business unit and do connector design and circuit simulation right at the customer's facility. For a few of our truly key customers, AMP has a resident sales engineer permanently at their site to interface directly with the customer's engineering, manufacturing, marketing,and purchasing people.

Industrial and high-tech manufacturers should provide their sales forces with the necessary tools to analyze a customer's needs and make recommendations much like a doctor does with a prescription or remedy for a patient. The Timken Company, the world's largest manufacturer of precision tapered roller bearings, is an excellent example of the kind of consultative selling tools that make salespeople true professionals. The Timken Company developed a software program that enables their salespeople to help customers—including Caterpillar, Boeing, and Mercedes—select the proper antifriction bearing with Timken's Select-A-Nalysis™ program. With customer information for about twenty conditions or constraints (including the RPM, radial load, heat generation, fatigue life, outside diameter, bore size, torque, and lubricant type) the Timken sales engineer can sit beside the customer's design engineer and select the proper bearing for his or her problem. The right bearing is quickly determined, and the customer immediately receives a bearing drawing. As the customer considers different what if conditions, the Timken sales counselor can immediately generate the appropriate bearing selection, and the Select-A-Nalysis™ also shows the Timken part number.

PRINCIPLE 4: SELECT THE APPROPRIATE ORGANIZATIONAL APPROACH

When organizing an industrial sales force to implement market strategies, the firm should choose from three basic structures: purely geographical, by product range, or by industry or market segment. A combination of the three can also be used. Each organizational form involves considerations of sales force effectiveness and efficiency. *Trade-offs will always be necessary.* The following sections describe each organizational approach and the advantages and limitations of each.

Geography

In the most basic sales organization, each rep is assigned an exclusive territory in which he or she then represents the supplier. The sales rep is responsible for all current and potential business in the defined geographic area regardless of the type of customer, market segment, and size of each account. If a company manufactures a limited range of products and technology for one market segment, this approach works well. This approach minimizes travel expenses because the geographic region covered is limited. A major function of sales management then is to design territories with similar sales potential, travel time, and workload. However, when a sales force carries an increasing number of products or more complex new products for many market segments, this approach can deteriorate to order taking. It can result in having geographic coverage but little or no penetration in specific market segments because the salesperson does not have the in-depth knowledge of the customer's operations and product benefits necessary to fully service the customer. To bring more focus to customer problem solving for a wide range of products, separate sales forces can be structured around fewer products or around distinct market segments.

Product Range

Product specialization is typically necessary when the products are more technically complex and/or are very numerous in number. For example, Parker Hannifin created separate sales forces for its seal, connector, and pneumatic product lines even though they sometimes call on the same customer. As a company broadens its product lines and because different technologies are often involved (such as with Parker's seal and pneumatic businesses), more specialized product and application knowledge is needed. A company often acquires new product lines or entire companies and then just "bolts on" the product lines to those already handled by its original sales force; the company then claims it has achieved efficiencies from the "pooled" sales force. Unfortunately, as a company adds new product lines to a salesperson's responsibility, the salesperson often becomes less knowledgeable about the individual products. After IBM acquired Lotus Notes, they decided not to integrate their existing computer sales force with the Lotus Notes sales entity. IBM realized that salespeople can only assimilate so much, and that salespeople then tend to promote only those products they are most comfortable with. Furthermore, if the salesperson now contacts different people at the same geographic customer location, the risk associated with trying to intelligently represent too many products or technologies is even greater—even though, on the surface, it often looks very efficient to have one sales force call on the "same customer" at one geographic location.

As Johnson & Johnson expanded its hospital product range, it created different sales forces, each with a narrower product range, to call on the same hospital location because the buying influences and technologies for surgical instruments *are different* from those for prescription drugs, which differ from those for surgical gowns or glucose monitoring equipment. At the larger teaching hospitals, Johnson & Johnson has as many as eight different sales forces calling on different hospital departments with a wide range of product technologies. Johnson & Johnson knows that *sales effectiveness must be considered against the assumed cost efficiencies* that might come from a geographically pooled sales force. Similarly, BetzDearborn has two different sales forces selling water treatment chemicals at the same paper mill location because the buying contacts, chemistry, and specifications are different at the "wet" and "dry" ends of the same paper mill.

Industry or Market Segments

Industrial companies are increasingly specializing their sales forces by industry or market segment. Pall Corporation, the world's largest and most successful maker of filtration products, has separate sales forces for their aerospace, industrial hydraulic, chemical, electronics, and biomedical markets. Sometimes the same Pall product is sold to different market segments by different sales forces and at different prices because the benefits and values of many of their products vary across market segments. The same Pall product often has different brand names in each market segment. The specific industry or market segment sales forces of Pall have been key to running trials and demonstrating lower total life-cycle costs (not just unit price), and they have helped Pall rapidly introduce new products by showing customers how they will save or make money with the new product. Finally, Pall typically selects distributors for each market segment-and not just by the geographical area the distributors may cover. For example, in central New Jersey, Pall has separate distributors for the petroleum, industrial chemical, electronic, and pharmaceutical market segments. This is called parallel distribution.

A market-focused salesperson should be an expert in the industry or segment on which they concentrate. Market-focused salespeople are especially well suited to run field trials, perform consultative selling, and launch new products. Quest, a unit of ICI Chemicals that makes brewing ingredients, has a global sales force that only calls on breweries around the world, even though that means crossing over the geographic territories of other ICI Chemical salespeople. Quest's product development and acquisitions candidates for brewery ingredient products are guided by suggestions from the brewery sales force. Furthermore, nearly all of Quest's brewery ingredients salespeople are ex-brewmasters who speak the language of brewery people.

The major disadvantage of the market-specific selling approach is that when customers in a market segment are widely dispersed throughout a country or region of the world, more extensive travel time and costs may be incurred than if they were organized only by geography. Sales organization by market or industry segment emphasizes sales effectiveness over sales efficiency, and, if greater market penetration and higher margins result, the added costs are a good trade-off.

Special Situations

In multidivisional companies there are often some product, customer, or market situations that require special attention. A few senior sales reps might be assigned to national or global accounts that need close coordination between multiple customer facilities and the supplier's many manufacturing locations. In another situation, a market or industry specialist might be located in Detroit or Tokyo to work with just automotive customers and another one located in Atlanta or Singapore to work exclusively with textile accounts, while the rest of the sales force is organized on a geographic or product basis.

In another specific approach, 3M created market focus within their geographically organized coated abrasives sales force. How? The 3M sales rep located in High Point, North Carolina, sells to all accounts in his geographic territory, but he also serves as a market specialist in the woodworking industry throughout the United States. Similarly, the 3M salesperson located in Pittsburgh is responsible for a geographic territory but is also employed as a national resource for steel manufacturing customers. Timken bearing sales engineers in New York City, Chicago, San Francisco, Tokyo, Frankfort, and London serve as specialists for rapid transit/subway rail car maintenance, repair, and overhaul needs. A global transit market manager works closely with the sales engineers in these cities and with the OEMs to get Timken products qualified and specified.

In still another situation, specification work and approvals might have to be performed at a central buying location or technical center before the product can be bought and used in another region. In this case, a "missionary specialist" might be assigned to trials and obtain approvals at a customer's facilities, but he or she would have no responsibility for sales. The primary job of a missionary person is to provide customers with product and application information and to get products approved and specified. These "salespeople" don't usually take orders from customers; they are typically low-key, and low-pressure influences. For new products that require a lot of technical education with immediate customers or with customers' customers to "pull" through the demand for a product, such a missionary specialist might conduct seminars throughout the country (or a region of the world) to begin the buying process, which is then handed over to a local salesperson or distributor. In such cases, one or a few product or market specialists would then be added to handle the additional education and missionary work. Finally, where a business unit believes its products are not suited for the existing geographic, product, or market-focused approaches, it will strike out on its own with a dedicated sales force for a more limited range of products, defined customers, or market segments.

PRINCIPLE 5: ORGANIZE ONGOING TRAINING

As mentioned earlier, today's sales job is far more complex than simply making calls to sell the product or taking orders. In addition to achieving sales goals, management rightfully expects their salespeople to build a strong consultative relationship with key customers by really understanding the business; by providing market feedback on customer needs, competitive intelligence and new application opportunities; and by selling a desired product mix. These same companies expect their sales forces to make value-added presentations that emphasize total cost and not unit price.

Rarely, however, does management give the salesperson sufficient training to accomplish all these objectives. Usually, the sales representative is provided with product knowledge, given a sales quota along with a pep talk, and told to get out there and sell. This is not very helpful to the typical salesperson, who is constantly faced with a choice of how to allocate his or her time among various products, customers, users, or other contacts that could influence the sale. Nor does it help him or her think through the specific actions that should be taken when the priorities have been decided.

Most sales training programs focus almost entirely on product features and fundamental selling approaches, such as how to tell the product story, combat customer objections, refute competitor claims, peak customer interest, and close the sale. This kind of sales training is, of course, useful. Every salesperson must have knowledge of these basics before he or she can make an effective sales call. But such knowledge alone is no longer sufficient in most cases to help the sales force do an outstanding job. To accomplish this, the sales force must have guidelines and information from marketing that help resolve such issues as the following:

- Which market segments offer the greatest sales and growth potential, and which specific accounts should be targeted based on documented value in that segment?
- What points should be emphasized (e.g., cost savings, product reliability, product performance benefits, ease of operation, system solutions, order lead times, technical service) with each market segment to provide genuine value and take the emphasis off price as the dominant buying consideration?
- How should selling time be divided among servicing existing accounts, prospecting for new ones, arranging for team visits, making capability presentations, and so on?
- How much emphasis should be placed on new product introductions, which applications represent the best targets for the new product, how can an agreement for an initial trial be secured, and how should the trial be managed?

Training the sales force is not an easy task. Battles are won because the troops are properly trained and given direction by marketing. Today's sales troops need new and better sales tools and ongoing training oriented to specific markets, applications, and customer problems; they need side-by-side competitive information comparisons; and they must be less focused on just getting the order.

Nowhere does the need for excellent sales training occur more than when marketing demands that the sales force develop and present cost-effective solutions based on a customer's documented total or life cycle-costs and not on unit price. In these situations, it is marketing's job to provide salespeople with the appropriate analytical techniques, schematics, and formats for framing a customer's costs. Whether such a selling approach is called "applied costs," "value received," or "customer ROI," the training program has to provide "how to" training in six areas:

1. How to develop a schematic of the customer's operation from procurement through after sales service and including the needs of the customer's customers.
2. How to uncover the customer's and the customers' customer's current requirements, future expectations, and unarticulated needs.
3. How to measure the customer's cost and savings per day, month, or year in terms of the tangible and intangible results of your product/service package.
4. How to set up and run a customer field trial to document and verify the customer's value received.

5. How to communicate the tangible and intangible benefits to multiple buying influences and various organizational levels.
6. How to price based upon the value received as compared with the customer's current system, competitive product, or your existing product as reference points.

Extensive classroom and on-the-job field training is necessary to make these "value selling steps" a reality. This always takes a lot of time, investment, and hard work. It never occurs with a superficial program or by providing a few examples of customer cost savings. The methodology must be learned and applied in a very disciplined manner with the customers' usage and cost information—that often must be developed in cooperation with customers and documented with an on-site field trial.

Industry and Application Knowledge

Once market segments are selected to counterattack and attack, in-depth knowledge about each segment and application must be gathered and disseminated in training sessions for the salespeople. Sometimes a sales force can develop this knowledge from past experience and specialization. Often they cannot. Selective and cautious hiring of people from leading customers in each target market is one sound way to build the industry knowledge base among your salespeople; these people should then train the other salespeople. Those hired from the target market segments should have at least three to five years of experience in the operations or technical area that you compete in; they do not usually come from the customer's marketing or sales areas. People recruited from customer operations have an in-depth knowledge of the manufacturing process, bottlenecks, customer's language, and competitors' products and services. Of course, a company should never hire a person from a current customer unless that customer is first notified and is in agreement with the switch. Recent retirees from the customer's organization are often a good source of full- or part-time help for training, developing industry specific literature, attending trade shows, and making joint sales calls with your direct and distributor people to customers in the segment.

The following examples show how hiring people from your customer's operations (or your customer's customer) can bring the customer's heart and soul to the center of your business:

- Crosfields, the England-based supplier of catalysts to segments including the petroleum industry, hired one process and one maintenance engineer from petroleum companies to train their salespeople and develop user-friendly literature in the operator's language.
- Johnson & Johnson's surgical business units, including Ethicon (sutures), Endo-Surgery (small incision products), and Codman & Shurtleff (surgical tools), have a long-time practice of hiring former operating room nurses for most sales positions. Former operating room nurses know the language, culture, and buying practices in these specialized hospital areas.

One of the better market-driven transformations I saw first-hand occured at the Cabot Corporation, a $2+ billion chemical manufacturer of carbon black, fumed silica, and tantalum products. Cabot was an old-line, product-driven company. After targeting a number of key market segments, Cabot carefully hired a number of sales and technical people from progressive customers in the segments as shown in Exhibit 7-1.

Exhibit 7-1

Target Market Hiring

Target Market Segments →	Employees Hired from
Automobile and truck tires	Major global and regional tire manufacturers
Coatings and adhesives	Dexter, Nippon Paint, Valspar, Lord
Semiconductors	IBM, AT&T, Rockwell

Companies such as those just described find it much easier to take experienced people from a customer's operations and train them in their own products than to do the reverse. Equally important, salespeople from the respective market segments are able to develop an in-depth rapport with the users because they intimately understand their business and operating conditions, speak the same language, and bring credibility to the supplier.

Sales Competency Quizzes

Attending a sales or new product-training workshop is one thing. Remembering what one "learned" may be another. After every training school at Sealed Air Corporation, they administer a two- to four-page multiple-choice quiz that covers the important points in the training program. Also, every Sealed Air new product training session concludes with a short quiz that covers the new product's tangible and intangible customer benefits, and side-by-side competitive comparisons. If a score of at least 80 percent is not achieved on each Sealed Air competency exam, the participant has to study and retake the quiz. Sealed Air also conducts a distributor management workshop for its sales reps that concludes with a five-page competency examination on distributor management. Sealed Air's professional training process reinforces former chairman and CEO, Dermot Dunphy's statement at the beginning of this chapter, "Sales professionals should have a doctor-patient attitude and aptitude."

The notion of giving competency quizzes after the completion of sales training has been commonplace for years in the pharmaceutical industry, where "detail" salespeople are extensively trained about the benefits, negative side effects, and competitive product offerings of the new drugs they present to physicians, who then test and prescribe those new products—much like an engineer who writes a new product specification. Because a physician is usually a technically astute buying influence, a well-trained drug salesperson is mandatory. Sales competency quizzes can help launch new products as if they were perishable fruit. When I suggest to industrial clients that they administer competency quizzes at the end of any sales training program as Sealed Air and a few others do, many sales managers strongly resent the notion. What could be behind their negative reaction to such a proven approach?

PRINCIPLE 6: TAKE ADVANTAGE OF ELECTRONIC ADVANCES

When today's consultative industrial salespeople open their briefcases, the last things they might take out are product samples or order forms. The first item they often remove is a laptop computer, which contains background information on the account. Laptop computers, software programs, the Internet, web sites, company databases, information networks, electronic data interchanges, voice and e-mail, faxes, 800 numbers, modems, pagers, and portable telephones have dramatically redefined the industrial salesperson's effectiveness and efficiency. All these electronic technologies are enabling factors that have permanently changed nearly every aspect of the salesperson's job. First and foremost, these electronic tools have allowed the sales rep to respond to customer needs faster and better. On-line networks help the salesperson instantly know how much of which items are located where. Previously, many telephone calls and callbacks were needed to provide the customer with the most basic shipping and scheduling information. When planning sales calls in an earlier career, I had to dig through file folders and telephone many departments to gather current pieces of information that were then manually updated. Sales reps can now just "key up" or enter new information into their laptop computers.

Laptops are also especially helpful in working with a customer to solve a design problem. Sales reps and customers increasingly sit down together in front of a computer screen, and with menu-driven software options, they can view what the configuration will look like, what customer benefits will result, and what the customer's total cost will be. For example, GE plastics sales engineers use laptops with the customer's engineers to apply failure analysis and to apply design to manufacturing and assembly models to determine the optimum design and to understand the system's total cost. As a result of this type of technical help, GE can frequently sell higher priced thermoset plastic because the sales rep can demonstrate how it lowers a customer's total system cost more than a lower priced option. Furthermore, if the customer is not thoroughly convinced that the solution is the best for his needs, they can be shown, using GE's database, an application story or testimonial from someone in that market segment who benefited from buying the same product. While in front of the customer, the GE rep can also access information about competitive products, prices, configuration notes, and the status of deliveries.

Computers are affecting even the traditional product training schools. The time and cost to fly people off to week-long product training schools is being reduced or replaced with CD-ROM and online training programs. For example, as copiers became more technical and buyers more sophisticated, Canon Copier's traditional week-long training programs were getting expensive and time consuming for the independent dealer salespeople. Canon developed interactive CD-ROM training programs that last for sixteen hours and that have reduced or eliminated some of the training schools. The training programs walk salespeople through the steps of selling copiers, and they give people the opportunity to interact with other people acting as customers. If a salesperson is having problems handling a certain objection, he or she can type in questions and get a series of possible answers. Common troubleshooting procedures and solutions can also be handled via electronic and videotape modules. A web site with FAQ's (frequently asked questions) is available to Canon reps, distributors, and customers. FAQs should be created for applications information, data sheets, available literature, technical papers and reprints, trouble shooting, locations, and contact numbers.

Sales representatives who are equipped with the available electronic technology have seen their customer effectiveness and productivity increase. Two short case study situations, one at Compaq Computer and the other at Pioneer Hi-Bred, a specialty farm seed supplier, show how electronic technologies can significantly improve an industrial sales force's efforts to be more effective and efficient.

Case Study #1: Compaq Computer

Compaq Computer Corporation is a $12 billion manufacturer of computers. A few of its products are sold by mass merchandisers, including Wal-Mart, but 90 percent of its sales are to business firms and dealers, where most of their sales force productivity gains have been achieved. Compaq's CEO describes its situation:

> We moved every one of our salespeople into home offices. In the process we also cut our sales force by a third, from 359 to 224 people in North America and saved millions annually in salary, rent, and travel time.

We decided to automate instead of populating the street with more inefficient salespeople. We first asked our customers. Many said they could not find our salespeople, or it took too long to reach a live one. Some of our reps were getting more than 40 voice-mail messages every day. The typical big-company response would be to hire more salespeople. We concluded that all of our existing salespeople were utilizing their time badly.

We shut down four of eight regional offices. Every salesperson's home office was equipped with a portable notebook computer, a 486 processor, a 200-megabyte hard disk, a color monitor, a wide keyboard, a backup drive, and a laser printer. Each home office also got a fax/copier, cellular phone, two phone lines, a desk, a bookshelf, and a credenza. We set up toll-free numbers to answer routine inquiries about products, pricing, and availability, freeing salespeople to focus on developing new business and servicing accounts. We paired inside customer service people with outside sales reps and called it "hunting in pairs"!

Every workday our reps log into our client/server network. The database includes a centralized account listing where Compaq people from different departments record their contact with each current and prospective customer. All customers have market segment codes. The system also contains marketing material, technical reports, application stories, and electronic mail. Sales managers, engineering, customer service, and other staffers can scan the network for updates.

Reps typically download the material they will need for their current day's meetings into a notebook computer or what they call their toolbox. They also have appointments, contacts, telephone numbers, charts, and graphic presentations on their notebook computer. If they want to leave a brochure or schematic with a client, they just produce one on the laptop computer.

When the reps return home, they type and print letters, respond to e-mail, and update the common database with the latest information about current and potential customers. If they need an engineer to follow up with more information, they input the contact's name, and when the engineer looks at his accounts in the database, he'll call the contact.

Automating our sales force and moving them into home offices reduced Compaq's sales, general, and administrative expenses (SG&A). As a result of this lower overhead and, more importantly, higher sales productivity, net income climbed as a percentage of revenues. In fact, we hope to get SG&A down further, making it possible for Compaq to live well amid further price cuts.

Case Study #2: Pioneer Hi-Bred

One of the most automated and better consultative sales forces in the world is found at Pioneer Hi-Bred International Inc., a $2 billion developer and grower of farm seed corn. Pioneer has used its sales force finesse and information technology to become the most profitable and largest corn seed company in the world, with a 45 percent market share in the Americas. Tom Urban, Hi-Bred's chairman and CEO, explained how their electronic sales force works at our annual senior executive workshop:

To begin, Pioneer tracks over 800,000 current customers and prospects in its database for the United States, Canada, and South America — a group responsible for 45 percent of the world's corn production. Our in-house database, which is consistently updated by the sales force, records who runs which farms, how many acres they grow of which crop, what type of seed corn they are currently buying, and who they are buying it from. Another Pioneer software program helps our reps track the yields (customer benefits) from 17,000 plots on which 150 different corn hybrids are grown, providing detailed comparisons of Pioneer seed yields versus the yields of our competitor's seeds. When Pioneer's reps (who are usually all former farmers) meet with customers, they are armed with laptops and printouts of customized reports generated from PCs at their homes. If a farmer doesn't currently plant a Pioneer line, the sales rep's goal is to get the farmer to plant a trial strip of Pioneer seed. The reps use other reports to show how farms with similar conditions have improved their yields with Pioneer.

Every rep can call up our databases to identify any of 50+ hybrids designed for unique soil or climate conditions and resistance to particular diseases or pests. In addition to improving our customer effectiveness, information technology has also dramatically improved the efficiency of our sales reps. Fifteen years ago, each rep typically had 70 to 80 customers. Today they have as many as 300, and they also update all the customer information and process all their orders electronically. We have also significantly reduced the number of first-level sales managers we now have in every country. Largely due to our computer-assisted approach to sales, our sales force productivity has improved each of the last five years.

Relationships Still Matter

Lately, it is not fashionable to talk about relationships in industrial buying situations. We are told it's simply a cold, calculating, and impersonal transaction devoid of people. In a web-based world where electronic connections are replacing some of the previous face-to-face meetings, many industrial marketers are re-thinking their customer relationships. The Internet is a tool that enables a professional salesperson to develop an even closer relationship with multiple people in the buying organization. In the more complex industrial purchases and integrated supply relationships, a host of voice-to-voice and face-to-face issues must be still resolved. Buying organizations still make many of their purchase choices after considering a variety of factors such as consistent quality, technical service, product support, and total costs.

Buying organizations are human and social as well as interested in economics and value. Purchasing people may claim to be motivated by intellect alone, but the professional salesperson knows that most customers run on both reason and emotion. In most industrial sales approaches, suppliers must persuade and then prove that their companies will handle all details as trouble free as possible. If well done, an effective relationship with a given supplier can be more important than the lowest price and little or no service. Few industrial buyers and sellers are connected by electronics alone. Most industrial organizations buy from people and suppliers that they trust and respect and who will go the extra mile for them.

Industrial suppliers frequently have to package or configure the most cost-effective solution for each customer. Trusted personal contacts, uncovering unmet needs, running field trials, and agreeing to specific solutions and supply contracts are not done on the Internet. E-mail and negotiations are most successful when the parties have a preexisting relationship. Successful problem solving and two-way dialogs develop trust. An increasing number of customers prefer to buy a total solution to their needs from one supplier, sometimes called systems contracts or integrated supply. More suppliers are responding with annual contracts as a marketing tool to secure existing business and develop new accounts. Professional salespeople still manage the overall process while electronic connections help speed up and streamline the process. However, we must remember that just schmoozing and socializing with customers today is no longer enough for any customer relationship to endure.

PRINCIPLE 7: LINK COMPENSATION TO BUSINESS GOALS

Many sales compensation arrangements work at cross-purposes to management's overall businesses objectives. For example, many companies still pay their sales representatives totally or largely on the basis of their sales volume, even though achieving a richer price or product mix, opening new accounts, or developing certain end-use markets and account profitability may be an equally or more important objective in terms of ultimate success in the marketplace. But what person in his or her right mind would spend time on longer-term sales development activities when the payoff is simply for volume taken today? Also, who would spend a lot of time negotiating value for a higher price when volume is the pay lever? Furthermore, who wouldn't constantly complain to headquarters that prices are too high when lower prices could provide a basis for meeting a quota based only on sales revenue or unit volume?

Setting Goals

Setting goals for a sales force has traditionally meant just setting sales revenue quotas. The quotas are usually expressed in sales volume and are too often dictated from the top down by a regional or national sales manager. The salesperson and his or her supervisor should mutually develop sales goals. *Any sales goal that is based purely on sales volume is wrong.* One-dimensional sales goals based solely on volume can undermine the profit and other goals of any business. If salespeople are rewarded solely on the basis of volume, they will focus on the largest customers and then negotiate the lowest possible unit price. Of course sales volume must be in every salesperson's goals but there must also be goals in other areas, such as territory and account profitability, new business, customer trials, new product sales, customer satisfaction ratings, and distributor management (where appropriate).

The role of sales management is to develop the appropriate multiple goals and weights for each salesperson. The multiple goals typically include sales volume, some measure of profit, new product sales, target markets, and new business at existing or new accounts. The switch to some of a person's pay being tied to profits is intended to stop salespeople from cutting deals that hurt his or her employer. Intense discussions usually occur when deciding how much of the pay should be tied to profits and if or where it should be capped. When IBM first moved its 30,000 salespeople from a pure-volume goal to pay-for-profit, only 6 percent of the compensation package was tied to account and territory profitability. Very little behavior change occurred. IBM's commissions are now based 60 percent on profitability, 40 percent on customer satisfaction, and 0 percent on sales. Customers are surveyed to determine how satisfied or unsatisfied they are with the local sales team. One of Hewlett-Packard's sales forces, which compete against IBM, pays its people a variable commission of up to 55 percent. My belief is that at least 40 percent of the variable pay should be tied to profit to encourage sales reps to behave more like businesspeople and less like bounty hunters chasing volume. Tying incentive payments to gross margin dollars generated is another way to pay salespeople. It links both volume and a profit measure into the account, and it's easy to explain and measure. An increasing number of companies require each salesperson to have at least an annual gross profit goal for each account and territory, and some leaders track the cost to service each account, and measure and pay salespeople based on net customer profitability.

Sharing Cost-Profit Information

Part and parcel of any sales compensation package tied to profits is the need to widely share product and customer profit information with the front-line salespeople. Salespeople need to know how much profit they are making, or giving up, at every account and on each transaction.

Without product-line and customer profit information, salespeople have little reason to care about how profitable an account may be. When a salesperson knows the margin on various products and the past and potential profit prospects at every account, they can rationalize services, emphasize the higher margin products, and better manage account profitability. I often hear managers say, "You can't trust salespeople with profit information," or "They will tell or go to the competition with the information." From my thirty years of experience, *competitors don't hire salespeople for profit information, they hire them for their customer contacts, product knowledge, application know-how, and professional selling skills.* Salespeople, like all other employees, must be trusted, empowered with information to make decisions, and evaluated as a businessperson. It makes good sense to drive profitability measures down into the sales force, giving reps the same accountability as middle management. Salespeople simply must have access to financial information about the business and their customers to do this. I also strongly suggest that each salesperson's territory be managed as a profit center-account by account and in total for his or her territory.

Sales Salaries

In some cases, sales salaries are so high relative to the incentive opportunity that incentive really doesn't mean much. Many companies have drifted into this situation by steadily granting salary increases instead of holding salaries constant at some level and increasing incentive opportunities. The company is then locked into higher structured sales costs that are tough to swallow when volume turns down and, more importantly, that make the salesperson too comfortable even if sales goals are not achieved. In other situations, the incentive is so small that it doesn't motivate the high performer. Many company bonus plans for salespeople are seen as inequitable and unfair. Most salespeople want some form of variable pay or gain sharing from the business unit, but many of these same people don't want pain sharing or a reduction in pay when the business unit doesn't do as well.

Commissions

The idea of earning a commission on sales appeals to many aggressive people and has a lot of merit in many situations. However, some commission arrangements that start paying off on the first dollar of sales encourage sales representatives to "skim the cream" or "cherry pick" from the territory by concentrating on quick volume from accounts-when the emphasis should be placed on developing the potential in the more profitable accounts. Several salespeople from one company that sold chemicals freely admitted that they set a daily volume quota for themselves that would yield enough commission to meet their standard of living. They were very comfortable with a lower, but adequate, income, and frequently bypassed new business that required more development in preference to sure-thing orders. The company had to get these people out of their comfort zone. In order to prevent salespeople from coasting for part of the year, a few companies have changed the bonus period from once a year to every six months or quarterly.

Seniority-Based Compensation

Other compensation systems are designed in such a way that they reward seniority rather than performance. This entitlement arrangement has a double-edged effect: Senior people relax their efforts, and young, aggressive people become frustrated, back off, or go to competitors. A company that competed in the semiconductor equipment market provides a classic example:

> Incentive payments were made out of a group bonus pot, and each person's award
> was based on a percentage of his or her salary. Since no adjustment was made to

reflect individual performance and since senior people tended to have higher salaries based upon automatic annual increases, many hard-working younger people became discouraged and left. Equally important, when management looked into the situation, it found that many of the senior salespeople were relying on the younger people to build up the pot and thus were not pulling their own weight.

Team or Group Incentives

Many industrial buying situations require that management, technical, customer service, and office staffs all work together to serve customers; thus, incentives and recognition systems for just the outside salespeople can de-motivate other members of the customer service team. As companies form sales teams or cross-functional groups to serve key accounts, the sales rep becomes more of an account leader and less of an account manager. In such team-selling situations, all team members should participate in the rewards and recognition. When everyone has a share of the rewards, healthy peer-group pressure comes into play. Less supervision is needed when work teams have group incentives. Self-managed sales teams take on tasks such as scheduling people and equipment that are traditionally done by supervisors. Team-based sales incentives motivate people to help each other and share ideas and information. Such informal work teams often already exist among sales, technical, and customer service people.

Every compensation plan has weaknesses, and some team compensation plans allow the lower-performing individuals to receive the same rewards as the heavy contributors. But, over time, peer-group pressures help many people improve their performance, and the team composition may eventually have to be changed. The sales team members may even have a hand in hiring and disciplining team members. Where everyone in the business unit or division has an incentive based on the profit return of his or her unit, individual and team-based performance is aligned. When team-based incentives do exist, it is necessary to share all sales, profit, customer satisfaction, and productivity information with all the employees in the business unit. In short, team-based incentives make everyone serving the customer work like a business owner and less like a hired hand.

Tailor the Objectives

In many cases, sales executives are so concerned with keeping their compensation plan simple that they fail to take into account key variables that affect sales performance. It is not at all uncommon to hear executives say something like, "We know our sales compensation plan is not right, but it is simple and we don't have any difficulty getting our salespeople to understand and believe it." In other cases, executives feel that once a system is in place, it should not be changed because the sales force will become confused or suspicious. Of course, making changes in midstream that are unfair to the salespeople should be avoided at all costs. But the fact is that business objectives do change frequently, and unless the compensation system is adjusted to reflect these changes, it is certain to drift out of phase with the company's business and marketing goals.

There is no way to prescribe a compensation plan that is right for everyone. However, every compensation system should be designed around five areas:

1. Achieve monthly, quarterly, and annual sales and profit objectives from direct sales, and, where relevant, for distributor sales. (No plan should ever just include sales volume.)
2. Ensure a balanced selling job by paying for new account openings, new applications, new product introductions, and other sales development activities essential to strengthen the company's short- and long-term market position.

3. Provide an attractive entry level for new salespeople, who will then provide adequate raw material to build the kind of organization necessary to achieve marketing objectives.

4. Provide an attractive earnings opportunity for career sales representatives so that there is a cadre of highly skilled, trained, and motivated people to serve as the cutting edge of the sales effort.

5. Draw a sharp distinction between the rewards for average and outstanding salespeople and the penalties for below-average performers.

PRINCIPLE 8: DEVELOP A SALES CAREER LADDER

A highly respected, professional, and high-performing consultative salesperson is absolutely essential for any industrial business that wants to sustain sales and profit growth. And those people who love the daily challenge and freedom of industrial sales and do it very well should not have to change careers in their company or go to a competitor for advancement and higher remuneration. Unfortunately, *many industrial companies have no sales career path* or pay steps based on expertise and performance within their sales organizations. Sales for many industrial companies are too often a dead-end street. This problem is usually greater in Europe than in the United States because many European industrial companies have not recognized the need for a really professional and high-performance sales force with matching pay grades and perks. A few progressive companies have developed a career ladder for professional salespeople (see Exhibit 7-2). Any advancement up the sales ladder should be based on performance and not just longevity or seniority. Pay grades should be related to each "step" in the career ladder.

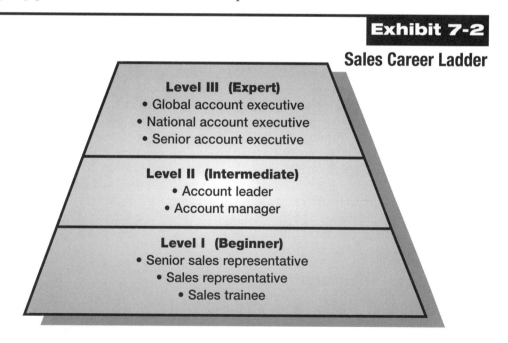

Exhibit 7-2
Sales Career Ladder

Level III (Expert)
- Global account executive
- National account executive
- Senior account executive

Level II (Intermediate)
- Account leader
- Account manager

Level I (Beginner)
- Senior sales representative
- Sales representative
- Sales trainee

PRINCIPLE 9: PROVIDE FIRST-LINE SUPERVISION

As companies equip sales representatives with more electronically automated information and empower them in decision making, it is less necessary for them to frequently report to a sales manager for permission or authorization. Furthermore, with the use of laptop computers, electronic mail and networks, faxes, and portable phones, the reps have less need to be in a traditional sales office, and the span of management control can also increase for sales managers. When the salesperson is able to obtain customer data and cost-profit information from a computer, develop training sessions through computers, and use e-mail or voice mail direct from headquarters, the sales manager's position as a communication conduit, data analyst, and information source has significantly changed. The more sales reps a sales manager has reporting to him or her (often from cars or home offices), the less face-to-face contact time he or she has to spend with each salesperson. In the old inefficient days, one sales manager for every four to six sales reps was needed; today there may be eight or twelve salespeople per sales manager.

However, most sales executives agree that *strong, first-line sales supervision is still a key ingredient* in their efforts to build an outstanding sales organization. The sales force is typically made up of a cross section of men and women with widely diverse backgrounds, experience levels, and perceptions; many are separated from headquarters by thousands of miles. The first-line supervisor is the only manager physically close enough to them to define and interpret company policy, direct their week-to-week efforts, and coach them in the company's marketing and sales approach for various products, markets, and customers.

Conflicting Demands

In some cases, the performance of first-line supervisors falls short because their jobs are structured such that they are supervisors in name only. They are really only super-salespeople or bureaucratic administrators, with the bulk of their effort focused on direct selling activities and/or paperwork.

I know of one company that relied on its branch sales managers to handle the first-level supervisory role. Each manager was expected not only to watch over four or five salespeople but also to take on a full sales territory of his or her own as well. The results were not at all what management expected. The branch managers spent the greater part of their time selling and developing their own territories, and thus they provided little, if any, real supervision for their sales forces. Actually, this should not have been surprising—any time good salespeople must choose between doing the sales job that is second nature to them and carrying out the difficult tasks inherent in any managerial role, they tend to take the path that is easiest and most enjoyable. My experience shows that most people who have a combined sales/supervisory role quite naturally and honestly get so deeply involved in their own direct selling activities that they have little time for the coaching, training, and follow-up activities that are the heart of the supervisor's job.

I am not suggesting that it is totally inappropriate for a sales manager to have any direct sales or account responsibility. In fact, a good case can be made that every sales manager should have some account sales responsibility to keep current with selling approaches and customer requirements. But this responsibility must be limited so that it does not take up a disproportionate amount of the manager's time.

Inadequate Preparation

In other cases, first-line sales managers fail to perform well because they do not know what the supervisory role is or how it should be carried out. This is frequently not their fault; surprisingly few companies provide any kind of training programs to help new supervisors learn how to perform their new responsibilities. Most sales managers need training in the sales management process that represents the heart of their job. In particular, they need to be shown the following:

1. How to make account, territory, market, or distributor analyses and determine sales volume and profit potentials.

2. How to administer sales compensation and incentive programs.
3. How to evaluate the performance of their sales personnel or distributors, identify training and development needs, and determine who can and cannot improve.
4. How to select new hires and dismiss poor performers.

In some cases, former star salespeople can never make the transition to manager, no matter how much training is provided. Often those who fail in this category are allowed to stay in their supervisory positions far too long. Eventually, the management career path becomes clogged with people who are going nowhere. Understandably, this frustrates the outstanding younger salespeople looking for early promotion and inevitably leads to a high turnover of people who should not be lost. A vicious circle ensues, resulting in mediocrity at the supervisory level and ineffective training and direction for the sales force. The sales career ladder, suggested earlier, would alleviate some of the problems.

Excessive Paperwork

In many companies, the call report sent weekly to headquarters is sacred because it gives management a feeling that they are on top of what is going on in the field. More than likely, however, all management has is a massive paper flow that is useless to headquarters personnel. Many companies look to their call reporting system as a reliable means of control. In reality, however, some salespeople simply go through the motions of filling out their forms while spending their time as they please. Clearly, some type of planning and control system is desirable in every sales organization, but it should be designed around a weekly or monthly cycle to minimize the paperwork. Also, it should primarily help the salesperson plan his or her time and set priorities. It should not be designed as an elaborate system for centralized control or Big Brother intimidation.

A good call report captures the right account information and meets three criteria:

1. They are easily generated and updated on a laptop computer that is networked to many databases.
2. Call reports should clearly identify all the contacts at the account and identify the market segment and applications, competitive purchases, and your company's historical sales at the account.
3. Finally, the critical issues or problems at the account, the status of trials, and the next step should all be clearly communicated.

A sound call report is vital feedback that summarizes the important issues at the account. The benefits of a good call report extend beyond the reports themselves. If a sales rep is transferred, injured, resigns, or dies, such complete and automated information can give a new rep a big edge at the account by not having to spend time reconstructing the vital information.

PRINCIPLE 10: DETERMINE THEIR BUSINESS PLANNING ROLE

The top sales management of any industrial company-that is, the national sales manager and his or her subordinates, who typically have responsibility for sales results in various geographic regions or market segments-should play an important role in the entire business planning process. They should be an integral part of any cross-functional team set up for any important strategic assignment. In developing target market plans, front-line sales reps experienced with accounts in the market segment should participate in the business planning process. Their participation is essential to ensure that the company's product and market plans accurately reflect the customers' needs.

It is also essential to gain the wholehearted commitment of sales management for the successful execution of the company's overall target market plans. If the sales force is enthusiastic about the plan and genuinely believes it can sell the volume and mix that is expected, it will do a good job. If the salespeople feel that sales expectations are unrealistic, or that unfair sales goals have been imposed on them, morale will suffer, and the plan will not be achieved. It is not unusual for sales representatives and field supervisors to charge, "Our sales goals have no rhyme nor reason and have nothing to do with the marketplace. They are just 10 to 15 percent higher than last year." With this attitude, how can they be expected to do all the hard work necessary to achieve demanding sales targets?

Considering the importance of sales performance to the success of target market plans, it is only logical to give sales management a real voice in the development of these plans. At the least, sales managers should be included in the following activities:

- Closing the feedback loop from the field by distilling and interpreting information on user requirements, local market conditions, competitive standing, and expected sales at key accounts.
- Discussing sales needs and opportunities with other functional managers and recommending alternative actions to build or defend the business overall and at key accounts.
- Participating in cross-functional discussions to evaluate the commitments and programs required to carry out various options and to weigh these against expected results.
- Agreeing on realistic volume and share of market targets under various options and helping to decide which options are most attractive.
- Suggesting product-line gaps and evaluating the merits of specific product development and acquisition candidates.
- Helping identify lead users for product development, schedule team interviews, field trials, and launch new products.

The experience of Owens-Corning Fiberglas, a large company serving the building products field, proves that significant results and improvements can accrue from tying the sales managers more directly into the business planning process. The top executives of this company were very concerned about a general deterioration in the company's sales effectiveness. Share position in traditional markets was slipping badly, and important new markets were emerging in which the company had no position at all. The company's product edge had been lost, and new product developments were not coming along, as they should. Finally, sales costs were increasing steadily, while productivity (i.e., average sales per salesperson) was trending downward. In short, the current situation was bad and the outlook worse.

In recognition of the seriousness of the situation, the general manager called in the product managers and key sales managers for an emergency planning session. Including sales management in the planning session was more of an afterthought than anything else because planning had traditionally been an isolated headquarters function while sales had responsibility for execution. To the general manager's surprise, the most imaginative and effective ideas came from the sales managers closest to the target markets. They recommended product modifications that could be made quickly, well before new products could become available to meet important needs of emerging markets. In addition, they suggested dropping a collection of low-profit products so that manufacturing could be simplified, the sales force cut back, territories enlarged, inside salespeople added, and overall productivity increased. These sales managers also proposed a volume discount plan that would provide the basis for recapturing business that had been lost with large customers while still preserving the integrity of the company's pricing structure. The general manager and the product managers were so impressed with the contributions made by the sales managers that they made it a regular practice to include them in planning sessions from that point on.

SUMMARY

Clearly, a host of things must be done to build an outstanding industrial sales force. Much has been written about the importance of motivating salespeople, territory layout, selling skills, and other important considerations for industrial selling. I have taken a different approach by emphasizing ten management principles that enable the sales force to function as consultative problem solvers and businesspeople and be at the cutting edge of a market-driven management team. I have found that these management principles equally apply to independent distributors or dealers that market a manufacturer's products. When management follows these principles, all the other activities necessary to make the sales force an effective implementation arm will be carried out as well. Neglecting any one of these ten principles will jeopardize the success of the business, no matter how well other sales activities are performed.

In nearly every company, implementation requires overcoming long-standing traditions and mind-sets. Extensive training of sales managers and salespeople alike is mandatory, and some personnel changes must eventually be made. However, all of these efforts are clearly worthwhile because failure to manage the sales force according to these management principles can cost a company a fortune in lost market opportunities and excessive selling costs. Many successful industrial companies have taken a hard look at their selling effort and have made the changes necessary to build these principles into their sales organization. In so doing, they have converted their volume and order-taking sales force into a respected consultative selling organization. This, in turn, has given these companies power in the marketplace to significantly strengthen their competitive positions and sustain sales and profit growth.

[1] "Mild-Mannered Hewlett-Packard is Making like Superman," Business Week, March 7, 1998, p. 111.

Working with Industrial Distributors

"One of the most difficult challenges facing manufacturing executives is distributor relationships."

Don Fites, Chairman and CEO
Caterpillar, Inc.

Most industrial manufacturers market a portion of their products with partners called distributors, or dealers. A significant percentage of the GDP every year is marketed through independent distributors. However, the marketing of products through distributors is frequently badly handled, and the results are often poor for both manufacturers and distributors.

Industrial manufacturers too often see marketing with distributors as an afterthought that does not get sufficient attention, resources, or competent people. Far too many industrial firms see the distributor as merely an intermediary for pushing products through and are continually disappointed with this means of serving end-use customers. Some manufacturers unfortunately see their distributors as customers rather than as partners serving a common customer.

Many industrial manufacturers treat their distributors as stepchildren and fail to get the cooperation they need to capitalize on the distributors' sale and profit potential when large amounts of profits are at stake. The same manufacturers often use bullying or brinkmanship tactics to achieve their goals without regard to the distributor's needs. Few manufacturing executives understand how distributors make and lose money. The result is a relationship that is far from a sound partnership. Other manufacturers go to the other extreme and become totally dependent on what distributors do or don't do in the marketplace. This inevitably results in little or no knowledge of end-use customers and their changing requirements-and frequently places the manufacturer at a serious competitive disadvantage.

WHY USE DISTRIBUTORS?

Industrial giants, including 3M, Caterpillar, Loctite, Parker Hannifin, and Mead Paper, market a major portion of their yearly sales volume through distributors. To counter competition from Japanese photocopy machine manufacturers, both IBM and Xerox contracted with independent distributors to market PCs, copiers and printers. Why do all of these companies use distributors? The reasons are clear: The cost to the manufacturer of making direct calls is frequently prohibitive in relation to the service needs of certain customers. In fragmented markets with many smaller users, distributors are the only cost-effective way for the manufacturer to serve these markets. The demand for just in-time (JIT) deliveries from customers requires frequent deliveries, and a local stocking distributor is well positioned to provide this service. Furthermore, if customers want to reorder or repair an item, they often want rapid service and delivery which is usually best provided by a local distributor who buys and maintains a local stock of products to sell and service customers. Furthermore, a good distributor can differentiate "me too" products with excellent customer service.

In the aftermarket or maintenance, repair, and operations (MRO) market, the industrial distributor is often the vital link between the manufacturer and users. When a bearing or hydraulic cylinder needs repair, the user usually wants the repair done in a hurry. Parts availability and rapid service are critical and usually best provided by a local distributor with the appropriate inventory (see the accompanying box). For more technically complex customer needs, the industrial distributor will be called to help solve specific problems, perform fabrication, or install an item. Technical service, or "engineering in the field," is vital product support to ensure repeat purchases for many industrial products.

Why Caterpillar Uses Distributors

Most people think of Caterpillar as a company known for making machines that are big and yellow. But Caterpillar dealers that sell, support, and maintain the equipment provide vital value to customers. Because of the importance of rapid repair, parts delivery, and field services in the construction equipment industry, Caterpillar believes local distributors can best serve local customers. Caterpillar is not just selling machinery; it sees itself as marketing equipment, parts, and service to support its products. The local distributor provides the basis for achieving maximum uptime or minimum downtime for very expensive machines. When a $300,000 machine is down because of a $50 part, every hour represents a significant loss of money to the user. To minimize downtime and the resulting financial loss to customers, local Caterpillar distributors carry parts for all Caterpillar equipment-including parts for equipment Caterpillar hasn't manufactured for the last 30 years.

When a Caterpillar road grader was an integral part of a road resurfacing crew in the Arizona desert, the breakdown of the grader idled four other pieces of road-building equipment, seven asphalt trucks, and twenty workers. The local Caterpillar dealer sent a radio-dispatched repair unit to the field with the appropriate parts for that model road grader. The 2.5-hour downtime could have been days had there not been a local distributor with the right parts in its inventory ready to provide prompt service.

Exhibit 8-1 shows the important *intermediate role* between manufacturers and users played by industrial distributors. Marketing with a distributor can save the user time and money in terms of the item's purchase price. Industrial distributors can reduce the manufacturer's selling cost and thereby reduce the selling price of the product to users. Thus, paying the distributor a profit is not always the same as paying a "double profit." If the functions performed by the distributor are shifted, they must be performed and paid for by the manufacturer or the user. When distributors perform these functions cost effectively and competitively, customers' benefit, and the distributors are entitled to a profit for their efforts. If distributors are not effective and competitive, the manufacturer may choose to serve the account direct or via e-commerce. However, while the Internet provides an intriguing and lower cost way to serve many markets and customers, manufacturers should not quickly abandon their existing distributors.

Exhibit 8-1

Distributors Link Manufacturers to Users

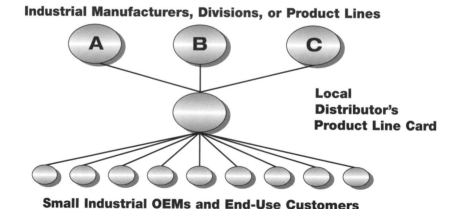

In many corporations, several different divisions often manufacture complementary products that are sold to common customers. In these situations, it is advantageous for the manufacturer to sell through a common distributor network. This enables the distributor to become a single source-shopping place where a customer can buy all related requirements. Just-in-time procurement and vender-managed inventory, and integrated supply contracts are well suited to local distributors. These all allow the distributor to provide more value. The common distributor concept has provided a focus to some manufacturers' acquisition and product development activities as they grow their company around an existing distributor network.

WHEN TO USE DISTRIBUTORS

The industrial manufacturer must decide which of its products and accounts are better served by a distributor than by direct sales. Several factors need to be considered. If any one of the following criteria is not characteristic of the product or market being served, the product should probably be sold to users directly by the manufacturer and not by distributors.

Stockable Standard Products

Most of the product line should be able to be stocked and serviced locally. This implies that catalog items manufactured in large quantities and sold locally off-the-shelf a few at a time are well-suited for distributors. Products used for maintenance, repair, and operations (MRO) are especially suited for distributor sales. Most custom-designed parts, specialty chemicals, and machinery, which are made to order, are easily eliminated as possibilities for distributors. In some special situations, a stocking distributor will place the order, do the paperwork, and offer credit while the manufacturer ships directly to the user rather than to the distributor's warehouse. In these "drop ship" situations, in which the distributor acts more like an agent than a stocking distributor, the manufacturer usually pays the distributor less commission than if the item were stocked by the distributor and sold from his or her inventory.

Small Purchase Quantities

Items selling for a few dollars are the most likely distributor products to be sold off-the-shelf. Nearly all MRO replacement parts fall in this category. If the yearly purchase volume of an OEM is large, it is usually not served through a distributor. Smaller OEM purchases are usually assigned to distributors to service. For example, bearings are used in tractors, motors, and machines. When they wear out, they need to be replaced in the aftermarket. The small unit dollar purchase rule also applies to heavy equipment items like construction machinery and trucks. The customer buys one or a few at a time and is often buying on the basis of service and parts availability. Repair parts for original equipment are nearly always of smaller unit dollar value than the new equipment. Many manufacturers have a minimum order size or minimum annual purchase amount to distinguish between a direct or distributor account.

Many Smaller Customers

The broader or more fragmented the customer base with standard product requirements, the greater the need for a distributor network. A market with many hundreds or thousands of users each buying at little at a time is usually better served by distributors. However, in most market segments, there are usually some large users that might be better served directly. For example, Navistar serves the large truck-fleet buyer directly, and the smaller owner-operator is required to buy through an authorized Navistar dealer. If only a handful of customers will ever buy the product, it is unlikely that a distributor will do as satisfactory a job as the direct sales approach to users. Manufacturers usually cannot sell custom-tailored products with distributors. For example, one company's special gasket product designed for customers' unique requirements was given to distributors to sell. Existing business rapidly declined, and virtually no new accounts were created. After several years, it became clear that the distributors received repeat orders only from the customers originally secured by the manufacturer's direct salespeople.

Rapid Availability

One of the most important factors is the need for rapid service, which is often stated in hours rather than days, weeks, or months. If the product is needed immediately because of equipment breakdown or operating supply shortage, the customer needs the item as quickly as possible. The driving force behind rapid delivery is also how practical it is to plan the purchase. The cost of downtime for an oil-drilling rig is more than $250 a minute; the downtime on an automotive engine assembly line is more than $200,000 an hour. Minutes can be a matter of life and death when a hospital operating room needs a small piece of surgical tubing or parts for a life-support machine. The waiting time of these customers is very short. These customers normally prefer immediate or very fast delivery. In all these situations, the greater the downtime, the more costly the situation and the greater the need for prompt service and delivery from local distributors with the needed items in inventory.

Product Support

Technical support to install, troubleshoot, or repair the item is critical to many products purchased from a distributor. This is sometimes called service backup. The greater the need for local product support, the more important the distributor is. Product support also includes pre- and post-sales counseling, selection and application of the product, operator training, repair, credit, and delivery and pickup. If you cannot service what you sell, you will eventually sell fewer products. Fast product support minimizes downtime. Superior customer service is a combination of product availability and technical support. A manufacturer may have an excellent product and/or a competitive price, but if good product support is missing from a local distributor, the end-user may buy from another distributor who provides better service.

MARKETING CHANNEL CHOICES

In order to achieve various market, sales, and profit goals, industrial manufacturers have to choose between different distribution options. The major choices industrial goods producers make include the relative balance between direct sales and through intermediaries, the type of intermediary in terms of each market and the relative intensity of distribution needed by geographic area.

There are four commonly used channels to serve market segments with products and services. The four basic channels are: **1)** direct sales to end-users; **2)** with industrial distributors to end-users; **3)** with manufacturer's reps to end-users; or **4)** with manufacturer's reps and distributors to end-users. Most industrial manufactures use a combination of these four approaches to achieve various product/market goals. Exhibit 8-2, titled "Going to Market," shows an overview of the channel alternatives for serving different markets and different sized customers. This framework enables managers to think through how they might market specific products to different market segments, evaluate the advantages and disadvantages of each channel and identify the present and potential conflicts between various channels.

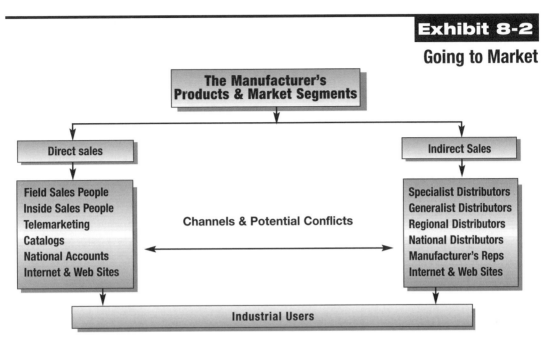

Exhibit 8-2

Going to Market

Industrial marketing channels have anywhere between zero to three levels of intermediates between the manufacturer and the end-user. Information technology also allows manufacturers to shorten the number of levels in their selling chains, even if it might risk alienating some partners. Information technology puts more speed in the channel and usually lowers the procurement, transaction and inventory costs. If the manufacturer maintains one or more regional warehouses, one could argue that they constitute another level and inventory in any warehouse is a high cost. Exhibit 8-3 shows the common levels of industrial marketing channels.

Exhibit 8-3

Industrial Marketing Channel Levels

Finally, when considering different ways to go to market it is usually helpful to draw a schematic of how the industry goes to market. For example, before Honeywell made any changes in their distribution strategy and policies, they developed Exhibit 8-4, a schematic for the climate control industry. Honeywell determined what specific products and quantities were sold direct to other manufacturers (OEMs), contractors, and owner-operators. The current and changing role to serve these users was further analyzed by determining whether direct sales, distributors, or manufacturers' reps were best for certain products and types of customers/market segments. Honeywell also used the schematic to identify where the specifications were developed in each channel. Such a schematic also helps to develop policies that will reduce the amount of conflict among partners in the channels.

Exhibit 8-4

Multiple Industrial Marketing Channels

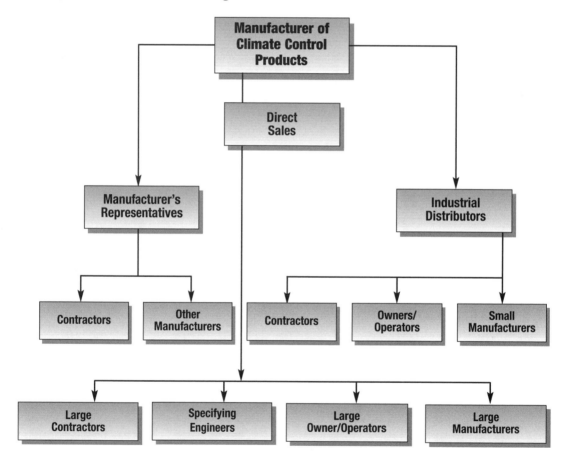

A manufacturer's channel strategy is part of the overall business stategy and as such should be developed within the context of the business unit's plan. A sound channel strategy first requires defined market segmentation and market facts about each segment's potential and your market share. Before developing a channel strategy, you must also understand the current industry trade practices, the process of specification writing, and how information technology can link partners in the channel.

TYPES OF CHANNEL PARTNERS

After a company has determined which customers and markets are best suited for distribution, they must determine what type of partners are needed, the available intermediaries, and the responsibilities of each channel partner. The industry practice, the products to be marketed, the market potential and the availability of channel partners in each geographic area determine the choice of channel partner. There are six different types of channel partners to choose from:

1. *Manufacturer's Reps or Agencies.* They usually have an exclusive territory and/or segment. They carry no inventory and are paid a commission on sales. They usually represent complementary lines, but not competitive products. Some manufacturer's reps are very specialized and technically competent in a market segment. Smaller manufacturer's tend to use reps to a greater degree, but larger producers recognize their value in certain industries and market segments.

2. *Exclusive Distribution.* They have a designated geographic area of prime responsibility, sometimes called an "APR," with no other distributor authorized to do business in the protected territory. These stocking distributors usually agree to not carry competitive lines. By granting an exclusive, the producer hopes to maintain more dedicated and knowledgeable selling. Some of those distributors are quite specialized. Exclusive distribution recognizes geographic territories, but usually not market segments.

3. *Dual Distribution.* Two distributors share the same geographic territory. For example, in a large city like Los Angeles or Frankfurt, the traveling time between distributor locations may be better served by having one other distributor in the region. If the exclusive distributor opens another branch location in the large metropolitan area, there may not be a need for dual distribution.

4. *Parallel Distribution.* In this situation, the distributor has an exclusive territory for a specific market segment(s) and specific products. For example, the Pall Corporation has a filter specialist for the petro-chemical markets in New Jersey and in the same New Jersey territory they have a biomedical filtration distributor who only serves that market segment. The parallel approach recognizes market segment differences within geographic territories. As a result, this approach often generates more market segment penetration in a defined region rather than just granting exclusive geographic coverage.

5. *Multiple Distribution.* There is no exclusive protection in these situations. In any given geographic area, there are multiple stocking distributors carrying the same product line. More intensive geographic and market coverage is the goal of this approach. There may be a combination of specialized and general line distributors in the same territory carrying the same manufacturer's products. In large metropolitan areas, multiple distribution is a common strategy.

6. *Internet Distribution.* Though still in its infancy, e-commerce has the potential for manufacturers to sell more customers directly without middlemen. This is called the threat of disintermediation. However, distributors with Web sites and the Internet are also offering e-commerce to their customers. Standard parts and catalog type items are most suitable to marketing on Internet channels.

DISTRIBUTOR RELATIONSHIPS

The relationship between manufacturers and distributors is always tenuous. Concerns about trust, loyalty, and fairness are forever present in the relationship. Because most manufacturers are larger than distributors and control the product and contract agreement, many distributors are paranoid in the relationships with many of the manufacturers they represent. Threats of cancellation, less product support, smaller territories, and even cancellations, are always possibilities. Some manufacturers and distributors see each other as competitors or enemies servicing customers. E-business is adding to the tension between manufacturers and distributors.

Why Difficult?

The relationship between a manufacturer and a distributor is one of the most difficult in business. Part of the difficulty stems from the fact that a distributor is both a partner and a customer. Distributors must be seen first as business partners and second as customers. If the manufacturer does not see distributors as partners first, they will be *selling to them* rather than *working with them*. When a manufacturer's field people are paid by what a distributor purchases rather than what a distributor sells to users, many conflicts result, including loading the distributor with slow moving items. A large number of manufacturers are openly and strongly "antidistribution," and their direct selling mentality gets in the way of working with distributors as partners. Manufacturers' attitudes toward distributors range from seeing them as unnecessary evils to customers we sell to, and only a few managers correctly see distributors as partners to serve a common end customer. The following statement by a marketing manager with a major chemical company captures the essence of this all too common problem:

> Since I've taken over this job, I've experienced a lot of difficulty in putting together an acceptable distribution system. Traditionally, our products have been sold direct to end-users. This worked well when all of our customers were large-volume purchasers. Within the last ten years, there's been a dramatic increase in the number of small accounts using the product, causing our firm to alter its strategy and sell through distributors. Sure, the prospects of added sales are fantastic, but listen to some of the problems we face: The discount system is falling apart because distributors are "giving away" portions of their discounts in the form of lower prices to gain business. Unfortunately, some distributors are even being forced into mergers and selling their business. Our distributor in northern California is just cherry picking the low hanging fruit; the Cleveland distributor is not utilizing our co-op funds properly. Although we have two distributors in Chicago, their sales are far below our market share goals; perhaps more distributors are needed there, our distributor in Atlanta only emphasizes part of our product range; and our distributor in northern New Jersey won't tell us who he's selling our products to. Top management of our division feels that these difficulties can be eliminated through a return to aggressive direct sales. I'm not so sure we can make any money that way with these smaller accounts.

Many distributor networks have been put together on a random basis that results in poor or no coverage in some markets and overlapping coverage in others. In most industrial companies, mergers and acquisitions have created overlapping distributorships in some territories and market segments. In most situations, there are nearly always too many marginal distributors. The comment of a progressive coated abrasives distributor in southern California shows the problems that can result from this kind of approach:

> They signed up anybody and anywhere in Los Angeles for so long that we all felt they were not really serious about distributors. Then they make product line acquisitions without considering the effect on their existing distributor network. I now get slow inventory turns from their line, and if the large margin wasn't there and they didn't have new products to sell, I'd drop them tomorrow.

Cultural Differences

There are many cultural differences between an industrial manufacturing business and an industrial distribution business. The two key words that separate most manufacturers from distributors are *bureaucracy* and *entrepreneur.*

The entrepreneurial industrial distributor will work with a manufacturer and follow its lead if properly coached. However, the distributor will never work for a manufacturer in a subordinate relationship. The industrial distributor is not typically an "organization person." In fact, the personality, speed, and independence of the distributor are often in direct contrast to the manufacturer's tendency to be slower moving, risk adverse, and more bureaucratic. Brent Grover, president of National Paper and Packaging, a major disributor, said it well: "Most distributors are fiercely independent small-business people. No supplier or manufacturer is going to tell us how to run our business!"

It is useful to examine the question of the distributor's independence more carefully, because it is such an important factor in any manufacturer-distributor relationship. Although manufacturers and distributors would seem to have the same objectives in terms of achieving sales and market share, their priorities are often different and even incompatible. To start with, the distributor is typically dealing with its own money and incurs all the risk, whereas the manufacturer has many stockholders, so the risk is syndicated. A slow-paying customer or bad debt is painful to any distributor. Most large companies' employees are immune to aging accounts receivable. The cost-profit structures of manufacturers and distributors are typically quite different. The manufacturer generally has a relatively high capital and fixed-cost base and a longer-term business horizon. It is interested in building volume, even at lower margins, to gain profit leverage after covering its fixed costs. The distributor's operation, however, is totally different. The distributor operates a buy-sell business with a low fixed capital cost and is interested in maximizing profit on each dollar of sales over as short a time period as possible. These economic and time differences help explain the different business orientation and value system that make the whole concept of working with distributor partners a lot easier to talk about than accomplish.

The successful distributor can afford to be independent. He or she can probably secure a competitive line if he or she is threatened or sees the possibility of a better relationship with another manufacturer. But their independence notwithstanding, distributor activities must be managed like any other business function. To develop, improve, and continually refine an effective distributor network always involves hard and uncomfortable work, and many industrial executives do not have the will, skills, or personality to do this job. Exhibit 8-5 shows there is often a "we versus they" relationship between manufacturers and distributors. The goal is to create a larger area of common interest so both can profitably grow together. The manufacturer must take the lead role to enlarge the area of common interest.

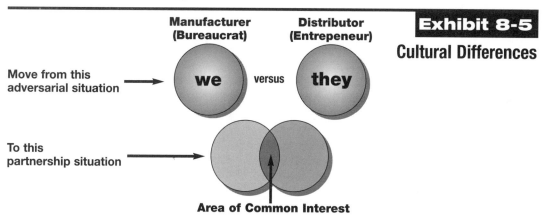

Manufacturer (Bureaucrat) **Distributor (Entrepeneur)**

Exhibit 8-5
Cultural Differences

Move from this adversarial situation → **we** versus **they**

To this partnership situation →

Area of Common Interest

Adversarial relationships may work when you don't have to see the bastards again. But when manufacturers and distributors must work together everyday to serve a common customer, they should work toward win, win, win approaches. First, the customer must win or the distributor and manufacturer will not survive. Second, the distributor should win most of the time, or he or she won't carry the line. Finally, the manufacturer has to take a longer-term view of winning the war even if a few battles are periodically lost.

E-BUSINESS RELATIONSHIPS

In today's digital age, suppliers, manufacturers, distributors, and customers are becoming increasingly wired together. Manufacturers' computers are increasingly linked directly to their distributors. The Internet allows customers and large corporate buyers from all over the world to band together, pool their purchasing power, and obtain volume discounts. For example, by pooling purchases of operating supplies from divisions, General Electric obtained price reductions from suppliers of up to 20 percent on more than $1 billion of goods purchased online. While manufacturers are grappling with the pros and cons of direct sales on the Internet, many distributors are creating their own web sites and using the Internet to their advantage. E-business is creating constant motion in the supply chain, with some distribution channels changing and most others waiting or pursuing a trial-and-error approach to going more electronic. While e-business is better suited to some products and market segments than others, channel trust, paranoia, and conflicts are inevitable results of the Internet and the addition of numerous web sites.

The growth of e-business consists more of tinkering and experiments than moving to a straight-line extrapolation of today's business plan. While e-business is still in its infancy, it is important to understand how it is evolving and how it will affect every manufacturer, distributor, and customer relationship.

Wired Buyers and Sellers

E-business can be defined as the application of information technology to facilitate the buying and selling of products and services over networks. The main difference between the web and other electronic media such as fax machines and telephones is that the web goes beyond just enabling transactions. The buyer and seller "face" each other through an electronic connection. There is no traveling to a company, no face-to-face salesperson, and no order book. Instead, there is a web site. Thus e-business represents a fundamental shift in how buyers and sellers interact. In this new electronic world, much of the ability to decide how business will be done is shifting from the seller to the buyer.

Before the web, buyers and prospects depended on people to answer all questions, offer advice, provide information, and solve problems as well as take orders. Companies have traditionally done their purchasing through professional buyers, who would scan catalogs, phone suppliers, and try to negotiate better terms. In e-business, the customer is the proactive navigator, and the web site meets the customer face-to-face. It is the site that "listens" to the customer's questions and responds with advice, guidance, recommendations, and pointers to other sources.

The Effect of E-Business on Cost

E-business affects four broad categories that determine costs of a firm:

1. *The cost of executing a sale.* Because an e-business web site is open twenty-four hours per day, seven days a week and available to a global market from day one, a business no longer has to build separate physical facilities to attract a larger cus-

tomer base. By providing product or service information online, customers can educate themselves about performance attributes and sometimes price. Prospective customers often arrive at a web site knowing as much as the supplier about product attributes. Therefore, subsequent contact between the customer and dedicated sales or support staff tends to be at a higher level. E-business usually reduces the errors in orders, and the outside and inside sales and service relationships are changing with e-business. The factory and distributors' sales and service people need to be knowledgeable helpers and problem solvers, not just order takers.

2. *The costs of procurement.* Web-based procurement of MRO supplies usually costs less than the traditional approach to MRO procurement with a purchasing person searching a variety of catalogs to find the right product, supplier, and price. Not surprisingly, the administrative cost for purchasing many supplies often exceeds the unit value of the product itself. Some industrial customers are now directly linked to preapproved suppliers' catalogs. Linking to electronic catalogs significantly reduces the need to check the timeliness and accuracy of supplier information. MRO procurement by many large companies previously was done through proprietary electronic date interchange (EDI) applications running on private value-added networks (VANs). Now, the trend is to move these activities to a web-based environment available to requisitioners (who had no access to EDI in the past) rather than the purchasing department (which may have used EDI but no longer needs to be involved in each transaction). EDI over the web costs about one-tenth as much as it does over a VAN. Not surprisingly, some of the largest corporate EDI users are migrating their EDI-based MRO procurement to the web.

3. *The costs of making and delivering a product.* Rather than increasing production and inventory in advance of actual customer demand, e-businesses are looking to make both their own supplier chains and those of their customers and suppliers respond in real time to actual sales. Visibility of the entire supply chain is necessary so that a business can analyze the interplay among interactions such as procuring materials, components, and subassemblies from various suppliers; shifting production among installations or business partners; and moving goods to the final consumer. Understanding relationships among all players in a particular value chain allows e-business to adjust to new contingencies in real time. Data storage and analysis tools help firms identify supply chain bottlenecks and better understand actual distribution costs. Lower operational costs, better collaboration with partners, and reduced cycle times are the big benefits. On the customer side, users are able to track the status of an order in real time.

4. *The cost of logistics.* E-business transforms logistics from simply packaging and moving goods and turns it into an information business. E-business changes the logistics business by tying carriers such as DHL and FedEx closer together with product shippers and their customers through electronic load tendering, inventory confirmation, and delivery tracking. As more businesses move to build-to-order process models and extremely low inventory levels, increased value is placed on prompt, accurate inbound and outbound logistics. Given the complexity of coordinating fast order fulfillment with the ability to track an order, it is no surprise an increasing number of web-based e-businesses are outsourcing order fulfillment to parcel delivery firms such as DHL, FedEx, and United Parcel Service (UPS). This outsourcing goes beyond shipping to include warehousing, packaging and customer support.

These four cost saving areas will continue to fuel the growth of e-commerce for some products and services. In many product/market situations, e-commerce changes the basic cost structure of sales, procurement, supply chains and logistics. Let's now determine what products are most and least suited to e-business.

E-Business Qualifiers

The value and use of e-business is highly product and service specific. For example, when the product configuration is very clear (such as this book's web site or item in a catalog) you have a candidate for e-business. On the other hand, the more variability and customization involved in buying a product or service, the more likely it is to require face-to-face human intervention, and, thus, it is less suitable for pure e-business. There are three basic categories of industrial products and services to consider for e-business, distinguished by how configurable the products are:

- *Ship-to-order products*—goods that have predefined options and little variability other than attributes such as color or size. Office furniture, computer peripherals, books, and most MRO and standard catalog items are examples highly suited to e-business. Customers expect the transaction to be completed instantly or in a few minutes.
- *Assemble-to-order products*—products that are more variable in their final form but are comprised of standard off-the-shelf components. Dell and Gateway computers and certain telecommunication equipment fall in this category for e-business. Customers expect the transaction to be completed in a few hours or in a few days.
- *Engineered-to-order products*—Products with highly variable configuration possibilities because the solution is more open-ended. These final products require more extensive technical interchanges between the buyer and seller. Products including many specialty chemicals and aerospace subassemblies are examples of configurations that are tailored to a customer's needs and are less suited to e-business. Customers expect the solution or final product in a few weeks or months.

Ship to order and assemble to order products are most suited to e-business. These relationships can be either direct to the end-user or from the distributor to the end-user. Engineered-to-order products are typically conducted directly between the manufacturer and end-user. In all three situations, e-business facilitates, reduce costs, and puts speed in the relationship.

Distributor Responses

When customers deal more directly with manufacturers, there is less value added from distributors who simply transfer goods or information. Distributors and middlemen must provide value. The Internet's promise of faster service and often lower prices can *disintermediate* or eliminate the role of distributors who assist in the transaction between the producer and the user. If e-business is about to threaten a distributor's business, the distributor can turn to two alternatives. The first is to become much more of a service-oriented model by offering for-fee consulting, for-fee training programs, and more value-added products and services. The second alternative is to use the Internet to get back into action as a large nationwide distributor, W.W. Grainger, did.

W.W. Grainger is a large, nationwide industrial distributor with annual sales of more than $4.5 billion, 500 branch locations, and about 1.5 million industrial customers. The company icon is a seven-pound catalog as thick as the New York phone book. Before the web came along, Grainger was a business built around a gigantic inventory of 210,000 MRO items in its 4,000-page catalog (called the "Red Book) used by factories, garages, military bases, hospitals, and school maintenance people. No other company (except Cisco Systems, Dell Computer and IBM) come even close to Grainger's web-sales volume. Some companies treat their web sites as just another 800 toll-free ordering line. Grainger rethought its business model and as a result reduced the search costs for customers. Grainger significantly reduced its own process costs as well. Grainger invested more than $50 million to build its web site.

Grainger builds online customized catalogs for any customer who negotiates discounts. When large customers log on, the web site automatically shows the company's discount. The customer enters the part number and places an order much faster than when they phoned Grainger and talked to a salesperson. Grainger's online customers spend nearly double the average order per purchase made by phone or in person. The cost of servicing an order placed over the Internet is a tiny fraction of what it cost Grainger to handle the same transaction.

Grainger dealt with one of the most difficult issues faced by manufactures or distributors going online by guaranteeing its sales force a cut of all e-commerce purchases by their accounts. Salespeople are given incentives to encourage buyers to use the web site. Even after customers move entirely online, sales reps keep getting commissions. Whether the accounts click in, call in, or walk in, the Grainger sales rep receives his or her commission. Compensation that includes the salespeople will reduce the perceived threat of e-business to a distributor's sales force.

Distributors who offer consulting, fabrication, and other services that customize their product/service packages will be less vulnerable to e-business. More and more distributors are designing extensive Web pages for their company's products and services. Being in the service business and competing with the Internet is requiring distributors to provide seven-day, twenty-four-hour-a-day order information; send phone, fax, or e-mail solutions; and conduct online dialogue and repair from a distance through computer diagnostics. Electronic auctions are being used by distributors for reconditioned equipment and for moving obsolete and discontinued inventory. In short, to survive and grow with the Internet, the middleman must find ways to add more value.

DEVELOP DISTRIBUTOR POLICIES

It is important to think through the common areas of potential manufacturer-distributor conflict and then set down in writing specific policies for dealing with these situations that are fair to both parties. These policies should be discussed with all existing and prospective distributors. At a minimum, specific policies should be developed to address the areas of pricing, inventories and returns, sales to large accounts, market coverage, market volume penetration, and end user information. For example, industrial manufacturers should have clearly defined pricing policies that encourage adequate distributor inventory levels. In many cases, the bulk of a distributor's capital is committed to manufacturers' inventories. The manufacturer's pricing practices can enhance, protect, or penalize the market value and profit margins on these inventories. Some enlightened manufacturers have a policy of paying salespeople who call on distributors only for what the distributor sells, and not for what he or she buys. This reduces the tendency to overload the distributor with inventory. It also aligns the manufacturer's salespeople with the interests of the distributor to serve end-users.

Manufacturers should also develop policies defining how large OEMs and specific end-use accounts will be served. Will large accounts that have been developed by a distributor ever be taken away from the distributor and sold on a direct basis? If so, when and under what circumstances will the distributor still receive a commission for developing the account, if yes, how much and for how long? Some manufacturers leave the distributor-developed account with the distributor as long as the distributor delivers an acceptable share of the account's business and can profitably serve the account within its normal price structure. This is admittedly a touchy subject, but specific written policies must be developed. Being completely open is the only way to minimize potential conflict and misunderstanding. There should also be specific written policies on the kind of end-use sales information the manufacturer requires from a distributor. Without information from distributors that shows who their customers or users are, who is buying how much, and what market segment they are in, the manufacturer will not know what amount of penetration, if any, exists in a particular market or account. Parker Hannifin has a policy, which is a condition of being a distributor, that calls for all distributors to report sales to every user by part number, customer name, SIC or NAICS, ship-to location, and bill-to location. Another manufacturer requires warrant cards to be completed and returned so it can track this same information. This kind of information enables the manufacturer to evaluate distributor performance, set distributor goals, add or drop distributors, and provide direction by market segments and specific accounts.

In considering such policies, one caveat is worth emphasizing. Industrial distribution channels are outside the manufacturing company, and therefore policies cannot be developed and implemented by simply issuing directives. This means that the industrial manufacturer must carefully develop policies that are fair and *consistently applied* with the idea of the manufacturer and distributors working together as partners to serve common customers over the long term.

Once the key areas and responsibilities of distributors are developed and written, they should be communicated to the manufacturer's salespeople and to all current and potential distributors. A sound manufacturer-distributor relationship should be regarded as a long-term partnership for profit, so the need to establish a solid foundation for that partnership is important. Exhibit 8-6 shows how Loctite has defined its Statement of Philosophy on Distribution. This exhibit states what Loctite's responsibilities are to distributors and what distributors should strive to do. Kevin Boyle at Loctite states:

> An understanding and joint commitment to these philosophies are most important to forming a profitable partnership. The mutual commitment is far more important than the contract most manufacturers and distributors sign.

Sales management in many companies often resists developing written policies such as Loctite has. They argue that being so specific often creates hard feelings among distributors and reduces their flexibility to deal with distributor problems. I don't believe this is the case at all. As long as the policies are fair and responsive to market needs, distributors will welcome them. And where there are honest differences of opinion, it is much better to get those into the open so they can be resolved. Allowing them to smolder under the surface will only lead to problems that will immediately strain the relationship with individual distributors and ultimately weaken the entire distribution network.

Exhibit 8-6

Loctite Statement of Philosophy on Distribution

I. Statement of Philosophy

Loctite Corporation recognizes and values the role of distributors in our free enterprise system. We are committed to establishing a strong working co-operative partnership with our distributors. The cornerstone of our distribution philosophy is the recognition of our authorized distributor as marketing partners, not as customers. Loctite markets products with our distributors to satisfy needs and solve problems in the industrial marketplace. We ask our distributors to help us establish a positive working relationship conducive to the sharing of marketing information, product knowledge, and technical selling skills, which we believe to be essential for continued growth. We further recognize the importance of maintaining a Distributor Advisory Council and active participation in manufacturer/distributor associations for the purpose of working with our distributor partners for the common goal of increased sales and profits. We also believe that it is counter-productive to our partnership goals for an authorized distributor to maintain competitive product lines. We reserve the right to reconsider our partnership commitment to distributors who elect to sell competitive products.

Loctite will always strive to:

- Maintain selective distribution by appointing an appropriate number of authorize distributors in a market area. Loctite shall have sole authority in determining the number of distributors in a geographic area.
- Provide strong profit margins and return on investment.
- Provide marketing programs, product training, sales development programs and technical assistance to aid in selling to industrial markets.
- Make joint sales calls with distributors to promote Loctite technologies and create new business opportunities.
- Make joint sales calls with distributors who actively promote Loctite's products and partnership program.
- Decline to make joint sale calls when another authorized distributor is known to handle an account, except when a distributor is requested by the customer to:
    - → Solve a problem.
    - → Consult on a new application.
    - → Provide customer training.
- Establish mutually agreed upon sales goals and objectives to be reviewed quarterly to assist in maintaining a close distributor/manufacturer relationship.

Distributors should always strive to:

- Use their best efforts to actively promote and increase sales of Loctite's products.
- Participate in Loctite partnership programs.
- Provide information and recommendations for the establishment of sales objectives and goals.
- Implement marketing plans sufficient to achieve mutually agreed upon sales objectives.
- Maintain adequate inventories and credit-worthiness to enable their business to grow and prosper.
- Support and participate in Loctite product and sales development training programs.
- Provide sales information for Loctite sales force measurements

MANAGING THE NETWORK

Attention to a few fundamentals is the key to developing and managing an effective distribution network. None of these fundamentals would be difficult to follow in a startup situation when a new network is being established. However, they are more difficult to implement in an established business with a distributor network already in place. Long-term friendships, cozy relationships, and bad old ways of doing things are serious roadblocks to thinking through and carrying out the required corrective steps. But because working with distributors is so necessary for many industrial firms, all levels of management must be concerned with building and maintaining an effective network. Lack of interest by any level of management, especially senior management, generally means the job will not be done the way it should.

Assign Responsibility for Distributor Development

In many manufacturing firms, no one person has responsibility for distributor development. In theory, the top marketing or sales executive bears this responsibility, but in practice it is often fragmented or even neglected. Merely writing the responsibility into sales representatives' job descriptions is seldom enough to ensure that the job is done properly. To most salespeople, loyalty to long-time distributors, the pressures of meeting the current quota, and earning bigger bonuses are usually more important considerations than the tedious job of keeping tabs on all the distributors in their group. Unless this duty becomes a real part of a salesperson's job performance standards, it will almost surely be neglected. Moreover, sales managers struggling to meet current quotas are unlikely to make distribution changes that might hurt the quarter's sales. Finally, marketing executives usually have more exciting and seemingly more profitable projects to think about, such as new-product introductions, sales promotion campaigns, and strategic planning needs. Not having the time or staff to spare, they will seldom be inclined to invest the necessary time and effort required to strengthen the distribution network. Some leading companies have established a position that is responsible for distributor development. However, the job really belongs to the marketing executives, and they need to make sure it is done. Field personnel and regional and/or territory managers are then responsible to implement policies and evaluate distributor performance. Manufacturers should provide their field people with the appropriate training and tools to work with distributors.

At Caterpillar, for example, the support and development of distributors is a concern that permeates the entire corporation. Caterpillar chairman, Don Fites, states: "We all approach our distributors as partners in the enterprise and not as agents or middlemen to pass products through. We worry as much about their performance as they do themselves."[1] Caterpillar dealers are effusive in their praise of relations with Caterpillar: "They have consistently supplied us with superior products, training, and a high-quality program of parts and product information."[2] The average Caterpillar distributor tenure is 40 years, and most stay within the family for generations. The company even conducts a course to encourage and show distributor families how the business can be passed on to the next generation. Caterpillar's loyal distributor relationships are quite possibly the greatest barrier to its competition and the greatest asset of Caterpillar. However, Caterpillar or any manufacturer's great distributor network will never appear on their balance sheets as an asset.

Recognize Market Segments

Once a manufacturer's target market segments are identified, it must determine the size, growth potential, and requirements for each segment and decide whether to serve that market with distributors or with its own direct sales force. Two manufacturers successfully serving the same market segment with similar products will usually use the same selling approach. If one manufacturer emphasizes the OEM market segment for the product, it will usually sell directly to users. If another manufacturer of a similar product emphasizes the after-market segment, it will sell primarily through distributors. Many industrial or technical product manufacturers think first in terms of geographic coverage and then of distinct markets or customer segments. Thinking this way can result in the wrong selling approach and limited sales. The marine and forest product industries, for example, are both located in the Pacific Northwest. But these two market segments generally buy the same product from different types of distributors in the same geographic area.

The marine customer buys mostly from a marine supply distributor who stocks special products for customers' needs, speaks their language, and knows marine applications. For this market, it is often necessary to have products with technical U.S. Coast Guard approval for salt-water corrosion resistance. The wood products customers in the same geographic area often require many of the same products as marine customers, but they buy from a distributor who primarily serves the forest products industry. Deere, for example, usually employs different distributors to serve its agriculture and construction equipment market segments in the same geographical areas. Caterpillar frequently uses different sets of distributors to serve the construction equipment and diesel truck engine markets in the same geographic territory. Parker Hannifin's Racor fuel filter division has different distributors to serve the commercial marine, pleasure craft marine, and diesel truck markets.

The specialized distributor serves and stocks the special needs of these respective markets, whereas a general distributor may not be as effective. If a manufacturer's existing distributors are not able to penetrate the different market segments in the same geographic area, management would be wise to consider different types of distributors to serve different or specialized market segments in the same city or region. If one manufacturer is already successfully penetrating the identified market segment, the second or third competitor coming into that market segment should carefully examine what type of channel or distributor the successful first entrant chose.

Matching Channels to Market Segments

There are different types of channels and distributors for reaching and serving distinct market segments. To reach and penetrate multiple market segments effectively, it is often necessary for the manufacturer to market through multiple channels. Exhibit 8-8 shows a manufacturer of diesel engines that markets to three general types of markets: governments and municipalities, OEMs, and MRO markets. The government market (federal, state, and municipality) is often a direct sale because of the buying practices of these organizations. The MRO after-markets require distinctly different channels to serve their respective users. However, OEM and MRO channels are not always totally separate. As Exhibit 8-7 shows, MRO engine distributors may sell to end-users, and engine rebuilders. As a consequence, some channels compete and create channel conflict.

Exhibit 8-7

Matching Channels to Market Segments

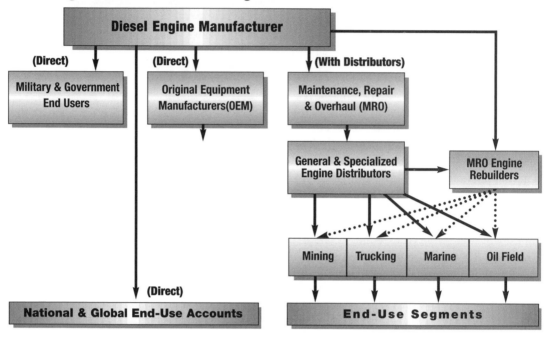

The particular diesel engine manufacturer in Exhibit 8-7 has further divided MRO engine rebuilders into four segments with distinct distribution channels: trucking, mining, marine, and oil field. Different marketing programs and distributors might be used to reach each of these sub-segments of the after-market. In situations in which there are multiple and complex channels and competition among a manufacturer's channel members, special care must be exercised when developing strategies and prices for each channel. For analysis and strategy development, it is helpful to develop a schematic such as that in Exhibit 8-7 before making policies. Such schematics also help identify market segment specification needs and pricing approaches, and helps "rationalize" a distributor network, especially where there is overlapping distribution from either having too many distributors in the first place or from an acquisition that never considered the effect on the distribution network.

Assign Markets, Territories , Products, and Potentials

A distributor's suggested territory may range from part of a large city such as Chicago to three or four counties within a state, the entire state or country region. If a distributor's business is based essentially on product lines from one manufacturer, the distributor will typically ask for some protection from other distributors selling in the same area. Some distributors selling more technical products that must be specified or "designed in" will usually want some kind of protection to prevent another distributor in the same geographic area from getting the business after he or she has done the specification, qualification, and approval work. Many distributors will simply not carry a manufacturer's item unless some specific territory is assigned to them. Their investment in space, inventories, and time is simply too great if they do not have the assurance that they will be credited for sales in their area.

Manufacturers, however, should be very careful not to assign "exclusive" or "protected" territories in which the distributor is compensated for all sales in the territory irrespective of whether it contributes to the selling effort. Generally designated territories can be assigned to specific distributors. But the manufacturer should not be trapped into paying a distributor standard commissions on direct sales to accounts that have the buying power to demand direct sales. Nor should the manufacturer be obliged to pay a double commission on occasional sales made in one distributor's territory by another distributor who has aggressively pursued the segments' business across designated distributor territories.

It is essential to state clearly what products the manufacturer wants the distributor to sell, what market segments or customer groups to focus on, and what geographic territory the distributor is expected to penetrate and serve. These ground rules should also spell out inventory stocking requirements and what sales volume of the items the manufacturer expects over time. If these conditions are not spelled out and understood by current and prospective distributors, a lot of time and effort will be wasted, and a lot of sales and profit will be lost to competitors.

Tailor Distributor Agreements

Every manufacturer-distributor is a legal relationship. Nearly all manufactures have distributors sign an agreement drawn up by their attorney. The main reason manufactures have these signed agreements is so they can cancel the relationship within the stated 30-, 60-, or 90-day period. The majority of these agreements are basically sales contracts that define the suggested trading area; list the product lines to be sold; describe termination, payment terms, returns, and use of brands and trademarks; and they usually have a nontransferable ownership clause. Distributors have different legal rights under the laws of each state and country. These differing legal rights must be known before signing-up a new distributor and when attempting to negotiate modifications to any existing agreement.

The spirit and process of developing a sound distributor agreement should build on the concepts of continually improving the distribution network. *A distributor agreement should codify the manufacturer's distribution philosophy and enumerate the responsibilities of both partners*. It should also include primary market segments of responsibility, direct accounts, unauthorized branch locations, carrying competitive lines, reporting user sales information; marketing responsibilities of each partner, a jointly developed annual business plan; performance reviews; and the duration period of the agreement.

Some distributor agreements have no renewal period. They are forever or "evergreen." An increasing number of manufacturers are writing three-year distribution contracts with an annual review that is part of the business planning process with the distributor. If a distributor is underperforming, the manufacturer might grant a one- or two-year contract. To avoid possible lengthy and costly future legal costs, it is wise to have a clause in the agreement that any dispute, which cannot be satisfactorily resolved between the parties, will be submitted to arbitration for a binding agreement. The manufacturer should have two or three people sign-off on each distributor agreement. The regional manager and one to two people at the corporate or division headquarters are the logical sign-offs to maintain continuity and consistency in the relationship.

Provide Sufficient Training and Support

Often the distributor's sales force is undertrained and undersupported by the manufacturer. This is commonly called "sign 'em up and then forget 'em." Training a distributor sales representative to sell a new product takes many hours of instruction. The manufacturer must demonstrate the product features, advantages, and benefits for many different user situations and applications and how it stacks up against competitive products. The more technical the product or "art" required to use or apply it, the more time necessary for training. Sometimes such training must be done by the manufacturer for both the distributor and the first customers who use the product. Product literature must be supplemented with trade magazine advertising to generate inquiries and sales leads for the distributor. The manufacturer, in turn, must promptly channel qualified inquiries and leads to the appropriate distributor to have a local sales call made.

Improving the effectiveness of industrial distributors can be approached in many ways. For example, a manufacturer can open regional warehouses or depots to provide the means for the smaller but growing distributor to expand its volume for the product lines. Sometimes a good cooperative advertising program that provides leads and inquiries will help get new accounts. Distributors tend to not follow-up on unqualified leads. Distributor-oriented manufacturers such as Parker Hannifin, Loctite and Caterpillar qualify leads and charge distributors a minimal fee for this service. In dealing with some customers, specialized sales support from the manufacturer may greatly strengthen a distributor's performance. Under extreme circumstances, it may be necessary to give the distributor financial aid in the form of longer inventory terms, equipment, or accounts receivable financing.

When a distributor needs technical field assistance for a potential new account, the manufacturer should ensure that such support is provided. Most manufacturers have regional sales representatives who can accompany distributor salespeople on calls and provide the first level of technical backup. Although some might regard this as an inordinate cost or a luxury the manufacturer cannot afford, it is often a smart investment. The manufacturer's sales rep, with his or her greater product and technical support and know-how, can help analyze an account's needs and get a product specified, which, in turn, will build volume six months to a year later. *It is usually a mistake to assume that distributors will get the manufacturer's product specified*. If a product requires some specification and qualification work that is not done by the manufacturer, the distributor will generate little or no business in that territory. In the health care market, drug company salespeople, or detail people (who explain the technical details of the drug to the physicians), must first influence physicians to specify or prescribe one drug brand over another before the local drugstore or distributor can fill and possibly deliver the order to the end user. Similarly, architects and construction engineering firms must be encouraged to specify one manufacturer's product, or the local building and construction material distributor will not get business from the local customers.

Sometimes a product is technically specified in one geographic area or country but is bought in another city, region, or country. For example, General Motors in Michigan specifies what make of valve it wants on machine tools it is having built by a machine tool builder in Ohio for productions line in California, Canada, and Mexico. To sell to the machine tool builder who is selling an automated production line to General Motors, it is first necessary to meet the specification and get approval by General Motors' corporate office in Michigan. Without General Motors' corporate approval, the Ohio distributor cannot serve the Ohio machine tool builder. It frequently pays big dividends for manufacturers to have a person who does nothing but get their products specified and/or qualified at OEMs, government agencies, automotive companies, and architectural and engineering firms. These specifications and approvals help "pull the business" through a chain of user buying influences and distribution networks.

Manage Distributor Councils

Industrial manufacturers should view the distributor first as a business partner with a common user and second as a customer with needs. The end-use customer does not "belong" to the distributor; because the distributor serves the customer with the manufacturer's product. The manufacturer assists in the marketing and specification process. *The manufacturer should become the distributor's marketing department*. As an aid to maintaining closer distributor relationships and ensuring good feedback on markets, customer needs, and competition, some leading manufacturers have formed very effective distributor councils.

A distributor advisory council should consist of six to twelve members who represent a diverse mix of sizes from various geographic regions and different markets. Each member serves for a maximum period, such as three years, and every year a specific number of members go off and new ones join the council. The rotating membership provides continuity and keeps distributor councils from becoming just social gatherings of old friends. The full council might meet twice a year and always has an agenda of five to ten topics. Council members sometimes have regional pre-meetings with the distributors they represent to raise and discuss common concerns. Minutes should be kept at meetings of the national distributor advisory council and then distributed to all distributors as well as to the appropriate manufacturer's personnel. The distributor meetings are conducted at a high level and address issues that include the manufacturer's policies, competition, sales, technical and promotion support, and needed products. Other topics might include return-goods policies, a quality problem with a particular product, the need for new catalogs, new industry standards, a product line gap, or the training of inside salespeople to handle distributor problems. General economic trends and business conditions are also useful discussion topics for council meetings, as long as they are tied to specific actions the distributor and/or manufacturer should take. A distributor council is not a sales meeting, good old boys club, bitch session, or distributor trade union. It is a forum for manufacturers to get feedback and advice from progressive distributors.

A poorly selected distributor council and ineffective council meetings are a waste of time and money for the manufacturer and distributor. Properly directed, a meeting of a distributor council is an opportunity for the manufacturer to capitalize on the distributors' direct contacts with hundreds of end-use customers. The council can provide reliable feedback on common problems that need attention from the appropriate division or from top management. The points of view expressed by council members can be very helpful to a division marketing manager or product or market manager attempting to think through a new program or policy.

EVALUATING DISTRIBUTORS

Distributors are not all alike. Manufacturers should continually be evaluating every distributor. Each authorized distributor evaluation should be rated as excellent, average, or below average. Improvement programs should be mutually agreed to and followed up at each branch.

Unfortunately, most distributor evaluations, if they are done, are superficial. At minimum, they only look at yearly sales growth and rarely identify the causes of insufficient sales growth. Too many regional and national sales managers "evaluate" underperforming distributors with bully tactics that never address the root causes of weak performance. Even fewer distribution evaluation programs identify areas for improvement at each distributor.

Uniform Format and Process

Evaluating each distributor branch will facilitate constructive communication between the manufacturer and the distributor. Specific areas for improving the distributor's sales and profits with your lines should be agreed to, and corrective actions should be put in place. This evaluation should not be viewed as a one-time event. It should be institutionalized as part of an annual or semiannual performance review and used to kick off the distributor's planning process for your products. Conversely, distributor marketing programs should be part of the manufacturers' business plans.

A uniform annual evaluation process covering many factors will help identify areas for improvement at each branch location. The ten common areas included in a distributor evaluation should include the following:

1. General management and leadership.
2. Sales growth versus the local growth rate.
3. Product knowledge and support.
4. Quality of outside and inside sales and service.
5. Marketing and sales programs.
6. Information technology capabilities.
7. Annual product line and customer gross profit.
8. Financial condition and credit policies.
9. Annual business planning for target markets and accounts.
10. Ownership and succession planning.

The starting point for evaluating distributor performance is a thorough knowledge of the market potential in each distributor's territory. To be meaningful, total potential should be established for each market segment in the territory. The manufacturer/distributor team should be able to determine the market segment or territory potentials in a county and for target accounts. No industry or marketplace is static: New uses are usually found for existing products. New products displace older ones. New market segment opportunities emerge, and other markets stagnate or shrink. As a result, end-use markets change in size and importance, and manufacturers' and distributors' market shares typically increase or decrease over time. Therefore, it is extremely important to continually track market segment changes in size, growth, and buying locations. Market facts provide the base information necessary to determine where stronger, more, or new distribution coverage is needed. Once market share data have been developed, distributor quotas should be established. The distributor's initial quota should be established from these market facts and then adjusted by sales and marketing management to reflect the manufacturer's marketing objectives, local market growth rate, and the realities of the competitive situation. (See Chapter 5, "Assessing Industrial Markets.)

The next step is to track distribution sales in each market segment. Many companies have no idea where their product goes after it leaves the distributor's shipping department. As a result, they lose touch with their ultimate customers and do not have a sound basis for evaluating distributor performance. Many sales personnel will argue that this kind of information is not available. This is not true. It is available and can be obtained with the distributor's cooperation. If a distributor is unwilling to cooperate or does not keep appropriate sales records, he or she shouldn't be allowed to carry the manufacturer's line. As I mentioned earlier, some manufacturers require each distributor to submit monthly sales information to them by product, customer name, and location as a condition of carrying their lines. When a motor, machine, or large piece of equipment is sold with a warranty, customer information is much easier to develop. Most of the end-users fill in and return the warranty card directly to the manufacturer. This means the manufacturer should be able to track sales to the end-user without any distributor involvement. However developed, a system that reports sales to end-users and back to manufacturers, provides invaluable information for a wide range of distributor and marketing management decisions.

Create Distributor Categories

Almost every manufacturer periodically faces the task of getting more effort out of their distributors. To accomplish this successfully, management must be able to grade the performance and potential of its existing distributors and concentrate its support programs on those distributors who can generate the most sales and profit dollars by achieving realistic goals. For example, bringing the distributors in the top twenty markets up to the average market share performance levels of the entire group would seem to be a reasonable goal and can often generate significant sales and profit dollars.

After conducting a uniform distributor evaluation, the manufacturer should be able to categorize the viability and growth prospect of each distributor. One coated abrasives manufacturer places each distributor in one of the following four categories:

1. *Premier.* The top 10 to 15 percent of their distributors who are progressive and do most things very well.
2. *Growable.* The 20 to 40 percent of their distributors who need and accept improvements.
3. *Declining.* The 15 to 20 percent who plateaued and may or may not be willing to rejuvenate the business.
4. *Nongrowable.* The 5 to 10 percent who probably should have been terminated years ago. Some are retired or dead, but may not know it!

The manufacturer's regional and territory sales managers must be trained in how to evaluate distributors and place them into three or four categories. The nongrowable ones should be terminated and replaced as soon as possible. The growable and declining ones need to be coached, and action programs developed with a timetable and followed up quarterly. Annual or semiannual business plans, mutually developed with a distributor, are a good vehicle to rally improvements around.

Complete and periodic distributor evaluations require considerable time, diplomacy, and follow up. When distributors have interests or goals that are not consistent with the manufacturer's market objectives in the defined market and geographic trading area, manufacturers should first try to explain what must be done and the payoffs for such efforts. If a distributor has not achieved satisfactory penetration or growth in a key market, the manufacturer should establish an improvement plan with milestone dates.

Terminating and Selecting New Distributors

Canceling a distributor is never a pleasant experience. However, to allow an underperforming distributor to remain will only weaken your network and provide the wrong signals to the entire network of distributors. Terminating a distributor in the United States is similar to terminating an employee in that you should create a documented paper trail of causes for dismissal. Having an arbitration clause in the original distributor agreement helps avoid a process where attorneys on both sides draw out a dispute to maxize their fees. There are a number of specific reasons to terminate a distributor including:

- Repeated failure to perform against uniformly applied evaluations.
- Spotty participation in the manufacturer's training and promotion programs.
- Repeated failure to follow-up on qualified leads.
- Failure to meet EPA, OSHA, or uniform quality standards.
- Removal of the manufacture's brand and/or company name from the product or package.
- Consistently late record of payment.

If no real improvement occurs with problem distributors, after a reasonable time and appropriate manufacturer assistance, a decision must be made. It is crucial to face up to the task of replacing distributors who will not or cannot upgrade. *Manufacturers cannot grow if their distributors don't want to grow.* The manufacturer's determination to improve a distributor network has proved to be the key to more than one outstanding marketing success story. For example, when Ray Snyder, the director of distributor sales at Reliance Electric, made an analysis of distributor sales, he found that the proverbial 80/20 rule was in effect. Twenty-two percent of the company's 400 distributor locations accounted for a little less than 80 percent of total distributor sales. Faced with the obvious question of why carry a lot of nonproductive distributors, he launched into a program to upgrade the distributor network. Within twenty-four months, the number of distributors had been reduced by nearly 20 percent, average sales per distributor increased by 25 percent, and total distributor sales were up sharply. In some areas, specialized distributors were added to serve new and emerging market segments.

After concluding that more, fewer, or new distributors are needed, a careful selection process must be followed so that the problem is not compounded. Many manufacturers frequently choose additional distributors who are already overloaded with products. The successful distributor is usually courted by numerous manufacturers and is frequently carrying as many product lines as it can effectively handle with existing sales and service capabilities. Manufacturers also frequently make the mistake of choosing the plateaued distributor with a successful history who has forgotten how to be aggressive. Some previously successful distributors plateau, and then their second- or third-generation owners may not have the entrepreneurial drive needed to grow the business. Admittedly, the credit rating on the younger, more aggressive distributor will rarely be something that excites the home office financial people. However, the manufacturer often errs by not attempting to find a way to help finance or support a newer distributor who could do a good job with the right kind of assistance.

Distributors are never very happy when they are told that they are being canceled or that an additional distributor is being authorized in what had been their exclusive territory. Many manufacturers are reluctant to take this step because they are unwilling to upset the long-standing personal relationship with the low-performing distributor. However, when the decision is made objectively on the basis of solid market facts and the distributors repeatedly lack improvement, the manufacturers' market position inevitably improves. Conversely, procrastination or rationalization of excuses typically lead to further market deterioration and a weak distributor network.

Identifying and adding the specific distributors are local or regional decisions. Regional or territory sales managers should be the first people to do an exhaustive search for new candidates. Because it is a local or regional decision, the search is frequently narrowed down to one or two key cities in the region. Trade directories and local Yellow Pages are typically used as sources for existing distributor candidates. Competitors, customers, and distributors who carry complementary lines are also sources of new distributors. If possible, manufacturers should try not to add new distributors who carry competitive lines.

Sometimes the number two person in an existing or competitive distributorship becomes a candidate to start a new distributorship. In some situations, the existing distributor may be interested in opening a new branch to provide the necessary coverage and is aware that if he or she doesn't, the manufacturer probably will find a new distributor for the area. As a last resort, some manufacturers will consider opening a company store on a temporary basis with one of its salespeople managing the distributorship. Often the manufacturer continues the person's salary, finances the new inventories, and provides management assistance to help get the operation running in the black. At this point, the company employee is often given the opportunity to arrange his or her own financing to buy out the manufacturer's inventory and leases and becomes an independent business that will remain and develop accounts in that territory. Aggressive employees of the manufacturer often make excellent distributor principals.

SUMMARY

For markets, customers, and products that are well suited to distribution, the manufacturer and distributor are very dependent upon each other. Therefore, they must coexist and work as partners, not adversaries, in growing sales and profits. To put it simply, they have a co-destiny.

Experience shows that all too few marketing and sales managers understand how to market products and services with distributors successfully. Industrial manufacturers with strong and loyal distributor relationships usually perceive distributors as business partners and not just as vehicles through which to pass products. Such manufacturers see that distributors must earn satisfactory margins and profits while serving their joint customers. These same manufacturers cement the distributor partnership with market guidance, training, and technical and promotional support. By avoiding mistakes in distribution and taking care of the essentials in evaluating, selecting, and developing distributors, manufacturers can substantially increase their chances of market success. Every manufacturer faces the need to replace or add new distributors. To not do so will only weaken the entire network.

Electronic connections with the Internet are dramatically changing the role and relationships among manufacturers, distributors, and users. As customers continue to demand more wired relationships, manufacturers must consider the value added role of any intermediary. Manufacturers must determine which product families, market segments, and customers are best served by an Internet strategy. That strategy may or may not include distributors.

A good distributor network is often the key to market leadership and overall business success. Because it takes many years of continuous attention to develop and maintain, a strong distributor organization is a big barrier to domestic and foreign competitors. Technology can be quickly copied; an outstanding distributor network cannot be quickly duplicated. Superior distribution can result in better customer service, customer satisfaction, and higher prices. Without a solid distributor network, even a manufacturer with a superior product can fail in the marketplace. A manufacturer that recognizes the importance of distributors as a major competitive advantage, can reap excellent, long-term sales and profit growth for itself and its distributor partners.

---

[1] "Caterpillar: Sticking to Basics to Stay Competitive," <u>Business Week</u>, May 21, 1997, p. 77.

[2] Ibid.

Knowing Your Costs

You can't sell your way out of a cost-structure problem.

Jim Kennedy, National Starch and Chemical Company
Chairman and CEO

When Dennis Hayes, the man whose name is synonymous with computer modems, sought Chapter 11 bankruptcy protection, it exposed not only the deep problems of Hayes Microcomputer Products but also how any business can rapidly fall if it doesn't manage its costs, even when it has the largest market share in a rapid-growth business. Hayes was the pioneer in modems, the devices that allow computers to talk to one another over telephone lines, and it dominated the worldwide marketplace with a 65 percent market share and more than $350 million in annual sales. Just as IBM first set the industry standard for computers and later tripped, the Hayes design was followed by every other modem manufacturer in the world. And again like IBM, Hayes watched nimbler competitors with lower cost structures run away with the market Hayes developed. Hayes was too slow to respond to the lower-cost suppliers who rapidly carved out hefty shares in a high-growth market.

Hayes Microcomputer first misjudged the lightning speed and cost-pricing ramifications of technological advances in product and manufacturing technology. Like microprocessors, modems generated very short product life cycles. A modem that could handle 1,200 bits per second (bps) of data used to be standard but is now obsolete. In just a few years, 14,400-bps, with both data and fax capabilities, became common; then 28,800-bps, with data, fax, and voice; followed by 33,600-bps modems; and then 64,000-bps modems were developed. But just as important, each new generation was manufactured at a lower cost and sold at a lower price. The combination of more product performance and lower prices resulted in a market explosion.

The industry is selling more modems than ever, but at lower prices, so sales revenue is growing much more slowly than modem unit sales growth, as shown in Exhibit 9-1. This is not a one-of-a-kind situation. The same pattern can be seen in personal computers, laser and jet printers, and many other industrial products.

Exhibit 9-1

Global Growth In Modem Sales

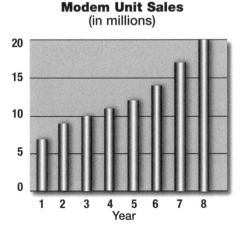

Modem Unit Sales
(in millions)

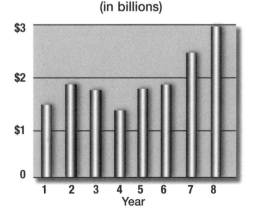

Sales Revenue
(in billions)

The Hayes bankruptcy came at a time of fierce Darwinian competition in a $2+ billion industry where the business units of market share leaders, Hayes and Motorola were losing money. A band of fast-moving and lower-cost suppliers, including U.S. Robotics and Zoom Telephonics, appeared on the modem scene with products that offered high speed at prices significantly below the higher-priced Hayes models. Smarter business customers were no longer willing to pay a premium for just an old brand name, something Hayes was counting on heavily. U.S. Robotics invested heavily in manufacturing technology that slashed costs and enabled them to undercut Hayes and other uncompetitive suppliers. They designed and made their own circuit boards (which Hayes outsourced to Mexico), created most of their own software, and got new products to market much faster than Hayes. U.S. Robotics' modem business generated gross profits of over 35 percent, compared with 26 percent for Hayes. An U.S. Robotics spokesperson said,

> Unlike Hayes, we don't have a lot of high paid executives and fancy facilities that inflate SG&A costs. Our lower cost structure allows us to be aggressive in pricing and profitably grow market share.

On the day before filing for bankruptcy protection, and in the midst of the industry's most important trade show (Comdex) the founder and CEO of Hayes Microcomputer, Dennis Hayes, said:

> Our past success, the growth market, and high prices attracted a lot of competitors that kept driving down prices 15 to 20 percent every year. The market prices came down faster than our costs. The problems of over buying components, production snafus in Mexico from our subcontractors, and the steady descent of prices left us cash poor, even though we had annual sales of over $350 million and over $50 million in firm orders to fill. It feels a little funny having to talk so much now about cost numbers. In the earlier years, we ran the company more on intuition. If I had been paying more attention to some of the financial details, the company wouldn't have gotten into trouble.

In its attempt to emerge from Chapter 11, Hayes was able to obtain $111 million in new financing from Asian investors to help pay off creditors. For this investment, Dennis Hayes had to surrender the CEO title and daily operating control to an outsider selected by the new investors. Nearly 40 percent of the company's people were terminated. *In short, you cannot run any company as a growth company over the long term without a sound cost structure, and you cannot hide a bad cost structure behind good revenue growth.*

SEVEN COST-PROFIT PRINCIPLES

If Hayes Microcomputer had better understood and managed around seven cost-profit principles, bankruptcy could have been avoided. Few truisms apply universally in the business world, but the following seven maxims are valid in every business situation:

1. Over the long term, it is absolutely essential to be a lower-cost supplier.
2. Being a lower-cost supplier applies to industries as well as to countries and regions of the world.
3. To stay competitive, inflation-adjusted costs of producing and supplying any product or service must continuously trend downward.
4. The true cost and profit picture for each product and for all key customers and target market segments must always be known, and traditional accounting practices must not obscure them.

5. A business must concentrate on cash flow and balance sheet strengths as much as on reported operating profits.
6. Productivity must improve relentlessly from year to year, driven by a side-by-side comparison with the best global competitors.
7. Cost-profit and productivity information must be shared with many people within the organization so that more what-if options can be generated and better decisions can be made.

These seven truths are more important than ever because there is less room for error in our increasingly more competitive global environment. Let's now amplify each of these cost-profit truisms.

LOWER-COST SUPPLIER

As products inevitably mature and become more similar, price competition increases, and the necessity to be a lower-cost supplier increases. IBM recently announced that it lost more than $1.5 billion on PCs in one year. Even well-run Hewlett-Packard doesn't make much money in the intensely competitive PC business. In today's global village, price competition comes faster, and the pressure for lower costs comes sooner. Compaq was a lower-cost supplier of PCs. Net profit margins were typically in the 7 to 9 percent range with gross margins between 23 percent and 26 percent, while many other billion dollar PC makers would just like to be in the black. Dell Computer's more efficient direct business model has replaced Compaq's as the lower-cost PC supplier. How does Dell out-earn rivals in a marketplace where razor-thin profit margins and profitless prosperity is common among competitors?

To begin, Dell keeps R&D costs low, typically only 1 percent of sales, while giants including IBM, HP, Digital, and Apple spend between 6 and 9 percent on R&D. In design, Dell, unlike IBM, is careful to not over-engineer any part in their machines. Whenever possible, Dell buys off-the-shelf components, and has standardized many parts across all its models. Dell leverages their suppliers' expertise. Dell also saves on promotion costs by piggyback riding on Intel and Microsoft, who mention Dell in the marketing of chips and software.

Another big Dell cost advantage is from productivity gains. From 1996 to 1999 sales per employee at Dell nearly tripled from $305,000 to more than $1,000,000. Dell Computer achieves a cost advantage of about 12 percent lower than Compaq's because it builds all PCs to order, barely carries any inventory, and sells direct to users via the phone and Internet with no dealers or middleman. For retail sales, Dell gets credit card customers to pay at the time they order which significantly decreases Dell's need for working capital. Machines are only assembled after an order is received. Dell turns its inventory about 30 times in a year while Compaq turns its inventory 12 times. *Dell substitutes information for inventory.* In contrast to Dell's lower cost structure, Apple Computer has had many years of declining gross margins and diminishing profits. Apple's gross profit margins plunged from 53 percent to 15 percent over a five-year period as shown in Exhibit 9-2. The difference between net profit margins of 4 and 7 percent at Apple translate into $360 million a year in bottom-line profit. This lesson is simple: *Your total costs must be trending downward, or a competitor will sooner or later do it for you.*

Apple Computer has been doing better since the ousted founder, Steve Jobs, returned to the CEO job. To reduce costs, Jobs hired some former Compaq managers. Over half of Apple's manufacturing is now outsourced to more efficient suppliers and by slashing R&D in half and accelerating the launch of a couple new products, profit temporarily improved. Overall market share is about 3.5 percent, down from its peak of 10 percent. Only time will tell whether or not Apple will survive as an independent company and sustain its improvements.

Exhibit 9-2

Apple Computer's Gross Margin Decline

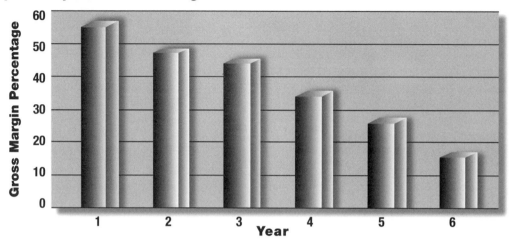

No industrial company can succeed over the long term unless it is a lower-cost supplier than most others providing equivalent products or services. Costs tend to over-accumulate in good times when there is no pressure to question every activity's effectiveness and efficiency. *Proprietary advantages never last forever.* All products eventually mature and decline, and prices and margins inevitably succumb to competitive pressures. As competitive product distinctions fade, price becomes increasingly important in buying decisions. A company should never compete purely on price if they don't have a cost advantage. The more successful suppliers relentlessly improve productivity and reduce costs. Thus, even when price pressures become intense, margins will at least be maintained. When this is not done, profits and market positions almost certainly fall. Summarizing retrospectively, Paul Allaire, the CEO and president of Xerox, stated:

> We were the undisputed copier king. Finally, we realized the Japanese were selling quality products for what it cost us to make them. We learned the hard way how quickly our competition can turn market supremacy into market oblivion. Our current business model is not sustainable.

Being a lower-cost supplier doesn't necessarily mean having the lowest cost among all competitors. Being a lower-cost supplier also doesn't mean having the lowest price. Nor does it mean that you can't or shouldn't have a strategy of producing at a somewhat higher cost and selling at a higher price. *But it does mean that one's total costs should be at or below the average of all competitors offering equivalent products or services to the same market segments.*

Costs include more than just production costs. Overhead or other costs such as design, sales, delivery, inventory, and services can throw the total cost structure out of line. The costs to serve a particular customer include sales time, special work, rebates, tech service, returns, and account receivables and can dramatically reduce net profit.

Inflation and price increases can be enemies that distort profit pictures. Price increases and inflation provide smokescreens for companies to avoid addressing their costs properly. In the "good old days" it was easy to frequently raise prices when costs went up because demand was bullish and often exceeded supplier capacity. Such situations led to a lack of discipline. The health care industry is a good example. For twenty years, it was a cost-plus reimbursement industry, where prices were allowed to rise with unmanaged costs. When third-party payers (government and insurance companies) and then employers finally came to their senses, a lot of health care providers who had let costs go uncontrolled got into trouble. Abbott Laboratories escaped that fate. Abbott's chairman said at our annual executive workshop:

> To simply raise prices along with the industry is not the Abbott way. Our overall corporate measure of productivity is sales per employee. Price increases don't get factored in. Paying close attention to such things as head count becomes second nature. You must develop an attitude throughout the company that you can always find a better and lower cost way to do things. Our constant effort to lower unit costs also makes more money available for new products and for price-cutting assaults. They help keep old competitors at bay and new ones away.

Logic suggests that, over time, the real inflation-adjusted costs of doing business should trend downward because, as organizations learn how to do things better, they also become more efficient. This is the underlying principle of the learning curve, and it usually works over time. The computer hardware cost of processing a million instructions per second dropped 76 percent for mainframes, 86 percent for minicomputers, and 93 percent for PCs over an eight-year period. In the manufacturing of industrial power tools, the cost fell 29 percent with each doubling of output over a ten-year period.

These continual cost reductions do not come automatically with volume, experience, or the passage of time. They require constant management attention in all matters for continual productivity gains and cost reductions. Too often products and costs drift out of competitive bounds, and no one realizes this until it is too late. Managers, who quickly claim that they are a lower-cost, or even the lowest-cost suppliers, rarely know their true costs and even fewer know how they compare with competitors. Even when clear evidence shows that competitors are selling at a lower price, many managers deny any kind of cost disadvantage. Instead, they say that "competitors are stupid," that "they're buying the business," or that "they aren't as concerned about profits as we are."

To know exactly what your costs are and to manage them well, you must carefully isolate various costs and match and assign them to specific products, customers, and markets. Such assignments are often handled poorly. The most common mistake is to work on the basis of average costs, as if all products and customers equally shared all costs. Average costing is like spreading peanut butter evenly across a piece of bread. Average costing ignores important differences among products and the fact that different products, different markets, and different customers require different costs. The broader the product line, the more distortions result from cost averaging, which nearly always leads to average price increases or decreases. In average pricing, some products or customers are overcharged, while others are subsidized. Across-the-board price changes ignore true product-line cost differences and differences in customer price sensitivities. Average costing that results in average price changes can lead to a loss of profit, reduced volume, declining market share, and the dulling of management spirit.

LOWER-COST GEOGRAPHIC AREAS

The second cost-profit principle applies equally to countries and to companies. When astute businesspeople discuss cost structures and productivity, they quickly compare the costs and productivity among different regions and countries of the world. *They look at the cost of labor and materials as well as the cost of highly skilled engineers and technical people.* Because most industrial manufacturing businesses have a significant amount of their total costs in design, materials and manufacturing employment, any meaningful decisions about sourcing, plant expansion, consolidations, and relocation must look at the respective costs, skills, and productivity in various countries. It is increasingly difficult to competitively design and manufacture most industrial products from a high cost country, not to mention the difficulty in making an attractive profit in the process.

For decades, Europe was the major source of productive and globally competitive output for industrial products. Unfortunately, some of Western Europe is now uncompetitive when it comes to global cost competitiveness. Germany is a prime example of a high-cost country. Germany was once the world model of a successful industrial economy, but it has been losing thousands of manufacturing jobs and future investments in markets it long dominated including advanced machine tools, telecom equipment, office equipment, optical equipment, chemicals, and automotive components. For decades, German productivity and ingenuity compensated for high corporate taxes, big government, and shorter workweeks. But in a global marketplace, German costs are numbing when compared with areas in Central Europe, Asia, and Mexico.

The low-cost central European countries (including Hungary, the Czech Republic, and Poland) are on the doorstep of Western Europe and are experiencing a rapid influx of industrial investment. The costs and productivity in Budapest, Prague, and Warsaw are on par with those in Malaysia, Thailand, and Mexico.

DOWNWARD-TRENDING COSTS

The third cost-profit principle is that no company can be successful over time if inflation-adjusted total costs do not follow a steadily declining pattern. For example, Hewlett-Packard was able to reduce its prices on computer workstations by 20 percent because its costs were significantly decreasing. Exhibit 9-3 shows how the cost of goods to produce a unit of Monsanto's Roundup herbicide dropped by 31 percent over the past five years. New technologies for improving the manufacturing process have led to higher volume throughout, shorter cycle times, and higher yields. These in turn have reduced waste, lowered raw material costs, and improved the use of capital.

Exhibit 9-3

Cost of Goods for Monsanto's Roundup® Herbicide

1996=100

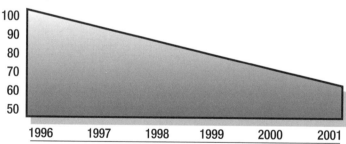

Source: Monsanto Company

Management must place unrelenting pressure on the entire organization for measurable cost reductions and productivity gains, year after year. The rate of improvement may vary annually but should never fall below inflation. This means that when inflation pushes salaries and wages up by a certain percentage, productivity gains must be made to more than offset this added cost. Vigilance is critical because it is so difficult to regain cost competitiveness once it has been lost. Costs should not be allowed to get out of line in the first place. And with all the company downsizing still occurring, one should ask, "Who let the cost structure become uncompetitive?"

As companies grow, any increments of capacity should be added grudgingly, especially in a slow-growth business. In today's fast-moving world, product life cycles are shorter, and payback cycles must be shorter. Before investing in new capacity, management should determine whether it is possible to better utilize existing capacity by going to more shifts, working six or seven days, or operating above current capacity. Furthermore, companies should evaluate any capacity additions and all capital appropriations against profits from the least profitable line in the plant; it may be possible to drop the less profitable line, not undertake the contemplated addition, or both. *The goal is to optimize the product mix in every manufacturing facility.*

If your costs have become noncompetitive, then traditional incremental expense reductions alone (cutting back here and there, reducing travel, freezing pay) probably won't do the job. Even deep cuts along the way generally won't do. You need to think differently: Eliminate big chunks of structured cost; design cost out of the product and the entire system; and greatly improve efficiencies everywhere in the organization, not just in manufacturing.

COST AND PROFIT PICTURES

The fourth principle is that the true cost and profit picture of each product and for all key customers and target market segments must be known and shared with people throughout the organization. An important reason companies get their costs out of phase with those of competitors is they don't usually know their own true costs. To ascertain costs, the following questions must be answered accurately for each major product line, account, and market segment:

1. What are the directly attributable and allocated costs for each major product line, from procurement to customer delivery, including post-sale service and warranties?
2. What is the present break-even point, how does it relate to capacity, and how much can volume be increased before it will have to move up?
3. What is the incremental cost and profit on each unit that is produced and sold over the current break-even point?
4. How do costs fluctuate with changes in volume? What costs are inescapable if volume declines?
5. How do the current cost structure, capacity utilization, and historical cost trends compare with those of competitors? What cost advantages or disadvantages exist?
6. What are the total costs to serve each account? Are some of our largest customers marginal or profit losers for us? Could we make more money with fewer customers?
7. Are there certain market segments in specific countries that are more attractive in terms of profits? Should we de-emphasize or withdraw from some market segments?

Managers in many multi-product-line businesses routinely make critical decisions without knowing these cost-profit facts. Executives at Armco Steel even managed to lose money on a special cost-plus contract because they didn't know their costs. Managers in rapidly growing businesses are often especially uninformed. Many high-profit businesses have primitive cost-profit information that no one has any confidence in, and they later get into serious trouble because they don't know their true costs.

Consider a manufacturer of plastic injection-molding machines with a twenty year record of successful growth and profits. The company generated reasonable profits during down cycles by reducing the work force and bringing back into its plant work that had been subcontracted out during good times. To improve margins, management heavily invested in automated equipment and greatly reduced subcontracting. Projected returns were very attractive, but in the next downturn in capital spending, losses accumulated for the first time in twenty years. The investment in automated equipment had significantly raised the fixed costs and the breakeven point. The latitude to reduce costs by eliminating direct labor hours and subcontract work no longer existed.

This point had not been raised when the company evaluated the new equipment.

What Accounting Schools Never Teach

Most managers agree that it is important to understand the costs and profits of their businesses, although often they don't know what this really means. Those who do know are often frustrated because their information systems don't present the data to develop this knowledge, and they don't know how to correct it.

Common Cost-Profit Ranges

To resolve this problem, let's go back to some managerial accounting principles. In Exhibit 9-4, we add target ranges for the key cost-profit components of most manufacturing companies and show a framework for developing an initial understanding of the cost-profit structure. The cost-profit ranges would be somewhat different for a process business because of the much higher plant and equipment investment, and the greater pressure for higher-capacity utilization. The opposite is true of the cost structure in most service businesses with lower investments and fixed costs.

Exhibit 9-4
Common Cost-Profit Ranges

Sales		100%
Cost of goods		65% and down
Gross margin		35% and up
R&D	0-15%	
Sales	5-15%	
General and administration	10-15%	
Total	15-45%	
Earnings (before taxes target)		15%
Assets employed		60%
ROA target (after taxes)		15% and up

The general manufacturing cost structure framework in Exhibit 9-4 is designed to yield a sustainable 15 to 20 percent pre-tax profit on sales, a 30 to 40 percent pre-tax return on assets (ROA) employed, and a somewhat higher return on equity, depending on the amount of debt leverage in the capital structure. These profit returns must be achieved to be a truly outstanding profit performer. Operating consistently within this framework requires the following:

1. Manufacturing operations must generate a gross margin (after all manufacturing costs, including variances) of at least 35 to 40 percent (and in many cases, much higher) to cover research and development and sales costs.

2. R&D activities for product and process technology obviously vary by industry but can range up to as high as 15 percent of sales, depending on the rate of technology change in the business and the stages in the product life cycles.

3. Sales expense typically runs in the 5 to 10 percent range—lower if sales agents or distributors are used, higher in the early stages of market development.

4. General and administrative costs are usually in the 10 to 15 percent range and should include all the overhead costs of conducting the business, including interest (at least for working capital) and allocated division, group, or corporate overhead.

5. Total assets employed for plant and equipment and working capital should not run more than about 60 cents on each dollar of sales in a manufacturing company, with variations in the split between them, depending on the type of business.

A company can be profitable if its performance does not fall precisely into this framework. In fact, the ranges show that there will probably be significant differences in the percentage for any cost element, depending on the industry and each company's market strategy. However, two numbers are crucial to meet or exceed the profit targets shown. First is the gross margin, which is the profit-generating fuel for any business. No manufacturing business can continuously generate satisfactory profits if gross margins drop much below 25 percent. Even this margin rate is questionable unless it is clear that R&D and sales, general, and administrative (SG&A) requirements are near the low end of the ranges shown. There simply aren't enough margin dollars to cover the costs of doing business and still generate a 15 to 20 percent pre-tax profit. The business may be able to generate attractive profit margins if it can operate with lesser R&D and/or SG&A expenses. Pursuing a "copier" or "fast follower" strategy means the R&D expense is probably on the low end of the range, but doesn't mean it is zero or that SG&A is necessarily less.

The 60 percent of sales allowed for total assets employed is the second crucial number. While this percentage again will vary widely depending on the nature of the business, it is a reasonably good standard for most manufacturing companies. It is clear that the business must generate higher earnings than indicated in our framework to yield the desired return if the percentage of total assets to sales is higher. Conversely, the earnings could be much lower and still yield a satisfactory return if the assets were lower, as they are, for example, in many distributor or service businesses.

None of this should come as a surprise to anyone who has had profit-loss responsibility. But it is surprising to find so many managers who continue to struggle to improve profit results by building volume without understanding and focusing on basic problems in their cost-profit structure. The problems become readily apparent in Exhibit 9-4. While it is always nice to have increased volume, the bottom line will not be helped if the cost-profit structure is out of line. As Jim Kennedy, CEO of National Starch and Chemical, often said at our in-house workshops, "You can't sell your way out of a cost structure problem."

The inescapable fact is that any industrial company must have a cost-profit structure that makes sense in order to be an attractive profit contributor over the long term. It is essential to first determine what it should be for each particular business and then to make sure the business actually operates around this structure. No amount of hard work or clever strategies will lead to outstanding profit returns if the business' basic cost-profit structure is not sound.

The Cycle of Profit Decay

When profits decline or disappear, companies often tighten the belt in the wrong way and in the wrong places. This can easily generate a self-feeding cycle of competitive decay. There is a natural tendency for managers to short-change sales or market development, R&D, or training or to forgo manufacturing improvements for the short term to make the business and profits look better. Exhibit 9-5 shows how a viciously deteriorating cycle can work itself into worsening conditions.

The most common (and almost hidden) factor that starts such a decay cycle is that of a management team operating with the wrong type of data—that of accounting rather than of cost control. Unfortunately, most management teams use data derived from accounting systems designed primarily to meet outside financial reporting requirements and not the needs of operating managers responsible for profitably making products and serving customers.

In addition, most accounting data presents aggregate numbers for large chunks of the business rather than the costs or profits for a number of discrete product groups and key accounts. Even when the data presents the cost and profit picture for product lines and major customers, they often focus only on gross or operating margins, not on the complete net profit picture after all technical, sales, and administrative overhead costs are taken into account. Finally, traditional accounting systems typically do not provide a clear picture of how costs and profits behave as unit volume moves up or down. Thus, they are not particularly helpful to managers who must evaluate sales, marketing, pricing, and manufacturing alternatives that involve different levels of activity.

For these reasons, some of the financial data must often be reorganized and reordered to capture the needed managerial information. This may require extra effort, but it is not as difficult as

Exhibit 9-5

The Cycle of Profit Decay

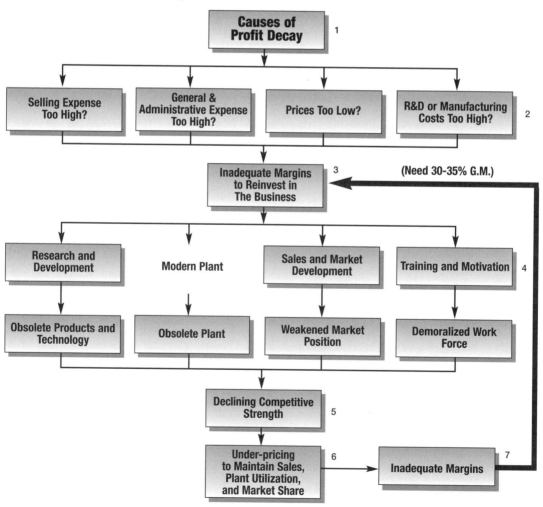

it sounds. A few commonsense cost definitions that provide the basis for categorizing all costs associated with each product line must be agreed upon. The following categories can provide a definitive framework for any manager:

1. *Bedrock fixed.* These costs are related to physical capacity and include plant and equipment costs such as depreciation, taxes, and facility maintenance that cannot be avoided unless the facility is sold or written off the books. These are the only true fixed costs. Typically, they are not as large a factor in the cost structure of companies as you would think, although they become greater as companies automate and when newer facilities are not depreciated.

2. *Managed fixed.* These costs are largely related to people and structure the so-called overhead of management, accounting, finance, and even activities such as advertising, sales, R&D, or market development. These costs tend to build up in good times and as a business grows. Once in place, managers often treat them as integral and bedrock fixed costs. They are not. You can and should manage them. Understanding their makeup is important to keeping them under control and distinguishing them from the overhead costs that organizations share.

3. *Direct variable costs.* These costs rise or fall in direct proportion to business volume. They are easily identified and can be traced back to the specific units produced or services rendered where, again, they can be better examined and managed.

4. *Shared costs.* These include all other costs incurred to support the business not immediately traceable to any one product line or activity. These normally include overhead of the corporation, division, and/or plant as well as SG&A expenses. They can also include operating costs for plant and equipment. All are manageable.

Agreeing on these cost definitions is the first step. The second step is matching the various costs to these classifications. In most businesses, few costs are either absolutely fixed or variable. Most costs lie in the vast area of "managed costs," shown in Exhibit 9-6. Make no mistake; costs

Exhibit 9-6
Managed versus Fixed and Variable Costs

Bedrock Fixed		Managed		Truly Variable	
Depreciation	Property tax	Supervision	Small tools	Telephone	Materials
Patent amortization	Rent	Inspection	Lighting	Receiving	Royalties
	Cleaning	Payroll taxes	Materials services	Spoilage	Overtime premium
	Maintenance of building	Payroll services	Machinery maintenance	Benefits	
		Office expenses		Wages	Supplies
	Insurance	Advertising	Lubricants		Fuel
	Executive salaries	Administrative salaries	Sales salaries		Power
			Entertainment		Scrap
	Auditing	Legal expense	Travel		Commissions
	expense		Uncollectable accounts		Freight

in the managed category are not fixed, even though they are commonly bundled under this label. Generally, as a business expands, costs tend to be far more variable than they should be, and when it contracts, they are far more fixed than they should be.

Reordering Cost Information

Once there is agreement regarding cost categories and definitions, the next step is getting help from the accounting or controller's department to determine how to divide, match, and allocate specific product/account/market businesses to the costs incurred in each of these categories. This is not easily done. Many accountants are reluctant to divide fixed costs into categories or to allocate shared costs to product families or specific customers because it is difficult to do this with the precision that accounting professionals normally use to develop traditional financial statements. Accountants have a natural aversion to shifting numbers around in an imprecise manner. There is simply no way, however, to know how well or how badly a product line or account is doing without making this cost information clear, that is, without knowing which costs are bedrock fixed, managed fixed, direct variable, or shared and without matching and allocating such costs to their various business units, product lines, and accounts.

At the divisional or business unit level, cross-functional teams of all department heads and the general manager should be responsible for hammering out the allocations according to the actual activity levels of each cost category. Some accountants don't like full or activity-based costing approaches because they demand a clear understanding of how a company works and a detailed understanding of all costs. It forces accountants out into the plants, warehouses, laboratories, and offices where the costs and activities are. Many accountants and controllers have no idea how to do this within each business. Yet, as Sam Siegel, Nucor's CFO and co-founder, states, *"A basic responsibility of the accounting profession is to match sales revenues and costs."*

In most cases, general management must ensure that data are reordered along the lines necessary for intelligent product/account/market management. Shared costs are a greater problem for most companies and difficult to attack as a lump. Shared costs must be broken down and matched to discrete business units or product lines, even if it means arbitrary allocations by some standards. Managers with hands-on profit responsibility will argue about the fairness of each type of allocation, but it is critical to take a stand or discussions will become endless and fruitless. There is no other way. Matching costs to the actual activities and then allocating the remaining costs is the only way to know what is really going on.

Better Cost-Profit Pictures

Exhibit 9-7 tabulates the results of changing to full-cost allocations in the instrumentation division of a large corporation. When complete, product groups traditionally regarded as the best profit producers were not as profitable as previously thought, and some of the worst were actually near the top. The instrumentation division overall had a reported gross margin of 45.6 percent and it generated 11 percent pre-tax profit of $30.1 million. Sales and gross margins were reported by product line, but pre-tax profit was reported only for the division overall. Reported gross margins for the product groups varied from a high of 54 percent to a low of 40 percent. Fully loading all production lines with their real costs resulted in adjusted gross margins that varied between 38.1 and 15.9 percent.

Because of their relatively lower reported gross margins, standard products D and E (at 41 and 40 percent, respectively) often took a backseat when the company assigned sales, manufacturing, and engineering priorities. When it analyzed and allocated plant, engineering, and SG&A overheads according to actual usage, it was clear that the standard products were being penalized by allocation methods that distributed these overheads according to sales volume. Adjusted gross

Exhibit 9-7

Full-Cost Allocation (millions of dollars)

Product Group	Annual Sales	Reported Gross Margin		Reported Pre-Tax Profit		Adjusted Gross Margin		Adjusted Pre-Tax Profit	
A	$42	$22.7	54%	NA	NA	$19.8	47.0%	$ 3.7	8.8%
B	51	26.5	52	NA	NA	23.4	46.8	4.0	7.8
C	37	17.4	47	NA	NA	15.9	43.0	3.4	9.2
D	83	34.0	41	NA	NA	38.1	46.0	12.1	14.6
E	61	24.4	40	NA	NA	27.8	45.6	6.9	11.3
Division -wide	$274	$125.0	45.6%	$30.1	11.0%	$125.0	45.6%	$30.1	11.0%

margin percentages for standard products D and E improved their relative pre-tax profit performance dramatically; gross margins on custom-engineered products A, B, and C declined by several percentage points once appropriate overhead costs were matched and allocated against them.

Looked at another way, products D and E contributed less than half (48.6 percent) of reported gross margin dollars but almost two-thirds (63.1 percent) of pre-tax profit dollars after all costs was allocated. It's obvious that the way management assigns sales, manufacturing, and engineering priorities can change drastically once the actual cost-profit pictures become clear.

Product-Line Net Profitability

Net product-line profitability statements also help bring management pressure on big chunks of overhead or shared costs (SG&A, engineering, manufacturing, and overhead at all levels) that are otherwise difficult to evaluate and control. When companies match and allocate these costs to specific products or profit centers, they show up as a charge against earnings, and managers responsible for profits carefully scrutinize and challenge them. This can be a powerful force toward reducing overhead costs and keeping them under control that would otherwise never be scrutinized by someone with a direct profit responsibility. To do this, many companies need to create more net profit centers and have more managers with full profit-loss responsibilities. Rarely does a company have too many profit centers or too many people responsible for net profit.

Knowing the true cost and profit structure for product groups is also an immense help in selecting products, customers, and markets for emphasis. Remarkably few managers consider profit potentials when they assess and select product/market segments. They more often focus on sales potential with the naive assumption that profits will follow. Managers can justify this in a product's early stages but can never do so later in the life cycle. When the fight for share in a stable, slow-growth, or declining market intensifies, managers must specialize in what is more profitable rather than in what is bigger. Companies that measure their success only by market share or volume rather than by profitability end up being the losers. *Most companies could make more profit if they made and sold fewer products and had fewer customers.*

Customer Net Profitability

After selecting the most attractive market segments to counterattack and attack and after knowing your product-line costs and profits, the next important decision is choosing which customers in those segments to get close to, deemphasize, or fire. Yes, those customers who are high levels of hassle, low or no sales growth, and low or negative profit should be fired, serviced differently, or given to distributors to serve. The notion of dropping or firing some of your customers is sacrilegious to many industrial firms conditioned to never lose an order and to keep every customer happy at any cost. These are usually the same companies that try to be all things to all people and have no understanding of the net profit from even their largest customers. These companies use the term "key account" when they talk about their largest existing customers, regardless of how profitable, marginal, or unprofitable they may be. In short, not all business is good business.

The decision of which customers to concentrate on is a complex one. First, if it is an existing account, the past sales, gross profit, and net profit must be determined or estimated. Most companies have no idea what their total costs are to serve each customer. The cost of sales calls, technical service, special new products, trials, rebates, discounts, freight, consignment, days of sales outstanding (DSO), and order transaction costs are all real costs that can be determined or estimated for every account. It costs every supplier a different amount to manufacture from different facilities in the world and to serve multiple customer ship-to locations across the globe. After completing this analysis, many companies see that between 20 and 30 percent of their customers are reasonably profitable, another 20 to 40 percent are marginally profitable, and between 20 and 35 percent are clear money losers. When determining which customers to emphasize, serve differently (possibly with inside people or with distributors), rationalize services to, or drop, one needs to consider both the present and potential volume and present and potential net profit of every account. Many companies only look at the potential volume of each customer and never even discuss the present or potential profit. If they happen to consider profit, typically only gross profit is mentioned. Astute companies know you can have a nice gross profit and insufficient net profit. *Smart companies develop a "cost to serve model" and determine the net profitability of most of their customers.*

PPG Industries was a $20 million customer for a pigment supplier. PPG's global procurement program, termed $AVE (Supplier Added Value Effort), requested that every supplier reduce its prices by at least 5 percent each year. For a $20 million supplier, a 5 percent reduction amounted to $1 million. After documenting the annual cost to serve PPG as shown, one PPG supplier was able to avoid the annual 5 percent reduction (see Exhibit 9-8).

Exhibit 9-8

Cost to Serve PPG

1.	New-product spray test panels	$ 75,000
2.	New-product automotive field trials	310,000
3.	Global regulatory compliance	48,000
4.	Styling presentations	95,000
5.	Special bar coding and labeling	10,500
6.	JIT frequent LTL deliveries	95,000
7.	EDI/electronic commerce requirements	150,000
8.	Supplier-owned inventory	210,000
9.	Supplier-managed inventory	37,000
10.	Returned goods and allowances	91,000
11.	Special rebates and discounts	89,000
12.	30 day terms averaged 45 days	75,000
	Annual total cost to serve PPG =	$1,285,500

Unfortunately, too few industrial suppliers know the cost to serve even their largest customers. Without an attempt to develop and share this important information, any business unit will limit their profit growth prospects.

Market Segment Profitability

Every business unit should trace sales revenues to specific market segments and then relate those revenues to the costs to serve each segment and as a result have net profitability statements by customer groups. In some companies with relatively few customers within a market segment, this analysis simply requires aggregating the sales revenue and subtracting the total costs to serve these customers.

Because market segmentation sometimes involves tailoring the supplier's product, services, and programs to groups of customers with similar needs, the annual sales revenues, costs, and profit results must be analyzed. For both strategic and tactical decisions, managers need to know the gross and net profit of market segments. Tracing the profitability of segments permits improved pricing, selling, advertising, and services offered. Ultimately, profitability by market segment helps to determine the attractiveness of various market segments in the resource allocation process.

Some companies address the profitability of product lines, territories, and a few customers. Relatively few companies ever attempt to assess the relative profitability of market segments. When armed with market segment profitability information, managers can more accurately vary policies and either increase or decrease various efforts to improve profit. Where the profitability of market segments is unknown or sparse, managers should begin working toward approximating and then developing more accurate market segment profitability pictures. Some of the costs can be fairly accurately matched to segments while others have to be allocated. In short, a profit-and-loss statement must be constructed for each target market segment.

Karl Bethell, Vice President of Henkel Surface Technologies, clearly recognizes the need for better profitability information when he stated at one of our workshops for Henkel in Dusseldorf, Germany:

> There is an old management adage that states if you can't measure something, you can't properly manage it. This saying pertains to our need for good cost-profit information for products, customers, and market segments.

If upper management does not demand cost analysis and profitability information by products, customers, and discreet market segments, the standard sales analysis will only report volume by products, territories, and large customers. These companies will invariably make many wrong decisions, many of which will negatively influence net profit results. Companies that have some understanding of segment net profit can ask many what if questions and they can make better strategic decisions. Without good cost-profit information, strategic market segmentation will be largely based on volume, not present or future profitability.

MANAGING CASH AND LIQUIDITY

The fifth management principle stresses the need to manage cash. Cash returns can be more important than reported profits. Cash returns lead to liquidity, and liquidity is a top priority whenever there are high risks and great uncertainties in a cyclical business. Cash and liquidity help withstand surprises, facilitate adaptation to sudden changes, and capitalize on the narrower windows of opportunity that are common in a turbulent environment.

Any entrepreneur or small businessperson who has survived a startup and built a market position knows the importance of cash and liquidity. Any business can go bankrupt while reporting record sales, just as Hayes Microcomputer did. But it will rarely go bankrupt if its cash and liquidity positions are strong. Most senior corporate executives and successful small businesspeople understand this but do not ensure that it is stressed or understood at the business-unit level.

The results are apparent in many large corporations. Capital expenditure proposals tend to be "wish lists" justified on projected volume gains or cost savings without regard to the availability of funds or to cash-carrying costs. Working capital is allowed to build without adequate regard for its carrying costs. Overinvestment in plant, equipment, and working capital often disguises sloppy business practices and control. These are practices that inevitably lead to a bloated investment base—too big for the business and too marginal for sustaining profitability.

Many operating managers are unaware of the costs of excessive capital tie-ups. For example, most will acknowledge that it costs money to carry their inventory (these days, usually 8 or 9 percent), but few know that total carrying costs should include storage, taxes, obsolescence, accounts receivable, and shrinkage and that total costs, including interest, actually run closer to 30 percent. The reason so few managers know this is that the costs of working capital are not charged against their business unit's earnings, even though they are real costs of doing business.

Cash management deserves far greater attention than it gets in most companies. Management must put greater emphasis on, and be held accountable for, managing cash. Planning and reporting systems should be modified to highlight actual cash flow and liquidity against objectives. Furthermore, the reward system should be adjusted to pay those who meet cash and profit objectives and penalize those who don't.

However, I am not suggesting that any growth company become obsessed with cash flow, as too often happens in highly leveraged companies, especially leveraged buyouts (LBOs). If all you do is maximize cash flow, you will be liquidating the company or, at best, dressing up a corpse for divestiture. You will always need cash for updating facilities, plant additions, research and development, maintenance, and activities that grow existing businesses and create new ones.

A manager who makes pricing, capital investment, personnel, and any strategic or tactical decisions without accurate cost information—and then does nothing to create a companywide discipline to manage costs—will face unpleasant surprises and serious questions of survival as the competitive world gets increasingly turbulent.

None of these actions is difficult if senior management has the will to carry them out and if the accounting system is set up to do so. They can be impossible, however, if the accounting systems are designed around big divisions of business rather than around discrete products, customers, and market segments and if big chunks of structured or managed fixed costs are not matched and allocated to smaller business units. Ideally, every manager should think like a small business entrepreneur whose own money is at risk and who seeks profitable growth. If more managers did this, we would see fewer companies with bloated balance sheets and marginal returns, and we would see a lot more with profitable top- and bottom-line growth.

PRODUCTIVITY MEASURES

The sixth cost-profit principle stresses the need for ongoing productivity improvements, measured by comparisons against the best competitors. Management must set goals and make action plans to facilitate the achievement of annual productivity improvements. After-fact financial measures alone do not get to the root causes of the competitiveness or uncompetitiveness of a business. Productivity measures provide earlier warnings than those provided by the traditional, backward-looking accounting measures. Basic types of ratios should be developed for any business and then compared with the best competitors, and improvement goals should be set with action and programs in place. If improvement goals and action programs are not developed, there is good reason to challenge any cost and profit structure. The performance ratios deserve examination in the evaluation of any industrial business because they are clear indicators of how efficiently the business is being managed. These performance ratios vary in importance, depending on the industry and products manufactured, but it is doubtful that any business can be healthy if they are out of line with industry standards or the best-managed competitors.

Using Productivity Measurements

The purpose of productivity improvements is to reduce the total cost per unit. These improvements allow a supplier to increase or maintain profit margins, reduce prices, or improve operating profit. There is no single measure of productivity that applies to every business, but ratios such as sales, shipments, production units per employee, and total engineering and labor costs per unit shipped usually indicate a direction or trend. TRW developed six productivity measures that apply to their diverse industrial businesses:

1. Sales per employee (constant dollars).
2. Sales divided by total deflated employee compensation costs.
3. Value added (sales minus direct material costs) per employee.
4. Sales divided by deflated materials cost.
5. Sales per unit of energy consumed.
6. Sales divided by plant and equipment replacement costs, less depreciation.

When factory labor was a product's primary cost component, single measures such as sales per employee were helpful indicators. With increases in automation, engineering, and technical services, labor costs have often been replaced with fixed investment costs. Therefore, the productivity measures must be related to your industry and then compared side-by-side with industry averages and the best competitors in your industry. The more common productivity measures for industrial manufacturers include yields, cycle times, lead times, and sales and profit per employee.

For example, a division of industrial manufacturer Emerson Electric measures its productivity in key areas and then compares itself with the best global competitor, as shown in Exhibit 9-9. After gathering information, Emerson Electric creates a third column, "Annual Improvement Goal," and action programs are developed to achieve the improvements. Emerson Electric continually demands productivity improvements, for which a slowing economy is no excuse for failure. Most industrial companies need at least 3 percent annual improvement in productivity to

Exhibit 9-9

Manufacturing Productivity Measurements

Measurement	Emerson Electric	Best Competitor	Improvement Goal
Quoted shipment time on standard parts	2 days	Same day	
Quoted lead time on specials	20 days	10-15 days	
Scrap and rework costs	3.5%	2.0%	
Machine set-up or cycle time	3-6 hours	2 hours	
Inventory turns per year	7 times	10 times	
Warranty costs (as % of sales)	2.0%	1.2%	

meet competition and generate resources for growth. Just think where consistently under-performing companies such as Westinghouse, Apple Computer, Air France, Digital Equipment, General Motors, Phillips, Bethlehem Steel, and Hayes Microcomputer would be if they had managed with productivity goals.

Because of the "soft" nature of a service business, some people incorrectly believe that productivity measures are less useful in these types of businesses. Highly efficient UPS religiously measures its productivity results against package delivery rivals that include FedEx, Airborne, Emery, and DHL.

Working Capital

Another major productivity indicator involves how efficiently the working capital is used. Enormous amounts of capital can be tied up very inefficiently if these ratios are out of line, and profit performance can suffer greatly as a result. Moreover, it is easy to develop a plan for increased sales that may do the company more harm than good if the costs of added working capital requirements are not adequately considered. These ratios also vary widely from business to business, but comparisons can be made with industry and competitive data. There is also a cross check against these ratios that applies in most industrial manufacturing companies. In most manufacturing industries, the investment in inventories and receivables should not exceed 35 cents for each dollar of sales. This rule of thumb may not always be applicable, but questions should be raised about the working capital investment when this amount is exceeded.

Dell Computer has built an extremely efficient business model that requires virtually no inventory or working capital. Product configuration is undertaken directly with each customer; then, with mass customization manufacturing techniques, Dell generates more working capital than it consumes. Dell's customers specify and pay for products before Dell has to pay suppliers. In contrast, Honeywell International has $3.5 billion tied up in working capital at any given time. Dell turns its tiny inventory 60 times a year. The effect of Dell's approach on total capital is eye-opening. Dell's customers finance the company's growth, so it does not have to take on debt. Dell collects money from its corporate customers 30 days after shipment or, for retail sales, on ordering, but pays its bills after 45-50 days. Mass customization also allows Dell to make only the products it has sold. Thus, there are no inventory write-downs or discounts to move obsolete or slow-moving inventory.

Reducing working capital yields three powerful benefits. First, every dollar freed from inventories or receivables rings up a one-time $1 contribution to cash flow. Second, the goal of reduced working capital forces companies to work smarter and faster because they don't have the luxury of large financed inventories from which to fill orders. Finally, reducing working capital creates a disciplined approach to reviewing all areas of the business where cash is involved. For example, one DuPont business reduced working capital from $50 million to $8 million over a two-year period in which their receivables shrank from 53 days to 42 days. Receivables fell from $11.6 million to $400,000 over the two years while divisional sales surged.

Producers to Supporters

A third indicator to examine is the ratio of what might be called "result producers" to "supporters" in the organization, also sometimes called "direct" and "indirect" people. This ratio does not reflect a traditional way of looking at a business, nor does it tie in with common definitions of work assignments. It is, nevertheless, a useful indicator of any operation's cost structure and profit-making capability. Anyone contributing directly to results should be included in the category of results producers. This includes direct hourly workers, sales personnel with specific sales assignments, engineers involved in designing products or responding to customer requests for special features, service technicians who install and/or maintain the equipment, and anyone else who performs a function directly linked to a company's design, manufacture, sales, and service capabilities. All other personnel in the organization fall into the category of supporters. They provide support services to the results producers. This group includes all full-time managers, all staff personnel, all secretarial and clerical help, and anyone else in the organization who does not actually design, make, sell, or service the company's products.

Ratios, of course, vary widely with different businesses, and what are correct ratios for one situation may not be correct for another. Moreover, there will always be arguments over definitions and the appropriateness of a particular ratio in a given situation. Despite these difficulties, ratios can be developed for any situation, and they can help determine whether the cost-profit structure is sound. It should not take long to determine what is a fair measure of performance for any particular situation. The value of each increment of improvement (each day's reduction in receivables, each added thousand dollars of sales per employee) can certainly be calculated to determine whether profit improvements can or should be made and whether enough emphasis has been placed on these improvements in the plan.

SHARING COST-PROFIT INFORMATION

The seventh and final principle demands that the information gathered in the previous steps be shared with enough people so that more what-if options can be generated and better decisions made. Having fact-based cost-profit and productivity information is one thing. The wide sharing of this information to encourage questions and make better decisions is another level of sophistication. Sharing cost-profit and productivity information is a lot more than just announcing year-end or quarterly results for the fickle financial community. It means communicating all relevant information monthly, weekly, or even daily to all employees within the business unit. In some companies this requires a 180-degree cultural change from a top down, need-to-know mentality. Salespeople need to know the cost and profit of products and accounts so they can move customers to higher margin products and service customers according to present and future profit prospects. To become more market driven, organizations must put a lot more information, trust, decision-making authority, and accountability in the hands of those closest to the customers, laboratories, and factories. These changes require a lot of learning and a change in many managers' leadership styles. In spite of the talk about teamwork, consensus, and participative decision making, nearly every company I have worked with has a few autocratic or dictatorial managers who don't delegate or trust their employees enough. I have often wondered if these managers trust a waiter in a restaurant with their credit card receipt. These same people inevitably have a restricted need-to-know mentality toward sharing cost profit information with associates in their organization. These managers need to have their minds reprogrammed to think and ask, "Who in the company doesn't need to know this information?" If these managers can't change their style, they should step aside or be moved out of the organization.

The old-style need-to-know management contributed to the decline of IBM. When the new CEO, Lou Gerstner, arrived, he found IBM's four information classifications to be wasteful, annoying, and dramatically opposed to an open culture. A rulebook explained which level of bureaucracy and which job titles should have access to each category of information. IBMers ended up branding millions of mundane paper memos as "confidential." The new CEO discarded the rulebook. Now one category, IBM confidential, is limited to new-product development, business plans, and customer lists. All employees now decide for themselves what qualifies as IBM confidential.

Trust Your Employees

In sharp contrast to IBM's previous close-to-the-vest and limited information sharing, their successful competitor, Hewlett-Packard, has always had a very open culture. Hewlett-Packard's decentralized divisions have been gathering and widely sharing cost-profit information for many years. With activity-based costing, HP's divisions calculate how and where overhead is being used on specific products and with large customers. At HP, cost-profit information is widely shared with the engineering labs so that everyone understands all the costs of a product before a product design is begun or frozen. Every design engineer at HP has real-time cost information at his or her fingertips. Tallies of all costs required to design, manufacture, sell, and service products are found in the desktop computers of HP design engineers.

Soon after a new product idea is hatched, HP engineers run sophisticated what-if cost, gross margin, and net profit estimates. Engineers frequently change the design on the spot to favor components that require less testing, thus reducing costs and time to market. In the past, HP engineers handed the design to accountants, who required several days or longer to estimate the production and other costs. The designers were often told much later that what they wanted was too expensive. To achieve this level of knowledge in using cost-profit information, HP had to conduct a three-day in-house workshop on "managerial finance" for nonfinancial people.

Marketing and pricing decisions at HP are guided by widely shared knowledge about a product and customer's total costs. Every department in HP holds "coffee talks" on a regular basis, where general and upper management meet with employees in the division to discuss product-line and customer costs, margins, and profit results. HP sales, margin, profit, and productivity results are described in detail, and time is taken to answer questions from engineers, manufacturing workers, and others. The wide sharing of cost-profit information gives HP employees a feeling of being respected, trusted, and valued contributors. This culture, in turn, causes most people to come forth with money-saving ideas time after time.

Trust engages employees' minds and hearts, not just their passive compliance to rules and procedures. Email, the Internet, and other electronic networks now give people the information necessary to think and act wisely, quickly, and with great flexibility. However, only when more companies and managers around the world become as open as Hewlett-Packard with good profit pictures, and trust all employees rather than try to control them, will they really tap the potential of their people.

Electronic Networks

The advances in computers, software, and data networks throughout every organization are giving a whole new meaning to the words "need to know." Global electronic networks enable people to communicate across the hierarchical and geographical boundaries of the formal organization and to interact based on ideas rather than organizational positions. Electronic networks enable people to be continually apprised of what others are thinking and doing all over the globe. With an open-book culture and wide information sharing, a more informal, faster-moving, and flatter organization should evolve.

Every company's bottom line is directly affected by many factors. Department expenses, inventories, labor and sales efficiency, engineering hours, material costs, warranty costs, and so on are all key numbers. This information must be available to or be shared with many people. Employees throughout the organization must be trained in how to understand and use the relevant numbers. When this information is widely shared, every employee becomes a "knowledge worker" by helping contain and reduce cost and waste. An open-book culture of sharing cost-profit information results in continuous learning throughout the organization. As more information is shared widely in the organization, all employees must be advised against sharing certain information with people outside the organization because "loose lips sink ships." Finally, with more information, every employee becomes more of a businessperson. Upper management personnel are no longer the only ones who worry about making money because everyone is trying to keep costs contained and trying to focus on profitability as well as growing sales.

Top and general management must walk the talk of sharing more cost, profit, and productivity information by simply trusting all employees more than they have in the past. Experience from my training programs, which encourages the wide sharing of information, shows that it takes at least one to two years to make the complete transformation from limited sharing and mistrust to wide sharing and trust throughout the organization. Top management must lead this change and convert, or ultimately replace general managers and department managers that resist the transformation to a more open-book culture that is fundamental to profitable top-line growth.

Never Believe One Number

I have known some CEOs and senior executives that view the maintenance of a high price-to-earnings ratio as far more important than sales growth, profit margins, and profit from operations. Accounting gimmicks and misrepresentations to manage earnings for Wall Street are so commonplace that many CEOs believe it is not only okay, but their duty, to investors. Delaying depreciation, using up future credits, capitalizing expenses, overstating goodwill, and putting capital gains into operating income are all acceptable accounting techniques that improve reported (but not actual) earnings in the short run, but they delay the inevitable day of reckoning. To hike earnings per share, a CEO could also simply sell assets, cut marketing and R&D, defer investments, or just buy back shares. Whenever I see that a company is capitalizing many items that a financially conservative management would expense, I am curious about the asset base, age of the equipment, state of technology, reported earnings, and especially how top executives are being paid. Revenue from sales of products and services should be recognized upon the shipment and use by customers, not earlier. Estimated product warranty costs should be recorded at the time of sales and periodically adjusted to reflect actual expenses.

I am equally suspicious of executives who try to manage and grow a business with just one financial number, like the currently popular economic value added (EVA) concept heavily promoted by consultants. EVA is a company's after-tax return minus the cost of capital to generate that profit. Of course, *it is very important in the long run for every company to earn more than its cost of capital;* otherwise it will be destroying wealth, and, for that reason, the EVA performance measure is one good measure. In a capital-intensive and cyclical business such as chemicals or steel and when the company has little debt (leverage), it won't look very good with the EVA approach, which some people see as just another form of short-term balance sheet management with no concern for long-term innovation and organic sales growth. EVA can cause a business unit to cut costs too deep and in the wrong areas, and it never addresses the advantages of a financially conservative company or the need for patient new-product and market development investments.

If just one financial measure is used in isolation, whether it is return on sales, return on assets, return on equity, return on capital, or EVA, it can puncture any attractive ideas for internally growing the top line. Some numbers are better performance measures than others, but *every resource allocation decision should be based on multiple measures of profitability that consider both the short- and long-term implications.* Finally, lower tax rates and favorable exchange rates can mask otherwise lackluster performance. Uniform international accounting standards; a profit reported in one country can easily be a big loss in another country. For example, in 1999 Daimler-Chrysler posted a net income of 615 million marks according to the more liberal German accounting standards, compared with a loss of 1.8 billion marks under U.S. generally accepted accounting practices (GAAP). Daimler-Chrysler has since stopped publicly releasing results calculated according to German regulations (although the company provides this information to the German authorities) and now reports publicly only according to the U.S. accounting practices or GAAP.

SUMMARY

In Chapter 3, I defined marketing as *serving customers profitably*. This chapter spotlighted the word *profitably*. Any book, training program, growth strategy, product line, or customer or market segment decision that does not emphasize the cost-profit dimensions is sorely lacking and of questionable value. All business is not good business. Without a sound knowledge of a business unit's cost structure, product line, and customer and market segment costs and profits, any talk of growth or strategy is shallow and academic. A sound cost-profit structure is a necessary foundation before profitable top line growth can begin and be sustained. Consistent with the underlying theme in this book that small is beautiful and profitable, many smaller business units have better knowledge and control of their costs than many large business units.

Internal and external benchmarking are critical for setting cost and productivity improvement goals. Side-by-side comparisons and estimates of competitors' costs and productivity should be developed before strategies are developed or changes made. This also implies that cost-profit information and productivity measurements must be a bigger part of the up-front decision-making process. It is important to remember that any one financial measure can distort reality. Always use multiple financial measures before making any business decision. And because marketing is defined as serving customers profitably, it is critical that anyone with a profit responsibility (general manager, business unit manager, product or market manager, regional sales managers, each salesperson) must join the charge to gather, widely share, and use cost-profit information for product-line, customer, and market-segment decisions. Profit-center managers and their business teams will then all become marketing controllers with the common goal of serving customers profitably.

Pricing for Profit and Position

*"If you price low enough,
you can have the whole market."*

Bill Hewlett, Co-founder
Hewlett-Packard Company

With more than $55 billion in annual sales, The Boeing Company is the largest player in the fast-growing aerospace industry. Boeing's long-range 747s, 767s, and recent 777s were technological innovations, and its medium-range 737 airliner is the industry workhorse around the world. After years of industry consolidation, Boeing now competes with only one competitor, Airbus Industrie, the European consortium based in France. With air travel and aircraft orders booming, these should be glorious times for Boeing. However, despite a record backlog of 1,700 orders for aircraft that requires down payments and progress payments, Boeing reported its first year-end loss in 50 years. Boeing's profitability is gradually gaining speed, but its high-profit-margin past is nowhere on the horizon.

What happened? To sum it all up, Boeing's obsession with protecting and growing its 65 percent market share initiated a brutal price war with Airbus as both companies fought for every order. Each time Boeing lowered its selling price, Airbus followed. When Boeing cut up to 30 percent off list prices and Airbus then offered about 40 percent off list prices, they turned a customized specialty business into a semi-commodity and possibly lost its long-time advantage of designing innovative products and controlling pricing with even its biggest airline customers. *Boeing simply let unit price become more important than product performance and life cycle cost.* For its most popular 737 model, which carries list prices of $45 to $50 million per unit, Boeing offered every customer rebates pegged to the lowest price Boeing charged any other customer for a 737 during the year. At these prices, the next four hundred 737s will be built at a loss of more than $1 billion to Boeing. They also gave extraordinarily generous terms to customers. Boeing then promised to deliver 515 planes within the year, up from 218 in the previous year, the fastest airline ramp-up ever. Because of the huge surge in orders, Boeing was unable to meet promised delivery dates. Large breach-of-contract penalties and customer lawsuits followed. Southwest Airlines, which flies only Boeing 737s, was irritated by Boeing's delayed deliveries because they caused Southwest to postpone adding cities to its route system for the entire next year. Boeing agreed to pay Southwest an undisclosed monthly fee for lost passenger revenue. Boeing also experienced a loss of major customers to Airbus. United Airlines, previously a Boeing-only customer for the past twenty years, stunned Boeing by ordering 100 Airbus A320s at a big discount. Singapore Airlines, worried about Boeing's production delays and resulting limits on their route scheduling, cancelled orders from Boeing for long-range 777 aircraft valued at more than $2 billion. Airbus got the Singapore Airlines business by offering firm delivery dates and deep price discounts. The price war with Boeing also caused Airbus to post a record $200 million loss in the same year-end, while its backlog also was the largest ever.

Today, it is difficult to see what benefit Boeing gained from starting a price war that resulted in a downward spiral of prices in a dogfight between only two players, or what economists call a duopoly. Such a pricing strategy and tactics can wreck the profit structure in any market segment or an entire industry for many years. Unfortunately, the Boeing and Airbus type of price competition occurs too often in industrial businesses. *If you get business solely based on price, you will most likely lose the business on the basis of price.* One secret of making money in any business is to get and keep more control over pricing than Boeing and Airbus did.

Few will argue that pricing is an important ingredient in the success of any company. Pricing is vital in the industrial world in which buying decisions are typically more rational and less influenced by emotion and advertising appeals. Despite its importance, little has been written that is useful to managers in thinking through alternative industrial pricing policies and actions. Most text material and articles on pricing deal with economic theory relating to supply and demand curves, retail products, or the pricing of pure commodities. Although interesting from an academic point of view, this information does not offer much practical help to industrial managers faced with the need to make strategic and tactical pricing decisions that can make or break the business. It is especially unfortunate that industrial managers too often make pricing decisions that literally destroy the long- and short-run profit performance for themselves and sometimes the entire industry. Examples to support this contention, such as the Boeing/Airbus example, are easy to find. Bad pricing decisions are a major cause of poor profit performance in industrial companies all over the world. What causes these situations? Why are examples of bad pricing decisions so common and widespread in every industrial business and country in the world?

Management's explanations for naive pricing actions vary little from one industrial situation to another. I often hear the following statements:

- We lowered our prices to gain market share.
- Our competitors are cutting prices, and we have to stay competitive.
- We needed the volume to keep our plant loaded.
- We cannot pass on all of our added costs and still maintain our position.
- We'll make up all the lost profit with a little more volume.
- Our competitors cannot survive very long at these prices.

However, these all-too-common explanations are not the real reasons at all. Rather, they are symptoms of and are related to fundamental deficiencies in management thinking that lead many companies into pricing problems, price wars, and usually poor profit results.

Pricing and price competition are some of the biggest problems facing all industrial executives. Industrial pricing is too cost oriented (if a company knows its costs); it is too often set independently of the market strategy; and it is not varied enough for different products, market segments, customers, and specific opportunities. Furthermore, the administration of industrial pricing typically lacks the needed discipline and consistency.

In this chapter, these deficiencies are examined in detail, and actions are suggested that management should take to avoid or correct them. I then outline the fundamental points that should be considered in thinking through and implementing a sound pricing approach for any industrial product line, customer, or market segment.

MANAGEMENT DEFICIENCIES

For purposes of clarity, the discussion of management deficiencies is structured into the following eight parts:

1. Inadequate understanding of market segments and customers value.
2. Inadequate understanding of competition in each market segment.
3. Inadequate understanding of costs and economics of the business.
4. Overemphasis on volume and market share.
5. Overemphasis on gross margin numbers.
6. Failure to understand inflation, deflation, and currency fluctuations.
7. Failure to link pricing to the market, product, or customer strategy.
8. Inadequate administration and discipline of pricing policies.

Let's examine each in some detail.

Inadequate Understanding of Market Segments and Customer Value

Many managers fail to develop a deep understanding of their market segments, nor do they understand how and where their customers generate profit and the value their products and services provide to market segments. These kinds of questions about the market and customers require specific answers to the following questions:

- How is the market segmented, and what channels serve each?
- Which specific market segments are we seeking to serve, and why?
- What is the value of our service/product package to different market segments and to individual customers?
- What non-price factors, including product performance, lead times, quality, and service, influence the buying decision in each segment?
- How price sensitive are specific market segments and individual customers?
- What present or potential pricing conflicts do we have between different channels (i.e. direct sales, distributor sales, and Internet sales)?

All industrial customers seek to reduce their total cost, improve sales and eliminate procurement hassles. However, *a higher unit price can often be demonstrated to result in a lower total cost for the customer.* For example, Engelhard Corporation manufactures a premium-priced pigment for paint formulations that reduces the paint manufacturers' total costs and increases the brightness of paints used by contractors and do it yourselfers.

Most industrial products provide different benefits and economic value to each market segment and to each customer and should be priced accordingly or with the outside-in approach. This approach is based primarily upon the value received by the user and is not based on the supplier's costs plus a desired profit goal. There are seven ways to provide value to a customer:

1. Reduce a customer's total costs.
2. Avoid a cost to the customer.
3. Increase a customer's sales.
4. Increase the customer's prices.
5. Reduce a customer's hassles or be easier to use.
6. Provide increased safety to users and the environment.
7. Provide any of the above benefits to your customer's customers.

Far too many industrial manufacturers price their service/product packages as if they had the same value to every market segment and customer. This cost-plus or inside-out approach to pricing, especially for new products and services, tends to leave money on the customer's table. *The real issue is customer value, not unit price.* Most industrial companies do not conduct customer field trials before they set prices for new products. When field trials are conducted and the supplier is not present, such companies then wonder why customers say the trials are usually unsuccessful. Most industrial companies do not know the value of their products and services to their immediate customers, and even fewer know the value of their service/product packages to their customers' customers. These companies spend too much time negotiating price and too little time communicating customer value.

Inadequate Understanding of Competition in Each Market Segment

The following questions should be asked and factually answered before any prices are set or changed:

1. What functional product substitutes do we compete with in each market segment? (Do not just consider like products.) Do we have a patented or proprietary know-how position that results in better performance and/or lower total costs over functional substitutes?

2. What is the competitive structure in each segment? What is the relative market position of each major competitor by country and global regions of the world? How do competitors match up on the factors that influence the buying decision? Have we benchmarked ourselves against the best global competitors' costs?

3. How much product or service differentiation exists? Are there grades of good, better, or best products, or are all the suppliers products largely perceived as commodities? Are any competitors able to usually get a premium price, and, if so, for what reasons are customers willing to pay even a little extra?

4. To what extent does market demand vary with price? Does product substitution for functional substitutes occur at various price levels? If so, how much price elasticity is there? What underlying factors cause the relative elasticity or inelasticity of the demand curve (such as a commodity product or unique or proprietary product advantages)?

5. Are new or foreign competitors using a penetration pricing strategy to enter markets and build a large market share position? Are foreign firms "dumping" products abroad by selling below their local country costs or the selling price in their home country, or is it simply geographic expansion or, free trade penetration strategy? Are there government tariffs or import quotas on certain products in specific countries?

6. How does global capacity for direct and indirect functional substitutes compare with total market demand? What significant changes in capacity are likely? Why? How does the changed capacity outlook compare with estimated demand for the future? How have industry or company pricing practices shifted in the past with changes in capacity or demand relationships?

All these questions about functional substitutes, competitors, proprietary advantages, demand, and global capacity provide essential background information to make intelligent judgments about how various prices, price changes, and price policies will be received.

Inadequate Understanding of Costs and Business Economics

I am amazed at the number of companies that do not know their costs and, therefore, cannot with confidence answer the following questions:

1. How much net profit is generated by each product line and each customer (after activity-based costing and formula-based allocations)?

2. How does the cost-and-profit structure for each product vary with changes in volume?

3. How and where in the design, manufacturing, sales, and servicing of the business are there significant costs, and where is customer value added?

4. How many dollars of assets are committed where, and what return is being earned on each major investment?

5. How sensitive are profits to changes in variables such as price, product mix, customer mix, and service costs?

6. What are the true idle plant costs for abandoned or underutilized capacity?

As you can see, these questions are designed to generate the information about the cost-and-profit structure necessary to quantify the effect of pursuing one pricing policy versus another. Chapter 9, "Knowing Your Costs," addresses these questions.

Without being able to answer these kinds of questions, it is impossible to make intelligent pricing decisions. For example, will a reduced price actually generate incremental volume? How much incremental volume is required to offset a lower price that reduces unit margins? Are competitors likely to react to a pricing action in a way that will damage the overall profit structure of the business? None of these questions can be answered without a deep understanding of the fundamental market and economic characteristics of the business. Managers typically rationalize their inability to answer these questions by claiming that their market research and accounting systems do not provide this information. To some extent this is true; most traditional information systems do not automatically generate the data necessary to answer these questions. However, this deficiency is not a valid excuse for not knowing the answers. The data do not have to be 100 percent accurate or complete. In the vast majority of cases, the information can be developed simply by reordering existing data or even by making estimates that allow intelligent judgments to be made. Blaming the system is simply an excuse for the kind of lazy thinking that inevitably leads to faulty pricing decisions.

Overemphasis on Volume and Market Share

The emphasis by naïve consultants and executives on the absolute importance of volume and market share for profit performance has misled many industrial managers into chasing unprofitable volume. The all out volume advocates claim that the producer with the highest market share will always have the lowest cost and greatest profit because of so-called economies of scale. Their reasoning is based on the experience curve concept that the total costs of a product automatically decline, approximately 20 to 30 percent in real terms, each time accumulated manufacturing volume is doubled. Believers in this notion advocate pricing below competition and sacrificing current margins as a means of gaining volume and market share. They argue that the higher profits achievable as volume grows and manufacturing experience is gained will more than offset the profit shortfall from lower prices.

There may be isolated cases in which this volume-based strategy pays off in the industrial world, but it is an impractical approach in the vast majority of cases. Although it is quite reasonable to expect and plan for 20 to 30 percent cost improvement during the early stages of manufacture of a new product (or even of an old product in a new manufacturing facility), the picture is quite different for almost any established industrial product. The potential for further gains through additional manufacturing experience diminishes rapidly after the process reaches maturity. This does not mean that manufacturing costs cannot be reduced by 20 to 30 percent after the initial learning period, but it will not happen automatically as manufacturing volume doubles and certainly not without major investment and a specific plan for achieving this kind of improvement.

Many companies have fallen into the trap of cutting prices with the expectation that increased volume or "tonnage" alone will automatically lower manufacturing costs to sufficiently offset lower margins and increase profits. The results have often been disastrous. Nothing is more painful to senior management than listening to a sales manager try to explain why profits are down although volume is far above plan. Anything the sales manager might say about gaining market share through aggressive pricing or about counting on some kind of volume curve to automatically improve future profits does not go over very well with astute senior managers whose experience tells them differently. *Any obsession to be number one or number two in any market segment, without an even greater desire to be a profit leader, is an ego trip that often leaves shareholders as the losers.* IBM, U.S. Steel, Xerox, and Kodak met the test of being number one or two in market share, but they were all profit losers. In one year in which General Motors had the highest market share, it lost $36 billion. GM is still the largest car manufacturer in the world, but its profit per car or truck is one of the lowest. Simply concentrating on increasing the number of units or tonnage often leads to big revenues, small profits, or profitless prosperity. Sometimes high profits come with a high market share. If market share and profit don't highly correlate, you may actually be more profitable with less volume, fewer customers, and a lower market share!

Overemphasis on Gross Margin Numbers

Any good CFO will caution managers with this maxim: *Never to make a decision based on one number.* In the early stages of a product's life cycle, the product should enjoy a higher margin, and companies need to price for high gross margins for new products that are demonstratively better than competitive offerings. In addition, without a sufficient gross margin, you will have a no-win cost structure. However, high margins at any stage of the life cycle can distort or mislead any executive. Managers who put too much emphasis on a product line or a customer's gross profit number, or even worse, just gross profit percentages—may end up with a lot of unpleasant surprises. You can have a good gross profit number but have unsatisfactory net profit results. A manager needs both gross and net profit return numbers before making a decision.

You do not want to let your largest customers squash your margins, but, just as importantly, all managers need to think in terms of the return on capital—not just gross margins. Many companies have not matched and allocated all costs to product lines and then to specific customers. Most companies have no idea what it really costs to serve customers beyond the gross profit measure. The annual costs of sales calls, technical service, customer meetings, product samples, prototypes, and special testing can be huge, and they all subtract from gross profits. Likewise, rebates, transaction costs, and slow paying and bad credit risk customers subtract further from gross profits and always create less net profits. Finally, many buyer-supplier contracts that employ just-in-time (JIT) deliveries and vendor-managed inventory (VMI) programs often resemble consignment sales terms where a customer only pays for goods as they are consumed. Such terms often require suppliers to have warehouses near or inside a customer's facility, and the supplier's employees do a lot of the work that customers previously performed. All of these activities occur after the gross profit number, and they all cost real money to perform and administer before you achieve any net profit.

Failure to Understand Materials, Inflation, Deflation, and Currency Fluctuations

It is essential to understand the effect raw material increases, inflation, deflation, and currency fluctuations have on pricing policy. Failure to recognize just how important these factors are and how to adjust pricing policy have triggered serious profit problems in many companies.

Raw material increases or decreases can dramatically affect the profits of any manufacturing business. For example, when airfares rise sharply for business travelers, airlines typically blame rising fuel costs because they are a significant part of any airline's operating costs. Just a 1¢ drop in the price of jet fuel means a $30 million improvement in annual operating profit for United Airlines, the largest carrier in the world. A 1¢ fuel savings for United also translates into a 17¢ increase in United's earnings per share. Many industrial suppliers set prices with raw material indexes or escalators that are then used to adjust prices up (and occasionally down) when raw material prices change. When jet fuel costs drop, airlines have little incentive to forgo fat profits by passing the savings to business customers because airlines do not tie their airfare prices to a raw material index as many industrial companies do. Some government-developed price indexes are notoriously inaccurate measures of costs to a company, and they should not be built into the pricing agreements. A few words to the wise: Be very careful when choosing indexes since they can go down as well as up!

No one has to look very far to find examples of companies that have been seriously hurt because of management's inability to operate effectively in an inflationary or deflationary environment. On standard products with short delivery cycles, there are myriad cases where costs escalated ahead of prices and profit margins showed a steady decline, frequently on the heels of greater volume. On longer-cycle products or systems sold on contracts that might call for delivery one or two years ahead, there are just as many cases in which anticipated profits suddenly turned into red ink because inadequate allowances were made for cost escalation during the design and manufacturing cycle. The pattern of profit decline may vary somewhat in different situations, but the cause is basically the same. Simply stated, if management does not anticipate or react effectively to the upward spiral of inflation or downward spiral of deflation, they will experience some unpleasant surprises.

The Inflation Spiral

Business managers in countries such as Brazil and Mexico, which have lived with an annual inflation rate of 40 to 50 percent, have a better grasp of the problems caused by high inflation and currency devaluation and have adopted economic and pricing policies to protect profits and assets against inflation's effect. Wages, rent, contract prices, assets, and other values that are affected by inflation are frequently and automatically indexed by government data, and managers must move aggressively to adjust any values that are not indexed so that parity is preserved. However, most managers in countries where high rates of inflation are a new phenomenon have not adjusted their thinking to the realities and tend to lag or fall short in their reactions. To start, they do not understand the extent that inflation affects profit requirements. Higher inflation demands higher returns just to stay even. Although this may sound like an amazing discovery of the obvious, far too many managers have not yet adjusted their thinking to the realities of inflation economics. They are content with profit returns that are excessively slim when the effect of inflation is taken into account. Therefore, the company's return on capital, and even its capital base, can actually erode while management thinks the company is turning a satisfactory profit. Also, most managers are far too slow to react, and price adjustments tend to lag farther and farther behind cost increases. Profit margins deteriorate, and the business is caught in a cost-profit squeeze. In some cases, managers simply do not move quickly enough, nor do they understand what is happening. In others, they are afraid the market won't accept a price increase and don't want to lose volume. Whatever the reason, profit results are severely penalized and never seem to catch up as costs move relentlessly ahead.

The heaviest penalties are inflicted on those who do not adjust prices to inflation at all. Because it is a good bet that we will be plagued with some inflation nearly every year, it is essential that managers start to think logically about the futility of chasing volume while costs continue to rise.

The Deflation Spiral

When deflation occurs, there is a decline in prices for various goods and services. *There are two different reasons for declining prices in any industry or product area.* The first reason for declining prices is usually good for manufacturers and is driven by productivity increases. The declining prices for semiconductor components and computers is an example of price decreases due to productivity improvements. In the electronics industry, prices go in only one direction, down. Intel and Dell are among the most successful firms in history because they aggressively achieve productivity improvements year after year. The second reason for deflation is usually ugly for manufacturers because it is *driven by excess capacity* around the world for commodity products. These products are undifferentiated, easy to compare, and highly interchangeable. In this second type of deflation, global excess capacity keeps prices down because too many goods are chasing too few buyers—a simple case of too much supply and not enough demand. Many managers have not lived through a period of deflation caused by excess global capacity. With excess capacity-driven deflation, suppliers have little or no pricing power and profit growth is dead. During deflation, manufacturers of the more commodity products face two decisions: cut prices and/or lower output. Price deflation will not retreat in this situation until some supply diminishes or demand catches up with supply. However, products and services that are unique, difficult to imitate, difficult to compare, and patented are less prone to the downward spiral of deflation pricing faced by commodity products.

Currency Fluctuations

Free markets and global competition have fueled constant fluctuations in currency exchange rates. The more global a company's operations, the more currency rates will favorably or unfavorably affect reported profits. For example, currency devaluation in Asia reduced FedEx's profits by $40 million in one year. Companies can choose one of four approaches against currency fluctuations. First, they can choose to hedge against currency mismatches by paying money for insurance to dampen the volatility. Drug giant Merck and Coca-Cola buy insurance to hedge all of their foreign cash flows. Such hedging involves putting your foreign cash flows in one- to five-year options to sell the currencies for dollars at locked in rates. The second approach is to hedge only a few specific contracts and not your overall foreign receipts and payments. For years, Eastman Kodak has chosen this strategy. The third approach is to locate plants in many countries where you do business so your costs are in the same currency as most of your revenues. This strategy reduces the impact of currency swings without hedging. By using locally earned revenues to fund the production of local goods, manufacturers reduce the hit to earnings that comes from exporting products from a strong-currency country to one with a weak currency. Cabot Corporation has chosen this strategy by building numerous small factories all over the world. Cabot has placed many of these plants in countries where demand is strong or emerging and where wide currency swings are common. The final approach, which 3M pursues, argues that ups and downs of currencies will even out over the long run. 3M does not hedge any of their foreign exchange exposure.

Failure to Link Pricing to Product, Market, or Customer Strategies

Few generalizations are useful in all industrial situations. However, one that is useful deals with the importance of ensuring that all parts of the business are linked together in a cohesive strategy that is geared to the requirements and unmet needs of the market being served. Otherwise, the effect in the marketplace will be diffused, and profit results will not be satisfactory. This general principle applies especially to a company's pricing policy, which should always be an extension of its strategy for the business unit, market segment, product line, or customer. For example, if the strategy is aimed at participating in a price-sensitive segment of the market, the business is likely to be structured around a narrow line of "bread-and-butter" products— high-volume, low-cost manufacturing operations with minimal engineering and service capabilities and a selling effort targeted at price-oriented customers. In this kind of situation, a pricing policy designed to achieve high-volume goals even at the expense of some unit margin probably makes sense. But this same pricing policy would make no sense at all if the strategy were focused on a segment of the market in which customized product design, superior performance features, and customer service were the key factors in the buying decision. Here a more logical policy would be to price at a premium and be willing to sacrifice volume to preserve unit margins and gain a reputation for superior product performance and customer service.

Differences in product design, manufacturing operations, and selling or service approaches obviously lead to substantially different cost structures for what may appear to be similar products. For example, a plant structured to produce a narrow range of products generally has more automated equipment, lower direct labor costs per unit, higher fixed and indirect manufacturing costs, and a lower break-even point than one set up to manufacture a unique product, for a custom market in small quantities. However, when the business comes under tough competitive pressure or when the market softens, these fundamental differences in cost structure are often forgotten, and pricing policies or actions are implemented that are totally at odds with the profit-making strategy management originally set out to follow.

During the past few years, Cleveland Twist Drill, a broad-line manufacturer of high-speed cutting tools, found that smaller, and often offshore, producers were hurting its business by selling below cost on certain lines with selected high-volume users. To preserve its position with these accounts, Cleveland Twist Drill matched the lower prices, but it did not intend to lower prices across the board. There are few secrets in the marketplace, however, and once the lower price was granted to certain customers, other customers heard about it and demanded the same treatment. As a result, the price eventually dropped across the line, and margins deteriorated. The narrow-line producers then retaliated with an even lower price and again started taking market share from Cleveland Twist Drill. Discussions with suppliers indicated that, even with the lower prices, at least three of the four offshore producers could still make satisfactory profits.

Inadequate Administration and Discipline

Once a pricing policy is defined, you might think that everyone would automatically follow it. Unfortunately, this is not the way it works in the real world. Unless management takes firm steps to ensure that the pricing policy is explicitly followed throughout the company, exceptions will occur at a phenomenal rate. A few exceptions to any policy are to be expected, but with too many exceptions, the pricing policy becomes nonexistent.

You might wonder how this happens, but it is easy to explain. There is usually pressure from people within the organization for a lower price. Salespeople the world over can always find persuasive reasons for prices to come in below policy; to be more competitive or to crack a new account or to get the follow-on business. A plant manager sees a costly gap in a near-term production plan and calls on the sales force to help him fill it by offering some short-cycle business (short period from sale to delivery) at reduced prices. A product or sales manager sticks to the published list price, but offers the buyer some form of price concession through extended terms, a longer warranty period, a break on return goods, a rebate, prepaid freight, or some other terms that cost the company money. When most pricing is below a published list price, you wonder why some firms bother to publish and distribute external list prices to customers. A systems marketing manager might accept an order within the current price policy, but delivery is set for 12 months from now with no escalation clause to adjust the price at delivery for inflation. In short, any salesperson, market, product, or plant manager worth his or her salt can always find a hundred reasons and ways to deviate from stated price policy. *Many of these concessions are a bribe for volume.* Unless top management exercises tight control and discipline, the company's pricing policy becomes a joke or, at best, simply the starting point for price negotiations and big reductions in bottom-line profit.

Most companies think they have the tight control necessary to avoid these situations, but, in reality, they do not. It takes a large degree of top management attention and discipline in an organization of any size to make sure that unauthorized price concessions or policy deviations do not occur. In addition, the plain truth is that management teams in many companies simply do not exercise the kind of tough-minded discipline required to make a pricing policy stick, especially from large customers who increasingly employ big guerrilla tactics with their suppliers. General Electric has nearly $120 billion in annual sales, and it purchases more than $70 billion annually from suppliers. Although GE has been flourishing for many years, it consistently applies bully tactics to many of its suppliers. (See Exhibit 10-1, a letter from GE's Medical Systems business, which makes X-ray, diagnostic imaging, and MRI scanning systems, to all of its suppliers.)

Exhibit 10-1

GE Medical Systems Letter to its Suppliers

GE Medical Systems

RE: Material Costs

The purpose of this communication is to advise you, as a key supplier to GE Medical Systems, of the severe cost pressures facing us and the action we must take to address them. These cost pressures are influenced primarily by macro-economic factors operating within the health care industry that are beyond our control. Equipment and service pricing threatens to deteriorate faster than we will be able to take cost out. As a result, we are entering into new and uncharted waters relative to successfully managing a business through times such as these. Global economic conditions are further exacerbated by worldwide over capacity in many industries, including ours. We believe that prices will also come under severe pressure from the newly industrialized countries in Asia. As these countries grapple with the economic forces that are sweeping through these markets, they will undoubtedly attempt to export their way back to sound financial footing. **These factors have led GE Medical Systems to conclude that price and cost pressure in the medical imaging industry will be deflationary.**

Our manufacturing strategy is highly leveraged toward outsourcing. A high percentage of the cost of our products are outsourced components and sub-systems. Because of this sourcing pattern, it is imperative that we address these risks and exposures to our business swiftly. While we would like to be able to discuss this matter with you in advance, it is a matter of utmost urgency and cannot await a more leisurely schedule. **Accordingly, effective with all new purchase orders issued to your company, GE Medical Systems will reduce the prices paid by 12% across the board.**

If you believe this action violates any commitment made to you by GE Medical Systems, please let me know as soon as possible. We understand that this letter may bring unwelcome news, and are prepared to discuss with you any alternatives that may serve the same purpose – which is to keep our product offerings, with your help, the most competitive in this difficult global market.

We appreciate your cooperation in this urgent matter.

Yours truly,

Vice President

The automotive industry has notoriously employed an approach like that of GE for decades. Many large, multinational, and multibusiness customers with huge purchasing power and global price information are today pooling their purchasing volumes and forming regional and global commodity councils to buy many supplies, even specialty items. These same large customers often demand annual price reductions from suppliers. These tactics were previously limited to a few industries and to customers in financial trouble. Today, even companies that are flourishing are increasingly applying such price-reduction tactics to squeeze money out of the "supply chain" or more appropriately, the suppliers' hide. However, if any purchasing manager does not ask his suppliers for a better price, he or she probably is not doing their job.

The supplier who quickly caves in to a request such as the one GE Medical Systems attempted to dictate can end up with a plant full of unprofitable business. Unfortunately, many customers do not care about their supplier's need to make a reasonable profit or even about the supplier's survival. Whenever a company sits down to negotiate with any customer, especially the largest ones, it must know ahead of time what the walk-away or lowest price will be, and it must then be prepared to walk. However, customers who consistently employ "hard ball" tactics, like those requested at GE's Medical Systems, over the long term may not end up with the best supplier base.

MANAGEMENT SOLUTIONS

Let's now turn to the actions management can take to prevent or correct these common problems. There are no easy answers or simple solutions. Preventive or corrective actions should be designed to keep a strong focus on bottom-line profits and the effect that changes in a product's cost structure and alternative pricing actions can have on these results. All these actions revolve around basic management requirements that are essential to success in any industrial operation.

Establish Top-line Growth and Profit Targets

The first requirement is to define and communicate an explicit set of growth and profit targets. To be meaningful, the targets must be balanced to cover the expected return on sales and capital as well as a profit growth objective. To be worthwhile, they need to represent a level of performance that yields an attractive return on capital and provides the means to create an attractive work environment for employees. For example, an after-tax return of 7 percent on sales, 20 percent on capital employed, and a 15 percent growth rate would represent a satisfactorily explicit and balanced set of targets. These target numbers are precise and require balanced performance. They cannot be achieved by concentrating on sales growth alone without regard for the investment in working capital required. Nor can they be achieved by sacrificing growth and scaling back investment and costs to improve returns. Conversely, some vague statement about earning attractive profits or achieving large sales gains would not be worthwhile. *The emphasis must be on profits and profit growth to counteract the strong volume orientation that commonly exists in most industrial companies.*

Given the dynamic nature of our business environment, these targets (like interest rates) should be reviewed regularly and adjusted for changing inflation rates and economic conditions. It is clear that profit returns, like interest rates, require upward adjustment with the rate of inflation. In other words, if management expects to earn a 10 percent after-tax return on its capital with inflation at 3 to 4 percent, it makes no sense at all to settle for the same return when the inflation rate doubles. In some countries, many companies determined that their growth and profit targets had to be adjusted when the annual inflation rate jumped to double-digit numbers. Although they may not know it, those managers who failed to recognize this need actually suffered erosion in their capital base when inflation rates exceeded profit returns.

A different set of targets needs to be developed for different countries. Country-specific targets must take into account long-term market goals and differing inflation and tax rates, as well as the inherent economic and political risks in each country. For example, it simply does not make sense to settle for the same profit returns in a soft-currency country such as some countries in Latin America or in areas of Asia, where high inflation or devaluation distort the monetary value each year, which is in contrast to a hard-currency country such as Switzerland, where inflation appears to be under control. Nor does it make sense to overlook the volatile political climates in some countries that greatly increase the risks of achieving an attractive payout on invested capital. Obviously, high-risk situations demand a higher return and more caution. In high-risk countries and with high-risk customers, you might reduce or eliminate credit or require prepayment before you ship anything.

Just as important as defining these targets is the need to ensure they are communicated throughout the organization and that everyone understands the market strategy and basic pricing policies designed to achieve them. Special emphasis should be given to explaining these targets to the sales force and relating them to the company's business plans and pricing policies. Communication with the sales force is crucial because the sales organization is where most of the pressure for volume and deviation from pricing policy begins. Getting the sales force to understand how the company's pricing policies relate to achieving overall growth and profit targets and also understand the importance of adhering to these policies will put a cap on a lot of this pressure. Paying a salesforce on profit, not only volume, also helps.

Determine Net Profit for Each Product, Customer, and Market Segment

A second requirement is to have an accurate picture of the cost-and-profit structure for each product line, customer, and market segment. Management teams in most companies have some means of knowing the relative profitability of their key products, customers, and market segments. Some rely on statements that show gross margin dollars and percentage of gross margin to sales; others use contribution dollars (sales dollars minus out-of-pocket costs equal contribution to overhead and profit). This data can lead management to wrong pricing decisions because they do not include all the costs of doing business and thus do not fully reflect the true cost-and-profit picture. Unfortunately, even so-called fixed costs tend to increase steadily when inflation rates are high. As a result, what are traditionally regarded as relatively stable overhead costs (insurance, taxes, and supervision) can escalate unexpectedly and dramatically affect any cost and profit structure. Relying on profit statements that do not take all these costs into account can easily lead to pricing decisions that generate more gross margin or contribution dollars but lesser bottom-line profits.

To keep the true profit picture in focus, net profitability statements need to be developed on a regular basis for each product family and then for each customer and, finally, for each market segment. This is not a quick task, but neither is it impossible. Most accounting systems identify the direct costs (labor, material, direct overhead) for each major product line. Allocations of indirect costs, including most group and corporate charges, should be matched or assigned to each product line on some kind of rational basis. Activity-based costing (ABC) helps the matching and allocation process. There will be plenty of arguments by those responsible for the profitability of one product line or another about the fairness of these allocations, and undoubtedly periodic adjustments will have to be made. However, all indirect and overhead costs must be completely allocated. None of them will go away, and they must be assigned somehow to specific product lines to reflect a true profit picture. The allocation process should not be arbitrary or left entirely to the accounting side of the business. Getting the managers with profit-and-loss responsibility involved is a good way to improve their understanding of the economics of the business, and it will also help gain agreement on the fairness of allocation methods to specific products and customers.

After net product line statements are developed, the net profitability of each customer must be determined. When customers differ in their requirements, the costs to serve them will likely differ as well. Unfortunately, for sound decision making, these cost differences are usually obscured in broad-brush cost allocation procedures. This means that the best that most firms can do is compare the profitability of customers according to their relative contribution margins after direct costs and overheads have been allocated. This inevitably provides a limited and misleading cost picture that ignores selling and engineering costs, quantity discounts, delivery concessions, and special terms or late payments. When costs are properly assigned to the customers who require or demand the activity, alarming results are inevitably revealed. The insights typically lead to a round of price increases, providing fewer services, less attractive terms and conditions, higher minimum order quantities, a shift to lower cost sales methods such as e-commerce or inside sales, assigning the account to distributors, or finally, simply walking away from the customer.

Once developed, these net profitability statements should serve as a starting point for regular review sessions to bring necessary management actions into focus. Estimated cost increases for labor, material, and overhead should be made frequently so that management can see how each product-line statement will be affected. Doing this should highlight the need for management action to reduce material or labor costs, cut back overhead spending, defer major programs, or initiate price increases. Management needs to use these statements aggressively. They should be reviewed regularly as a formal part of the management process so that problems can be quickly pinpointed. Once problems are identified, strong action to raise prices and/or reduce costs should be initiated to ensure target profits for each product line are achieved. Finally, management must take a hard line on product lines and customers that do not meet profit objectives, and they must be willing to drop those lines if necessary unless realistic plans to achieve satisfactory profits are presented. The whole idea is to get a regular and all-inclusive look at the cost and profit structure for each product line, customer, and market segment so that appropriate actions can be taken to achieve satisfactory profits for the total business.

Know the Country Laws and Practices

When making pricing decisions, managers must consider not only what is profitable but also what is legal and practical in each country. Price fixing, collusion, and cartels are illegal for U.S. executives who are constantly under scrutiny from the Justice Department and its antitrust division. General Electric's emphasis on profit results at any cost is possibly one reason GE has been plagued over the years with scandals in power generation equipment, with defense contracts, and from its Kidder Peabody bond trading scheme.

U.S. managers are prohibited by the Foreign Corrupt Practices Act of 1977 from paying or accepting bribes, but many foreign competitors do not operate under any such constraints. In many countries in the world, price fixing is not a crime, but it is in the United States. In global industrial markets with few suppliers and a clearly defined number of large customers sold on a direct basis, it is easy for suppliers to fix prices, limit capacity, and allocate market shares.

Today's global industrial economy and consolidation of suppliers and buyers provides many opportunities for cartels to occur. The fewer the number of suppliers and buyers, the easier it is for suppliers to influence one another and control the customer base. Competitors outside the United States frequently contact each other before they change prices. If collusive arrangements are made openly outside the United States, they are called a cartel. Each firm in a cartel agrees to produce less than it would under unrestrained competition in an attempt to drive up the price. One of the better-known pricing cartels is the Organization of Petroleum Exporting Countries (OPEC), which consists of 12 major oil-producing countries including Saudi Arabia, Iran, Venezuela, Libya, Nigeria, and the United Arab Emirates. In large cartels such as OPEC, there is usually dissension, and when individual members of the cartel refuse to abide by the production quotas and chisel on price, the cartel's influence quickly weakens.

Segmented Pricing and Terms

Industrial manufacturers in the United States and throughout the world can legally practice many forms of *price discrimination* (also called discriminatory pricing), which is when the same product or service is sold at two or more different prices regardless of any differences in costs. When different market segments and different customers are charged different prices for the same product or service, price discrimination occurs. Quantity discounts for different volumes of the same product do not have to be justified based on the supplier's costs. Different prices can also be charged for the same product or service based on the time it is used. Public utilities vary their rates to commercial users by time of day and season. Telephone companies all over the world charge different rates by time of day and day of the week. FedEx, UPS, and DHL charge different prices for next-, second-, or third-day deliveries for the same weight packages. Airlines, hotels, and movie theaters employ time-based yield pricing to increase utilization and total revenue. Such price discrimination works well when the market is clearly segmented and the price can be tailored to the needs of each market segment.

In countries in which buyers lack sufficient hard currency to pay for their purchases in cash, they offer items as *barter.* Caterpillar has accepted steel pipe from Romania and water buffaloes from India for payment of their machinery. Daimler-Benz and Mercedes in Brazil accept bananas from Ecuador, which, in turn, are sold to a German supermarket chain for hard deutsche marks. Caterpillar and Boeing have full-time staffs that advise equipment distributors and customers on how to initiate a barter or countertrade transaction. Many barter sales are a blend of inventory and cash. Some federal, state, and local governments frown on barter trade because they might not be involved in receiving the appropriate sales taxes or import-export duties.

The number of days that a sale remains an account receivable varies significantly from country to country. In the United States and Germany, 30 to 35 days sales outstanding (DSO) are normal practices. In Italy, 85 to 90 days is the customary period from the time a customer receives goods to when they pay their bills, and 120-day terms are common in Chile. Because Finland has a federal law requiring all invoices to be paid within 25 days, they are one of the fastest paying countries. Some customers, especially large ones, routinely take discounts offered for paying within the stated terms, even if they pay much later. In situations where customers and distributors take longer periods to pay or use your money, you will need either more aggressive accounts receivable or higher margins to meet your profit goals.

When a supplier begins giving rebates for quantity purchases, they are difficult to stop. Many purchasing agents are incentivized by the amount of rebates they can negotiate. Rebates are a bribe for quantity purchases because they are usually not related to any economics of the buyer or seller. Furthermore, rebate programs play havoc with any outside-in pricing approach that is based on the value that customers receive, from your service/product package.

Develop Pricing Strategies and Policies

The next requirement calls for top or general management to define the pricing strategy and articulate the pricing policy. Later, the administration and discipline are the greater challenges. Although it sounds difficult, setting prices is not the toughest part of the job. To begin, there are a limited number of pricing alternatives to choose from for any market segment or customer. They are:

- Tie price to the customer's value received.
- Price high to hold or improve margins.
- Match certain competitor prices.
- Price low to build volume and market position.
- Be a price leader or a price follower.

The key is to determine which of these policies is most appropriate for each market segment, key account, or the business unit's overall market strategy. Exhibit 10-2 shows the network of interrelated considerations that need to be evaluated before setting a pricing for any product line, customer, or market segment.

As Exhibit 10-2 shows, within each of the four steps, a number of questions should be asked. These questions should serve as a checklist before setting or changing a price. Far too many suppliers price only from inside-out, or with steps 3 and 4. This cost-plus approach is done too often and is commonly pursued without knowing the total costs and the sales and profit goals. Companies that do not scout and analyze the competition as shown in step 2 will be setting prices in a vacuum. Since few companies know the value of their service/product packages to customers, they do not start by asking questions in step 1. Market-driven pricing starts as an outside-in process with steps 1 and 2, and then considers the inside-out steps in steps 3 and 4 before setting a price.

Industrial pricing strategy decisions are, in effect, investment decisions that commit the resources of the firm and that, therefore, must be directly linked to the business unit's market strategy. It is not necessary to define pricing policy in a way that covers every conceivable situation or set of circumstances. Broad but definitive statements such as, "We intend to adhere to our standard list or discount structure," or "We intend to price in a way that achieves our margin objectives and value to customers," or "We want to price at a percent premium over certain competitors," are usually adequate pricing policies.

Exhibit 10-2

Setting Prices

Outside-In Steps

1. Customer/Segment Value
- Tangible benefits
- Intangible benefits
- Services needed
- Life cycle stage
- Proprietary situation
- Credit risk
- Cost to serve
- Gross and net profit

2. Segment Competitive Structure
- All functional substitutes
- Number and size of competitors
- Existing global capacity
- Planned global capacity
- Competitive delivery and lead times
- Competitors cost structures
- Competitors profit goals
- Side-by-side comparisons

Inside-Out Steps

3. Internal Cost-Profit Analysis
- Your capacity utilization
- Fixed/variable cost relationships
- Unit costs at different volumes
- Competitive cost comparisons
- Break-even points

4. Internal Sales Growth & Profit Targets
- ROI versus company profit goals
- Sales volume and growth rate
- Market share versus profit growth
- Short-term v. long-term profit growth
- Aggressive stretch goals

Enforce Pricing Policies

Top and general management should provide strong follow-through to ensure that pricing policies are administered. The most difficult part of management's job is to take the actions required to show that the policy is not just words. To start, someone with an eye for profits must have the responsibility of monitoring individual pricing actions to ensure that unauthorized deviations do not occur. In some cases, the general manager may want to maintain this responsibility. In others, especially where multiple product/market businesses are involved, general management may delegate the responsibility to a product, market, or business-unit manager. In still other situations, the general manager may decide to give this responsibility to the controller as part of the overall accounting control assignment. It is better to err on a more restrictive approach of enforcing prices than to delegate too much. John Davidson, the vice president of marketing at Henkel Surface Technologies, states:

> Henkel is a fairly decentralized company, but when it comes to administering pricing, we are more centralized. To begin with, we do not delegate pricing authority to the sales force, but we train, motivate, and strongly encourage salespeople to demonstrate to customers the total cost savings of our products and services or how to value sell our products and chemical management services. We discourage selling that is based primarily on unit price and tonnage or volume. We try not to give a price until after we run a field trial for a new product. If we must provide a price before we can run a trial for a new product, we call it a "developmental price." Our centralization of pricing also relieves the salesperson from receiving pressure from purchasing people and the large OEMs. We do not want our salespeople continually shaving prices to where customers view the salesperson as a source for getting the lowest prices rather than respecting them as a valued resource. Furthermore, our more centralized and disciplined approach to pricing prevents inconsistencies across customers, segments, and countries. Regional pricing is coordinated through our global business teams to minimize inconsistencies and to maximize customer value.

Whoever has this responsibility must clearly play the role of enforcer. Carrying out the job will not win popularity contests, because it involves such things as ensuring that orders that deviate from policy without appropriate authorization are returned—and that the responsible party is ordered to explain the situation to the customer—and seeing that those who try to slide around established price policy in some clever way get noticed—and that everyone knows about it. Admittedly, actions such as these are tough medicine, but they are essential so that everyone knows that top managers really mean it when they say: "This is our pricing policy, and we intend to make it stick."

Internet Pricing

The advent of the Internet has introduced many changes and pricing strategy is no exception. It is too early to tell which industrial products, services, markets, and customers will be most and least affected by Internet purchases and pricing. Overall, Internet based pricing does a good job at emphasizing unit price and a relatively poor job at recognizing customer value, especially for the non-price factors. Since Internet based purchases stress unit price over other tangible and intangible benefits, Internet pricing tends to drive prices downward. When suppliers display their prices on the Web they encourage a lot of competitive comparisons based on unit prices. The Internet automates price comparisons for standard products by enabling a customer to rapidly price-shop at a virtually unlimited number of locations in order to find the lowest unit price – without leaving his or her computer.

Auctions are an example how the Internet stresses unit price over the near exclusion of non-price factors that may be important to customers. There are two types of auction formats, the Yankee, and Dutch auctions. The more common Yankee auction is where one or more supposedly identical items are offered for sale at the same time. When the Yankee auction closes, bids on items are ranked in order of price, then quantity, and then time of the initial bid. The other type of auction, the Dutch model (also called a reverse auction), is where buyers post a starting price they are willing to pay for a product or service. Bidding starts at that price and it is lowered progressively until a buyer claims an item by calling "mine." The reverse or Dutch auction is designed to push prices down.

Since the Internet creates unprecedented ability for customers to unit price shop, it puts even more emphasis in knowing your costs before setting or committing to any prices. The last chapter, "Knowing Your Costs," addressed this vital management need. Some industrial companies that have been marketing and pricing on the Internet have been pursuing very aggressive pricing to get the business at any price. Many start-ups offer untenably low prices in a rush to capture market share. Unfortunately, many of these same suppliers are pricing products and services below their true costs. After twelve months of Internet transactions, a well-known manufacturer of adhesives did a cost analysis of their Internet sales as shown in Exhibit 10-3.

Exhibit 10-3
Internet Sales

1.	Average revenue per customer	=	$160.01
2.	Adhesives manufacturing costs	-	$119.22
3.	Average gross margin	=	$ 40.79
4.	Marketing cost per customer	-	$ 42.68
5.	Average cost to service each customer	-	$ 19.83
6.	Average net loss per customer	=	($ 21.72)

This adhesive manufacturer concluded that their direct Internet market strategy and/or pricing approach was ridiculous. The group president said, "What are you doing selling below our cost—do you really think you'll make it up on more volume?" The company is reevaluating the economics of their business model on the Internet. How many industrial companies are similarly pursuing aggressive pricing strategies on the Internet without knowing their costs, economics, and resulting profit or loss? Any e-commerce pricing strategy that emphasizes low selling unit prices over any non-price factors requires very accurate cost information, a need to manage costs, and a close look at net profit before and after going electronic. In the absence of facts, intuition is driving many companies Internet pricing strategies. Furthermore, many incumbent industrial firms that offer prices on the Internet have cannibalized some of their existing customers with lower prices and less net profit.

FINAL GUIDELINES

Once the previously explained management solutions are in place, top and general managers need to relentlessly take steps to remain competitive, and, at the same time, the entire organization must be disciplined to stand firm when a market turns soft. Let us now expand on these two final guidelines.

Strengthen Ability to Compete

Beyond actions designed to ensure tight control over pricing, other management actions are required to make it practical to stick to a firm pricing policy in the face of competitors who may not follow that practice. Continued or even increased investment is required in product-development activities to build greater proprietary value into the product or service offering. It is essential that the salesperson is in a position to emphasize new-product features, shorter delivery cycles, quality assurance and reliability programs, product training, or any other conceivable advantage that provides genuine value to the customer. Training salespeople with these tools enables them to sell in a way that takes the emphasis off price and encourages the customer to *think about total costs instead of the lowest unit price.* Furthermore, with some customers, you must first lose the business based on a competitor's lower price and later get the business back when the other supplier slips up in some way—and you should get it back at an attractive price.

Management must also place relentless emphasis on measurable annual cost reductions to help offset inflation-driven increases in material, labor, and other product costs that are certain to occur. Successful programs that take costs out of a product and the organization without penalizing quality, performance, or service are essential to preserving profit margins without passing every increase on to the customer. When inflation is running at a double-digit rate, however, it is unlikely that even the most successful cost reduction programs can completely offset spiraling cost increases, so timely price adjustments must be implemented along with the appropriate customer explanation. Timely means planned well in advance, and not waiting until accounting records show that profit margins have declined. This is not as difficult as it might sound. Most cost increases are predictable, and operating plans should include schedules that show both the cost-reduction programs and the pricing actions that will be taken to preserve or enhance profit margins.

TRW invented and developed the market for automotive airbags twenty years ago. But TRW's market share for airbags has fallen from 36 to 26 percent now that domestic, European, Latin American, and Asian competitors have entered the high-growth business. The airbag business accounts for 20 percent of TRW's $11 billion in revenues but are a big drag on overall profits. TRW used to price the driver side airbags to automotive OEMs at $250 each; it now sells dual front airbags for a total of about $150 per set. A safety engineer and airbag expert at Ford stated, "It's now hard to say one airbag is different from another. Airbags have increasingly become a commodity. We are interested in effective total systems that cost less." If TRW doesn't find ways to add value and/or reduce costs, competitors will increasingly do it for them, and TRW's shareowners will suffer.

Stand Firm When the Market Turns Soft

The acid test of management's determination to stick with a firm pricing policy comes when the market turns soft and a struggle develops to achieve volume goals. When this occurs, management can expect to see proposals to lower price as a means of picking up incremental volume or marginal contribution to help absorb overhead. On the surface, these proposals have a lot of appeal. Why not lower price to pick up volume you could not get otherwise? Why not take your price down even below full cost to pick up added volume that will help absorb a fixed amount of overhead that you have to pay anyway? There may well be times when it is smart to lower price to achieve objectives such as these, but in most cases, the proposals are ill-conceived notions that represent a snare and a delusion.

Think about what happens if competition matches or goes below a lower price and, as a result, captures some of your established business or customers. Consider how effectively you can compete if your action to lower price triggers an all-out price war among competitors who also have idle capacity and would like to have incremental volume to fill it. Or assume you are able to pick up low price volume that absorbs overhead without competitive retaliation. Have you really achieved an economic gain? If you take on lower-profit business when you have open capacity, will the lower-profit business stay and occupy the position of high-profit business in an up-turn? Is there a real advantage in wearing out machines and people just to gain contribution dollars instead of scaling back capacity so that underutilized capital can be redeployed?

Pricing actions such as these are never made in a vacuum. Aggressive competitor reactions should be anticipated, particularly in slow-growth market situations in which demand is relatively inelastic and competitor share positions are relatively stable. This does not mean that such pricing actions should never be taken. It does mean, however, that management must be judicious and must also consider likely competitor response scenarios and the ultimate economics of such actions until all factors have been taken into account. Many times the economic ills and excess capacity in one country affect the price for commodity-type products in another country. Imports quickly find their way into the faster-growth countries and put supply pressure on price reductions in the growth country.

When it looks as though the market is turning soft, management needs to move quickly to cut back costs; otherwise, the fears of those arguing for lower prices will prove valid, and lower volume will create an intolerable profit pattern. If management is on top of the business, it should be able to anticipate soft-market conditions so that actions to reduce inventories, staff levels, and indirect costs can be initiated before the actual volume decline occurs. Waiting until the condition impacts the profit-and-loss statement is at least several months too late and often leads to panic reactions that penalize the firm over the longer term.

In most industrial manufacturing businesses, the economic structure of the business is not totally dependent on volume; market declines tend to be cyclical rather than permanent; and demand varies between market segments, geographical areas, countries, and regions of the world. Given these characteristics, it is surprising how well profit margins and even absolute profits can be preserved if management moves quickly and aggressively to focus on the less cyclical market segments or to scale back costs in anticipation of lower demand. As a general rule, a volume shortfall from plan of up to 5 percent—and in some cases up to 10 percent—should be absorbed without penalizing planned profits if the plan is soundly conceived and if management moves quickly enough to make appropriate changes in its cost structure. If the volume shortfall is deeper than 10 percent, contingency efforts should be implemented to gear back the business so that planned profit margins are achieved on a much lower volume base.

Admittedly, these are demanding objectives that cannot be achieved with a "kid glove" approach to running the business. But it is clear that they can be achieved. History has recorded plenty of examples of businesses that actually generated the profit dollars and margins necessary to achieve these objectives on lower volume as they grew through various stages to their present size. During a recession, one of Reliance Electric's plants operated at about 35 percent of its rated capacity and still broke even. It was able to do this for two reasons. First, the plant was basically an assembly operation, and the fixed-cost base and break-even point were relatively low. Equally important, operating management anticipated the decline in business and moved quickly to reduce both its direct and indirect costs. The entire workforce was put on a four-day week, and a companywide "gain and pain" profit-sharing system was in place. When the backlog softens, too many companies make drastic cuts in people and programs that later hurt them in the long run.

With proper management, a business can generate the same profit dollars and margins as volume slides down. To be successful, management must understand that discretionary costs tend to be regarded as variable when volume increases and fixed when volume goes down. These discretionary costs are the ones that must be attacked and scaled back to ensure a cost configuration that will yield satisfactory profit margins and profits on a lower-than-planned volume base. Belt tightening is always tough, but it is a necessary course of action for management when the market turns soft. In addition, it is the only way to build real integrity and believability into a company's pricing policy.

Of course, if the economic structure of the business is volume sensitive, as it is in many industries that operate with an unusually high percentage of fixed costs, there may be no alternative to lowering prices. And if at some point the total market really dries up, prices may have to be lowered and lower margins accepted in any business just to keep the doors open, since some contribution to overhead and profit is better than no contribution at all. However, unless the business is extremely sensitive to volume, cutting prices should be a last resort and should always be seriously weighed against the alternative of developing new products or scaling back or exiting out of some segments of the business so that resources can be redeployed in areas in which profit opportunities are more attractive.

SUMMARY

Pricing policies are a vital part of the decision-making process for any industrial company, and such policies need management attention if they are to foster the long-term success of the firm. Panicky decisions under pressure from large customers, naive decisions made without accurate market and cost-profit information, and attempts to chase short-term gain at the expense of long-term success are common in industrial firms, although they need not be.

Most of the trouble stems from management deficiencies such as not understanding the market, costs, and economics of the business; not knowing the value of the product/service package to customers; overemphasizing volume and market share; failure to reduce costs and keep a step ahead of inflation; failure to link pricing to the market strategy; and failure to administer a pricing policy consistently and carefully. All these mistakes can cost the company profits and even its very existence.

Certain procedures can take the mystery and the danger out of pricing. Quantifiable top-line growth especially for sales and profit targets, must be communicated throughout the company. Another procedure is to determine actual product-line and customer costs; some industrial companies in nearly every industry still do not know their costs. Only when you learn about the value of your products to customers and market segments can you communicate and price according to user value.

One of the most important implementation issues is to define and enforce a pricing policy and to stand firm when the market turns soft. Management with a clear idea of where the company is going and a solid grasp of its economics and value to customers can develop and administer a consistent pricing policy that will work to the company's advantage and make profitable top-line growth a reality.

Top Management Leadership

"The day once was when being named the CEO was considered the culmination of a career. Today it is the start of leading your company to new heights."

Jack Welch, General Electric Co.
Chairman

The top management team, which includes the CEO, group presidents, and general managers, must create the right culture for profitable top-line growth. The top management in New York are grappling with the same top-line growth challenges that executives in London, Frankfort, and Tokyo are encountering. One unmistakable by-product of globalization is that the challenges and opportunities facing industrial business leaders everywhere are becoming increasingly alike. There have always been and will always be external factors that are threats to achieving profitable top-line growth. Great leaders anticipate and plot winning strategies around obstacles. These same great leaders always accept the blame for less desirable results. In short, they are not excuse managers—those who always blame external events for mediocre results. They make industrial marketing the entrepreneurial compass for the enterprise. Top management in these companies are obsessed with profitable top-line growth, and they create a risk-taking growth culture with aggressive goals. These leaders provide business teams with broad strategic growth guidelines, appropriate planning formats, and an organization to focus resources. Finally, these leaders pay business teams for results, not for just length of service and by job grades.

Let's now explain more specifically what the top management team must do to accelerate profitable top-line growth.

STOP BEING EXCUSE MANAGERS

Excuse management statements have taken over the business press, management reviews, and the annual reports of far too many companies. Many poor-performing executives only blame external factors for their mediocre results. *There are nearly always a combination of internal and external causes for poor performance.* Real internal problems, such as a bad acquisition, old products, flawed new products, or noncompetitive costs, rarely get aired by top management. Whenever there is bad weather or an economic downturn in one area of the world, that region gets blamed for weak company performance. High inflation in Brazil, the Arab oil embargo, El Nino rains, excessive snow, and woes in Asia are all convenient ways to shift blame to "uncontrollable external causes." Following are two typical examples of excuse management at industrial firms:

> A publicly owned adhesives manufacturer reported a 24 percent decrease in income on a sales gain of 20 percent. The public announcement stated: "Major events affecting sales included bad weather conditions in North America and Latin America that hurt the packaging business, slower economies around the world, the Asian crisis, and raw material shortages for most items that drove material costs up."

> Another manufacturer reported record sales of $2.7 billion, but profits of $114 million

that fell significantly short of the previous year's $171 million. The annual report stated profit was lower due to "a poor Asian economy, the Brazilian currency crisis, lackluster global industrial markets, the dumping of foreign imports in the U.S., key customers reducing orders, and power outages at two of our mills."

Many shortfalls in the preceding excerpts were internal and clearly caused by management. When most publicly owned companies do poorly or do not meet analysts' expectations, they usually claim that external factors were the only culprits. These same companies praise their own leadership when results are good. My close friend and former CEO of Johnson & Johnson, the late Phil Hofmann, saw through such external scapegoats when he frequently stated at meetings: "Management is the cause of good and poor results—all else is effect." Hofmann realized that external events could sometimes slow down or even derail plans, but he also believed that good leaders anticipated and plotted their way around even the most turbulent situations. Complacent, incompetent and weak leaders typically lack a sound understanding of the business, have little or no vision, are not well-rounded businesspeople, or lack courage and people skills to lead others. They are the corporate bosses that are coming and going at an unprecedented rate.

When confronted with the facts of internal causes contributing to lackluster performance, many top and general managers go into denial. There is something in the nature of general managers and CEOs—pride, vanity, a primal need for control, an obsession with success or power—that makes many executives look like fools when results turn against them. They rationalize. They justify. They then circle their wagons, build their bunkers, and mollify their lieutenants and sergeants. They see themselves as helpless victims of the environment. These people have trouble admitting that they and their companies "screwed up."

In these faster moving times, denial is more popular than ever, according to Intel's chairman, Andy Grove. Grove believes that most executives are vulnerable because they have trouble adjusting their mind-sets and adapting their navigation systems. There are many CEOs who are in constant denial. They are high-profile chiefs whose companies once basked in high praise and good press. They lead companies with once secure market positions and golden reputations. They have tasted success, but now they are in clear and present danger of becoming tomorrow's case study of another company in decline. And the CEO may be the last to know it. What these CEOs, group presidents, and general managers need is a big wake-up call. But who's going to tell this to a CEO? Many top managers are surrounded by people who say "yes, sir" "yes ma'am" and feed their delusions; this includes rubber stamps on the board of directors who "vote yes" for every whim the CEO proposes.

Alcoa Inc., the world's largest and best-run public aluminum manufacturer, is not run by a bunch of excuse managers in denial. Alcoa's 7 percent net margin in a "commodity" metals business far outshines Alcan's 3 percent and Reynold's 1 percent net margins. The ability to make money in a down market is a consistent skill of Alcoa. While the aluminum industry in general suffered through a protracted slump in pricing for the last five years, Alcoa has seen its profits rise. For the last six years, the London Metal Exchange (LME) price for aluminum has dropped while Alcoa's earnings have increased. Alcoa's astute chairman, Paul O'Neil, explains why Alcoa does not accept most outside excuses for profit slippage.

> We've always insisted on making a rate of return on our assets, rather than focusing on the tons, throughput, or production figures that are deluding many of the other metals companies. Alcoa is well integrated, but we get 75 percent of our sales from thousands of different fabricated products, everything from car and truck wheels and aircraft wings to window frames and bottle caps. Diversification of aluminum products, markets, and countries helps growth and spreads risk. Furthermore, aluminum is slowly replacing steel in car and appliance making. About one-third of our business is done with distributors, which helps reduce a lot of costs.

We have just-in-time inventory control, small batch production, flexible production lines, quick machine tool changes, and minimal waste. We seek to "pull" rather than "push" goods through the manufacturing process. In other words, products are made in response to a customer order like they are at Dell Computer, not churned out merely to keep equipment running. We have over 200 locations in 31 countries, yet we need just two days to close the books after the end of a quarter. Our selling, general, and administrative expenses (SG&A) is 5 percent of revenues compared with 6 percent for Alcan and 7.6 percent for Reynolds.

After acknowledging that management must accept some of the responsibility for disappointing results and not be in denial of the facts, the top leadership must support the notion that everyone is in marketing. As more managers realize that they are part of marketing, the entire organization becomes rejuvenated and in more control of their destiny.

MAKE MARKETING THE WHOLE COMPANY

I have had CEOs of some of the best known and largest industrial companies ask me privately, "What the heck is industrial marketing all about?" and others have said, "How do we make our company more market driven?" After asking a few questions, I quickly realize that some of these executives equate marketing with just selling, or even worse, many CEOs and general managers think of marketing as just literature, public relations, and glitzy sales presentations. Even fewer CEOs and general managers realize that the service/product package is a strategic variable that can be tailored to groups of customers at different prices to create customer value, competitive advantages, and differentiation. These same unknowledgeable executives have no understanding that strategic market segmentation is the method by which a business unit develops the right capabilities to deliver a service/product package that brings superior value to customer groups and profit to shareowners. Nearly all of these industrial executives have had backgrounds in engineering, manufacturing, and/or sales. Many have or had titles in marketing, but they have no idea what industrial marking is all about. Very few senior industrial executives have ever participated in a practical industrial marketing workshop or read a sound book about industrial marketing. Not until industrial marketing receives the necessary level of understanding and commitment from top management, which starts with the CEO, group presidents, and general managers, will the industrial marketing concept be implemented in any industrial company. Likewise, the quality movement never got started until top managers understood and supported quality across the enterprise with extensive training.

For any industrial organization to make marketing a stronger force for profitable top-line growth, the first essential step is to obtain the understanding and commitment of top management teams to the practices underlining industrial marketing as discussed throughout this book. If these senior executives don't learn what marketing is, they cannot make the necessary commitment to make and keep marketing the entrepreneurial compass of the enterprise. *At least 90 percent of the CEO's, COO's, group executives, and general managers in industrial firms do not have a clue as to what industrial marketing is or should be to guide profitable top-line growth.* This subject is thoroughly covered in Chapter 3, "Everyone is In Marketing."

After learning what industrial marketing is and ending excuse management responses, top managers must create a growth culture that encourages risk taking, and tolerates failure. These same top executives must share the power and fun with those who do the growing. With the right organic growth values, corporate goals, and empowered business teams, more companies will achieve top-line growth from implementing the industrial marketing concept.

CREATE A GROWTH CULTURE

In great growth companies, the top management has an obsession with internal or organic growth. These managers are always talking about top-line growth, market positions, new products, and the need to move into new markets, new countries, and new continents. If they discuss acquiring a company, it is typically a logical business or product line that they want to pump up into a bigger business or bolt onto an existing business to fill a gap. These same top executives value customers, and they realize the need to let employees achieve dreams and be champions of ideas to grow the business. Because many of the CEOs in these companies had successful experience building a division or business in the company, they know the importance of supporting ideas, being patient, and recognizing and rewarding employees who create customer and share-owner value. In the great organic growth companies, which include 3M, Sealed Air, Hewlett-Packard, and Johnson & Johnson, I have watched successive generations of CEOs and group presidents stress the need for aggressive growth. These successful growth companies are always concerned that they might evolve to complacency from past successes and become less venturesome. Rick Steber, President of Goulds Pumps, Europe, repeatedly reminds his business teams of the need to aggressively go for growth as he states, "Aim high and hit high." In short, these executives assume that their companies will have less of an urgency to grow as they get bigger. They counter the real threat of complacency by emphasizing the need for risk taking and growth at every appropriate event. These top managers know that no company is too big to grow and that no company can save or shrink its way to greatness. They know that the strategy of increasing profits from internal efficiency has a limited future. *They expect their companies to grow faster than the economy or the industries they serve.* These top managers usually put building and growing businesses ahead of buying businesses because they know that even if 25 to 35 percent of the acquisitions add to shareowner value in the long term, they must continue to grow the acquisitions to justify the purchase price and keep good people.

It is far easier to maintain a growth culture in a company such as 3M or Hewlett-Packard than it is to create one in a company that has been stagnant, drifting, shrinking, or downsized. In a company where there has been deep cost cutting or autocratic top-down management, the morale is often low, and people are afraid to speak up with growth ideas. The rumors and lifeboat mentality prevalent in most downsizing, restructuring, or top-down organizations are not conducive to profitable top-line growth. In these situations, top management must work twice as hard to build confidence and encourage people to step forth with new business opportunities. Waves of early retirement programs often leave these same organizations without the highly experienced people who could have served as mentors to younger people. New hires are typically brought in, but they have to first learn the business and earn other people's trust and respect before they can lead teams that plot winning growth strategies.

Encourage Risk Taking and Tolerate Failure

There is a need for developing and maintaining an entrepreneurial capability in every company, especially the larger ones. It is the responsibility of top and general managers to create an environment in which people have the freedom to propose new avenues of growth. Profitable top-line growth requires creativity and risk taking. The old adage "Nothing ventured, nothing gained" is very accurate. With the rate of change in products, processes, and information technology, the ability to respond quickly to opportunities is separating the winners from the losers. However, in workshops all over the world I hear middle managers repeat the following common statements:

"There is little or no tolerance for failure in this company."
"Our top management is too top down to let risk-taking occur."

"There are no rewards but a lot of penalties for taking risks here."
"Our headquarters and group executives micromanage so much that not many opportunities percolate up."

These are not isolated statements. I hear them throughout the week at many workshops. The existence of autocratic top or general managers fuels the cynicism. Even when people laugh and say, "It is better to ask for forgiveness after you do something," it implies that the culture is not right for risk taking and rejuvenating profitable top-line growth.

Many CEOs talk about risk taking and a need for more urgency in the organization, but they reward conformity, short-term results, and small incremental changes. With the risk-averse climate in many corporations, no one in their right mind will stick out their neck and be a crusader for a new opportunity. Even when new ownership or new leadership wants people to take risks, most have not forgotten that it is far safer to keep your mouth shut and not rock the boat. If top management really wants a risk-taking culture it must ask for it, demand it, be patient, and tolerate mistakes. Building a risk-taking culture also requires seeing failure as a mistake and necessary part of learning. In short, top management must create a risk-taking culture that *unleashes the ideas in people that have been waiting to be hatched.*

Share the Power and Fun

Too many business organizations are still molded after and act like a military organization, whose officers and generals hold nearly all of the power at the top. That model works in the military but is outdated in a multibusiness and knowledge-based for-profit organization that operates in many fast moving markets with different technologies, in numerous countries, and that should be managed close to the customer. But contrary to all we've heard about participative management and empowerment, there are still a lot of autocratic CEOs and general managers in many industrial companies. *The wrong leadership style will bury good ideas and creative people.*

A number of CEOs and group-level executives have great difficulty relinquishing any of their power. Their need for power too often creates compliance from everyone else rather than questioning, challenging, and raising needed, but politically unpopular, issues about resource allocations and profitable growth. When power is concentrated in too few people, there is no room for the rest of the organization to venture out and experiment. And without sufficient freedom and decision-making power (now called empowerment) for business teams, organically generated top-line growth will never make much progress. A CEO who is uncomfortable with the word "empowerment," is usually "leading" a top-down organization. When top management shares some of the power with business teams, the organization will grow because people can pursue some of their dreams. If power is not shared and people given a larger space to operate within, creative people will either leave to start a business, join a competitor, develop more outside interests, or be demoralized and become cynical about the organization. What kind of people will be dedicated to a culture in which they cannot have fun at work and in which they cannot realize some of their dreams? In the great growth companies, many people can't wait to get to work, and those same people give reasons beyond money as to why they like to work there. I have been close to Hewlett-Packard for more than 15 years. Many of their employees in northern California could join another company in Silicon Valley the next week at higher pay. But the challenging HP work environment, no-layoff policy, gain- and pain- sharing atmosphere, and good benefits keep most people happy. And the people at Hewlett-Packard continually make explicit connections between the company's financial success and their contributions.

The vast majority of employees at every company are trustworthy and honest. Most employees want to do their jobs well. Most want the company to do better than competitors, and most employees want to excel. Every CEO should ask these questions:

1. How many company mission statements state that risk taking is expected as a key value throughout the organization?
2. How many companies have multiple methods to encourage and evaluate innovative ideas beyond the often hilarious suggestion box?
3. How many companies readily make money available for up-front market research or to conduct a special experiment or feasibility study?
4. Do people frequently use the words "freedom" and "fun" when they describe their work?
5. Do people have to leave the organization to pursue growth opportunities?

If any company's top management can't answer all these questions favorably, it has to change its culture or else there will be little or no organic growth. These same sleepy companies will have difficulty attracting and keeping the most creative and aggressive people.

Good and Bad Growth

All growth is not good growth. Before choosing where to focus your business and which products and services to emphasize, a company's top management should consider good and bad growth or where it does and does not want to grow. A company is not necessarily better because it is bigger. By itself, there is no virtue in growth for just the sake of volume or size. General Motors has for long been the largest U.S. carmaker while also being the least profitable. More sales volume is healthy only if it produces higher overall productivity. In the short term, higher volume might be justified, but if it is tracked and doesn't contribute to overall productivity improvements, it should be considered bad growth and subject to surgery.

Every organization needs to think through its growth strategy. It is very helpful to ask: If we were not already making this product or not already serving this market segment or customer, would we do so now, knowing what we know about this market or product? Healthy growth requires freeing up resources for the most attractive opportunities. You cannot successfully capture opportunities if resources are dedicated to keeping yesterday alive longer, defending the obsolete, or making excuses for continually having unproductive resources and results. You must plan for healthy growth by first fixing, then selling or closing down the bleeders and low-performing situations. Every business needs sound growth strategies and ways to distinguish between good and bad growth.

A good business unit growth strategy requires a focus and product/market concentration. The most common mistake in a bad growth strategy is to try to grow in too many product/market areas at once. A sound growth strategy should think through the targets of opportunities—that is, the product/market combinations in which a company's capabilities are most likely to produce attractive sales and profit growth. Another growth guideline is to find profitable ways to grow that competitors cannot quickly imitate. That is the essence of a competitive advantage.

An investor only wants to increase or grow their investment if it generates an acceptable rate of return. The acceptable level of return is at least the firm's cost of capital. If a business is growing but the returns are inadequate to cover the cost of capital, the company must use investor's money to ante up for a below-par return. As long as a business is not at least returning its cost of capital, it is destroying shareowner value. Most industrial companies have business units that consistently destroy shareowner value because they don't earn their cost of capital. If the corporation has a cost of capital of 11% and it doesn't earn at least this percentage, its owners are going backwards. Failing to rapidly grow a high-profit business also limits the creation of shareowner value. In the longer term, say, five-year periods, the stock market favorably recognizes public companies that create shareowner value. Exhibit 11-1 shows the four possible business situations that either destroy or create shareowner value.

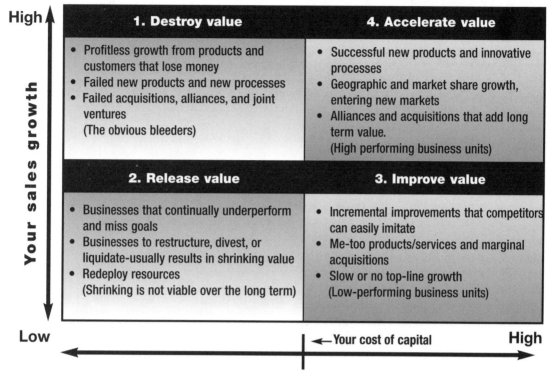

Exhibit 11-1

Growth That Destroys or Creates Long Term Shareowner Value

Your sales growth (High / Low)

1. Destroy value
- Profitless growth from products and customers that lose money
- Failed new products and new processes
- Failed acquisitions, alliances, and joint ventures
  (The obvious bleeders)

4. Accelerate value
- Successful new products and innovative processes
- Geographic and market share growth, entering new markets
- Alliances and acquisitions that add long term value.
  (High performing business units)

2. Release value
- Businesses that continually underperform and miss goals
- Businesses to restructure, divest, or liquidate-usually results in shrinking value
- Redeploy resources
  (Shrinking is not viable over the long term)

3. Improve value
- Incremental improvements that competitors can easily imitate
- Me-too products/services and marginal acquisitions
- Slow or no top-line growth
  (Low-performing business units)

← Your cost of capital (Low / High)

Your rate of return versus the industry and S&P 500

Exhibit 11-1 Notes:
A. The strategic implications of this framework apply to divisions, business units, productlines, customers, market segments, countries, and regions of the world.
B. If a business is not at least covering its cost of capital, why should investors ante up more money? Only when a business has a strategy that returns its cost of capital and more will it create shareowner value. Cells 1 and 2 never create shareowner value; Cells 3 and 4 do.

Companies that continue to invest and maintain businesses that repeatedly have negative or mediocre returns, relative to the company's cost of capital, destroy value. The obvious bad businesses to fix, sell, liquidate, or close down are the bleeders, shown in Cell-1 of Exhibit 11-1. The longer it takes for management to make the obvious decisions with these businesses, the more they destroy shareowner value. Only when management is able to successfully fix and turn these businesses around will the business become a value creator. Restructuring, downsizing, and focusing are ways to "fix" a value-destroying business in Cell 2 of Exhibit 11-1. Investments in Cell 3 are viable as long as the return is greater than the firm's cost of capital. *The most viable growth strategy for high performance companies is to move, or keep business units, products, customers, and markets in Cell 4.* The failure to rapidly grow a business in cell 4 will limit value creation.

The top management team must see the organization as creating customer and shareowner value—not just running plants and pushing products. This same management must clearly articulate a focused vision and then excite and stimulate others throughout the organization to capture the vision by creating more customer and shareowner value. This visionary leadership responsibility must start with the CEO, group presidents, and general managers or it will never get started. This is the most basic responsibility of the top management team—to articulate where the organization is going and where it is not going. If an organization does not clearly know where it is going, it will drift and go backward for all the stakeholders—namely, employees, customers, suppliers, and shareowners.

SET GROWTH GOALS

Everyone must know the sales and especially the profit goals set by top management. For example, the Andrew Corporation, a global manufacturer of wireless phone and data networks, has developed the following minimum long-term goals:

- 15 percent increase in annual sales.
- 15 percent increase in annual earnings.
- 7 percent annual return on sales.
- 16 percent annual return on stockholder's equity.
- 30 percent of sales from new products less than five years old.
- 50 percent reduction in time-to-market.

The top management of Andrew Corporation communicates these minimum goals to all of its 7,000 employees. These goals also appear in bold print on the inside cover of every annual report to show the company's commitment to achieving them.

At minimum, *every company needs clearly stated quantitative goals* that serve as a basis to evaluate decisions. Top management should have fairly consistent goals from year to year, especially for profit. I am amazed at how the profit goals or hurdle rates get changed from year to year, at many firms—and then the top managements at those firms wonder why few business teams ever achieve the goals. Top management must make an explicit commitment to profitable growth goals and then expect them to be achieved in every unit's business plans. For example, the top management of AGA, the Swedish industrial gas giant, stated that it wanted to grow 20 percent faster than the world market for industrial gases and to at least earn the company's cost of capital, which was about 11 percent. At the division or business unit level, AGA's managers had to determine which markets they would emphasize to achieve the ambitious corporate growth goals. Their market segments included gases for eye surgery, carbonating soft drinks, circuit board manufacturing, welding, mobile homes, and patient-enriched air for hospital and home use. AGA had a wide range of products or gases to possibly emphasize, including nitrogen, oxygen, acetylene, propane, helium, neon, and krypton. After analyzing the market segment growth rates for certain gases in specific countries and regions of the world, business teams developed strategies for product/market combinations that would achieve the CEO's sales and profit goals. They also had to consider the right services and "packaging" of the gases which included various sizes of cylinders, bulk truck transport, and on-site generation systems for certain market segments and key accounts.

Balance the Short and Long Term

All public companies have short-term profit pressures. Nearly every public company has constant *tension between the short term and long term*. To create a balance, the firm should *achieve both its short- and long-term goals*. Planning for a balance between long- and short-term profit growth is something that top managers must also articulate clearly and widely throughout the organization. Poor short-term performance often makes long-term progress more difficult. However, an obsession with short-term, quarterly performance and yearly bottom-line numbers can create a behavior of fear, small increments and too much cost cutting. In these situations managers indefinitely postpone investments in new products, equipment, and training. These managers run companies like a banker with a cash "portfolio" and quickly move cash around a Monopoly board like a riverboat gambler—not like a long-term builder of great companies which requires patient investments in people, new technology, and markets.

Why Have Stretch Goals?

Most top-level executives I have worked with complain that many of their people lack a sense of urgency. Many CEOs and general managers say they would like to see their people work more like an entrepreneurial startup company, where everybody's juices are flowing, high targets are set, and people push each other to achieve heroic results. Many upper-level executives do not realize that a sense of urgency starts when the top and general managers set clear and simple stretch goals. Most top management must re-energize their companies before they can achieve faster and more profitable growth. Top and general management need to push themselves and their people to go beyond just incremental improvements.

Stretch goals help people break out of developing plans each year that do the same things, just a little better. With annual improvement goals of 2 to 3 percent, who could expect people to have a sense of urgency? Incremental goals and plans all too frequently create mediocre results. If managers don't demand something out of the ordinary, they won't get anything more than ordinary results from people. These same companies rationalize average goals with statements including, "We're in a cyclical industry," or "We have too many foreign competitors," or "We're in a mature market." These statements often come from "leaders" who have become complacent and comfortable.

Most people get cozy, comfortable, and complacent, especially in paternal or historically successful organizations. People must be removed from their areas of comfort and challenged or pushed to tap their strongest instincts—those that guide survival. You don't have to create a crisis. There are always plenty of real crises and threats to rally people around.

With smarter customers, shorter product life cycles, descending margins, and more resistance to price increases, it is getting increasingly difficult for companies to just earn their cost of capital. For many companies, setting and reaching heroic goals is not an option, it's a necessity, especially when you see threats on the horizon or just around the corner. Stretch targets are not all-financial goals, even though most goals ultimately translate into improved financial results. Stretch goals should be set in many areas including sales growth, profit returns, entering new countries and adjacent market segments, new products as a percentage of sales and gross profits, quality, cycle times, time to market, safety, and cost reductions. For example, when CSX, the huge U.S. railroad, set challenging goals to reduce its freight car fleet from 150,000 to 125,000 units in two years, the goal was achieved. Capital expenditures for the smaller fleet shrank 25 percent from $825 million to $625 million a year. Such challenging goals are better than incremental ones. Moving from 4.7 inventory turnovers a year to 4.9 will not do as much for a business unit as achieving seven turns per year. Reducing the time-to-market cycle time from 25 months to 20 months will not do as much to the top line as a 15-month time-to-market period will achieve.

3M's enthusiastic CEO, Desi DeSimone, was convinced that sales from new products were mostly just replacing products that were being phased out. Furthermore, DeSimone saw a profit shortfall coming from the annual 10 percent increase that 3M always sought. After conferring with many people throughout 3M, DeSimone unveiled an ambitious stretch target. He said, "We must accelerate innovation to the point that 3M is generating 30 percent of its sales from products introduced within the past four years." This goal replaced 3M's revered 25 percent and five-year goal. The new goal sent tremors throughout 3M's divisions and laboratories. The resulting pressures caused 3M to shelve low-impact projects and concentrate more resources on blockbuster products that would significantly accelerate sales and profits.

EMC is hardly a household name. With revenues of $8.5 billion, EMC dominates the data storage computer industry at the expense of once high-flying computer companies including IBM. EMC's spectacular growth and success is partially due to the way the company creates a sense of urgency by setting aggressive quarterly goals for managers. EMC's CEO, Michael Ruettgers, explained this process at my annual new products seminar:

> "People compare the intense atmosphere at EMC to that of a start-up. A sense of urgency primes us to seize opportunities that are only just emerging, as well as to execute our existing plans. We fuel this sense of urgency by setting quarterly goals for the 800 or so managers in the organization. We measure and pay people against quarterly goals. I continue to be amazed at companies that still have annual goals for executives. I can understand having a profit target for the year, but I can't imagine just turning them loose and saying, 'As long as you get this done by the end of the year, it's okay.' We all know that it will probably be significantly more valuable to the company if it is done within two months. Related to this urgency is our emphasis on results and personal accountability. People have to deliver. There are no excuses. And this results-oriented focus applies to senior management, too. Employees know if senior managers make their goals or not."

Clear and Measurable Goals for Everyone

Far too many companies set goals that are nothing more than buzzwords or warm and fuzzy statements. The converse of these shallow statements are often hilarious. Common useless goals include the following:

- We will become the best company. (Would you want to become the worst?)
- We will have world-class competencies. (What the heck is world class?)
- We will be a visionary company. (Would you want to be a myopic or blind company?)

These statements sound like a politician running for office or a consultant peddling the current buzzwords. Furthermore, many companies' so-called vision statements are superficial generalizations that don't really get people's juices flowing rapidly in the same direction.

Many startup and successful small companies set and achieve aggressive goals. The always-present real threats of survival often help these companies create a strong sense of urgency and achieve or exceed audacious goals. Once clear, simple, measurable, and compelling stretch goals are set by the CEO and top management team, employees must see the need to act smarter and faster. Even if a wolf is not at the company's door, people must get out of their traditional and comfortable ways of doing things. Getting employees to endorse stretch goals in the absence of a perceived crisis is sometimes difficult. Stretch goals must be true and convincing to employees. Employees must realize that if they don't improve and change, they will fall on hard times. Company pride and peer group performance pressure between business units can help achieve aggressive stretch goals. Once ambitious but achievable goals are set, top management must get out of the way and let people in the labs, plants, and field, generate ideas, proposals, and strategies to achieve ambitious sales and profit goals. *Clear and measurable stretch goals create stress, tension, and a sense of urgency throughout the organization and thus avoid the tendency for people to plateau.*

Setting stretch goals and engaging all employees is not only the job of a CEO. Managers at every level and department need to set stretch goals with every team member. Ultimately, celebrations, recognition, and pay must follow the achievement of ambitious milestones, or stretch behavior will diminish over time.

Ensuring High Performance: Management Compensation

Quantitative goals provide top management with performance standards to motivate and monitor business units. In high-performing companies the quantitative goals are achieved with more regularity than in run-of-the-mill corporations. By *performance standards,* I mean the usual financial targets that top management uses to control and reward business units and individuals who achieve predetermined objectives.

People around the world go to work to earn money. Although people may work for other reasons, an acceptable level of monetary reward is always a concern. Money counts and it counts as much for the lowest paid employee as it does for the CEO. Deciding how to compensate people to achieve a company's goals is an extremely important responsibility of top management. The compensation methodology for many low-performing companies has an insignificant amount of variable pay at risk. Instead, these sleepy companies have management pay schemes that resemble a civil service organization, and the pay schemes for general managers and above have the appearance of a country club of "good old boys" who are well paid regardless of how their business unit or overall company does. In some companies, compensation is treated more like an entitlement or seniority program than as a way to recognize and reward outstanding performance. Compensation should be structured to provide big rewards for outstanding performance and meaningful penalties for poor performance. Low ability, lazy, and risk adverse managers will be attracted to companies with bureaucratic compensation systems that largely ignore business-unit and individual performance.

Deciding on the specific compensation amounts and time periods for long-term incentives can be a fairly complex subject, well beyond the scope of a book. However, to create an entrepreneurial climate across the organization, short- and long-term incentives should have a significant amount of every profit-center manager's and team member's pay "at risk" based on the performance of their business unit.

It is also important for people throughout the organization to know what kinds of businesses, markets, and customers should be avoided and what capital availability or constraints exist. The top management of well-run companies usually provides this information in the form of broad strategic guidelines for all their operating units.

PROVIDE BROAD STRATEGIC GUIDELINES

Top management strategic guidelines are essential to providing parameters for people actually doing the strategic thinking and planning in the various business units or divisions. The key here is to make sure that the guidelines are rational, in line with the realities of the business, and don't create a bureaucracy.

A good example of top management strategic guidelines to help set the stage for effective planning is provided in the following memo from the president of an industrial firm to the company's division managers:

> As you know, our end purpose is to earn a return for our shareowners that is more attractive than they could expect from other investments with similar risks and at least achieve our cost of capital. To do this means we must consistently compound our earnings at a rate that is 3 to 5 percent higher than inflation and achieve a return on stockholder equity in excess of 20 percent. For the corporation to achieve this kind of performance means that each operating unit must compound its earnings growth at the same rate and achieve an after-tax return on assets of at least 15 percent. In most cases each business unit will need to improve our after-tax return on sales to 5

percent or better to achieve the target return on net assets. These goals are mathematically compatible given our capital structure, debt limitations, and dividend requirements. Even more important, they are achievable. In fact, the leading company in our industry has done better over the past several years.

As you commence your strategic thinking and planning, be sure to keep the following five broad guidelines in mind:

1. We want to reduce our dependence on the OEM automotive industry to no more than 20 percent of sales so that we can achieve a more stable earnings pattern from after-markets and less cyclical market segments.
2. We want to shift our focus from selling products to sellong systems and serving selected markets (e.g., coatings, oil field, copiers, medical equipment) that we believe have more attractive growth prospects than the overall economy.
3. We want to have at least 50 percent of our sales from outside the United States within the next three years, and we are especially interested in rapidly growing our positions in Southeast Asia, China, and central Europe to achieve geographic diversity.
4. We want to achieve a goal of 25 percent of sales from products introduced in the last five years (in our electronic imaging businesses it should be about 35 percent and in our fluropolymers businesses about 20 percent).
5. We don't want to put new capital into any business that does not offer the possibility of achieving our profit goals within the next three to five years.

This short memo does an excellent job of providing some broad direction without putting anyone in a straightjacket. Continuing emphasis on these kinds of targets and guidelines forces the strategic thinking in each business unit into areas of business with the potential to accomplish company goals and to fix or get out of business areas where this possibility does not exist.

DEFINE THE PLANNING UNITS

It is usually unrealistic to develop plans for an industrial business as a whole. It makes more sense to segment the business according to some combination of product, market, customer, or application. These segments should be the building blocks for planning rather than the large operating units typically shown on corporate organization charts. "Small is beautiful" is an appropriate reminder to any business planning team. It is much more meaningful to develop strategies for many discrete product/market segments than for a big organization unit that houses multiple businesses with quite different customers, competitors, technologies, product requirements, and growth prospects.

Companies that are successful at strategic thinking and planning often break five or six major organization units down into forty or more discrete product/markets for strategic planning purposes. Reliance Electric is a case in point. Although the company is managed around five major organization units (Electrical Products, Mechanical Products, Toledo Scale, Telecommunications, and Federal Pacific), the business is planned and controlled around more than 80 separate product centers, each with its own plan and net profit responsibility. The "small is beautiful" motto applies to the need for smaller planning units. The goal is to create the spirit, soul, and speed of a focused, small business but with the resources of a large company.

ESTABLISH PLANNING FORMATS

In companies with many divisions or business units, a wide variety of interpretations are possible if top management does not provide direction as to the end business plans expected. The trick is providing adequate direction without confining anyone. The following memorandum sent to all operating managers by the president of a multidivisional company illustrates how direction can be provided without an elaborate set of forms and procedures:

> **To all profit centers: As we move toward our planning review dates, it is important to agree on what your business plans should look like. I think you can summarize everything we want to see on a few slides or frameworks, as follows.**
>
> 1. Define in a paragraph or two what customer value and strategy your business is seeking in a way that provides the rationale for the growth and profit goals you have set. In other words, state the overall mission you have defined for your business unit and how you intend to accelerate sales and profit growth, with customer value.
> 2. Show a five-year history of sales, market share, earnings before taxes, return on sales, return on net assets, and cash flow, and compare with our corporate targets. Do this for your division overall and for each product line or market segment for which you have prepared a strategic business plan.
> 3. In a side-by-side comparison, show how you stack up against the best competitor on factors important to customers. Indicate where you have competitive advantages and disadvantages and the basis by which you will develop a competitive advantage that translates into customer value and attractive shareowner profit.
> 4. Show three-year projections of sales, market share, earnings before taxes, return on sales, return on net assets, and cash flow for your division overall and for each product family or market segment you're planning around.
> 5. List the key strategic issues, strategies, and programs required for your division and for each product or market segment. If major capital or expense commitments are required, be sure to highlight these and indicate the probable timing. Also, be sure to comment on your priorities in the event that corporate cannot fund everything you want to do.
> 6. Describe what strategic alternatives you could pursue to accelerate your profit growth, assuming no constraints on capital or short-term profit requirements.
>
> **Be sure to have the backup detail to respond to questions that are likely to be raised during your presentation. You will undoubtedly want to have your whole management team with you so that questions can be directed to those most directly responsible.**

The actual format may vary somewhat from industry to industry. However, the objective should always be to avoid unnecessary details, forms, and schedules and to concentrate instead on end results that bring the strategic issues and growth options into sharper focus.

As a kickoff to the planning process, top management spells out what they expect in terms of sales and profit goals for the corporation over the next three- to five- year period. With these quantitative goals and other top management guidelines, each business unit shows what sales and profit results it can generate in the time period laid out by top management. The differences between the goals set by top management and the projections of each business is a performance gap. If there is a gap between the aggregate outlook for all the company's business units to meet the overall growth and profit goals, the question is, "How big is it?" If there is a gap, what are the alternative ways to close the gap? Chapter 13, "Developing a Business Plan," explains how sound business planning bridges any gaps between top management goals and the planned results of divisions or business units.

In developing business plans, most managers and their business teams need instruction, hands-on learning, and coaching. At a bare minimum, management training, developed with top management, is needed to describe the broad strategic guidelines, define the planning units, explain the planning formats, the quantitative growth goals, and provide a timeline for the strategic planning and review process. For a company that is just embarking on a strategic management process, more lengthy training is needed to build the necessary skills into the organization. In companies whose previous strategic thinking and planning was essentially a budget, a lot of management development work is needed at the division or business-unit level, where good bottom-up plans originate. Since profitable top-line growth is all about focusing on customer value and developing winning business strategies and plans, management development is usually needed for the cross-functional business teams developing each plan.

ORGANIZE FOR GROWTH

Management in many companies tends to devote too much time and emphasis to alternative ways to perfect or strengthen the organization, and the danger of frequent reorganization or overstructuring is very real. The organizational structure is one of the trappings frequently pointed to by management as an indicator of its commitment to accelerating top-line growth. However, by itself an organizational structure is nothing more than lines and boxes on a chart; it does not in any sense ensure solid sales and profit performance or market leadership. It is all too easy for managers to delude themselves into thinking they have an outstanding company because they have a large or highly structured organization. In short, these companies are often breeding grounds for bureaucracies and political agendas that tend to interfere with or even thwart the achievement of the organization's very reason for being.

A carefully thought-out organizational structure is the only logical vehicle for directing and coordinating the diverse but related activities of large numbers of people toward common growth goals. Moreover, with increasing emphasis on expanding products and markets all around the world, it is clear that the need for organizations that work effectively is not likely to decline. What I am suggesting, however, is that management must recognize how easy it is for any organization to become bureaucratic, particularly as it grows larger. While bureaucracy is a problem for any organization, it is devastating to activities where crisp, responsive cross-functional decisions and actions are crucial to meet customer and market needs. Recognizing bureaucratic symptoms, is a continuing management responsibility. Even more important is the need to constantly assess how the organization is functioning and to think through alternative ways to focus growth and how the decision-making process can be streamlined to avoid the development of bureaucracy.

Given this perspective on organization structures, let's examine alternative ways of organizing activities and the considerations that will lead to making marketing the headlights of the business and everyone's responsibility.

Basic Considerations

The correct structure for any business function or operating unit is always a lively subject for discussion since there are so many different approaches that could be followed and so many different "expert" ideas of what is right or wrong. Looked at in fundamental terms, the organizational structure for any business unit is simply a framework for carrying out the key activities essential to the growth and success of the operation. Designing this framework requires careful thought; there are always a variety of ways it can be structured and major penalties to be paid if it is designed incorrectly. It is unrealistic to think in terms of a perfect solution to any organizational question because there is not likely to be a perfect match between people's skills and the needed job requirements. For this reason, compromises and trade-offs are almost always involved in developing any organization. The objective should be to seek the right balance between an organizational approach that theoretically makes the most sense and one that is practically possible given the realities of the situation—existing skills and capabilities and time or cost constraints.

There are probably more inherent difficulties in organizing the marketing department (if one still exists) effectively than there are in organizing most other functional areas. To start with, all marketing activities must be structured in a way that will ensure leadership and direction to all other functional disciplines, which is the very essence of the industrial marketing concept. In other words, there is very little chance of having a successful industrial marketing effort if the functions outside marketing go their own way without looking to the marketing department for leadership. Also, a large number and wide variety of activities may be a part of the marketing department, including market research, strategic market planning, commercial development, distributor management, and direct sales activities. This means the strategy and programs developed in the business groups must be translated into action programs across the organization. Given these conditions, it is clear that careful thinking and analysis are required to determine how the enterprise can be structured to overcome departmental barriers and meet the requirements of target markets.

As functionally organized firms grow and focus they typically add product, market, and/or business unit managers to manage the more traditional marketing activities. These management positions are described later in this chapter. As the company learns about sound industrial marketing, it increasingly becomes the soul and philosophy of the business. *Industrial marketing should become a business process used by everyone in the organization and especially the cross-functional teams that horizontally serve customer groups.* When industrial marketing becomes the whole company and not just one department, the classic marketing department is less needed.

The organizational principles in this chapter should be used as guidelines, not controlling considerations in any company. By definition, guidelines are just that, and they can be violated if it makes sense to do so. For example, the old saw that authority should be consistent with responsibility does not hold true in the case of product or market management in which the manager has all kinds of responsibility without commensurate authority. Also, some quantitative limit on the span of control, such as five or seven people reporting to a superior, is not a rule that should be followed rigidly. There are plenty of industrial organizations that have as many as ten or twelve individuals reporting to a supervisor who carries the responsibility very effectively. The number of individuals reporting to a superior depends entirely on what is required in the way of supervision, not solely on some firm principle of organization.

When to Make a Change

The need to change or restructure the organization depends on two factors: how effectively the current organization operates and how adequately it provides the focus necessary to capitalize on future product and market opportunities. Deciding that the organization is or is not functioning effectively at a certain point in time is obviously a judgment call, but there are several questions you can ask to help make this judgment:

1. Is the organization responsive to customer needs, competitive actions, and/or shifting market requirements? Is it easy for customers to do business with the

organization? Are quoted delivery dates met? Are customer inquiries or requests for quotes on special items handled promptly?

2. Does the organization produce creative business strategies and solid business plans that result in a competitive advantage for each of its priority products and markets?

3. Do product, market, or business managers fulfill their role as the lead function of the business and ensure that all key functions are properly geared to serve the company's target markets? Are the communication links with manufacturing, sales, engineering, and finance clearly aligned to the target markets?

4. Does the organization achieve planned market performance and profit objectives? Are prompt corrective actions taken when actual performance falls behind plan? Is it clear who is accountable for results in each product line, segment of the business, and for each major program?

If the answer to any of these questions is negative, some kind of change is required. It may well be that a structural change in the organization to provide for better planning, closer coordination with other functions (such as R&D), stronger sales management, or some other such improvement is the answer. However, it is also essential to determine whether the problem really stems from a fault in the structure or in the people involved. Performance evaluation is especially important. No organizational structure will ever work effectively with inadequate performers. Nor are inadequate performers likely to work any more effectively under a new or changed alternative structure. A lot of time can be wasted shuffling boxes on a chart or putting names in different boxes if management does not face up to fundamental weaknesses in the people involved. People must know the industry, the technology, and the needs of customers. Training is usually needed to help cross-functional business teams develop a winning business strategy and cross-functional plans.

Looking to the future, the key questions to ask are these: What are the product/market areas selected for emphasis? How do we ensure the strong management and entrepreneurial drive to capture the business in these areas? If major opportunity areas are not specifically assigned in a way that brings these skills to the forefront, some organizational change is in order. The change may be as simple as giving some individuals dual-role assignments (e.g., continue as regional sales manager and also be responsible for planning growth in the marine market). Conversely, the change may require a major restructuring of the organization to provide stronger product or market management. Although different approaches may be used to achieve proper product/market assignments, the objective should always be the same: to ensure that someone feels the burden of responsibility for profit growth in each product/market area. Otherwise, these areas will be fun and interesting to talk about but nothing much will happen to advance the company's position.

MANAGE EACH FOCUS

We now turn to the management or administrative side of the market segmentation process. Over the years as industrial or business-to-business organizations have grown, they have evolved from a functional or departmental marketing organization to a cross-functional and horizontal process of managing markets, customers, products, and services. The basic organizational approaches to managing many products and markets are product management, market management, industry managers, and the use of business unit managers.

Product Management

As the number of products proliferates, a functional marketing department cannot manage them. A product management organization also makes sense when the company's products are quite different and flow into a single market or a few markets. Product managers usually report to the marketing department or a business unit manager. A product manager's job responsibility falls into ten areas:

1. Maintaining product leadership for existing and new product platforms by making certain that product design, cost, and performance characteristics not only are broadly responsive to customer needs in all markets, but also are not inadver tently altered to meet the needs of one market segment at the expense of the company's position in another market.
2. Ensuring that the product platform is responsive to market needs while at the same time avoiding changes that will clutter the engineering and production process with a proliferation of small-lot, custom, or special orders; in effect, they temper market managers' enthusiastic customer orientation with sober judgments on operating capability and economics.
3. Ensuring that production scheduling, lead times, inventory control, and capacity are intelligently planned to profitably meet the current and anticipated aggregate demand of various markets.
4. Being responsible for consistent quality, product-line cost reductions, warranty costs, and product and customer support.
5. Providing the in-depth technical and/or product knowledge and training required to support direct selling efforts on major and complex systems and with distributors.
6. Conducting side-by-side competitive comparisons, especially with the best competitor.
7. Being responsible for a business plan and accountable for gross and net profit results.
8. Protecting the pricing integrity of their product—that is, seeing to it that the pricing policies and practices in one market do not jeopardize the company's position or cost/profit structure in another.
9. Developing product specific information, bulletins, and literature.
10. Being responsible for product-line and customer rationalization.

The qualifications and functions of consumer goods and industrial companies are quite different. Consumer goods product managers (often called brand managers) typically come from advertising agencies because much of the job involves emotional customer needs, media spending, and working with advertising agencies. Industrial product managers are usually older and often have a technical background, and they spend more time with customers and their company's technical people. Industrial companies rarely have brand managers because advertising is a relatively small part of their business success.

Product managers often give too little thought to new products other than modifications, cost reductions, and line extensions to their existing products. The *new product manager concept* is often very effective when a company has managers marshal a product through development and well into the launch. At 3M, new-product managers are called product champions, and they might be encouraged to form a small, formal or informal, new venture team to develop a new concept.

In addition to not developing really new products, the product management organization has a number of weaknesses. Product managers usually have insufficient authority to carry out the listed responsibilities. Empowerment simply doesn't exist to carry out the job. Instead, they must rely on internal selling and persuasion to get cross-functional cooperation. Sometimes product managers are nothing more than glorified schedulers. To overcome these deficiencies, some companies have created cross-functional teams to work with the product manager in developing business plans and responding to the short-term needs inside and outside the company.

Market Management

When a manufacturer sells products to a number of distinctive and diverse markets, a market manager gets the nod. Market managers typically report to the marketing director. Market managers might be called market development managers, market specialists, or industry managers. A "specialist" title might be a permanent or short-term responsibility to get a product specified in an industry or to do missionary work in a specific industry or market segment. A market or industry manager may be responsible for one defined market (paint coatings) or a related group or markets (wood finishes, carpet coatings, caulks, and tape joint compounds), each requiring a focused business plan. A market manager's job responsibility falls into ten areas:

1. Developing a comprehensive understanding of customer and end-user operations and economics and specifying ways that the existing product and service package can be improved to provide a competitive edge in defined segments.
2. Developing a reputation for industry expertise and company capabilities among key customers and end-user groups and bringing this know-how to bear on the training and development of field personnel and negotiation of major orders.
3. Identifying product line gaps, new products and services, or systems that represent attractive opportunities for profitably enlarging the company's participation in defined markets through internal development, alliances, or acquisitions.
4. Drawing together at regular intervals an organized summary of the most attractive opportunities in the marketplace, specifying what must be done internally to capitalize on them, and recommending a first-cut strategy for the business.
5. Developing an understanding of the competition in each market segment, their strengths, weaknesses, and likely next moves.
6. Developing a value statement and business plan for each market segment and coordinating direct key accounts and distributor sales.
7. Developing market-segment-focused communication programs in the language and benefits of each target segment and participating in the appropriate trade associations, technical forums, and trade shows.
8. Setting prices for each market segment, key account, and focused distributor.
9. Being responsible for product-line and customer rationalization.
10. Being accountable for sales volume, margins, sales terms, and gross and net profit results.

Both Product and Market Managers

Because product and market proliferation have greatly increased in a large number of industrial companies, many find themselves selling multiple products in multiple markets with no neat product/market match. Under these circumstances, planning from one perspective—product or market—tends to be self-defeating. Neither one nor the other can be downgraded in the planning process without severe penalty.

If product managers are chosen, each one is likely to concentrate on selling his or her assigned products rather than on determining what it takes to serve the markets more effectively. In so doing, the managers will probably miss important opportunities in related products and services. Even more importantly, without sufficient focus on the market, the chances are good that product lines will lag behind competitive offerings or even become obsolete because the managers find themselves unable to keep up with changing user needs. If market managers are selected, each will tend to focus on meeting the requirements of his or her assigned market without regard for the effect that these actions or recommendations may have on the company's ability to meet the needs of other market areas with the same product line. Thus, if a company has exceptionally strong or persuasive managers covering one or two market areas, it can very easily end up with product plans or actions in these markets that seriously jeopardize the company's position in other market areas.

How does a company ensure the right planning emphasis and balance in this kind of situation? A growing number of industrial companies that I work with have found that the only solution to this dilemma is to stop trying to decide between product or market managers and, instead, use them both. Under this dual arrangement, market managers have an external focus toward the market and are responsible for determining what the company should do to be more responsive to market needs. The product manager's job is to seek a balanced response to the needs and opportunities in certain markets without jeopardizing the company's position in others and without placing an unfair burden on manufacturing and engineering.

With the dual approach of having product and market managers, the potential for conflict is automatically created. Both of these jobs fight for attention and time from engineering, manufacturing, and sales for their assigned products or markets. Let's look closer at the inner workings of this healthy conflict.

Because market managers' primary responsibility is to identify and meet market needs, they quite naturally seek modifications in the existing product or service packages without regard for any other market or the functional difficulties that may be created. And because product managers are responsible for keeping their product lines responsive to the needs of all the company's markets in terms of costs, design, performance characteristics, pricing policy, service, and warranty arrangements, they cannot bend indiscriminately to the requirements any one market manager perceives. Although inevitable, the conflict arising from the interaction of product managers and market managers should not be viewed as negative. In fact, this kind of conflict is specifically what the dual-management concept is designed to produce, and it should be regarded as a positive force. If it is properly managed, the conflict should help uncover a multiplicity of market opportunities that would otherwise go unnoticed and, at the same time, provide a mechanism for sorting through these opportunities so that the company's overall interests are best served.

DuPont has learned how to channel the always-present conflict with the dual approach of product and market managers. *The dual approach is a true matrix organization with shared authority.* As an example, DuPont's textile fibers business has separate product managers for five product families (nylon, rayon, orlon, acetate, and dacron) and five dedicated market managers (men's wear, women's wear, automotive, home furnishings, and industrial customer groups). DuPont views their market managers as the headlights of the business, and they see their product managers as suppliers to the market managers. DuPont's market managers closely resemble business-unit managers in other companies.

However, the dual approach adds costs because it requires both sets of managers, and there are still questions to address in three areas:

1. How should product development priorities be set? If manufacturing is shared, how should facilities be scheduled, and how should capacity additions be planned?
2. How should the sales force be organized? (Should the sales force be organized geographically or more specialized by either products or by markets?)
3. Who should set prices for the existing and new products in each market? (Usually, the market manager is responsible for the pricing of the product.)

Business Unit Managers

Business unit teams, staffed by full-time specialists reporting to a business unit leader, are an increasingly popular way to achieve market focus and cross-functional cooperation across the organization. Many companies evolve their organizations from product manager to market or business-unit managers, and then, as it grows, a new division with a general manager is formed. The business unit has either regional or global profit responsibility and is like a mini general manager with its own full-time technical and salespeople. Manufacturing facilities are usually shared, but they may also be dedicated to the business unit. Business unit teams must have full profit responsibility and at first usually report to the marketing director. Over time their reporting relationship should be to a general manager. The effective use of global business-unit managers, often with counterparts in other regions of the world, is reducing the need to have regional general managers or regional vice presidents. Country managers may still exist in the major countries. A business unit (sometimes termed a strategic business unit or SBU) must meet these criteria:

1. It must have a set of external customers with some common needs.
2. It must have a clear set of external competitors.
3. It must have control over its own destiny (what products to offer, how to obtain supplies and resources, how to set prices and whether to use shared resources such as research and development and a sales force).
4. It must be a profit center and be measured by its sales and profit results.

With the flattening of organizations, leaner structures, information technology, and more of a bottom-up approach that pushes decision making down to front-line teams, the business-team concept will continue to flourish. When a business unit is defined in terms of customer groups with similar needs, a more market-driven organization will evolve. Market-defined business units start with customer groups and then utilize the organization as a horizontal process to profitably serve the targeted customers. When a business-unit team is defined only around products, there is a big risk of products becoming obsolete, because market segments are more enduring and have identifiable and measurable needs.

Finally, recognition and equitable pay, based on results, are what keeps a business team performing. The drive for teamwork, especially through cross-functional business groups, is way ahead of the pay and recognition systems currently in place in most companies. Cross-functional or group performance appraisals, compensation, and recognition systems are lagging in many companies. The whole movement to business-unit teams for managing markets, key customers, and products will increase when team-based rewards become a significant part of everyone's incentive on the team.

Global Business Teams

Henkel KGaA is a $12 billion (US dollars) specialty chemical company headquartered in Düsseldorf, Germany. They are the world's largest manufacturer of adhesives, oleochemicals, chemicals for surface metal treatment, and industrial cleaning chemicals. Henkel prides itself on being a truly global company with more than 56,000 employees worldwide and about 41,000 people working for the company outside of Germany. Some of its global brands include Loctite, Ecolab, Cognis, and Henkel.

Henkel has done a good job of creating global business teams. Each global business unit guides the development of business plans for discreet target markets and key accounts in each region of the world. Every global business team is accountable for net profitability. Cross-functional global business teams helped Henkel change from a hierarchical emphasis with "silos" in manufacturing, sales, and technical areas, to more of a horizontal or matrix organization as shown in Exhibit 11-2. In the new cross-functional business team organization, target market plans and customer selection were more focused. Faster decision making took place. Customers were served faster, and customer satisfaction and customer profitably became a responsibility of everyone. Under CEO Dr. Harald Wulff's leadership, the global business planning teams and regional counterparts accomplished the following:

1. They divided the world into four geographic regions: the Americas, Europe, Japan, and Asia Pacific.
2. They established global market segment definitions and common application codes across the world.
3. They developed bottom-up country, regional, and global business plans that helped the company move from being a multinational to a more global enterprise.
4. They reduced the duplication of R&D efforts, and developed more global products with cross-functional and cross-continental business team inputs.
5. They shared more market segment, technology application knowledge, and customer contacts among countries and regions of the world.
6. They better served and coordinated large global customers around the world.
7. They created global centers of excellence for businesses with multinational or global opportunities, and the global strategic business units (SBUs) are led by global business unit managers, and regional counterparts
8. They eliminated many general manager and regional vice president positions by empowering business unit managers and their teams.
9. They have country managers in most of the major countries of the world.
10. They maintain very small regional offices in Germany, the United States, and Singapore.

Exhibit 11-2

Serving Global Market Segments and Key Accounts

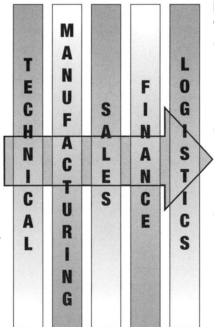

Outside-In Planning

Is done geographically by:
- Countries
- Regions
- Globally

1. Market segments are selected to counterattack, attack, deemphasize, or withdraw from

2. Key accounts are prioritized as defend, attack, deemphasize, or withdraw from the target market segments

Inside-Out Strategy

- Led by global business unit managers (SBUs) and regional counterparts

- Managed by cross-functional business teams with net profit responsibility

- Regional cross-functional teams develop business plans for each target market and key accounts are coordinated between regions of the world

Henkel's *organizational structure followed their strategy* to become more of a global company. It is important to realize that their organizational structure *followed* a well thought out global business strategy. Their global strategy was not constrained by outdated management practices and a historical multinational organization with country and regional fiefdoms.

SUMMARY

The number one item on nearly every industrial company's agenda is profitable growth. This chapter stresses what top management must do to accelerate profitable growth. Because top management creates the culture and values, sets the goals, controls resources, and determines the organizational design, if they do not provide the right kind of leadership in these areas, there will be little, if any, organic growth. Profitable top-line growth starts with top management doing the right things or it doesn't get started. The mindset of profitable top-line growth starts at the top, but it must be fully supported by every general manager, and then valued and implemented all the way to the bottom of the organization. Top management, who doesn't also delegate responsibility and authority to business teams, will have difficulty becoming a great growth company.

Top management must set aggressive goals, establish business planning units and organize the enterprise for sales and profit growth. It is also important that top management and their general managers read and understand the concepts in this entire book so they can speak the language of their associates and commit to the organizational structures, infrastructure systems, and rewards that make marketing the needed force to drive growth on a country, regional, and global basis. With the right culture and empowered business teams in place, top management should step aside, never micromanage, coach only as needed, and then judge teams by their business plan and results. If top management follows these prescriptions for profitable top-line growth, they will lead their company to new heights.

Winning Market Strategies

"A good industrial market strategy is a series of integrated actions leading to a competitive advantage and sales and profit growth."

Andy Grove, Intel
Chairman

Andy Grove, chairman of Intel, is one of the few executives that clearly understands that industrial marketing and strategy are synonymous. The basic building blocks of strategy are customer segmentation, differentiation, customer value, product/market selection, market share, positioning, and profitable growth are all concepts from industrial marketing. Furthermore, sound industrial market strategies should always be developed with an understanding of customer needs, competitive comparisons, and profitability considerations. In short, industrial marketing concepts play a vital role in developing winning strategies and effective implementation programs.

WHAT IS STRATEGY?

There is considerable confusion among businesspeople, consultants, and academics about what is a strategy. The word *strategy* has been overused and misunderstood. Many confuse corporate strategy (what businesses we want to be in) with strategy at the divisional or business unit levels (what markets, products and services we want to be in). A business unit strategy is a compilation of one or more product/market strategies, and the corporate strategy is basically an aggregation of the company's business-unit strategies. Many people call any activity in R&D, manufacturing, or sales a "strategy" when they should be called "programs" to implement a corporate or business unit strategy. *Market strategy at the business-unit level is about delivering customer value that translates into attractive sales and profit growth for the supplier.* The focus of this book is on market strategies done within and by divisions or business units for markets, products, and services. Let's now strip away all the buzzwords, describe market strategy and stragegic thinking in business units, and then provide some proven market strategies to grow sales and profits.

Developing a sound strategy is a relatively straightforward process, and yet the subject of strategy has become obscured and overcomplicated by pseudo-intellectuals and those with their own hobbyhorses to ride. Strategy is about identifying and capturing opportunities and coping with blows and surprises. Strategy can also be defined as attacking and counterattacking markets, defeating rivals, and making an attractive profit. Strategy has unfortunately become remote from those who need it the most—business managers fighting to create and deliver products and services that customers prefer over competitors' offerings. Market strategy is most useful when it is used to bring business discipline to each cross-functional business team. Business units are where strategies to create customer value and shareowner value are developed. Therefore, business teams need to know how to develop sound product/market strategies. Top management should review and approve business unit strategies—but never develop them.

Corporate or Business-Unit Strategy?

In a multibusiness organization, "corporate strategy" is somewhat of a misnomer because the head office staff has no products or customers, only overhead costs. Corporate strategy, which has been popularized by consultants and academics, is usually an alien imposition on decentralized business units. Corporate strategy, which is the firm's overall strategy of what business it wants or does not want to be in, comes from headquarters. Corporate strategy is concerned with the growth and profits from a mix of businesses. The corporate office should review bottom-up-developed strategies and businesses plans and then decide which businesses to invest in and which others to deemphasize, withdraw from, fix, close, or sell. Desi DiSimone, CEO of 3M, stated this well at our annual senior executive workshop:

> We have no grand corporate strategy at 3M. We let technology and our division people tell us where to go. But we do have clear financial and new-product goals that all of our people are aware of.

The corporate or group executives should act as a bank that approves or disapproves loans. They should do this by ranking all the business units for investment – from most to least attractive and then go about prudently allocating resources. Corporate headquarters should provide overall measurable goals, a business plan format, and sometimes general guidelines for the development of strategies.

Many so-called corporate strategies are headquarters-driven acquisitions that they initiate, set up, and then pass off to someone else to run and be on the hook for. Divisions or business units should identify most acquisition candidates, conduct the due diligence, and then be held responsible for the business they wanted to acquire. At most, corporate staff people might assist with the financial analysis and some of the tax and legal concerns of an acquisition. Anyone who wants the acquisition should be held responsible for it after it is acquired. Likewise, those who implement any strategies should be those who developed the strategies. The most dangerous strategies (including acquisitions) are those dreamed up by some corporate headquarters staff members or remote CEO that claim they have "a vision." Many corporate-level strategies end up destroying shareholder value. Equally risky are strategies developed by a "strategy" consulting firm that doesn't intimately know a company's technologies, products, customers, market segments, capabilities, or company culture. Consultants are rarely accountable for their strategy recommendations.

Marketing Is Strategy!

Marketing concepts play a central role in developing strategies and implementing cross-functional programs in any business unit. Sound marketing strategies always start with an outside-in analysis of customers, competition, and the environment. Andy Grove, the chairman of Intel, clearly sees industrial marketing and strategy as synonyms:

> A good industrial market strategy is a series of integrated actions leading to a competitive advantage to increase sales and profits. I still sit on the major capital authorization meetings, but only as an observer. But I can't stay away from the market strategy meetings where it all gets put together. I often wonder how CEOs or upper management who don't intimately know the business and understand marketing can evaluate and even much less develop sound market or business strategies that nearly always require significant investment and risk.

As shown in Chapter 4 "Segmenting Industrial Markets", the definition and selection of market segments is the most important decision facing every firm. Everything else follows the selection of market segments—it guides competitive analysis, *drives strategy development to secure competitive advantages,* and determines what action programs and capabilities are needed across the business unit to achieve the sales and profit goals. Without proper business segmentation and the selection of target markets, the strategy development process in a division or business unit can become a fairly academic exercise in form filling and making broad generalizations.

Mostly a Bottom-Up Process

In a multibusiness company, strategy development should be mostly a bottom-up process, conducted by cross-functional business teams to achieve or exceed the top-down goals. The most successful companies concentrate on developing strategies that are part and parcel of the management process for each attractive market segment. These same companies develop strategies around the key issues they identify for each market segment and, in some cases, for a key customer. They place emphasis on outside-in thinking and utilize information about market segment growth rates, customer trends, unmet needs, technology, and side-by-side competitive comparisons. In situations in which there are global customers who demand global coordination and local adaptations, regionally coordinated strategies are needed for these customers. Regional business teams should develop strategies for market segments, and key customers and a global business team leader would then coordinate the strategy and planning process between the regions.

At the division and business unit levels, strategies are needed to answer three decisions:

1. *Where to compete.* Companies must choose whether to compete in one market segment (or a small number) or in many different market segments with focused programs. An undifferentiated strategy would ignore any different needs among market segments.
2. *What basis to compete on.* A differentiated strategy would stress specific benefits for each target market segment. An undifferentiated strategy would stress one consistent message to all customers. However, there are big risks in trying to be all things to all people.
3. *Who to compete with.* A differentiated strategy typically recognizes different arrays of competitors in each market segment and not for just like products supplied to each segment. An undifferentiated strategy would consider a broad array of competitors.

The questions of where to compete, on what basis to compete, and who to compete with are all referred to as *positioning*. Positioning is the decision to design a product/service offering so that it occupies a distinct and valued place in the minds of target markets and customers.

MARKET STRATEGY OR BUZZWORDS?

The business world, especially in America, is full of trendy words that supposedly describe strategy and paths to success. These nonsense words, largely developed by management consultants and academics, fuel the confusion, fads, and fashion in market strategy. *Buzzwords are usually a clue to shallow, fuzzy, and simple-minded thinking.* Exhibit 12-1 lists a few of the more common buzzwords that create much of the mystique and many of the misconceptions about strategy in the industrial world. Whenever you hear any buzzwords in a discussion of strategy, planning, or business growth, speak up and ask pointed questions or run for cover. I can't figure out why so many businesspeople fall for these catchy phrases and then start using them without even thinking about their meaning. Many are just new words or hype created by spin doctors. Most buzzwords are simply nonsense. The latter part of this chapter describes practical and proven market strategies in plain talk that managers can put to work—not in buzzwords that sound like some politician running for office.

Exhibit 12-1

Common Strategy Buzzwords

Buzzword	Description
1. **Best**	This buzzword is often used in vision statements, quality banners, and in annual reports to describe a company's products, services, technologies, people, or overall company. How do you define and measure "the best" in goals people can relate to? If the converse, "the worst," is hilarious, therefore so is "the best." Great companies continually try to get better because they never see themselves as the best. It is always safer to underestimate your strengths and overestimate the competition, and never arrogantly see your company as the best at anything.
2. **Core**	Anything that was previously called key or a strength is now preceded with the word "core." It is a new word applied to the old concepts of existing customers, existing technologies, employee skills, company values, and company strengths—all of which have been now relabeled as "core competencies." If a company has core competencies, it probably also has core incompetencies, or what were formerly called weaknesses. In many companies, any business that is not making sufficient money is now considered a "noncore" business and is usually for sale.
3. **Diversification**	This usually involves taking cash from a successful existing business and buying a more glamorous one or a "new leg" that has no technical or commercial unity with a company's strengths. Purely financially driven strategies are often a diversion of company resources, resulting in "worsification," and later a divestiture, which are now called "demergers" by balance sheet managers.
4. **Internal customers**	When companies don't understand how to attract or keep outside customers (the only ones with real money), they talk about how to keep each other happy within the organization; meanwhile, the real customers (the external ones) may leave, and in turn, cause everyone to lose their jobs. There is only one real customer—the one who needs, pays for, and uses your end products and services.
5. **Leverage**	Financing with debt is called leverage. This is one way a company finances its growth. Equity and cash are other ways to finance growth. In the UK, leverage is called "gearing." Most academics and consultants are not aware of the many ways that high debt can work against a company. Leverage is also now being used in place of the older buzzword "synergy" whenever people are unable to explain more precisely how they will use or do something across the organization, they simply say they will "leverage it."
6. **Outsourcing**	This refers to farming out what a company can also do internally. This century-old industrial word is a "make-or-buy" decision. Progressive companies have always considered the strategic value, cost, and proprietary reasons for doing anything inside or outside their organization.
7. **Portfolio**	This word too often refers to thinking and acting like a stockbroker or trader who periodically buys and sells stock or securities. This simplistic notion sees the company as only a bank that channels cash around the enterprise. It doesn't usually involve thinking like an entrepreneur and getting beyond the numbers and ratios to develop sound strategies that detail how to profitably grow sales in each business.
8. **Stick to your knitting**	Popularized by the book In Search of Excellence, this concept implies that you stay with your existing capabilities (now called core competencies) and current customers (now called core customers). Business history is full of losers who myopically stuck very close to their knitting (existing capabilities), missed a trend, and then went backward or even bankrupt. If many of a company's healthy and growing customers now prefer to buy cotton over wool products, and if a company doesn't change by supplying its customers' new needs, it may eventually die by sticking to its knitting of wool products.

9. Sustainable advantage   This buzzword assumes that a competitive advantage will be ongoing, maybe forever. With the rapid movement of information, technology, and management know-how, it is far safer to assume that all advantages are temporary and short lived. With shorter life cycles, smarter customers, and global competitors, nearly all advantages are increasingly temporary and not sustainable.

10. Synergy   With synergy, 2 + 2 should equal 5, but often ends up equaling 3 or less. It should more appropriately be called negative synergy. Furthermore, when companies don't have a clue of the cost savings or the real technical or commercial fit, an acquisition is termed "synergistic." This buzzword is often used to rationalize an acquisition made by headquarters or recommended by consultants or investment bankers.

11. Vision   Any manager who thinks beyond the next month or quarter is now said to be a visionary. Vision is what successful entrepreneurs have always done to focus, survive, grow, and thrive. Rather than talk with such abstractions, leading companies articulate what kind of business(es) and markets they are in, don't want to be in, and want to be in, communicate this widely, and then inspire and reward people to capture the most attractive opportunities.

12. World class   This buzzword refers to vague things required of companies, their people, and their products and services. Many overengineered and high-cost suppliers favor this buzzword. This word is often seen in vision statements, flashy annual reports, and sales presentations. This term, like most buzzwords, is fuzzy. How do you measure world class? Is a world loser the opposite of world class?

Some buzzwords are called "smart talk." Companies all over the world are vulnerable to smart talk that sounds good and is elegant but is often devoid of substance. Smart talk is unnecessarily complicated and abstract. The empty words of most mission statements are an example of smart talk. Most mission statements sound very much alike. They all extol the values of integrity, respect for the individual, the need for teamwork, the importance of customers, and the need for satisfying shareholders. When were customers unimportant to a for-profit enterprise? The motherhood mission statements are then hung in public company places to ward off evil spirits. Pop-art management books, esoteric business professors, and managers with little or no experience building an organization are especially attracted to superficial smart talk, fads, and buzzwords that don't translate into viable and practical growth strategies. Superficial smart talk is the essence of much of the "management education" at many of the esoteric business schools in the United States and Europe. Inexperienced "business" professors teach students how to sound smart in classroom oral presentations where they never have to implement their eloquent recommendations and be measured by the results.

Questionable Strategy Consultants

The value of smart talk is reflected in the most popular career choice of leading business school graduates—management consulting and especially the big-bucks strategy consulting. Most strategy consulting consists of buzzword questions, buzzword reports, and more buzzword presentations. Armies of consultants in offices around the world bill clients billions of dollars every year for meaningless buzzwords. A few so-called strategy consulting companies now claim that they participate in the implementation, but their clients claim that it is merely a smokescreen maneuver for scheduling and sitting in at many meetings and, of course, more big billings.

Beware of any "growth" or "strategy" consultants who simply try to impress you with the latest slogans or buzzwords. Intel's Andy Grove calls most of these advisors "a bunch of muddled fad mongers." Many growth or strategy consultants are far more interested in creating economic value for themselves than they are for their clients. Some strategy consultants stay inside the client companies forever. Who are the addicted firms that hire these consultants with multiyear and often million-dollar-plus annual fees? AT&T, Lucent Technologies, and many underperforming and confused big companies hire these consultants to supposedly get them out of trouble. When John Walter came from outside AT&T to become its new president, he asked the CEO, Robert Allen, "Why is AT&T spending over a billion dollars a year for advice from many strategy consultants instead of relying on its own people to develop and implement strategies?" John Walter said, "Our managers must learn how to fish and we don't want to have somebody fishing for us." Unfortunately for John Walter, his outspokenness caused his tenure at AT&T to be short lived.

After years of big fees to reengineer and downsize, many of the same consultants renamed their jargon and old techniques as "growth strategies." Most have little or no background in practical industrial market strategies to profitably grow the top line. Most don't intimately know a company's business. Consultants should not create the actual business strategies—that's the job of the business team. How can an outsider, who does not know your industry, your company, your customers, your competition, or the relevant technologies, develop a sound market strategy? They typically generate a "one size fits all" strategy of raising prices, cutting costs, selling assets, and acquiring "diversified" or businesses that have no technical or commercial unity with your existing businesses. Most strategy consultants simply interview employees for advice, add buzzwords to the employees' suggestions, and then package and present the "findings" in nice binders with fancy graphics and a large fee. When this situation occurs employee moral and motivation drops, and respect for top management who hired the consultants continues to decline.

Most companies have had a checkered record of using strategy consultants. Sam Siegel, Nucor's long time CFO, calls the smart talk of consultants the "Baffle them with bullshit people." Companies such as Nucor that have a bias for plain language and practical concepts try to avoid the trap of smart talk. These organizations realize the value of direct language and no nonsense concepts.

The risks of using outsiders to plot your marketing strategy were evident when a consulting firm recommended that Cabot Corporation, the world's largest manufacturer of carbon black and fumed silica, diversify into some more glamorous businesses. At Cabot, carbon black, which is used in tires, paint, copier toner, and a wide range of plastic and rubber products, was the so-called cash cow that consultants channeled money from and used to acquire unrelated businesses in specialized crystals, semiconductors, ceramics, and safety products. Cabot had no technical or commercial linkage to any of these new businesses. The future profits from these "attractive" acquisitions failed to pan out. Cabot was later in such financial stress from these acquisitions that they downsized and sold nearly 50 percent of their assets. Under the direction of a new chairman, Dr. Sam Bodman, major investments were made to modernize their outdated carbon black facilities, and they began to look for organic new business opportunities from within their existing businesses. Sam Bodman described the situation as follows to me:

> When I arrived at Cabot, there had been very limited investment in the base businesses for years. Some outside consultants had convinced the company that you could milk a cash cow and never feed it; and as a result, some of the cash cows nearly died. Think of the message you send to employees in your existing businesses when most of your actions are diverting resources to totally unrelated businesses where you have limited knowledge. We went back to our carbon black and fumed silica businesses and found some unmined diamonds. We made major investments in technology and training over a five-year period. In addition, more than $250 million was invested in product and process R & D. In essence, we chose to invest in ourselves. Proprietary new products were developed for new applications including inkjet printing and semiconductor wafer processing, copier toner, and additives for adhesives and coatings. We moved from being a manufacturing-driven commodity

chemical company to become a market-driven specialty chemical company with business units focused on attractive market segments.

A major problem with many of the academic and consulting people is that they look only at short-term cash flow as a result and not as a cause of doing the right things. The best use of cash might be to counterattack and grow your cash cows and not milk them dry. Why take money from cash cows and divert it to unrelated question marks that are typically acquisitions and that, more often than not, fail? Surplus cash can be used for a number of good purposes—product or process development, updating facilities, sales force improvements, reducing debt, or giving dividends back to shareowners.

To understand why everyone in consulting and academia is now in the strategy business, we must ask why CEOs and general and business-unit managers are outsourcing their responsibility for developing and reviewing strategies to unaccountable outsiders. If managers are well versed in the issues and know how to develop a winning growth strategy, an outsider should not be needed to generate a strategy that insiders must place their careers on. Business teams need to learn how to develop a sound market strategy and business plan, which is the purpose of this book and our workshops. Top managers who periodically call in strategy consultants usually have no confidence in their own managers or themselves. If top management calls in consultants to do the work of your managers or to second-guess your business teams, you have some fundamental weaknesses in your top management, the business teams, or both. When a general manager or the business team leader is deficient in strategy development skills, you first fix it with training, and if that doesn't work, you put more qualified people in those jobs, and don't circumvent the problem with unaccountable consultants. *At most, outside strategy helpers should train CEOs, group presidents, and business teams in how to use concepts, and frameworks to develop a sound strategy and then leave and stay out of the way.* Companies could save millions of dollars by turning to their own employees, who know a lot more than consultants. In short, top management should train business teams, turn them loose to develop sound strategies to profitably grow the businesses, review their plans, and then pay them well for good results—something no strategy consultant is accountable for.

The Vision Thing

Strategic thinking is what "the vision thing" is about. Vision is the art of seeing somewhat invisible connections. Vision is simply where someone or a team identifies a market need and connects a solution to the need. Unfortunately, many managers are nearsighted and never connect opportunities to solutions. In short, more people, in every business unit, need to be visionaries. Many times these people have been overlooked or are buried somewhere in the organization.

Every company faces the challenge of identifying, evaluating, and selecting opportunities that will accelerate sales revenue and profit growth. As a successful company becomes a larger one, they cannot depend on the vision, intuition, energy, and direction of one or a few top executives to plot attractive avenues of profitable growth. The vision thing capability must increasingly become more of a bottom-up process from general managers, their department heads, and front-line people in the organization. In larger companies, top management should primarily act as a venture capital bank by soliciting visionary growth opportunities and then investing in the better ones that will meet or exceed the company's sales and profit growth goals.

To achieve higher profit growth that meets or exceeds stated profit goals, one must ask two questions throughout the company. First, do the business unit people have enough time and resources to identify *directions for high-profit growth?* Once the time exists with business unit managers and their people to generate opportunities, can they identify or achieve *competitive advantages* that translate into sales and profit growth? In short, every company should ask, do we have sufficient organizational creativity, time, and skills to conduct an opportunity analysis and then develop service/product value packages that translate into higher profit results?

Strategic thinking requires a different type of thinking than many department managers have experienced. Some general managers have difficulty thinking strategically about external threats and opportunities, generating options or directions for the business, and developing or exploiting advantages that accelerate sales and profit growth. Business units led by myopic managers tend to drift and are not sensitive to new opportunities, and they let competitors determine their destiny. These tactical managers typically make small incremental responses, and they do not see the bigger picture and big moves needed to rejuvenate profitable top-line growth. These same tactical business unit managers usually focus on their narrow past experience. Furthermore, tactical managers too often find excuses or reasons for not pursuing new opportunities or challenging the organization to go in related but different directions.

The strategic thinker is always scanning the environment for trends, threats, and opportunities. Strategic thinkers see most threats as opportunities. *Strategy is about breaking out from thinking about just cost reduction and operating efficiency.* Strategic thinking demands providing specific service/product value in defined market segments. This type of thinking provides focus and a sense of urgency to everyone in the business unit. In decentralized and entrepreneurial growth companies such as 3M and HP, this type of strategic thinking and entrepreneurial management is expected within each division or business unit. However, most companies do too little strategic thinking. Top–down companies rarely encourage or allow business teams to think strategically. Many general managers are great plant managers or salespeople, but too often are inexperienced as strategic thinkers. Still others might be good engineers or financial managers, but they still don't think broad enough.

Creative, break-out thinking about customers' current and emerging needs is necessary. The next section lists some break-out thinking guidelines that can help a company develop unique service/product packages so they can profitably grow faster than a market segment or industry is growing.

Break-Out Thinking

At the division or business-unit level, aggressive growth strategies require different ways of thinking about a service/product package. Let's describe five of these areas and then discuss how to put break-out thinking to work within any industrial company.

1. *Break out from being a me-too supplier or company.* Being different and better to the customer is the foundation for developing competitive advantages in product performance and customer service. Winning with profitable top-line growth must be based on competitive advantages that bring more value to customers and attractive profit to the supplier. With "me-too" thinking, one may remain a follower and never be a leader. Who needs another me-too supplier in an era of supplier reduction? Do not just catch up to competitors, leap beyond them with advantages that are difficult to imitate. If a competitor is doing it, it doesn't mean it's good or should be copied. Don't just clone a competitor's solution; improve on it, and, in the customer's eyes, make it better, and unique from any other supplier's offering.

2. *Break out from thinking about the industry you are in.* Customers and markets have needs and they don't care what industry or technology best serves their needs. The way things are done in a narrowly defined industry will constrain any break-out thinking about new solutions. If you are in the steel industry and laminated wood beams serve a customer's needs better, that customer will buy the better solution. If laminated wood beams are more architecturally pleasing than steel in certain

applications, how can steel beams be adapted to serve the application better than laminate substitutes? If the steel beam cannot be made better for customers, the steel supplier might choose to build, buy, or market laminated wood beams as well as steel beams.

3. *Break out from thinking just about products–think of service needs.* Most industrial customers first buy a service, then a particular product. Selling productivity improvements and system solutions demands that astute suppliers learn about a customers' total operation and perform R&D on customers' service needs. Customer cost reductions, just-in-time delivery, outsourcing, maintenance, and productivity improvements create opportunities to bundle, unbundle, and adapt the service/product package. In short, suppliers need to think in terms of supplying a cost-effective package of services with product solutions, not just a fixed product.

4. *Break out from confusing tactics with strategies.* Strategy is about the longer-term direction, customer value, and competitive advantages that translate into attractive sales and profit results. Tactics are the short-term actions used to implement a market strategy. Operational excellence, such as total quality, six sigma, and cost reductions are important, but they do not substitute for thinking about the strategic directions where you want to profitably grow and where you do not want to grow. Marketing is all about strategy. R&D, manufacturing, and sales are means of implementing a market strategy.

5. *Break out from your current company practices.* Ritualistic budgeting and strategic planning are too often simply extrapolating the past into future years and a means of reinforcing some of the company's mindless traditions that may be a hindrance to profitable growth. Many managers are unable to think beyond their own company's current practices. Most company cultures have some outdated aspects when they benchmark against high-performing companies. The "way we do things around here" may be the bad, old ways. Learning organizations question all their practices and challenge every assumption.

Caterpillar conducted break-out thinking on the service needs of their end-users and dealers, and they found that repair parts availability for a "down" machine or engine was the most important need of customers. The study emphasized that when a CAT machine was down, every hour of downtime represents a significant loss in revenue to the owner. After reading the market study, a product support manager for Caterpillar in South America had a "crazy" idea. He said, "If the CAT dealer didn't have the part and it took as long as five to seven days to get it to the owner, why don't we offer customers a guaranteed three-to four-day delivery or the part would be free?" After extensive discussions and brainstorming, the company committed to deliver any part within forty-eight hours anywhere in the world or it was free. To implement this break-through service strategy, CAT installed new capabilities including: information systems, regional warehouses, and dealer inventory levels to support their unique customer value strategy. Today Caterpillar ships more than 99 percent of the parts a dealer does not have on the same day the order is placed, and if most parts are not received within forty-eight hours, the item is free.

Break-out thinking helps you generate a number of options and develop a vision of where you need to go. Such out-of-the-box thinking helps a company design, reengineer, and accelerate growth with unique service/product packages. Break-out thinking helps reach corporate stretch goals, and fill future sales and profit gaps. This type of thinking enables a business unit to be proactive and to take advantage of the ever-changing environment. Most importantly, break-out thinking requires people to think about larger system solutions to customers present or emerging problems. (Chapter 3, "Everyone Is in Marketing," describes more approaches to think with customers to create breakthrough products and services.)

COMPETITIVE ADVANTAGES

Many managers do not understand what is meant by a competitive advantage and how it is needed to develop a sound market strategy. Market strategy is about creating advantages that translate into high profit growth. Without domestic and global competitors, there would be no need for strategies. And without a competitive advantage(s), why compete? Companies without the vision, energy, and capability to develop competitive advantages will experience profitless growth and all the negative consequences that brings to employees, shareholders, suppliers, and the communities in which they operate. *Most competitive advantages are temporary and not sustainable.* Today, competitors all over the world are quick to copy any advantage. *The only sustainable advantage lies in a company's ability to learn and create new advantages faster than competitors.*

Commodity products with little or no competitive advantage and differentiation are most vulnerable to global capacity and pricing pressures. Virtually all industrial commodity products, which are highly interchangeable among suppliers, are now available on electronic commerce. Smart customers can access these products on the Internet; read the specification; shop around for the best prices, terms, and delivery; and then click orders and make payment over the Internet. For these routine items, buyers increasingly prefer to meet salespeople via their telephones or computer screens rather than in their offices. The main buying factors in these situations are availability, an acceptable level of quality, and price. If suppliers of these commodities do not differentiate their products with meaningful services, customers will view these products like grain and livestock bought on a commodity exchange or auction, where unit price is everything. If a company puts its mind to it, any product can be differentiated and made better in the eyes of customers.

Be Different and Better

To develop a winning strategy, a supplier must be perceived as being "better" to a group of customers. Being different and better to industrial customers means reducing their costs, increasing performance, improving their sales, and/or reducing their hassles. In an industry known for intense competition, how can a new entrant compete profitably against entrenched industry leaders? The answer: By differentiating its product/service package and avoiding direct price competition. Consider the case of Nucor Steel's Vulcraft divisions; they produce steel joists and joist girders from strategically located U.S. facilities. Vulcraft is the largest fabricator of steel joists in the United States, and with more than 60 percent of the market, they usually charge a premium over competitors for a "commodity" product. Vulcraft's civil engineering-degreed sales force provides a construction engineering consulting service, and the guarantee of on-time delivery service makes them better than their rivals' product/service package. If Vulcraft differentiated its offering solely by cutting their price, it might be perceived in the construction industry as having lower quality or as "cutting corners." Furthermore, if Vulcraft reduced its consulting and on-time delivery services to keep costs and prices down, it might alienate customers.

When industrial customers select one supplier over another, it is also helpful to think of the choice as an act of risk reduction rather than simply as choices based upon the appearance of a particular brand. Successful industrial marketers find deeper meanings in the way they attract and help customers. Consider the following example from Parker Hannifin Corporation. In the high-pressure stainless-steel tubing and pipe fitting industry, the Swagelok Company had been the pioneer and entrenched supplier with a big lead over Parker Hannifin. Swagelok had dominant market shares for its stainless-steel fittings and valves in high-purity applications that included nuclear power stations, semiconductor manufacturing, and food and drug processing plants. Stainless steel valves and fittings sold to these segments demanded ultra-high-purity and leakless connectors. In side-by-side competitive trials, Parker Hannifin's stainless steel valves and fittings performed as well as Swagelok's, but Swagelok's were perceived as better because they were the first-to-market pioneers.

Parker entered the high-purity markets as a late follower, but by reducing the customer's risk and stressing how their high-quality manufacturing process assured users of the highest quality on the market, Parker successfully penetrated many market segments. Parker Hannifin's trade advertisements and salespeople's presentations showed how their manufacturing process, in a former high-tech aerospace facility, resulted in superior products. The ads and sales presentations showed a 100 percent inspection rate, the use of an electron instrument to test every piece for defects, and a batch numbering process on the fittings and valves that would allow traceability to each production batch. Industrial customers in nuclear plants, R&D labs, semiconductor facilities, and food and drug customers began approving and buying Parker Hannifin's products because they perceived Parker's products as better than any others because of their quality assurance checks and manufacturing process. Over time, Parker overtook Swagelok in some target markets and was often able to command premium prices. Eventually, Swagelok reacted with the same "purity" approaches, and Parker's premium price narrowed. Parker's competitive advantages didn't last forever, and they had to seek continual improvements to maintain their position in the high-purity markets. However, the lesson is that Parker was able to successfully establish a premium beachhead and large market share over an entrenched competitor by showing how their product reduced the risk of a leak better than the competitor's product.

Industrial suppliers can secure a market segment in one of two broad ways: through an undifferentiated or a differentiated product/service package.

An *undifferentiated strategy* is when the supplier ignores market segment differences and goes after the whole marketplace with the same product/service package. This approach emphasizes generic customer needs rather than differences among groups of customers. Undifferentiated marketing is commonly practiced when products are highly interchangeable and when the suppliers haven't figured out how to differentiate their offering. In the absence of meaningful differentiation among the offerings of suppliers, the customer has no resource but to buy on the basis of a low unit price. The undifferentiated strategy fits a production-driven mentality of keeping costs and prices down. In the absence of uncovering unmet market segment needs or performing any segmentation research, the undifferentiated strategy tends to serve the more price-sensitive customer groups. An undifferentiated strategy can rarely make one product/service package that appeals to all customers. The undifferentiated market strategy often results in intense price competition and the neglect of market segments that desire more service, quality, or a different product/service package.

A *differentiated strategy* is where the supplier intentionally designs and delivers a product/service package of benefits for each market segment it chooses to emphasize. When these suppliers serve different market segments, they develop a product/service package tailored to each segment, even if the tailoring is relatively minor and done only with application stories or benefit-based literature. The differentiated strategy often creates more total sales than the undifferentiated strategy, but it also increases the costs of doing business. Some of the increased costs of business from a differentiated strategy could include product modifications or special tooling, more expensive production costs from shorter production runs, higher inventory costs, and higher administrative and sales promotion costs. However, if these higher costs are offset by higher total sales—and especially higher prices—greater profitability can result from the differentiated strategy. A successful differentiation strategy makes price less critical to target customer groups, thereby often leading to a premium price and higher margin to cover the higher costs.

Anything can be differentiated by altering the product and/or the services offered. ***Product differentiation*** includes better performance, quality, or reliability. ***Service differentiation*** includes better customer consulting, troubleshooting, customer training, product availability, on-time delivery, vendor managed inventory, kits, installation, and maintenance and repair. Both product and service differentiation attempt to reduce the customer's total cost, improve their sales, and/or help their customers' customers save time or money.

Difficult-to-Copy Advantages

A successful product/market strategy should provide customers with value that is difficult for a competitor to copy. Some types of differentiation are more enduring than others. Few, if any, advantages are forever or sustainable because competitors eventually learn how to benchmark, copy, and improve. Even patentable products have a shorter effective life as competitors engineer around them. Nevertheless, the best competitive advantages are harder to copy or imitate. Furthermore, *many intangible benefits are harder to copy*, such as good sales counselors, excellent service, a unique service company culture, or a great company name that consistently gives customers high satisfaction from their products and services.

When most managers talk about differentiation, they usually only think in terms of making their physical products different and better than competitors. There are always opportunities to add services to your product/service package. The Milliken Company, a large textile manufacturer, sells shop towels and rags to industrial launderers, who rent and clean them for factories. Even though the towels are easily interchangeable with competitor's products, Milliken commands a premium price by offering services that "decommoditize" their rags. Milliken's people train their customers' salespeople, do coop advertising, and supply their customers with qualified leads. The industrial launderers pay a premium because Milliken's services improve their customer service, sales, and profitability. The global information system that Federal Express provides to customers for tracking provided a three-year advantage over competitors including UPS and DHL. Because service and product benefits are nearly always short-lived competitive advantages, progressive suppliers should constantly be searching for viable new ways to differentiate their product/service package.

Every manufacturer has the option of *bundling or unbundling their products and services* for any given market segment and then charging accordingly. Manufacturers need to know how much it costs them to provide each service and then estimate the effect it will have on sales and net profit. After identifying and verifying the needs of market segments, the manufacturer can accurately determine what products and services to bundle or not offer to specific market segments. Full bundling involves offering all services at a premium price. New entrants to a market sometimes enter with a strategy of little or no-frills service; as they get established and become better known, they often add services, and charge for them in bundled pricing.

Lower Cost Is Not an Option

To be successful in the long term, every manufacturer must strive to reduce its costs and improve productivity in all areas of the enterprise. If every firm does not relentlessly attempt to lower costs, a competitor with an equal or better product/service package will figure out how to do it for them. I draw a distinction between a lower total cost supplier and being the lowest total cost supplier. If there are six competitors in a market segment, I would never want to be the highest total cost supplier but wouldn't necessarily mind being in the middle. Sometimes the largest competitor has the lower total unit costs because they can spread their fixed costs over more units. Optimal-size manufacturing facilities may also create real economies of scale. Many companies that say they are the lowest cost supplier are just having delusions! When you look at their large overhead costs, company jets, pricey headquarters facilities, big inventories, many services, wide product range, personnel costs, and high break-even points, they may in fact be the highest cost supplier. And because of imperfect competitive intelligence information, manufacturers rarely know who the lowest total cost supplier is.

A lower-cost advantage can be used to invest in product development, automate manufacturing, provide more services, support lower prices, or provide higher profit returns. Being a lower-cost supplier doesn't necessarily mean that you must choose to be the lowest priced. The ideal strategy is to be a lower-cost supplier and offer enough differentiation to command an above-average or premium price. Later in this chapter this is described as the dual strategy.

Costs play a central role in the short- and long-term health of every company. The frugal-minded company assumes that most costs are variable in good and bad times. The under-performing company assumes that most costs are fixed or uncontrollable in the short and long term. Chapter 9, "Know Your Costs", describes the nature of costs and those that are fixed, semi-variable, and truly variable. Furthermore, a frugality culture throughout the organization in good and soft times are necessary to remain a lower-cost supplier.

To develop sound strategies, you must look at each market segment, first from a customer perspective and the competitive offerings to that segment, and then from a perspective of costs to design, make, and serve the segments. Armed with the perspectives of customer differentiation and lower costs, you are better able to understand the nature of a dual strategy to counter-attack or attack any market position.

The Dual Strategy

Being a lower-cost supplier does not necessarily have to be associated with low prices. And being a lower-cost supplier does not mean you are the lowest cost supplier. It does mean, as I stated earlier, you are not the highest-cost supplier. An emphasis, and sometimes an obsession, with either low cost or just differentiation can leave any manufacturer vulnerable. *Most companies should emphasize both lower cost and differentiation, not one or the other.* The dual strategy is about differentiating your product/service package while also emphasizing lower cost through operating efficiencies in all areas of the enterprise.

Parker Hannifin has lower manufacturing costs and nonunion plants in small towns and higher volume throughput than many of its smaller competitors. Parker's selling prices are rarely the lowest, but it has very fast and differentiated customer service provided through electronic data interchanges, regional warehouses, and a strong and loyal global distributor network that does not carry competitive lines. Much of Caterpillar's success is due to its lower manufacturing costs achieved through high volume and modern plants and the relocation of some manufacturing to lower-cost countries or lower-cost regions within a country. Furthermore, Caterpillar's global dealer network is able to provide repair parts and service to any user in the world within hours. Caterpillar rarely has the lowest retail prices, and their customers' repair bills are not small. Caterpillar's dual strategy is to sort out which product/market segments it wants to be in, differentiates itself with good products and outstanding service and continually reduce costs in each product line. Superior product/service differentiation and lower total unit costs underlie Caterpillar's and Parker's dual approach to strategy.

The ultimate goal of the dual strategy is to have declining lower total costs (maybe not the lowest) and to differentiate product/service packages to certain market segments and key accounts with higher competitive selling prices. In short, the dual strategy assumes that a strategy does not have to be either a differentiation or low-cost approach—both are needed for short- and long-term success.

Strategic Collaboration

Increased sales and earnings pressure, rapidly moving technologies, global competition, and the failure rates of many mergers and acquisitions are causing more and more industrial companies to enter into agreements, partnerships, joint ventures, or alliances. Strategic alliances with complementary partners, suppliers, distributors, or even with competitors may be the fastest and most efficient and effective means for achieving immediate access to market windows, new technology, manufacturing capabilities, sales and distribution channels, or geographic growth. Our recent study of the reasons for the growing use of many types of alliances included:

1. To rapidly gain market share.
2. To rapidly grow geographically.
3. To rapidly access or leverage new technology.
4. To rapidly be first to market.
5. To rapidly gain local manufacturing capacity.
6. To rapidly gain sales and distribution.
7. To rapidly leverage your strengths.
8. To share the costs, risk, and rewards.

Such successful collaboration and agreements are often less risky than a full-fledged merger or acquisition. An alliance can be quickly formed and disbanded when either of the two parties' needs is no longer being met. Furthermore, strategic alliances can allow companies to enter into trial marriages before making a more substantial commitment, or they can serve as a stepping-stone to going it alone. However, strategic alliances, like any relationship or partnership, require some sound foundations and operating practices. There are three broad "fits" that must exist in any type of successful alliance or partnership agreement with another company:

1. The strategic fit—growth in areas you want to grow alone or with a partner.
2. The operating fit—complementary technical or commercial contributions that leverage each other's identified strengths.
3. The human chemistry fit—common values, goals, and similar time frames.

Any collaboration or alliance is also a legal relationship. Before you start, you must finalize technology ownership and protect your intellectual property, or you may be just creating a new competitor. Furthermore, any such agreement and strategy should state when and how you may each exit—such as when goals are met or the partners have become incompatible with different goals and longer-term ambitions.

For decades UPS was a lone ranger. In the last years, they have entered into dozens of alliances. UPS CEO Jim Kelly is so fond of their successful alliances that he stated at one of our senior executive workshops:

> Without strategic alliances, UPS would be a much smaller company, be less global, have less technology, and we would have diverted resources to areas we are not good at. We were a lone ranger in everything for years. Now we are a lot more open to considering collaborating as a way to more rapidly grow and become more efficient.

GETTING STARTED

After a profit-center manager and his or her cross-functional business team understand what a market strategy is and the need for competitive advantages, they are ready to begin thinking more specifically about the strategy they will pursue for any given market segment or product line. There are ten industrial market truisms that should guide the team's development of growth strategies. After considering the truisms, every manager must consider competitive advantages that translate into customer value, sales revenue, and bottom-line profit.

Industrial Market Truisms

Companies that excel year after year never let buzzwords, traditions, or wishful thinking influence their strategic thinking. Their management teams are well aware of the ten principles that greatly influence the growth outlook for any industrial business, and they ensure that their market strategies are consistent with these ten proven market truisms:

1. *Strategic thinking must always start with clearly defined market segments.* This is particularly true now when market growth and profitably are no longer "givens." In the 1980s and 1990s, it was not unrealistic to think in terms of 4 to 6 percent real growth for most businesses because gross domestic product was growing close to that rate in real terms in the United States and Europe. Regional and country differences in segment growth rates must be recognized in any strategic thinking, planning, and resource allocation process. Global competition has increased, and an increasing number of industrial market segments are likely to be flat or shrinking in some regions and countries of the world, while rapidly growing in other areas. This does not mean that growth is impossible or should be forgotten in slower growth markets. But it does mean that sound strategies must be geared to the facts of each market segment, country, and region of the world.

2. *Rapid growth for any growth market is always limited.* No market in any country is forever a high-growth one. New products and many new competitors quickly find their way into faster-growing markets. The high market growth in certain Asian countries eventually slowed. The high market growth for many electronic-related segments will eventually slow. However, any boom market can mislead management in its strategic thinking. The importance of market share is often overlooked when sales are growing rapidly from a big growth wave. The need for fully competitive costs and products is often obscured because a rapid growth market temporarily absorbs marginal producers and products. The euphoria of a growth market never continues forever. Marginal producers and products fail as the market moves into a slow growth stage. In the slow-growth stage, being a lower-cost supplier is not an option—it's a mandate.

3. *Rapid growth usually does not return to a slow growth market.* Although it is possible for a flat or declining market to experience short growth spurts, strategy should be guided by the market's long-term growth prospects. There are exceptions to this generalization when rapid growth does return to a slow-growth industry. It usually occurs because of some major change in the underlying or disruptive technology. For example, for many years the industrial scale market was essentially saturated, showing very limited unit growth. However, then the technology shifted from mechanical to faster and more accurate electronics. The significant advantages of electronic scales, which also offered a computing capability and a total packaging approach in many segments, prompted many customers to replace mechanical scales that were still perfectly usable. The combination of replacing a large number of scale sales plus higher unit volume for the packing solutions triggered a growth rate in the market that was significant for the next five years; then maturity again occurred. New technology and a better service/product package can help you grow significantly faster than the overall growth rate of the market segment.

4. *Competition is more intense in slow-growth markets.* A company in a high-growth market can often profitably increase its sales without taking market share from its competitors. When a market is flat or declining, however, top-line growth occurs only at the expense of other competitors. Capturing market share in such an envi-

ronment is not easy because competitors retaliate viciously to preserve their market position, utilize their capacity, and absorb their costs. The staying time of even the weakest competitors is usually underestimated. Macho attempts to destroy the competition typically end up hurting shareowners the most. Being a lower-cost supplier in a slow-or no-growth market becomes vital. A business unit facing a stagnant market is generally a much greater managerial challenge than one in a high-growth market. Many company weaknesses and management incompetence are masked in a rapid-growth market. In fact, I would argue that it is impossible to tell how good managers really are until they have proven themselves in a flat or declining market.

5. *Innovation continues even in stagnant industries and markets.* Technology improvements, both in new products and processes, and continuously lower costs provide customers with greater value. For instance, the technology for producing steel has improved dramatically during the past decade, despite greatly increased global competition and unfavorable market trends. Nucor has profitably taken market share from competitors because its new technology and productivity-based pay enable it to be one of the world's lower-cost suppliers. Stagnant demand, therefore, does not mean stagnant technology, and it does not imply that management can forget or downplay the need for continuous product, process, and service innovation. Companies that underinvest in innovation frequently never catch up. Furthermore, the development of new technology is now occurring all over the globe. In less fertile product technology, the innovation emphasis should be on new process technology and innovations in sales, distribution, and services.

6. *Product performance, service, and price are the basics of any industrial or business purchase.* A competitive disadvantage in any one of these areas simply cannot be offset by hard work or by just having bright people. In situations in which competitive disadvantages exist, the product/market strategy must focus on ways to correct or overcome these deficiencies. Side-by-side comparisons of competitive product performance are the beginning of this process. Most companies do not compare how their services (ordering ease, availability, on-time delivery, customer consulting) compare with competitors. When competitive products are highly interchangeable, service advantages can be very important market-share factors. Any competitive comparisons must evaluate how a company stacks up on deliveries, consistent quality, troubleshooting, and after-sales service. These non-price factors are typically very important to many groups of customers. The judge and jury of the non-price factors and competitive comparisons is always the customer, not folklore or unchallenged assumptions.

7. *Having a high market share doesn't necessarily translate into high profitability.* An all-out effort for market share or to be number one in any market can be a prescription for suicide. An obsession with sales volume or tonnage by dumb companies has ruined firms and entire industries. Bill Hewlett, the legendary cofounder of Hewlett Packard, said it well at one of our workshops, "You can have the whole damn market if you price low enough." To begin with, the companies in any market segment don't have the same products, margins, services, prices, or cost structures. Many companies simply don't know their costs, and even fewer know their competitors' costs. Furthermore, not all companies have the same profit goals. A privately owned company with no debt, better products, and low costs can take some very different approaches than a publicly owned company with excessive debt, antique products, and a bloated cost structure.

8. *It is usually harder to protect a profitable high market share than it is to build from a low or nonexistent share position.* A high market share typically attracts many competitors to the feast. In Asia there is a saying that the higher a monkey is in the tree, the more visible and vulnerable it is. Even strong proprietary positions can be undermined by clever competitors. If the high-market-share supplier does not figure out how to profitably defend its market share, competitors will figure it out for them. The defender should identify and carve out subsegments before competitors develop a toehold, which can become a beachhead, and then can turn into all-out warfare. Product enhancements, new products, and process improvements are needed to defend a high-share position. Total costs and productivity must be trending downward. Monsanto's 20+ years of high margin success with its Roundup herbicide product put all these actions to work to maintain its high-share and high-profit positions.

9. *In market segments you select to counterattack or attack, choose either a first-to-market or fast follower approach.* A first-to-market firm is simply, "being first with the most." Many companies set out to be a leader or to leap-frog the leader and end by default as a close or late follower. It requires vastly different mind-sets, cultures, and company capabilities to be either a first-to-market pioneer or a fast follower. However, being first-to-market isn't always the most profitable position. Strong competitors often emerge over the dead bodies of pioneers who didn't have the necessary strong proprietary know-how and other capabilities in place. The second mouse sometimes gets the cheese. Furthermore, a company must be fast in product and market development to succeed as either a first-to-market or as a fast-follower.

10. *Market segments tend to be either concentrated or fragmented and have varying degrees of cyclicality.* In a concentrated market segment, the bulk of the business is with a handful of customers. Many OEM market segments are characterized by a few customers who account for 80 to 90 percent of the total market, and each customer has tremendous buying power over any supplier. In contrast, fragmented markets have a wide customer base, and because they are more costly to serve, distributors, regional warehouses, or regional manufacturing are sometimes needed to serve them. In highly fragmented markets, no one customer has tremendous influence over the suppliers. However, with all the mergers and acquisitions, many fragmented markets are consolidating and becoming more concentrated. A wide customer base and market segment diversification can lessen the cyclical nature of any manufacturer's overall business. Whenever any one customer accounts for 15 percent or more of a business unit's business, or if more than 30 percent of sales comes from one market segment, there is a high chance of vulnerability and cyclicality. Furthermore, market segments that serve basic consumers needs such as food and health care, will be less cyclical than equipment, automotive, or steel markets that are dependent on capital expenditures, country interest rates, the regional economy, and global capacity.

Given these ten facts about industrial markets, a successful product/market strategy must be developed around one or more competitive advantages, such as offering products with distinctive performance or cost benefits, improving the customer's manufacturing process, offering superior service, or achieving a cost advantage by some other means. Whatever the approach, the objective is always to establish a clear and favorable advantage over competitors that provides more value to customers and sufficient profit value to shareowners. Without such an advantage, it is unlikely that any product/market strategy will allow the business to compete effectively and generate satisfactory profit growth over the long term.

Four Proven Market Strategies

Companies that compete most successfully in the industrial world develop their product/market strategies around four basic approaches, all designed to achieve and sustain a competitive advantage:

1. *They concentrate on growth market segments within the industries they serve.* Even the most stagnant markets usually have attractive market segments—a particular customer group, specific countries, or specific geographic areas that offer better-than-average rates of growth. Electronic test and measurement equipment sales for Hewlett-Packard (now called Agilent) have sustained attractive growth rates during periods when total industry sales were flat by focusing on hospitals, medical laboratories, and the commercial aerospace segments, all of which were growing. By following the shift of semiconductor manufacturing to Scotland, Malaysia, and Taiwan, Parker Hannifin achieved better-than-average growth by focusing on these regional market segments. Vulcraft, the steel fabricating division of Nucor that serves the cyclical construction industry, has emphasized fabricated steel products for prisons and schools, two growth segments that are less affected by fluctuating interest rates. The definition of market segments, and the selection of the most attractive segments must be done before the strategy can be developed.

2. *They emphasize consistent quality and a service/product package that provides demonstrable value to target market segments.* They avoid any business that is sold only on unit price because if market share is gained solely on price, it will likely be lost on price. They emphasize the non-price factors important to customers. Innovations, especially proprietary expertise, are difficult and expensive for competitors to imitate. More importantly, they keep a product from becoming a commodity with product enhancements and services and thus allow a company to compete on a basis other than just unit price. Toledo Scale took the lead in moving the slow-growing mechanical weighing industry into electronics and enjoyed a proprietary product advantage for several years. The company picked up significant market share and profits by introducing sophisticated computing scales for parts counting and other industrial applications that no one else could match for a few years. In short, a company should continually develop competitive advantages that translate into value for market segments and sufficient profit for shareowners.

3. *They often cannibalize or obsolete their own products rather than wait for competitors to do it to them.* They regularly upgrade or replace their existing product lines and stay ahead of competition even if the new product generates less profit. These same firms follow an orderly process of cannibalization in specific market segments and with certain customers, and they use pricing strategies to help control the rate of cannibalization. A counterattacking mentality with cannibalization is often the only way that market leaders can stay leaders. By avoiding cannibalization and staying with a product too long, a market leader is encouraging competition to obsolete their products. Furthermore, some companies offer their customers competing technologies, often supplied by different divisions, and then let the customers make the final choice of what's more cost effective in their application.

4. *They identify, evaluate, select, and attack attractive adjacent market segments.* An adjacent segment is a new product/market combination that has some similarities to a segment a company is currently serving. Adjacent segments are essentially stepping stones or "lily pad" opportunities rather than great leaps from your existing strengths or capabilities to more remote market segments. Going after an attrac-

tive adjacent segment is often a less risky and more profitable move than going after a more distant segment with little or no similarity to your existing segments and strengths to serve them. Every business unit should ask the following questions: What is the possibility of adjacent segment competitors entering our existing markets? What adjacent segments are our domestic and foreign competitors in? What specific competitors are in each adjacent segment? What factors are critical in each of the adjacent segments? What unmet need(s) can we serve in each adjacent segment? What specific adjacent segment(s) should we consider entering or targeting? And finally, what are the highest priority adjacent segments?

These proven market strategies should help every business team develop winning strategies and that grow sales and profits. The following analytical frameworks will help business teams develop strategies and implementation programs that meet or exceed a company's growth goals.

GROW NORTH-BY-NORTHEAST

The two axes of the grid in Exhibit 12-2 reflect the company's return on assets (ROA) and sales growth targets (16 percent return on average net assets and 7 percent on sales growth). The grid is divided into four quadrants: high profit/low growth, high profit/high growth, low profit/low growth, and low profit/high growth. The ultimate aim, of course, should be to move all products, customers, and market segments into the upper-right quadrant (the high profit/high growth category) in a north-by-northeast direction. In reality, you might first manage the business in a east by northeast direction to build sales volume before you improve profit toward the northeast. Businesses in the lower-left quadrant (low profit/low growth) should obviously be under pressure for significant improvement as strategic plans are developed. Arrows can be used, as shown, to indicate the direction the management team intends to go with any particular product, customer, or segment, and solid circles can be drawn to show the current profit and broken lines for the potential profit. The size of the current and future sales and profit amounts can also be inserted next to each year.

The north-by-northeast framework is always a good starting point for developing strategies because it avoids the rhetoric of why things are better than they look; it simply first shows the sales and profit facts as they currently are. Moreover, it provides a useful framework for demonstrating how a business team and its strategy will move the business toward the company's profit goals. The framework can help top management decide on resource allocations and the fate of poor or marginal performing business units, product lines, customers or market segments. In short, the north-by-northeast framework can be a roadmap to show where you are and where you want to be in the next 1, 2, 3, or more years.

Exhibit 12-2

Grow North-by-Northeast – Current & Future Positions, Product Line Profit, & Sales Growth

Profit Measure

RONA, ROI, or ROS

(circle one)   %

Product A	90
Product B	70
Product C	65
Product D	45
Product E	30
Product F	25
Product G	20
Product H	18
Product I	14
Product J	12
Product K	10
Product L	7
Product M	1
Product N	-2

Compounded Average Growth Rate from Multiple Segments (1998-2001)

-6%	-4%	-2%	0%	2%	4%	8%	10%	12%	14%	16%	18%

3. High Profit/Low Growth

4. High Profit/High Growth

Up or Out?

Up or Out?

2001

2002

X 2003

Your company profit goal before taxes - must be above your cost of capital

1. Low Profit/Low Growth

2. Low Profit/High Growth

Cross-functional Team Guidelines:

1. Plot your current sales and profit positions with sales and profit numbers.
2. Plot where your business team plans to go over the next two to three years.
3. Insert the sales volume and profit numbers next to your team's future positions.
4. Instead of products, this framework can be used for customers, market segments, countries, and regions of the world.

Plot Your Current and Future Positions

Before any company can plot strategies and develop cross-functional programs, they should know which existing product lines, customers, and market segments are profitable, marginal, or money losers and what the future prospects are. *Not all business is good business.* Unfortunately, many business teams enthusiastically develop strategies without current product line, customer, and market segment growth and profitability information. Some of these same teams are regrettably comfortable with gross profit numbers or just gross profit percentages, and then they make questionable million-dollar resource allocation decisions.

Many managers talk a good game about making a factual assessment of the performance, competitive standing, and outlook for their business, but few really do it in a realistic manner. Instead, too much emphasis is placed on excuses for why sales have not materialized, why profit returns are low, or why competitors seem to have an edge. The objective should be to strip away all the buzzwords and excuses that generally accompany any discussion of weak business performance and simply look at the past sales and profit facts on Exhibit 12-2. One of the best ways to examine the facts is to plot historical sales growth and profit patterns for each product line, customer, or market segment on the North-by-Northeast grid. Plotting sales and profit performance over some period of time will show how well each product, customer, or market segment has performed against corporate profit targets and how much improvement is required to bring the business up to par. Once the information is plotted for products, key customers, and market segments, you can consider various ways to profitably grow the business.

Final Choices

The ultimate goal of a winning growth strategy is to improve sales and, especially, operating profit. Growth in revenue, margins, and operating profit has always been a priority for well-run companies. Increasing sales and operating profits can be considered in three broad ways: A) from revenue increases; B) from margin increases; and C) from reduced structured costs. The profit growth levers shown in Exhibit 12-3 suggest that companies focus simultaneously on growing revenue and increasing margins. High performing industrial firms demonstrate that there isn't a trade-off between margin growth and revenue growth. In fact, you'd better have it all. It's a bankrupt strategy to just grow sales revenue at the expense of margins. Likewise, it's unhealthy to grow margins at the expense of revenue growth. Companies that consistently grow both sales revenues and margins create above average returns for shareowners.

The most common strategy to turbocharge *revenue growth* is to pursue new geographies or countries (as National Starch and Chemical has done), to enter new market segments (as Sealed Air has done), and to focus on higher growth market segments (as Loctite has done). *Higher margins* typically are enjoyed by new products (as 3M does) or by serving smaller customers with distributors (as Parker Hannifin does), and from cost reduction programs and annual productivity improvements (as Emerson Electric does). When companies, including 3M, Cabot, Loctite, and Sealed Air, *simultaneously pull multiple revenue and margin levers in Exhibit 12-3,* revenue and margin growth are often dramatic.

When the return on capital for the buisness unit is less than the firm's cost of capital, employing the revenue and margin levers in Exhibit 12-3 may not be enough. When a company has geared-up to a certain sales volume, and then volume significantly drops, they often can't take out the costs fast enough. In such situations, the levers in Category C, Structured Costs, may need to be considered to change the business unit's cost structure. In short, when developing any strategy, management teams need to consider all the profit levers shown in Exhibit 12-3.

Exhibit 12-3

Ways to Increase Operating Profit

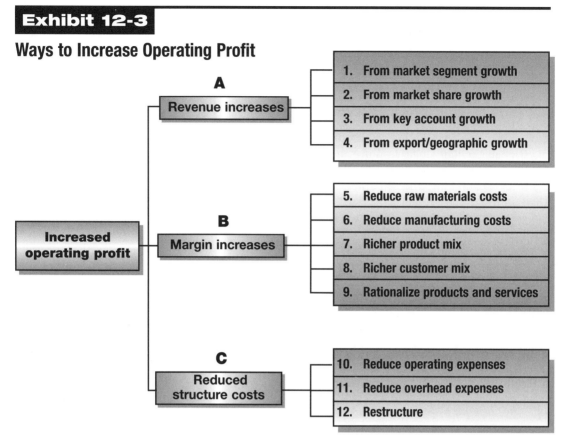

A
Revenue increases
1. From market segment growth
2. From market share growth
3. From key account growth
4. From export/geographic growth

B
Margin increases
5. Reduce raw materials costs
6. Reduce manufacturing costs
7. Richer product mix
8. Richer customer mix
9. Rationalize products and services

Increased operating profit

C
Reduced structure costs
10. Reduce operating expenses
11. Reduce overhead expenses
12. Restructure

SUMMARY

Companies should not fall into the trap of using meaningless buzzwords to develop or describe a strategy. Developing market strategies for selected product/market combinations requires facts, industry experience, analytical skills, and judgment. Unaccountable consultants should never develop the strategies that managers are held responsible for. A cross-functional team, experienced in the business, should perform the analysis, raise the key issues, select the best product/market opportunities, develop sound strategies and implementation programs, and then be rewarded for their results. Break-out strategy thinking should precede any strategic planning to avoid being a form-filling process. Every business team should identify ways they can make their service/product package better for each market segment. The dual strategy is a sound way to develop advantages and winning growth strategies with a differentiated service/product package and an emphasis on operating efficiencies. In order to develop winning strategies for products, markets, and customers within each division, country, and region of the world, business teams need to use the north by northeast framework. Companies need to clearly define where they do and do not want to grow and then develop strategies that will keep or move many product/market combinations to the "northeast" and meet or exceed their sales and profit goals. Many of the thought processes needed to guide the strategy development process and ways to increase sales and profit are provided in this chapter. When this bottom-up strategy process is done within every business unit, top management can make better decisions as to what opportunities to allocate resources to for profitable top-line growth.

Developing a Business Plan

"The business plan must be developed by a cross-functional team, never just a marketing plan generated by one or two people."

B. Charles Ames, Reliance Electric
Chairman and CEO

The business world would be a lot easier if management could simply forget or wish away the whole idea of annual business planning, but no one yet has been able to figure out how to get business plans into written form without a great deal of hard work. If anything, planning is likely to become a more important management tool in the future because it helps cross-functional teams focus on the more attractive market opportunities and develop the necessary action programs across the organization.

WHY BUSINESS PLANNING IS IMPORTANT

Business planning, both strategic and operational, has been an accepted part of the business management process for many years. The discipline of planning helps avoid the mistakes that are bound to occur when managers simply try to ad-lib their way through a complex business situation. *Planning has taken on added importance in recent years,* as the world has been caught up in change that has greatly increased the risks and chances of failure for any business venture.

Many argue that it is impossible to plan in an environment characterized by such volatile change and uncertainty. Actually, these conditions have made planning a more critical function because it is essential to try to anticipate changes and think through possible responses before the changes actually occur. It is the only way to avoid getting caught off base with no idea of how to respond. It is essential for management to devote much more time to considering (1) what positive and negative trends are likely to affect the business (there is always some good even in a negative trend), (2) what can be done to minimize the risks or capitalize on the opportunities that are likely to occur as a result of these changing conditions, and (3) what alternatives are available if things turn out differently than expected. Developing answers to these questions is essential for survival and success in a period of accelerating change and increasing uncertainty.

Despite the obvious need for, and inherent logic of, formal business planning, very few companies are truly satisfied with the results achieved, compared with the time and effort involved. The comment of a general manager for a major electronics company exemplifies the frustration and disappointment of many executives with business planning:

> We knock ourselves out every year with a major time commitment to put together a strategic plan for the business that is heavily based on marketing input. But we can't really point to any substantive benefits that are directly traceable to all the extra effort. As I see it, we have not done the job we should, in thinking through a strategy. If it had, we'd have a lot stronger edge in the marketplace. At this point, I am not sure whether it is something important that we ought to do better or whether it is just an exercise that conventional wisdom says we should do.

When it comes to business planning, small or highly entrepreneurial organizations are even more critical. The president of a $400 million private company told me:

We read many books and had fancy consultants show us how to do strategic planning. We don't need all the complexity and paraphernalia that others suggest. We now only have simple budgets that we plan and manage from. I know we are basically doing the rest on the fly and just adding capacity or throwing up plants. We need a very practical method to think, plan and control around.

Why should these reactions be the rule rather than the exception? What are the pitfalls that cause planning results to fall short of expectations? Most important, what lessons can be learned from the experiences of those companies that can honestly point to concrete results from their business planning efforts?

COMMON PLANNING PITFALLS

Most managers are well aware that effective planning depends on market and economic facts, that it results in detailed operating programs, not just budgets, and that it provides the best basis for measurement and control. Most managers are also very familiar with the various approaches to formal planning that have been emphasized in business literature and the academic world over the past several years. Yet major problems continue to crop up when many companies try to put some kind of formal planning approach into practice. These problems fall into four categories:

1. Confusion over types of planning and who does what.
2. Over-emphasis on form filling at the expense of substance.
3. Failure to tailor the process to the company's specific needs.
4. Lack of alternative strategies or options.

Let's examine each of these categories more closely before moving on to see what steps successful companies that have an effective approach to business planning have taken.

CONFUSION OVER TYPES OF PLANNING

Confusion about the distinctions among corporate strategy, business-unit strategy, and operational planning leads to major difficulties in accomplishing the planning job. These are all distinctly different types of planning, and the terms cannot be used interchangeably without creating confusion. To start with, it is useful to point out the differences and relationships between strategic planning and operational planning.

Strategic versus Operational Planning

The distinguishing feature of strategic plans is that they typically involve the commitment of resources (both human and capital) to a particular course of action. Once these resources are committed, *it is difficult to change direction without some kind of penalty.* This is not to say a commitment to a strategic course of action is irrevocable, but a penalty is most certainly incurred if directions are changed once a company begins implementing a strategic decision. For instance, it is impossible to reverse a decision on a new production plant once ground has been broken or to retract funding commitments for new-product or market development once the project is under way without suffering considerable time and cost penalties.

The time frame involved is another distinguishing characteristic of strategic planning. Generally, strategic planning covers a period of several years. *Three to five years is a reasonable period for strategic planning* in most manufacturing companies because most strategic decisions (e.g., building a new manufacturing facility, developing new products or a position in new markets) can be implemented within this period. Heavy manufacturing and aerospace companies that depend on long-term development programs may need to plan over an even longer period.

Operational planning, on the other hand, is typically done annually and should be designed to implement business unit decisions. Operating plans also provide management with an annual budget for controlling performance year-to-year, quarter-to-quarter, or even month-to-month. Many of the cost and time commitments reflected in the operating plan are the result of strategic decisions to develop and introduce new products, build new plant facilities, strengthen positions in new markets, or make acquisitions. *The operating plan is a vehicle to help implement the strategic plan;* therefore, it is obvious that these two types of plans must be directly linked together. In effect, the first year of a strategic plan should serve as next year's operating plan.

Product and Market Planning

Another category of strategic planning is product and market planning. This is the basic building block in a bottom-up organization. When this bottom-up process is performed all around the world, one can see the country-specific, regional, and truly global opportunities. I noted earlier that a separate plan is needed for each attractive market segment and key product. A well-defined market strategy should show where the business is heading and what kind of growth and profits can be expected. Product, market, or business-unit managers have the major responsibility for developing product/market plans by answering the following ten questions:

1. Is the business focused on the right market segments to counterattack and attack where you can provide more customer value, sales and profit growth? If not, how should the focus be shifted by deemphasizing or withdrawing from some segments?
2. What external factors or trends are likely to affect sales growth and profit potential favorably or unfavorably in each target market segment? How can any regulations and environmental issues be turned into opportunities?
3. Is the company's technology even with, ahead of, or behind the fastest growing competitors in the targeted segments?
4. Is the basic cost and profit structure of the business competitive? If not, what does it take to get marginal product lines and customers on a competitive footing?
5. Should investments be made in engineering, sales, or manufacturing to enlarge the business?
6. Should investments be made to integrate forward to strengthen market positions or backward to improve the profit structure and/or ensure a stable source of supply?
7. Is plant capacity available to handle increased volume expectations? If not, when and where will new capacity be needed and how much?
8. How much new capital is required for which projects, and what is the expected payoff?
9. What are the sales, profit, and cash-flow outlook for the target segments, and what is the probability of achieving these results or better in different countries and regions of the world?
10. Finally, does the market or product plan meet or exceed the corporate profit goals? If not, what other product or market situations would be more attractive?

Companywide Profit Planning

Once market and/or product strategies are developed for each business unit, general management has the basis for deciding what strategic moves, if any, are required companywide. This leads to the second type of strategic planning typically done by top or corporate management, which is designed to answer two fundamental questions:

1. Does the aggregate outlook for all the company's business units meet overall profit growth goals?
2. If not, how big is the gap, and what are the alternative ways to close it?

Exhibit 13-1 illustrates how a gap can be calculated by aggregating the planned performance of all business units and comparing the result with overall corporate goals. As you can see, the company's operating divisions have projected earnings well below the corporate objectives of 15 percent compounded growth each year, and an earnings gap of $1.20 per share is expected. If I assume that there are 5 million shares outstanding, the company needs to pick up $6 million of after-tax earnings over the next five years to close the gap. In this kind of a situation, corporate management has basically three alternatives:

1. Change the corporate earnings target.
2. Revise division plans to close the gap.
3. Redeploy capital into new technologies, market segments, or businesses with sufficient earnings power to close the gap.

Clearly, some combination of these alternatives is often the most prudent approach to follow when a strategic planning gap occurs. Whatever the decision, it is likely to change the direction or structure of certain business units and perhaps of the entire company.

Exhibit 13-1

Calculating the Aggregate Outlook

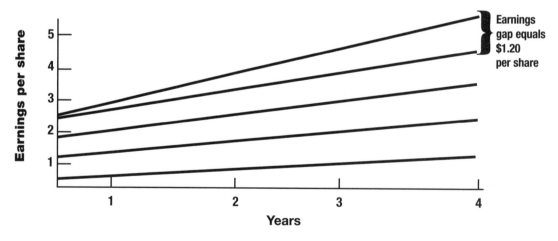

Strategic planning gaps can cause companies to expand certain businesses, make acquisitions, form alliances, or take other strategic actions to reshape the character and earnings stream of the company. When you read about a company that has sold one of its business units or moved into a new business area, you are seeing real-life resource allocation decisions resulting from corporate strategic planning. The company's corporate management has decided that the present structure of its businesses is not satisfactory to achieve its profit goals and has carried out a decision to change that result.

How Sales Forecasts Tie In

The pivotal factor in any plan is the sales forecast from each bottom-up product/market plan. Manufacturing levels as well as expense budgets are related to the sales forecast when the operating plan is put together. The sales forecast is also the most variable or least controllable set of numbers in any business plan. Manufacturing costs are far more predictable; generally there is an experience base from which manufacturing costs at various volume levels can be predicted with a fair degree of accuracy. Also, expense levels for most SG&A activities are known from prior experience and are therefore more predictable. Sales results, on the other hand, depend on a host of uncontrollable factors such as the economy, competitor actions, new-product sales, sales force effectiveness, and so on.

There are a variety of techniques for making sales forecasts, ranging from simple trend-line extrapolations to sophisticated statistical and computer-based projections developed around relevant market and economic indicators. The more accurate sales forecasts are a bottom-up process that start with key accounts and market segments in each country in which a company plans to defend and attack market positions. Regardless of how the sales forecast is made, however, it is still a guess about future events with all the risks and uncertainties of any prognostication. In most manufacturing companies, multiple forecasts are prepared by different individuals or groups within the organization, and it is general management's job to sort out these forecasts and ensure they are properly used to plan, manage, and control the business. Let's examine the different types of sales forecasts that are likely to be made in any industrial concern.

To begin with, most sales representatives are asked to make a "grass root" sales forecast for their accounts and territories. The aggregate of individual or bottom-up sales forecasts typically reflects the optimistic view of an enthusiastic sales force and is generally an unrealistic set of numbers for making strategic, operating, or financial commitments. Recognizing this, sales management usually scales back the sales representative's forecast and recommends a lower set of numbers for planning purposes. If market, product, or business-unit managers are involved in the organization, they will make sales forecasts for their assigned areas based on their best estimates of market conditions and the competitive situation. The aggregate of the account/product/market forecast is a good cross check against the forecast made by sales management, but it also may be on the high side since it is unlikely that all customers, markets, and competitors will act exactly as all managers expect.

Finally, it is not unusual for manufacturing management to second guess any or all of these forecasts and make a forecast of its own to schedule its manufacturing operations. A manufacturing manager for a medical equipment company put it this way: "The sales guys always have a 'pie in the sky' forecast that they never make, and I am not going to build inventory or product to a forecast like that."

It is general management's job to make certain that everyone in the organization has a clear understanding of what forecast is going to be used for what purpose. Probably the best approach is to use one of the more optimistic forecasts as a basis for setting sales quotas, establishing incentive programs, and evaluating individual sales performance. Then sales goals fall in line with what the salespeople feel they can achieve and this, hopefully, will stretch the sales force toward better performance. *A second, more conservative forecast, however, should be used to make operating and financial plans and commitments.* It is always much easier to adjust these plans and commitments upward if higher sales are achieved than it is to scale them back if actual sales results fall below forecast. Following this approach can help management avoid the embarrassment of explaining that profits suffered because sales were lower than forecast and/or because operating costs and expenses got out of line.

OVEREMPHASIS ON FORM FILLING

Many companies have developed comprehensive planning systems that define formats and procedures in great detail. Although some structure is unquestionably necessary, in too many cases the system is so detailed and so highly structured that it acts as a hindrance rather than a help to the planning process. The bulk of the time and effort goes into completing schedules and forms defined by the system rather than into the strategic thinking and discussion that lead to innovative plans.

Of all the roadblocks, this is the most frustrating for managers charged with the responsibility of doing a good job of planning. They recognize that good planning is hard work and cannot be done without a certain amount of hard work. But they bitterly resent demands for excessive writing or forms completion that serves no practical business purpose. A product manager for an electronic equipment manufacturer voiced his frustration over a planning system prescribed by the corporate headquarters:

> As part of my planning responsibility, I have to follow a format prescribed by the headquarters that calls for a point-by-point discussion of history and a laundry list of problems and opportunities and a whole series of analyses and schedules that are irrelevant for my business. I'm "gigged" if I don't cover every point and complete every form, and there's no way to do it in less than 30 pages of schedules and text. That takes a lot of time to prepare—mostly wasted time. All the product managers are sore about it. Much of what we end up writing is a rehash of the same old things year after year. In effect, we're being discouraged from concentrating on the aspects of the business that are really critical. What they want to see, apparently, is a nice, neat set of plans that all look alike. It just doesn't make sense.

Unfortunately, situations like this are not unusual. Some overzealous staff person designs a series of forms that are completely out of balance with the realities of the business. The resulting paperwork eats up great blocks of precious time without producing anything more than a lot of schedules and a written description of what would have been done anyway. *Planning is more than simply completing forms.* In fact, most forms are a hindrance to strategic thinking.

FAILURE TO TAILOR THE PROCESS

To a large extent, the disappointing results encountered by many industrial companies reflect their failure to recognize two distinguishing characteristics that dictate the need for a planning approach tailored to their specific needs. The first is the large number of product, market, and channel options that are available to most industrial companies. A typical multiproduct industrial manufacturer sells multiple products to a wide range of different markets, often through different channels. For example, it would not be uncommon for a manufacturer of electronic components to sell a broad array of different products in as many as 20 distinct markets (e.g., automotive, aircraft, marine, military), facing different technologies and competitors in many of these markets. It doesn't make much sense to try to cover this complex network of products, markets, and channels with a broad-brush business plan for the company as a whole. Instead, there should be a number of discrete plans, one for each product/market target that should be treated as a separate entity.

Juggling a large number of product/market businesses is not the only problem facing managers in industrial companies. Because the success of individual business plans depend on activities in all key functional areas and on the share of total company resources each product/market business receives, it is unrealistic to expect product managers, market managers, or even general managers to develop plans for selected product/market segments by themselves. It requires a cross-functional team effort with the full participation of operating managers throughout the entire planning process. Thus, the role of the business unit manager in an industrial company is to analyze and interpret product/market requirements for the business and then, with key functional managers, determine whether and how these requirements can be met. A product, market, or business unit manager should play the lead role in drawing plans together for the assigned product/market. But as Chuck Ames, the former chairman and CEO at Reliance Electric, said, *"The plan must be a complete business plan developed by a cross-functional team, never just a marketing plan generated by one or two people."* General management must also be involved throughout the process to set priorities and settle disputes that are bound to occur whenever several discrete product/market businesses depend on shared resources and effective implementation.

Obvious as these points may seem, they are frequently overlooked. Many general managers try to turn the entire job over to a marketing person or the division controller. Traditional marketing people just prepare sales forecasts and controllers just develop budgets—neither develops focused business plans. After several years of frustration with the resultant plans, they are ready to write off the whole planning effort as a monumental waste of time. The real source of their disappointment lies not in the planning concept, however, but in the way it has been applied. Here is a good example of how this can occur.

A major chemical company ran into trouble when it added a group of six market managers to its marketing organization, gave them a planning format to follow, and told them to write a plan for achieving a stronger and more profitable position in their assigned markets. Half of the six market managers had MBAs from some of the "best" schools but lacked an in-depth knowledge of their markets and respect from within their own organization. All six managers, eager to prove themselves, embarked on a massive fact gathering, analyzing, and writing effort. Some of the MBAs were referred to as "Masters of Business Analysis." After several months, hundreds of pages of plans and supporting documentation had been written, but no one in top management was much impressed. The general manager of the silicone manufacturer put it this way:

> I'm being generous when I say the end products are only slightly better than useless. Admittedly, we have some better market facts now, but the plans are based on a lot of vague ideas for product and market development that just aren't in line with the needs and trends we are seeing. On top of that, they've left out a lot of customer needs and technical considerations that really count. I've concluded that our market managers are simply too far out of the mainstream of the business to do an intelligent job of planning for us.

Not surprisingly, the market managers felt that they too had good cause for complaint. As one of them put it:

> The first month of effort was worthwhile. We were putting a fact base together that is essential for intelligent planning. But after that we were flying blind. We never had any idea from top management on the kind of business the company wanted or didn't want, the minimal profit return it expected, or the kind of support it would be willing to make in various markets. Worse still, we had no cooperation from the development group, the plants, or even the sales force, where decisions are made that really influence the business. The planning we did was bound to be a bust.

Unfortunately, this has been the experience of a great many otherwise well-managed industrial companies. Far too many planning activities get plenty of lip service but little real attention or involvement from general management and functional managers who have to make the plan work.

LACK OF ALTERNATIVES OR OPTIONS

Given the dynamics of most industrial markets, it is surprising that so many managers have tunnel vision when thinking about alternative ways to respond to change and improve the business. I believe this causes many industrial companies to be chronically plagued with poor results. They continue to plan for and run the business by making small incremental improvements to what they have been doing in the past. Their thinking is blocked by past experience, and statements such as, "We're in a mature market" or "We can't raise prices." They need to break out of their traditional "boxed-in" way of thinking. (Revisit Chapter 12 "Winning Market Strategies," and the topic "Breakout Thinking".)

The tendency to base current plans on past practices alone was exposed in a textile machinery company when each business-unit manager was asked by top management to outline alternative strategies for developing his or her assigned business and to summarize the commitments (e.g., financial, personnel, facilities) required and the payoff expected (sales, profit, return on investment). The request drew a complete blank. Despite all the new technology in textile manufacturing, massive textile plant closings, and declining domestic markets for U.S. textile machinery, these managers were so locked into their accustomed ways of thinking about their business that they could not conceive of a different approach that made any commercial sense at all. They had no real plan to aggressively follow the textile market to Mexico, Central America, or Southeast Asia. How can a business unit improve or even survive in such a different environment when its managers fail to recognize how the business has changed and what must be done differently?

This problem stems from a deficiency that has plagued business seemingly forever. Far too many managers have let their businesses "die on the vine" or have completely missed major opportunities because they thought only about making and selling their existing products and technologies instead of serving target markets with whatever it takes. Admittedly, it is difficult to think about moving away from traditional products, technologies, and business beliefs to preserve or secure a stronger position in selected markets. However, the tendency to limit one's thinking to existing products and technologies without regard for the realities of the market segment is a critical weakness. The CEO of a major chemical company stressed the importance of this point when responding to a question about the loss of vitality in American industry:

> To my mind, one central reason is this—our strategies have become too rigid. In trying to make our companies more manageable, we've constructed formula after formula that tell us how to run our businesses, and too often we get so tied up in the formula, we forget the changing real world that can break any business if it is not flexible and fast to respond. We're too much like a football team that sticks to its game plan in the fourth quarter even though it's losing 21-0.

In order to overcome these common planning pitfalls, a number of corrective actions need to be taken. The corrective approaches include direction from top-management, more strategic thinking, the use of issue management, and then empowerment of business teams. Let's start with direction from top management.

DIRECTION FROM TOP MANAGEMENT

Top and general management in leading industrial companies clearly recognize the strong role they must play in the planning process if they are to be effective. This doesn't mean they do all the planning, but certainly they are the ultimate architects of the plans for their business. Business unit or general managers must lead the development of strategies and implementation programs across departments. The group president within the test and measurement group of Hewlett-Packard demonstrated the importance of this point with the following comment:

> It took me three years to realize that our people couldn't come up with the kind of plans I wanted for our products and markets unless I worked closely with them. They have always been able to develop a picture of where our markets are heading, identify the opportunities that exist, and interpret what we have to do to build the business. The many considerations and options require a general management approach to marketing that no one department can come up with. Unless I set the basic direction and targets for our buisness, specify who is to plan what, see to it that technical, manufacturing, and sales really work together to provide what is needed, and then challenge and contribute any ideas on how our buisness can be developed, the whole planning effort is nothing more than a paperwork exercise.

This statement underscores several ways in which top and general management must participate in the planning process to make it successful. The top management must spell-out the rules of the game before strategic thinking and strategic planning begin.

First, the CEO and the upper management team must spell out the profit goals and what are acceptable and unacceptable profit returns. It is also extremely important that everyone in the organization know what products, markets, and customers should be emphasized; what kinds of businesses and customers should be avoided; and what capital availability or constraints exist. Strategic thinking and planning guidelines are essential to provide parameters for people actually doing the planning in the various business units. The key here is to make sure that the guidelines are rational, in line with the realities of the business, and that they make people stretch. The planning requirements of top management were described in Chapter 11, "Top Management Leadership" and in four topical areas; 1) set growth goals, 2) provide broad planning guidelines, 3) define the planning units, and 4) establish planning formats. You may want to review these four areas.

HOW STRATEGIC THINKING CAN THRIVE

In my management development workshops around the world, I repeatedly hear the following statements by top and general management:

> "We have little or no dialogue about the real issues facing us."
> "We continually confuse a strategy with tactics and operating plans."
> "We develop plans as if the world hasn't changed."
> "We don't think out of the box."

Why are these statements so commonly raised in industrial companies all over the world? These statements are very common because *most companies do too little strategic thinking and too much ritualistic form filling* where people confuse precise numbers with inaccurate observations and assumptions about their business environment.

Even though strategic planning has saturated the corporate environment, the key to profitable top line growth lies not so much in long-range planning as in the clarity of a company's strategic thinking. *Managers often confuse the process of strategic thinking with the process of strategic planning.* They are distinctly different. Strategic thinking should be directed at what the overall corporate, group, divisional and product/market strategy should be rather than how to get there. A strategy is defined as a framework that guides choices about products and services, the geographical growth and customer groups or market segments the organization wants to serve.

Strategy also includes the company's capabilities to develop and support the chosen products and markets, its growth rate and profit return, and its allocation of resources. *Strategic thinking is the cerebral process of deciding which businesses, markets, and technologies to be in.* Strategic thinking requires a lot of market facts, knowledge of trends, an understanding of your know-how, and relevant technologies. Only after strategic thinking has been done properly should strategic planning begin. *Strategic planning is simply a process of documenting the steps to be taken and the mileposts for achieving strategic thinking.*

The choice about products, services, and markets determines the focus of the enterprise. If these choices are made within the context of a strategic framework, the company's direction is clearly under the control of the executives. If these choices are made in the absence of a strategic framework, the executives will abdicate the focusing decision and run the risk of pursuing a direction that is in the hands of whimsical choices. Products and services are planned and designed to serve markets. The product and service is a variable, not a given in the strategy. *Strategies should be developed for products, but even more so for markets, because markets are longer lived than products.* In market-driven industrial companies, market definition, market attractiveness, and market selection should come first, and the choice of the product/service should follow. For example, Alcoa, an aluminum manufacturer, might choose to serve the residential housing market by supplying aluminum siding, windows, gutters, and downspouts. Alternatively, Alcoa could elect to supply aluminum sheet stock and coils to independent fabricators of the various residential building components. The market, in this case, might be broadly defined as residential housing. The product options are semi-fabricated materials, building components, or end-use products. Other Alcoa product choices may be whether to make a full line or narrow line in any given product area; whether to offer high, medium, or low quality; and whether to have a full range of sizes or to offer only a limited product range.

Strategic planning and day-to-day decision making should flow from the strategic thinking. Many product-, technology-, or manufacturing-driven companies fail to separate the formulation of strategic thinking from planning and operating decisions. These same companies confuse effective operations with an unclear strategy. Such companies often cannot make up their mind as to what specific kind(s) of business markets it should be in, and the result is too often a "hodge-podge" of products and markets with elusive competitive advantages and mediocre results. Longer-term growth in shareowner value in these companies is limited and often destructive. These companies lack direction because their CEO and general management do not have a clear picture of what markets and products they should and should not be in for the future. In short, many companies haven't really decided who they are and what kind of company they want to be to increase shareowner value.

A sound strategy statement should preface every business plan. A sound strategy statement describes what type of business the team is trying to build, what market(s) are targeted with stated superior value for each market and the necessary cross-functional implementation programs. A sound strategy statement should conclude with quantitative sales and profit goals over a three to five year period.

Any strategic plan that is not preceded by lengthy and constructive discussions of the strategic issues, possible scenarios, and growth direction(s) is not worth the paper forms it is done on. Yearly weekend retreats and off-site meetings dedicated to strategic planning, with little or no strategic thinking, are largely a waste of time and money. Strategic issue management can provide a practical linkage between strategic thinking and strategic planning.

STRATEGIC ISSUE MANAGEMENT

Most companies claim that their environment is becoming more turbulent and unpredictable. On a scale of 1 to 10, with 10 being the highest level of turbulence, they consistently rate their market environment as more turbulent today than ever before, much closer to the 9 or 10 level than to level 5. At the same time, however, they realize there has not been a company-wide adjustment of priorities or strategies to deal with this increased turbulence. Even more alarming, they uniformly express concern that their general managers and management teams do not have the knowledge or tools to make the necessary changes to respond faster. Most executives claim there is a growing incidence of events that come from unexpected sources and that can quickly affect their company. The speed of unexpected issues is often too fast to allow timely identification and response within the annual strategic planning cycle. The need for the development of more options as was discussed earlier in this chapter, can be helped with the use of strategic issue management. *Strategic issue management helps capture opportunities and cope with blows before it is too late.* A strategic issue is a likely forthcoming development or present event, from either inside or outside the organization that is likely to have an effect on the enterprise if it continues. An issue can be a *welcomed external opportunity* to be captured in the environment, or an internal strength, that can be exploited to the firm's advantage. An issue can also be *an unwelcomed external threat,* or an internal weakness, that may reduce success or even threaten the survival of the enterprise. Strategic issue management is essentially a strengths, weaknesses, opportunities, and threat (SWOT) analysis for a product line or market segment. The strategic issue management process is outlined in Exhibit 13-2.

Exhibit 13-2

Strategic Issue Management Process

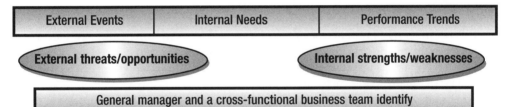

External Events	Internal Needs	Performance Trends

External threats/opportunities   Internal strengths/weaknesses

General manager and a cross-functional business team identify
the strategic issues for a market segment or major product line with a SWOT analysis

Exhibit 13-3 shows the strategic issues from a SWOT analysis that a ABS brake system manufacturer did for the sport utility vehicle (SUV) market segment in Europe.

Exhibit 13-3

SWOT Analysis Example

Market Segment and Region = Sport Utility Vehicles, Europe

Strengths:
- Good market share at most OEMs
- Company name well-known
- U.K. and German facilities
- New Czech facility

Weaknesses:
- Time to convert customers
- Late product development programs
- Customers want total systems
- Reduced aftermarket potential

Opportunities:
- Rapidly growing segment
- High bill of material per unit produced
- High margin business
- Global standards and approvals

Threats:
- How long will the SUV fad continue?
- High price of petroleum
- Eastern European competitors
- Planned new industry capacity

Many general or business-unit managers kick off their planning process with a session aimed specifically at reaching agreement on key issues and priorities for each market segment or major product lines. As one general manager stated:

> Our past planning has typically evolved into a number-crunching and form-filling exercise all too quickly, and we never took the time to really think about the need for fundamental changes. Now we spend the first day talking about issues facing the business in each segment and product line and the need for shifts in priorities and direction. This is strictly a thinking, discussion, and what-if session where we identify external opportunities and threats and examine the internal situation that may hinder us. Anybody that tries to take up much time with cost or sales projections at this stage gets shot down.

Most strategic planning is too rigid or slow to anticipate and react to unexpected events that occur throughout the annual planning cycle. There is a need to have more simplified, flexible, and action-based planning done by each cross-functional business team. Some companies have substituted strategic issue management for some of the unnecessary form filling in strategic planning. They have reduced the amount of strategic planning and added strategic issue management to their planning process. Business teams are increasingly using strategic issue management to develop more strategic options and to be better prepared for an uncertain future. Scenario planning helps stimulate thinking about the current and future issues facing the business.

Scenario Planning

Among the many tools a manager can use to develop more strategic thinking, scenario analysis or "what if" planning stands out as one of the most useful team approaches for assessing the effects of warning signals, trends and uncertainties. Scenario planning helps cross-functional business teams expand their visions by seeing a wider range of possible futures and thus be more prepared to take advantage of opportunities that come along.

Good scenario analysis challenges assumptions and cause-effect outcomes by creating a deeper appreciation for the myriad of issues that can shape the future. Scenario planning requires intellectual honesty, an open mind and courage to accept evidence and opinions that do not fit your current values and attitudes, even when they may threaten your very existence. The following statements are from executives who would have benefited from scenario planning:

> "There is no reason for any individual to have a computer in their home." (Founder and CEO, Digital Equipment Corp., 1987)

> "With over fifty different car models already on sale in the U.S., the Japanese auto industry isn't likely to carve a big slice out of the crowded U.S. car market." (Chevrolet Division General Manager, General Motors, 1980)

> "Plastics and aluminum will never replace steel in automobiles and household appliances." (Former CEO, U.S. Steel, 1984)

> "We lose more photocopier machines in shipping than the Japanese export." (Former CEO, Xerox Corporation, 1989)

These statements were made by executives who were no longer visionaries. Even worse, these management fossils underestimated the competition and overestimated the competitiveness of their companies.

Scenario planning differs from contingency planning and sensitivity analysis. Contingency planning examines only one uncertainty, such as "What if we only sell 50 percent of the forecast for the new product?" Contingency planning presents a base case and an exception. Scenarios explore the joint effect of various uncertainties. Sensitivity analysis examines the effect of a change in one variable, keeping all the other variables consistent. Scenario planning considers the interaction of many variables.

Developing Scenarios

Business teams can benefit from scenario planning in many situations, including the following:

- When the amount of strategic thinking is low or nonexistent.
- When the company or business unit has experienced too many surprises in the past.
- When the industry has experienced significant consolidation or is about to.
- When new competitors have or are about to enter your market.
- When a market segment is flat or shrinking.
- When you are entering a new market or country and you are trying to gauge customer acceptance and the competitive reaction.
- When you are considering investment proposals that project cash flow at several levels.

The reasons for doing scenario planning are endless. In short, scenario analysis is applicable to any situation in which managers would like to imagine how the future might unfold. Identifying, discussing, and evaluating different scenarios turns strategic thinking about options into a learning process for everyone. Furthermore, the team of people might want to attach probabilities to the likeliness of each scenario occurring. The end result should stretch and focus everyone's strategic thinking and preparedness.

Because windows of opportunity are opening and closing at a faster rate in most industries and market segments, issue management and what-if scenario planning can help minimize the blows or turn threats into opportunities. Top and general management must create an open culture that encourages everyone to speak up early about issues. Bad news is good news if it is communicated early! You cannot have a kill-the-messenger mentality and effectively use strategic issue management and scenario planning.

BUSINESS TEAM PLANNING

A lot has been written about the effective use of business teams. One of the most important uses of business teams is to develop business plans that are truly the effort of a cross-functional team, with a team leader and with regional or global teams to ensure successful planning and implementation. Let's now amplify how business teams are a vital part of the process of putting a business plan together.

Cross-Functional Members

If I could stress only one point in this chapter, it would be this: *Any planning in industrial companies that does not actively involve a cross-functional team from the very beginning is an exercise in futility.* Give and take among the entire cross-functional business team is really the heart of any industrial business planning process. It is during these discussions that marketing presents the requirements of the marketplace and the other functions discuss feasible responses. With all the opportunities and issues out in the open, the business team has a good basis for deciding how to allocate resources. The cross-functional business team planning process helps make marketing the whole company.

To plan and execute as a cross-functional team, *all the people involved with a product line or customer group need to continuously communicate about customer needs, competitive solutions, product-line and customer costs and profits, and the business unit's capabilities.* These same people must all be involved in identifying and prioritizing the key issues in each target market segment. Next, the same group of people must be involved in developing the strategy, goals, and cross-functional plans. The same team of people does the development and implementation of the strategy. When a cross-functional team of people in a business unit has input in developing a business plan, the process will inevitably require more front-end time. But this up-front time is well spent because the team-developed plans will be more speedily executed across the organization because everyone performs what they have agreed to do. Finally, this cross-functional group of people must communicate the focus and priorities of the business unit to many others in the organization so that they understand the implementation programs.

Business Team Leaders

Some profit-center managers may think that the use of cross-functional teams to develop and implement market-driven plans involves giving up their authority. The opposite is true—cross-functional teams more clearly identify the responsibilities of each person, thereby increasing the manager's influence on each team member. When a team of people is involved in selecting target markets, setting sales and profit goals, and developing action programs, more people will be committed to and feel responsible for the results. *A good cross-functional leader manages the team process.*

After participating in one of my market driven management workshops that emphasized the power of cross-functional teams, a product manager from Hewlett-Packard said:

> I first realized that my sales forecasts must be more accurate, detailed, and responsive to market changes or else I'd lose total credibility with all other functions. No longer do manufacturing and materials management develop their own forecasts. We now hold our monthly operating meetings at the plants so more people can be involved in discussing and solving the key issues. The cross-functional process has caused many engineering and some manufacturing people to spend more time in the field with customers and distributors. Our new-product designs now have more of a customer focus, and the final designs are more closely integrated with manufacturing capabilities and cost targets. Overall, our cross-functional approach to being more market driven has resulted in sensitivity to customer needs and competition advantages, costs, and capabilities that just weren't here before. Problems are even informally raised in the hallways and right then discussed and brainstormed until a good solution emerges. But before we adopted a cross-functional team approach, I was, as a product manager, nothing more than a glorified scheduler or a special accounts salesman trying to negotiate with each department silo.

Participative leadership is especially needed in cultures where people historically have not stood up to higher ranking or more senior people. Rather than be a take-charge gladiator in the business planning process, the cross-functional team manager must be skillful at group problem solving, reaching consensus, and managing differences of opinions.

Regional And Global Market Planning

As global companies such as Alcoa, BASF, Caterpillar, DuPont, Michelin, Nestle, Unilever, and the automotive companies increasingly move toward global specifications and procurement, global suppliers are supplanting local and regional ones. Suppliers unwilling to become global players also face the risk of losing their local business to more global suppliers. Buying from a handful of suppliers with operations around the world eliminates the customer's need to qualify new local suppliers. Emerson Electric has about 48 percent of its sales outside the United States. Emerson increasingly seeks global U.S. suppliers with willingness to "co-locate" and support Emerson outside the United States in their global locations. Emerson's U.S.-based suppliers, whose defensive strategies are to only operate and sell in the United States, are finding it more difficult to grow their business with Emerson.

The Timken Company has done a good job of following its bearing customers all over the world. They followed Caterpillar to Korea, John Deere and General Motors to Europe, Ford to Brazil, and Freightliner to Shanghai. Conversely, Timken's OEM bearing business with Toyota in Japan, Mercedes in Germany, Volvo in Sweden, and Rolls Royce Aircraft in England, all helped establish Timken as a global supplier on all seven continents. For business planning purposes, Timken has identified six broad industries for bearings—auto, truck, mobile, railroad, general, and precision—and over twenty market segments within these industries. Tom Strouble, the corporate vice president at Timken, led the transformation to manage the bearing business around broad industries, discrete market segments, and regions of the world as shown in Exhibit 13-4.

With customer consolidation from mergers and acquisitions, a number of Timken's market segments have become increasingly global. For example, heavy-duty trucks are managed as a global market segment with major players including Mercedes/Freightliner, Volvo, Navistar International, Scania, and Hino. A global business unit manager in the United States is responsible for this market with counterparts in Europe, South America, Japan, and Asia. Because computer disk drive bearings are used by OEMs in Singapore, Malaysia, Scotland, and the United States, counterparts are located in these regions and they report to the global business manager in the United States. The global managers and their geographic counterparts meet a few times a year to discuss issues and trends, develop strategies, and coordinate global and multi-regional customer requirements. Global electronic networking and teleconferencing sessions reduce the need, time, and cost to have more face-to-face meetings. Some market segments, including railroads and steel mills, are primarily domestic players so only country strategies are developed for these target markets. However, over time and with increased industry consolidation, more of Timken's growth opportunities are not limited to one region of the world.

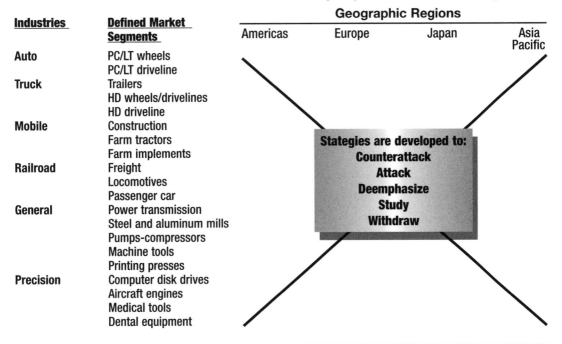

Exhibit 13-4
The Timken Company: Global Market Segments

Geographic Regions

Industries	Defined Market Segments	Americas	Europe	Japan	Asia Pacific
Auto	PC/LT wheels				
	PC/LT driveline				
Truck	Trailers				
	HD wheels/drivelines				
	HD driveline				
Mobile	Construction				
	Farm tractors				
	Farm implements				
Railroad	Freight				
	Locomotives				
	Passenger car				
General	Power transmission				
	Steel and aluminum mills				
	Pumps-compressors				
	Machine tools				
	Printing presses				
Precision	Computer disk drives				
	Aircraft engines				
	Medical tools				
	Dental equipment				

Stategies are developed to:
Counterattack
Attack
Deemphasize
Study
Withdraw

Although some companies may want to eliminate foreign competition through short-term protective trade legislation, the better way to compete long-term is to continually improve products at home and expand into foreign markets. Many companies would prefer to remain domestic if their home market was large and growing fast enough. A company does not need to be large to market globally. Small- and medium-sized firms can practice global nichemanship by designing globally and adapting locally. And, if most industrial suppliers do not think and act more globally, foreign competitors will attack them in "their" home market. Finally, since industrial products, technology, and investment capital do not have passports and country borders are blurred, there is really no longer such a thing as a home market.

SUMMARY

Business planning is undoubtedly one of the most important activities in the whole process of management. Who would consider for a minute supporting anyone interested in any type of a business venture without some kind of a business plan? Some companies' bureaucratic plans are nearly useless. I have observed and worked with many companies that talk a good game of planning and go through all the bureaucratic motions required to develop plans for their business. Yet, when the facts and issues are known, many of these plans have little effect on the way the business is conducted. I strongly suggest the need for many discreet business plans for specific target markets rather than a thick plan that quickly dies on a shelf. When business plans are developed for strategic market segments the entire process is more focused. Target niches to counter attack or attack should guide competitive analysis, technology solutions, growth rates, customer needs, and product development.

The cross-functional business team responsible for the implementation must do the strategic thinking and development of any business plan. The generation of strategic issues and scenario development help the team think strategically about the business before the strategic planning process begins. The use of strategic issue management and scenario planning can make strategic planning more proactive and future based rather than looking through a rearview mirror to develop the plan. Companies with rigid hierarchies and vertical silos will have difficulty with strategic thinking and with target market planning that must be done horizontally by cross-functional business teams on a regional and increasingly multi-regional and global basis. The prescriptions outlined in this chapter can help any company achieve improved results through better strategic market planning on a country, regional, and global basis.

Evaluating a Business Plan

"A team developed business plan should document superior customer value, have a sound strategy, and describe the necessary cross-functional implementation programs."

Chuck Knight, Emerson Electric Company
Chairman

While management in most industrial firms recognizes the importance of planning and prepares both long-term business plans and annual operating plans, there are wide variations in the quality of the plans. Some are very useful instruments that provide the basis for communicating a direction, pulling the different departments together, and dramatically improving results. Unfortunately, many others lack the substance to be a useful management tool.

Of course, no one can guarantee the success of any plan, and there is no ready-made checklist that will show absolutely whether a plan is a winner or a loser. There is, however, a logical thought process that will greatly assist management in deciding whether a plan is a solid vehicle for moving the business ahead or just a lot of words and numbers without real substance. My intent in this chapter is to describe how to use this thought process to determine whether proposed plans are soundly conceived and worth the commitment of resources or whether they should go back to the drawing board for more work. There is nothing sophisticated about the procedure. It simply requires getting answers to three general questions:

1. Is the plan properly structured and focused?
2. Is there anything about the plan that detracts from its credibility?
3. Is the business team's enthusiasm and strategy sound?

Although these broad questions may be obvious, the answers are often obscure, and it frequently takes much digging to bring the answers into focus.

STRUCTURE AND FOCUS

To start with, *the business plan should be a complete and self-explanatory document*, which means that even without prior knowledge of the business, anyone should be able to read the plan and decide whether it makes sense. That is, they should be able to understand the direction the business team has in mind for the business, why this direction was selected, and how it will be pursued. The strategy statement should also explain the value customers will receive from your product/service package, what cross-functional programs are needed to deliver customer value, and the sales and profit goals expected over the next two to five years. I am not suggesting that simply because a plan is understandable and reads well, it is necessarily sound. However, unless it has these basic attributes, it isn't worth further review. Far too much time will be wasted trying to figure out what the plan really means, what the cross-functional team intends to do, and whether the proposed actions are worthwhile.

Customer Value Statements

The purpose of having a customer value statement at the beginning of a business plan is to focus everyone and every program on providing documented customer value. A superior customer value statement differentiates your product/service package and causes people to buy from you. *And without any superior customer value, why even develop a business plan?* Because most industrial products and services provide different value to different market segments, separate customer value statements are needed for each market segment or group of customers you want to differentiate your package to. If the definition and selection of the most attractive market segments have not been done, it is unlikely that the plan will have different customer value statements for discreet market segments.

Unfortunately, most business-unit and general managers cannot articulate their business strategy in terms of the customer value they create. These same managers talk fluently about products, technologies, manufacturing processes, or broad goals, but they do not think in terms of the specific customer value they will develop, communicate, and deliver. The first key to developing a sound market strategy is to have a superior customer value statement. Ordering the marketing department to write a customer mission statement, maybe with an advertising agency, will never correct the situation. When everyone in the business sees and understands a superior customer value statement as the starting point in developing a winning plan, the plan is on the way to being a good one.

Before determining what is a good customer value statement, let's first examine examples of *bad customer value statements*. The following statements are typical of what a customer value statement should not be:

We supply high-performance products.
We design and make value-added solutions.
We are a world-class supplier.

These are not customer value statements. These are simply arrogant statements and resemble the kind of spin we see in annual reports and presentations to the financial community to hype stock. They have no measures, time frames, or explicit statement of what customers will receive. They are vague platitudes of self greatness and buzzwords.

Let's now look at some *good customer value statements* that are better than the last ones:

- We will reduce the noise, water usage, and weight in each machine.
- We will improve the wear resistance of components while reducing the number of parts and assembly time.
- We will eliminate the need for synthetic sizing additives, and improve the ink jet printability for the customer's customers.
- We have the best customer service for standard items and customer specials.

These customer value statements have identified the specific variable(s) by which they are different and better to users. The next step would be to document how much better their solution is than existing customer solutions. The claims must be quantified and then presented in terms of money or something saved for customers.

The following are two examples of *superior customer value statements*. They both show something saved per day, month, or year. A heavy-duty airbrake supplier developed the first superior customer value statement:

For heavy-duty truck vehicles and one of the large manufacturers, we will reduce the OE's assembly costs for airbrakes by 18 percent, and we will reduce their current warranty costs from 13 percent to 1 percent. The lower warranty costs will result in savings of $2.5 million per year for XYZ Company; fewer component parts for a saving of $150,000 per year and assembly costs will be reduced by $400,000 per year. This will also result in vehicle weight reduction, a reduced number of suppliers, and less warranty hassles.

A lubricant supplier developed the second superior customer value statement for automotive plant customers:

We will replace the current plant lubrication processes with our total lubrication-management service; customers will contract all lubricant procurement, inventory management, maintenance, and disposal of lubricants to us. Their total production costs will decrease between 1.5 and 2.5 percent. More specifically, automotive manufacturing customers will receive the following value:

1. 3-5 percent less unscheduled downtime due to machine component wear and machine failures currently caused by inappropriate maintenance and lubrication procedures. This will result in total production cost savings of 0.8 to 1.2 percent. [The actual money saved was omitted for proprietary reasons.]
2. 10 to 20 percent less scheduled machine downtime caused by use of inferior lubricants with shorter drain intervals, thus avoiding direct maintenance and part replacement costs (e.g. ball-bearings), worth another 0.3 to 0.6 percent in total production cost savings.
3. Over 25 percent lower direct cost of lubricant waste disposal, since disposal will be handled by us rather than a contractor, plus the less tangible regulatory and liability costs caused by less safe disposal, worth another 0.2 to 0.3 percent of cost savings.
4. Lower overall procurement costs associated with inaccurate and untimely payment and followup of lubrication invoices and storage costs, all worth about 0.1 to 0.2 percent lower procurement costs.
5. Lower inventory and environmental compliance costs currently caused by drum delivery of lubricants and to be replaced by totes and bulk delivery all worth an estimated 0.1 to 0.2 percent in savings.

Pricing: To be priced as an annual fee, proportional to lubricant volume usage, and about 40 percent below the total cost savings the customer realizes.

In both of these excellent examples, the suppliers were not just meeting or matching the competitive customer value. They exceeded the value supplied by competitors. *A superior customer value statement must exceed the tangible and intangible value of customer alternatives.* If you just equal or match a competitive offering, you can frequently get into a macho price war in which shareowners suffer. If you have just equal customer value, there is a possibility that the strategy and business plan are not winning ones.

In every planning review session, business teams should be asked about what benefits the product/service provides; how these benefits compare with competitors, and how they will price the product/service package relative to the customer's reference points. *If those questions are answered insufficiently, the business plan should be sent back for rework or not approved.* The message from such disciplined business plans and reviews are especially strong to people in R&D, product development, and manufacturing who quickly learn that a product cannot be assumed superior by some inside-out engineering criteria. The constraint of a customer value statement works well to focus R&D, manufacturing, and other departments that develop, make, communicate, and deliver customer value. When a company demands that its business plans start out with the specific benefits customers will receive, there will also usually be more *up-front work to document the favorable economics for customers and yourself—two big keys to a winning business plan.* (For more guidelines on customer value statements, see Chapter 3, "Everyone is in Markrting", and the topics "Provide Superior Value" and "Customer Value Statements".)

Sound Strategy Statement

The plan should next be prefaced by a brief summary or strategy statement explaining what type of business the team is trying to build, what market(s) has(have) been selected as targets and why, and the basis for believing the plan can be accomplished. A strategy statement provides a link between the superior customer value statement, the needed capabilities, and the cross-functional implementation programs to achieve the stated focus. The customer value statement described in the previous statement can be part of the strategy statement, or it can be a stand-alone opening statement. All that is needed here is a summary of the team's intent and the under-lying rationale. Why waste time wading through a total plan if the basic intent and rationale do not make sense? Here is a well-worded strategy statement from a plan to build a business in the telecommunications equipment market:

> Our continuing objective is to build a $90 million business in the telecommunica-tions equipment market within the next three years. We intend to concentrate our efforts on the equipment area involved in the "subscriber loop," where we have a sig-nificant technical base. We do not intend to get into switching or toll transmission, nor do we intend to get into the interconnect business. (R&D repeatedly wanted to develop technically interesting devices.)

> We will achieve this objective by introducing several new products with significant cost and/or performance advantages that will provide telephone companies with superior value by reducing their labor costs by 6 percent and prolong the useful life of their existing equipment by about 8 percent (customer value statement). These new products will account for 50 percent of our volume growth each year through 2003. We will also have to acquire several new products and platforms of technology that we do not now have to serve this market.

> Accomplishing this plan will enable us to sustain a real growth rate of better than 10 per-cent a year, bringing our after-tax ROS to 10 percent and our after-tax ROA to 25 percent.

A clear strategy statement such as this one, which explains in broad terms what the cross-functional team is seeking to do and how it intends to do it, is the hallmark of any good busi-ness plan. It states the customer value that it will provide to telephone companies: "reduce their labor costs by 6 percent and prolong the life of their existing equipment by about 8 percent." It states a precise objective and a time frame for reaching it. It defines the market segments the team has targeted and explains the competitive basis for believing the business can be enlarged. It defines the focus of attention—both what will be done and what won't be done. It states the type of actions the business team intends to take, and it states the expected sales and financial results.

One point about defining a strategy statement for the business is worth emphasizing. *It is sometimes equally important to define what you don't want to do as it is to define what you do want to do.* Defining what you don't want to do is like getting a no answer in the old game of 20 Questions. Even though a no answer is negative information, it often provides useful insight into the ultimate solution. Similarly, a statement defining what you don't want to do in a business helps bring into focus the strategic direction you do want to take. Note how the telecommunica-tion strategy statement achieved precision by naming the business (interconnect) in which the company would not participate.

Now let's look at a not-so-good example. Here is a strategy statement that management in a programmable-controller business prepared:

> We intend to grow our business in programmable controllers at the fastest possible rate and maximize profits. We intend to broaden both our distribution and customer base and gain market share. We will continue to reduce costs and build value into our products with world-class manufacturing. We will need an especially strong selling effort and will achieve this through superior sales training.

As you can see, this statement doesn't really describe any kind of a business concept. It doesn't establish any parameters on the size or scope of the overriding business objective, does not define any target market segments, makes no attempt to define a strategy for accomplishing this objective, and says nothing about financial implications.

Testing a strategy statement against the obverse highlights the lack of thought. This test holds that if a statement doesn't make much sense when the obverse is stated, it probably isn't worth saying. Now, think of the strategy statement for programmable controllers. Does it make sense to think in terms of growing the business at the "slowest possible rate," to make "minimum profits," or to "increase costs" supported with a "very weak selling effort" or "inferior sales training"? Hardly. And yet, the phrases "fastest rate," "maximum profits," "reduce costs," and "superior sales training" don't mean much more. And finally, the buzzword "world class" is so vague it says nothing.

Needed Cross-Functional Programs

Following the strategy statement, *the plan should outline a series of initiatives linked to the business strategy and customer value statement.* There should be cross-functional programs to deliver the customer value and the projected sales and profits. Given the summary statement for telecommunications, you would expect to see recommended actions and programs designed to develop new or improved products for the subscriber loop market and thus improve profit margins to the 10 percent level. If planned actions and programs do not fit this pattern, the logic is faulty, and there is something fundamentally wrong with the plan. Laboratory or, preferably, field trial data would be shown in the plan to support their customer value statement.

To be meaningful, all the recommended actions and programs should be defined in sufficient detail to provide the basis for effective execution and management control. For example, do the key programs proposed to improve performance show the major steps to be taken, the costs involved, the timetable for accomplishment, and the personnel responsible for each step? This level of detail is important. How else can you be sure that there is reason for successful execution? Moreover, it is the only way to ensure that appropriate corrective actions can be taken if something goes wrong before an accounting "scorecard" comes out at the end of a time period.

Another question to consider is whether there are any parts of the plan in which actual performance cannot be measured. Many companies are saddled with information systems that do not provide the means of tracking costs and profits for individual products, customers, or markets or that have other critical gaps. If this is the case, plans to improve sales and profits for these individual product or market segments—or for anything else in which actual results cannot be determined—cannot be measured or controlled. Since it doesn't make sense to plan something you can't measure or control, any part of a plan that falls into this category should be discounted until some basis for control is defined.

Finally, the plan should be summarized in a series of sales, cost, and profit projections that are also consistent with the strategy statement. In the case of the telecommunications plan, these projections should reflect a growth pattern that heads toward a $150 million business in three years. Profit results should show a 10 percent after-tax return on sales (ROS) and a 25 percent after-tax return on assets (ROA). If the projections show a different picture, there is obviously something wrong that needs to be corrected before the plan is subjected to detailed review.

Summing up, step 1 in distinguishing winning plans from losers is to quickly examine the plan document for completeness and logic. Is it understandable, and does it make sense? Is there a value statement that describes the benefits customer groups will receive? Is there a brief strategy statement that clearly explains what management is trying to do with the business? Does this statement sound reasonable, and do cross-functional actions and programs that are logical and cost effective support it? Are the actions and programs sufficiently detailed to ensure effective execution and measurement? Do the sales, cost, and profit projections make sense in light of what management wants to do and the actions and programs that are proposed?

Clearly, this first step in the review process does not entail any kind of in-depth analysis. It shouldn't take more than half an hour or so to do. If it takes longer, the plan is too complicated and verbose. There is no use spending time getting into details if the basics are not right. And any plan that cannot pass this initial examination of its structure and content should be reworked before more management time is wasted reviewing a business plan that is inherently unsound.

CREDIBILITY ISSUES

Assuming the plan is structurally sound, step 2 should be to look for weaknesses or inconsistencies that detract from the plan's credibility. Five questions will help ensure that there are no fatal flaws in the plan: (1) Is the plan's fact base sound? (2) Do the sales, cost, and profit projections make sense? (3) Does the risk/reward ratio make sense? (4) Has adequate allowance been made for contingencies? (5) Have cross-functional plans been developed for each key function and project?

Fact Base

A solid fact base is crucial to good strategic thinking and planning. It is the whole foundation for management's evaluation of the product, market, and competition and, ultimately, cost and profit projections. Few will disagree with the importance of solid facts to good planning, but very few managers are sufficiently tough-minded when searching for the real facts. Over the past several years, I have seen many presentations presumably based on facts. However, when many of these purported facts were challenged and the truth really emerged, I found that purported facts were not facts at all. Instead they were statements that fell into some of the following categories:

1. *Folklore facts* have grown up with the business and have never really been challenged. One such example is, "We have the best product or offer customers the best value." It is hard to think of any division or marketing manager that doesn't make such a claim. But, in most cases, such a claim doesn't stand up when the necessary digging and side-by-side competitive comparisons are performed to get the real facts.
2. *Assumed facts* are necessary assumptions about the future, but not facts. For example, statements that GDP will grow or inflation will run at a certain rate, costs will increase by a certain amount, or competitors will react in a certain way should be clearly labeled as assumptions and not presented in any way as facts. Undocumented claims such as "we're the low-cost producer" or that a "premium priced product" provides customer value are just vague and self-serving statements.
3. *Reported facts* tend to be given unwarranted validity simply because they have been published by some association or industry expert. Who published the data?

What is the source? How valid or complete is the source? How old are the data? Until these questions are answered satisfactorily, the data should not be regarded as factual.

4. *Hoped-for facts* represent situations management would like to believe but that do not accurately reflect the situation. "We are the most profitable company" or "We have the best sales force" are typical examples of delusions, arrogance, denial, and self-serving statements without any sound evidence.

5. *Half-true facts* have a certain amount of validity to them but are misleading. For instance, "The market has grown at an average rate of 10 percent a year over the past five years" may be a true statement, but it is misleading if five years ago this market dipped to an unusually low level and much of the 10 percent grown was simply catching up to where the market should have been. What is the base point? Where is it in the secular trend? What is the growth rate if we shift the base point back or forward? Have price increases distorted the unit growth?

In many situations, distinctions between facts that are real and facts that are not so real may not be important. Attorneys often like to play head games with so called "facts." But in business planning, the distinctions are critical. The whole plan is worthless if it is based on anything other than real facts. There is no way to make certain that proposed actions and programs are based on incontrovertible facts without hard-nosed questioning that challenges some of the facts and places the burden of proof on those presenting the plan. What are the data to support this statement? What is the source for these data? What is the proof that we are competitive or have a demonstrable advantage? These are all fair questions that must be answered to prove that facts are truly facts.

Sales, Costs, and Profit Projections

How do you determine whether a plan's sales, costs, or profit projections are sound? What do you look for when making this kind of an evaluation? You don't have to be a financial wizard, but you do have to have a solid understanding of cost and margin relationships and how they change or should change as volume moves up or down.

A few caveats are worth emphasizing. First, watch out for sales projections that call for a faster rate of market growth than historical patterns show or that require a significant gain in market share. Market growth rates or share positions may increase, but not as easily or as quickly as those presenting the plan expect. New or improved technology, even with clear customer advantages, seldom grow the business as fast as their optimistic sponsors think they will. Moreover, every perceived opportunity for market gain is usually accompanied by some risk or threat that could cause a decline. In most cases, risks or threats are overlooked, and only opportunities are emphasized. A commonly overlooked threat is the likely reaction by competitors. When the success of a plan depends on accelerated sales growth, especially with market share improvement, it is crucial to explore the reasons the change is projected, ensuring that they are valid. It is generally much safer to bet on a business plan geared to a conservative sales forecast— and then scramble to exceed the plan if the market opportunity develops—than on a plan with a higher sales forecast that will require a cutback in costs and operations if the anticipated market opportunity does not occur. Losing sales dollars because a market opportunity is missed always hurts. But it is not as painful as the losses that occur and the explanations that go with those losses when the whole plan is based on a sales forecast that is far too optimistic.

Also, if cost and profit projections show sharp improvement from past patterns, look for the reasons for this change. Remember, cost and profit patterns do not improve unless someone does something to make it happen. Who is going to do what? When will it be done? What is the evidence that it can be done and will yield the desired result? Watch out for long-term projections (three to five years) that are much more favorable than projections for one to two years. Long-term projections are easy to make; it is difficult to hold anyone accountable for them. Long-term improvements usually represent wishful thinking rather than a realistic plan.

Be sure that gross margins are adequate to cover all related expenses and generate a satisfactory profit margin. Of course, gross margins vary widely across businesses, but it pays to be very suspicious of the profit potential of any industrial business with a gross margin [sales dollars less all manufacturing costs (including variances) to convert the product from raw material to finished product] that is much less than 30 percent. In some cases—particularly in a process industry or where the business is based on the sale of a relatively few high-ticket products or systems—sales, marketing, and administrative expenses may be sufficiently low to permit a satisfactory profit level with a lower gross margin. Nevertheless, a gross margin under 30 percent should be viewed as a red flag and should be examined to determine whether the entire cost-profit structure makes sense with the lower ratio.

Check to see that anticipated cost changes for labor, materials, and outside services are adequately reflected in profit-and-loss projections. In today's volatile economic climate, it is all too easy to underestimate cost changes up or down, leading to erroneous profit projections. The only way to avoid this possibility is to ask very specific questions about the allowances for cost changes that have been factored into profit projections. For example, ask purchasing what price changes are expected on raw materials and other purchased items and when. Ask human relations management what kind of wage or benefit increases are anticipated for both hourly and salaried workers and when. Ask insurance management how much allowance has been made for increasing costs of medical, disability, and liability insurance and why. Obviously, all of the responses must be checked for consistency with current market and economic conditions. The controller should then ensure that all of these allowances have been correctly factored into the plan.

Examine expense levels for key areas to ensure that they correctly consider prior spending patterns and the job that needs to be done. In some cases, planned expenses may be too low. There is a tendency on the part of some managers to cut back on expenditures that should be made in critical areas so that their current profit looks good, even though this may jeopardize the long-term health of the business. In other cases, planned expense levels may be too high, especially with an overly optimistic sales forecast. Sloppy planning practices enable many managers to automatically increase their budgets for advertising, promotion, sales, and other areas that can move up or down very easily without regard for what is really required to support the plan.

Industry comparisons that will help determine whether a particular expense level is too low or too high are generally available through competitor reports, trade association data, or industry publications. If sales, advertising, or product development expenses are out of line with published industry data, it is important to ask why. An answer frequently given to this question is that the comparisons are not valid; apples to oranges are a common claim. Don't settle for this response. There may very well be differences in what different companies include in various expense categories, but if the ratios are significantly different, there is a good chance that something is fundamentally wrong.

It's also helpful to present the sales cost and profit projections in three cases: An optimistic case, a pessimistic scenario, and the most likely pro forma is shown as Exhibit 14-1. A break-even analysis should also be done for the pessimistic, most likely, and optimistic projections. This analysis is especially needed for new products and new facilities. When products have been in the market for years, an accurate pro forma income statement is easier to construct.

Exhibit 14-1

Pro Forma Income Statement

	Low (Pessimistic)	Medium (Most Likely)	High (Optimistic)
Sales	$35,000,000	$45,000,000	$55,000,000
Cost of sales	$25,000,000	$34,000,000	$43,000,000
Gross margin	$10,000,000	$11,000,000	$12,000,000
Expenses			
Direct selling	4,570,000	4,800,000	5,120,000
Advertising	1,570,000	1,680,000	1,800,000
Transportation and storage	280,000	380,000	470,000
Depreciation	150,000	150,000	150,000
Credit and collections	120,000	140,000	160,000
Financial and clerical	290,000	380,000	470,000
Administrative	550,000	550,000	550,000
Total expenses	$7,530,000	$8,080,000	$8,720,000
Profit before taxes	$2,470,000	$2,920,000	$3,280,000
Net profit after taxes	$1,280,000	$1,518,400	$1,700,400
Cash Flow	$1,430,000	$1,668,400	$1,850,000

Finally, be sure that profit on incremental volume is satisfactory. In any business with a sound economic structure, higher volume should generate higher profit margins, hence, significantly higher earnings, since it should be possible to achieve leverage on the fixed-cost component. *Unfortunately, most costs tend to be far too variable as volume increases and far too fixed when volume declines.* As a result, the profit gain from added volume does not vary as directly with volume as it should. It is reasonable in most manufacturing companies to look for a 30 percent increment of profit on incremental volume and to insist on a clear explanation whenever this is not projected. Conversely, if volume should decline, it is reasonable to expect the same profit margins to be maintained, and profit dollars should not be any lower than they were when the business grew through this volume to a higher level.

Risk/Reward Considerations

When reviewing opportunities, it is important to remember that every opportunity involves some degree of risk. *The degree of risk and reward varies widely from opportunity to opportunity.* It is always worthwhile to ask what is the risk/reward ratio—that is, for every dollar at risk, how many dollars of profitable gain can we expect? When evaluating the risk and reward, the most common combinations are shown in Exhibit 14-2.

Exhibit 14-2

Risk/Reward Combinations

Risk		Reward	
1.	Low	High	
2.	High	High	The Most Attractive Opportunities
3.	Low	Low	
4.	High	Low	The Less Attractive Opportunities
(Investment)		(Sales Revenue, Payback Period, and Profit Goal)	

It should be obvious that every plan involves some degree of risk—no one can predict future events with absolute certainty. However, the degree of risk varies widely from plan to plan, and it is essential to ensure that the opportunity for reward is commensurate with the degree of risk involved. Let's examine two plans to determine how the degree of risk varies and what the factors are that cause these differences.

1. *Example A.* A business team for a manufacturer of specialty chemicals submitted a plan to double sales volume for one of its new product lines. Doing so required a plant addition involving a $20 million investment and a significant investment for added working capital. The company's sales of this product had doubled during the previous four years, and the total market was projected to more than double during the next five years. This total market projection was not out of line with past growth trends and was supported by a growing customer base that perceived real economic advantages in the company's product. Product cost estimates had proven to be valid, and projected profit returns on sales and investment were well in excess of the company's accepted hurdle rates. Payback on the new plant addition was planned in 2.4 years.

2. *Example B.* A business team in a machine tool company presented a plan to take the company into robotics. The plan emphasized the growing interest in robotics in both foreign and domestic markets and projected a dramatic increase in robotic sales during the next decade. The company's product development group had developed a modular concept for a line of robotics that appeared to offer opportunities for major cost savings in the manufacturing process. Product development also claimed that their line of robotics would have better speed, range, and load-carrying capability than any other competitive offering. Pictures of a design or break-board prototype were presented to prove the feasibility of product development claims. Continuation of the program required additional funding of $2.7 million for further product development activities and a joint venture with another independent research firm to ensure the necessary control capability. The product development group was committed to having a prototype for the machine tool show in the fall of the following year, and marketing expected to capitalize on the introduction of the new robot with an integrated sales and promotion campaign to major potential users. The company had manufacturing capacity available to meet projected sales requirements, and no immediate investment was required for new plant or equipment. Total costs of pursuing the plan were about $5 million, with product development and market development expenses accounting for the great bulk of this sum. A payback period of 4.5 years was projected, and profits beyond that point were expected to grow at a much faster rate than anything the company had ever experienced.

It doesn't take much insight to see that the potential risk/reward ratio in Example A is much more attractive than that in Example B. Both situations are based on exciting market characteristics, and both appear to offer attractive growth opportunities. However, the plan in Example A is based on a proven product with an attractive sales and profit history, while the plan in Example B is based solely on claims by the product development group of what they can do against a formidable array of competitors. Moreover, the payback period in Example A is of much shorter duration, and the company's exposure to potential loss is much less.

All of these points are relatively easy to see when the examples are succinctly described on paper. They are not nearly as easy to see in a real-life situation, especially when an enthusiastic and articulate management team, who, quite rightly, has the utmost confidence in their abilities, presents the plan. Therefore, it is always worthwhile to ask two specific questions: (1) What is the risk/reward ratio; that is, how many dollars of gain can we expect for every dollar at risk? (2) What happens if customers or competitors react differently than anticipated?

Clearly, the degree of acceptable risk, regardless of potential rewards, varies from company to company, depending on size and financial condition. In a high-risk situation, the potential reward should be six to ten times the dollars placed at risk in a relatively short time frame. Isn't this what you would want if you were investing your personal money in a high-risk situation? When the risk is less, you can settle for reduced reward opportunities because of the greater certainty of achieving planned results. In any event, a plan should never be approved unless those proposing the plan can respond to questions about the risk/reward ratio in a manner that demonstrates they have given it serious consideration.

Allow for Contingencies

Many business plans compare their explanations to a road map, and, for the most part, this analogy is correct. Like a road map, the plan shows where you want to go and how you should get there. However, you can be much more certain that you will get where you want to go when following a road map than when following a business plan, no matter how brilliantly the plan may have been conceived and prepared. Unexpected road construction or detours might keep the driver from following the route exactly as planned. But these difficulties are minor compared with the roadblocks that any business plan is likely to encounter. Unforeseen changes in economic climate, competitor actions, customer or user requirements, and internal performance or capability breakdowns all represent uncertainties that are much more severe than those facing a driver trying to follow a map.

Unless adequate allowances are made for these contingencies when the plan is developed, it is almost certain to be too optimistic. It is not prudent to accept any business plan when successful execution requires all the pieces to fall into place exactly as planned. There must be some margin for error. How much depends on the penalties involved if the plan is not successful. When the penalties are very severe, the plan should not be accepted unless there is a high probability of success. Murphy's Law (everything that can possibly go wrong will) will prevail more times than not, and results will not be achieved as expected.

The best way to make this determination is to ask a series of what-if questions. For example, what happens to planned results if:

1. Sales volume is 5, 10, or even 20 percent below forecast?
2. Critical costs are above estimates by a significant amount?
3. Deadlines for product development are missed?
4. Material shortages or unusually slow deliveries occur?
5. Competitors cut their prices by a significant amount?

Naturally, the questions will vary with each situation, but the technique remains the same. Simply look for the key variables and ask what happens if any of them go wrong. Inadequate answers probably indicate that insufficient thought was given to the possibility of things going wrong as the plan was developed.

Planned Improvements

Most plans include expectations of major improvements in many areas. It is common to find statements such as "Manufacturing costs (or cycles) will improve by X;" "Inventories will be reduced by Y;" "Product redesign will take Z out of total costs;" or "Time-to-market will be cut by 50 percent." While these are certainly admirable objectives, they are nothing if not backed by detailed plans showing who is going to do what and when and the specific result that will be achieved. It is very easy to be misled into believing improvements will be made because objectives such as these are included in a plan presentation when, in fact, nothing has really been planned to make the improvements.

In short, cross-functional plans should exist for every key function and project:

- Research/development and engineering
- Manufacturing
- Inventory
- Procurement
- Cost reduction
- Productivity improvement
- Quality improvement
- Sales and distribution
- Manpower
- Capital expenditures
- Cash flow

All of these plans should be developed and ready for review and discussion.

BUSINESS TEAM APPROACH AND ATTITUDE

Two final points must be considered to complete the evaluation. First, it is important to determine whether the plan is integrated and truly reflects the thinking and requirements of the entire business team or whether it is simply a brainchild of one or two people and that none of the other departments know anything about. It is important to determine whether the entire cross-functional team believes in and is committed to achieving the planned results.

Integrated Across Functions

One of the most common and serious deficiencies of industrial business plans is that they are not integrated; they do not have input from all key functions of the business. This is the primary reason so many plans have so little meaning and make so little contribution to management and the decision-making process. When plans are developed in a vacuum, sales forecasts are discounted or second-guessed by manufacturing, and inventory levels inevitably get out of line. Product development activities are too technically directed and thus out of phase with market needs and what the other departments should do. The sales force operates with an unhealthy emphasis on volume and too little focus on selected customer groups or market segments that could make the business stronger and more profitable.

It is not difficult to determine whether a business plan is integrated to help manage the business. The first clue is the name of the plan. If it is called a marketing plan, it probably is just that, and it probably has all the shortcomings identified earlier. It must be an integrated cross-functional business plan. The second clue is how it is presented. If it is written and presented completely by traditional marketing people, it is a fair bet that other functional departments have not been adequately involved.

Another way to check if a plan is integrated is to ensure that all functional departments are represented when the plan is presented and to ask relevant questions. For instance, ask manufacturing if they agree with the sales forecast and if their inventory and production plans are actually geared to it. Ask if the planned mix of sales is comparable with existing production capabilities or if this factor was even considered when the sales plan was developed. Ask the controller if the department has determined the relative profitability of alternative sales strategies and if this information was considered as sales plans were drawn together. Ask engineering to identify their planned project priorities and show how engineering labor-hours will be allocated to these projects. Then ask marketing to explain how these priorities and allocations tie into their assessment of marketing needs and opportunities. The answers to such questions will clearly and quickly indicate if the plan is based on a true cross-functional business team effort. If not, it isn't worth much and should be rejected.

Business Team Commitment

Commitment to a plan is a difficult concept to define and probably the most difficult area to probe. At the same time, it is in many respects, the most crucial area. A deep-rooted sense of commitment is why certain business teams are able to overcome all obstacles and still achieve planned results. It is the same ingredient that enables a team to win against tough competition even though their best players are injured or all the breaks in the game go against them.

Without attempting to be a psychologist, there are several things to look for to determine whether this sense of commitment exists:

1. What has been the track record of those submitting the plan? It is a positive sign if they have a history of fulfilling commitments. Conversely, if the group has not met its commitments in the past, it is essential to find out what has changed to make their commitment to the current plan any more meaningful.
2. Is there evidence that individuals understand how a failure to meet their personal or functional commitments would jeopardize the ability of the whole group to accomplish its plan?
3. Is there any indication that anyone in the cross-functional team feels that their function has overcommitted or that they have been pressured into making commitments that are unrealistic?

It is unlikely that anyone will admit they are not committed to a plan they developed and recommend. But questions directed to each functional area about the certainty or difficulty of achieving its part of the plan help everyone see what must be done to successfully implement the plan. Such questioning helps to establish the importance of each individual's personal commitments, not only to the plan but also to the rest of the organization. In a sense, it helps to develop a form of peer pressure, which is just as important in the execution of the business plan as it is in other walks of life. No one enjoys being in the position of having let teammates down.

Challenge Assumptions

If top management truly wants to find ways to significantly improve profits and growth, it must constructively participate in the review of market strategies by challenging underlying assumptions. Most strategic decisions, particularly those that involve a change in direction, require the experience, perspective, and "feel" of upper management—not just its blessing. To be sure, many top executives try to do this, but the way they do it often stifles rather than encourages new ideas. They must avoid any atmosphere of an inquisition and, instead, encourage an open exchange of ideas and having people raise what if options. In such an environment, one idea leads to another, and the management team soon finds itself exploring new and imaginative ways of developing the business.

A cross-functional team give-and-take discussion with top management led a high-speed elevator manufacturer to adopt a new strategy that gave its parts operation a chance for survival:

In this company, as in many others, parts sales had traditionally been a major source of profits. Now management was concerned because "parts pirates" (local parts producers) were cutting sharply into their business. Asked to develop a market strategy that would reverse the trend, the parts manager first came up with a plan that called for adding three salespeople and cutting prices on a large number of parts to be more competitive. As he acknowledged, his plan was essentially no more than a holding action.

During the preliminary planning review session, in which all functions took part, the general manager encouraged everyone to take an entrepreneurial look at the parts business and to try to think of different ways to grow it. Predictably, fresh ideas were hard to come by in a business that had been run the same way for years. But eventually three break-through ideas emerged that were considered worthwhile: (a) build a service organization and sell contracts for maintenance service instead of just parts, (b) decentralize the parts business as a separate business and set up local parts and repair shops to compete head to head with local competitors, and (c) develop parts interchange tables and start to buy and sell some parts from other manufacturers' to spread overhead costs and serve customers with a full product line.

The long-time parts manager was naturally somewhat reluctant to do any of these things, since they would revolutionize his end of the business. But with top and general management backing and encouragement, he did the required analytical work and came back with two possible strategies, based on the first two ideas, that offered a much more attractive outlook.

This process does not always lead to an aggressive strategy because it is not always easy to overcome the scarcity of fresh ideas characteristic of a business run the same way for years and with a "mature market" mind-set. Moreover, alternative strategies are not always visible on a first pass. But upper management in the more successful companies insists on seeking alternative strategies and avoids getting locked into a self-defeating business-as-usual pattern of thinking.

EMERSON ELECTRIC COMPANY—A SHINING EXAMPLE

Emerson Electric Company is a $14 billion manufacturer of electrical, electromechanical, and electronic equipment that employs more than 80,000 people. In 2000, Emerson marked its forty-second consecutive year of improved earnings per share performance unmatched by any other publicly traded U.S. manufacturing company. According to a study by A.T. Kearney, Emerson is one of only eleven U.S. corporations that outearned its cost of capital during each of the past twenty-seven years. Their business units are very decentralized and autonomous, with names such as Alco Controls, Skil, Copeland, Rigid, Rosemount, Appleton Electric, Asco, Xomox, and Micro Motion. Twenty-five percent of 2000 sales were from new products less than five years old, and the goal for year 2001 is 30 percent. Emerson's sixty divisions make a wide range of industrial products that are not household names, even though Emerson is one of the better-run companies in the world. Emerson consistently makes profits in a manufacturing business that many observers consider mature and not glamorous. Emerson's corporate headquarters is small. In another attempt to reduce bureaucracy, the company has no published organization chart because they want people communicating around markets, plans, projects, and issues, not along an organization chart that would take away from their flexibility. The company does not have groups or sectors or other combinations commonly found in large, diversified companies. Emerson's chairman, Chuck Knight describes their planning process:

At Emerson, developing business plans is a line job, not a staff function. The people who develop the plans must be the people who implement the plan. We also believe in keeping our plans simple, our communication simple, our implementation simple, and our organization simple. It takes a lot of discipline to keep planning and implementation simple. Emerson's planning process emphasizes setting firm financial targets, planning carefully, and following up closely. This process is fueled by dynamic annual planning and quarterly review cycles.

Set Consistent Financial Targets

The first step in our planning is to set financial targets. Consistent high performance requires ambitious but consistent targets. Once we fix our financial goals, we do not consider it acceptable to miss them. The financial targets drive our strategy and determine what we have to do, the kinds of businesses we are in, how we organize and manage them, and how we pay the management team.

We have not modified our other financial goals, despite pressure to do so. During the 1990s, for example, we were criticized because we refused to increase our debt position. Given the then-prevailing attitudes toward leverage, our financial position appeared unduly conservative. But we regard our finances strategically; maintaining a conservative balance sheet is a powerful competitive weapon. When we see an opportunity that we can finance only by borrowing, we have the capacity. By the same token, we're not encumbered by interest payments, which are especially burdensome during economic down-turns.

Identify Investment Opportunities

The second step in our planning process is to identify specific market/product opportunities that will meet or exceed our criteria for growth and returns. In other words, we identify business investment opportunities. It is the role of our division presidents and their business teams to bring forth the better business investment opportunities. Since we are a big decentralized company, this bottom-up process of identifying opportunities that meet our top-down financial goals is the only way we know to run a large, close-to-the-customer company. We push the divisions to think through different scenarios and to plan actions that will reach our financial goals. We require only a few standard planning formats. While there are only a few planning formats, they require substantial planning and backup data to develop the small number of exhibits. To prepare properly requires the division general managers and their business teams to really understand the customers, technology, competition, and economics of the business.

Side-by-Side Competitive Comparisons

Our third step is to stress the importance of analyzing and understanding the competition in each attractive market segment. Simply comparing ourselves with ourselves teaches us nothing of value. We use the products and the cost structure of our competitors as the measures against which we assess our performance. We do this in detail, legally and ethically, taking apart competitors' products, analyzing the cost of components, knowing regional labor rates and freight costs, and more. If we want to make intelligent decisions about investing millions of dollars in a new plant to make circular saws we must assemble as clear a picture as possible of the cost structures and overall plans of both our domestic and global competitors.

When most companies consider adding capacity, they typically compare the anticipated returns for the new facility with the existing plant's return. But at Emerson, the management demands that the proposed capital expenditure for a new plant be compared to the return at the lowest cost competitor's plant anywhere in the world. In one situation, if the business team requesting the capital could not beat the lower cost of a Taiwan competitor, they could not get the funds. Before Emerson added the capacity, through judicious intelligence gathering, they knew what Makita's, Bosch's and Black and Decker's costs were. At Emerson, we figure out what the competitors' costs are before building any new plants.

Focused Strategy

Once we understand the needs of our customers and the plans of our competitors, we develop a focused strategy to develop better products, produce more competitively, and provide better service. Among other things, this strategy means staying close to customers and providing them with documented customer value. The financial targets are the parameters for the strategies. We don't have any grand corporate strategy—that's determined by each division and business units within each division. However, we have recently adopted strategies to exploit common sales and distribution channels and share technologies. Our division strategies are often based upon both product design and process improvements. The latter, process engineering, we are especially proud of because it addresses always-needed cost reductions. Every winning strategy must provide superior customer value and attractive profit returns.

Successful Implementation

Once we identify the most attractive investment opportunities in each division, the next step is to successfully implement. This is where many companies fail. Often implementation goes astray because the people who plan are separated from the people who have the responsibility to make the plans work. The plans too often go to the bottom of an operations manager's drawer, and that's the end of them. At Emerson, the people who plan are the people who execute. They have ownership and involvement; it's their plan, not a corporate plan. That ownership makes all the difference. Sometimes people fail to execute because the same people who developed the plan are not permitted to complete the implementation. Many companies put high-potential people on a fast track by giving them more responsibility and promoting them. For the benefit of implementation, we avoid moving people who are in the middle of implementing business plans. We focus on the person's projects rather than status; we compensate people based on the importance of their job, not on the number of people reporting to them or the arbitrary need for a promotion.

For implementation, we use a technique called ABC budgeting: an A budget applies to the most likely scenario, a B budget to a possible lower level of activity, and so on. As a result, our managers know well ahead that, if their business environment changes, they have a well-thought-through set of actions they can take to protect profitability. This contingency planning is particularly helpful in an economic downturn; we are not paralyzed by bad news because we've already planned for it.

Tracking Performance

Our next step is to closely track performance and address deviations immediately. Each division submits monthly operating reports indicating how well they are doing, the criteria being sales growth, profitability, and return on capital. Each division has a board that meets monthly to review and monitor performance. In addition, the president and chief financial officer of each division meet quarterly with corporate operating and financial management to discuss short-term operating results. Each division president along with their appropriate staffs, meet once a year with seven corporate officers for corporate financial reviews. These reviews occur late in the fiscal year and are a review of performance against the financial plan.

Management Development Planning

The last step in our annual business planning reflects the importance we place on human resources. This part of the planning process usually requires an additional half-day meeting centering on the human resource issues in each division. In preparation, a division will evaluate all managers who are department heads or higher. We talk about each manager's length of service in a particular assignment and his or her potential to move to a more difficult job. We try to identify those people who look like future "high potentials," and we develop career plans to offer them a series of assignments and training programs to enhance and augment their skills. We maintain an organization room at headquarters, where we keep personnel charts on every management team in the entire company. Every year we update this information, which covers more than a thousand people, on the basis of organization reviews. The charts include each manager's picture and are color-coded for areas such as function, experience, and career path. They provide a powerful visual aid to human resource planning. When a position opens, we know quickly which candidates are most qualified and which people might succeed the candidates we move up. For the purpose of follow-through and implementation, this approach also lets us know which people should not be moved.

Since about 95 percent of all our promotions come from within Emerson, we believe that this approach to management development, as part of our business planning process, helps to create continuity, maintain our culture, and foster high morale. Nearly all of our general managers come from within the company or from an acquisition we made. We only hire from the outside when we need specialized experience.

SUMMARY

The process of developing a business plan, including the thoughts the business team puts in it before they began to develop it, forces everyone to take an objective, critical and unemotional look at the business in its entirety. The finished product—a business plan—is a roadmap that if used properly, will help the business team manage the business and work more effectively toward success. A winning business plan documents superior customer value, has a sound strategy, effective implementation programs, and expected results of the business team. It communicates a common language among the team and for top management to review.

This chapter developed a no-nonsense approach to evaluating a sound industrial business plan. By taking the role of a CEO, board director, or venture capital firm evaluating a business plan, guidelines for developing a sound industrial business plan will also emerge. None of the business review guidelines raised in this chapter should be difficult to achieve if the business unit's plan has been properly put together and is integrated across all key functions of the business. The cross-functional business team should be able to answer any questions clearly and directly. Long, vague, or indirect answers are a good indication that the plan is not solid and should not be approved until the right facts and answers are in place from the business team. Finally, a straightforward and relatively simple planning cycle should exist in every organization. The guidelines described in the previous chapters and the many examples in this chapter should help any company develop a better planning process. A certain amount of structure is needed for uniform planning outputs, but the process should be kept as simple as possible.

Correcting Your Weaknesses

"If you think of this practical management workshop as an expense, just try ignorance as an alternative."

J. I. W. Anderson, Unilever Chemicals
Chairman

Later in this chapter, I come full circle back to the growth rating scale introduced in Chapter 2. The previous chapters described what it means to be market driven in all aspects of the business, pinpointed common problems that interfere with profitable growth in most companies, and described some of the practices that leading companies have followed to make the concept pay off. After reading these chapters, a cross-functional team should be in a much better position to employ the rating scale as a diagnostic tool to assess the growth capabilities in any company.

I have discussed the challenges of profitable top-line growth being a market-driven business with hundreds of managers from a broad range of industries at my training workshops. I have drawn three conclusions from working with a cross section of managers. First, because most managers rate their performance for most factors on the low side, there appears to be a huge need for improvement in most companies. Second, even those managers who were generally positive about their performance were still very critical about certain factors and felt major improvements were needed. Third, most companies have some learning disabilities that slow or stop any improvement on their deficiencies. High-impact management training is usually needed, with cross-functional business teams, to eliminate learning deficiencies and consider new approaches. Before we revisit the market driven growth rating, everyone must determine if their company is a learning organization.

DO YOU WORK IN A LEARNING ORGANIZATION?

In order to apply the concepts in this book, the organization must have a culture that is open to trying new ideas and continually seeking to improve itself. Unfortunately, many industrial companies are not learning organizations. A learning organization must have a lot of openness throughout the culture and a strong desire to get better regardless of how good they might be. The following ten questions help assess the presence or lack of an openness in your company to learn.

1. Do you find that most senior managers in your company are quite receptive to ideas that they or other senior managers in your company did not come up with?
2. Do middle managers have an open view of employees' opinions that come from anyone, regardless of their job title and pay level?
3. Do most managers encourage people to speak up and challenge the way your company has been doing things?
4. Does your company provide sufficient formal or informal time for business units to share ideas with other business units?
5. Does your company provide sufficient formal or informal time for business units to share ideas between continents or regions of the world?
6. Does your company often try new ideas from competitors in your industry?
7. Does your company try new ideas from outsiders to your industry?
8. Does your company usually cite some internal factors, rather than just all external factors, as the cause for underperformance?

9. Does your company openly discuss mistakes and learn from them without ostracizing people?
10. Do most people feel it is safe to stick their neck-out or to speak-up when top or middle management is present?

If you answered no to two or more of these questions, it is likely that your company's culture is part of the bad old ways of doing business and your company has a need for a lot more openness if more learning is to occur. If an openness to share ideas from within and from outside your organization does not start with the CEO and general managers, the organization at best, will be a slow learner.

Let's take this quick assessment of a learning culture one step further. Another measure of whether your company is a learning organization is indicated by a nonstop commitment to learning and the development of employees for broader responsibilities. The following questions help gauge the degree of commitment to learning in any company:

- How much does your company invest per year and per person in management development workshops? How do these amounts compare to your most progressive or best competitors? Is the management-training budget highly vulnerable to economic swings or is it a firm annual investment?
- Does your company espouse the importance of promotion within? How much does your company spend annually on management search firms? How does the expenditure for search firms compare to your company's annual investment in formal management training programs?
- When management openings occur, are a number of people prepared, and ready to assume the added responsibility? Is there frequently more then one person ready, willing, and able to fill the open position or do people usually take on new responsibilities with little or no formal training?
- Are management development needs identified in every manager's annual performance review? Does your company have a mandatory number of hours per year and per person, such as 30 or 40 hours, for management development and skills training? Does your company measure and track the effectiveness of formal development programs?

If you had difficulty coming up with favorable answers to these questions, there is a good chance that you and/or your company is not committed to learning. Let's now see what it takes to become and remain a learning organization.

A LEARNING ORGANIZATION

Buckman Labs, a global specialty chemical company based in Memphis, Tennessee, is a leader in sharing and managing knowledge. Robert H. Buckman, chairman, described their learning organization at our annual senior executive seminar:

> We recognized early on that the greatest knowledge base in our company did not just reside in a computer database, but in the heads of our individual associates worldwide. All employees or associates have access to the knowledge base of the company. The company's global network and laptop computers are rapidly replacing desktops as a way to instantly create and transfer knowledge.
> The Bulab Learning Center, where most of Buckman's formal training and education is concentrated, is an on-line educational center, which delivers the classroom to the

student anytime and anywhere. Since instituting a knowledge management culture at Buckman Laboratories, we have reduced the global response time to the customer from days and weeks to a couple of hours or at most, a day or two; people that share knowledge are identified for advancement; and finally, the percentage of sales from new products that are less than five years old has significantly improved because of our sharing of knowledge inside and outside the enterprise.

In the long run, the rate at which your organization learns faster than the competition is the only source of competitive advantages. *Superior company performance depends on superior learning.* Underperformance is usually the result of using the good old ways from the bad old days and not learning from your failures and the experiences of others. A learning organization is always experimenting with new ideas, products, processes, and management approaches that may create new sources of growth.

In highly structured and bureaucratic organizations, the person at the top is expected to figure it all out and come in with grand schemes and good answers to everything. This model says, "The top thinks and the rest follow." In more complex organizations and a dynamic world, it is no longer sufficient to have one or a few people figuring it all out. The companies that will excel in the future will be the organizations that know how to tap everyone's knowledge and have the capacity to learn at all levels in the organization. The companies who figure out how to stimulate the collective genius of the people in their organization are going to be the most profitable market leaders.

Most industrial businesses are cyclical. However, companies that cancel training programs with every economic downswing often end up shooting themselves in the foot. Firms that see training as the first item to go in the slightest downturn and the last item to add in an upturn, are not learning organizations. Some of these same companies claim people are their number one asset. People always get outdated and periodically need formal learning to stay at the leading edge of management practice. Would you cancel the preventive maintenance on an aircraft? You should not cancel preventative maintenance for your people. Similarly, would you want to be treated by a physician who was not current and aware of the latest remedies and approaches?

Organizational Learning Disabilities

The chances are high that most readers of this book will see their companies plateau and underperform during their working career. In companies that underperform or fail, there is abundant evidence in advance that the firm is in trouble. The strong warning signals and evidence go unheeded, even when a number of managers are aware of it. Key executives cannot recognize the impending threats, cannot understand the implications of those threats, and cannot come up with viable alternatives to restore their performance. These disabilities are not only prevalent in a dying organization. Many industrial companies are poor learners - they lump along and survive, but never live up to their potential. In light of what the organization could be, many corporations are actually mediocre and going backward. Their employees and shareowners do not usually do very well.

Some industrial companies are slow or poor learners despite the efforts of bright, hard working, and committed people at all levels. Often the harder these companies try to solve their problems of decline, the worse the results. These companies have a number of learning disabilities. When learning disabilities in children and companies go undetected, they are tragic. We attempt to quickly diagnose and treat a child with a learning disability so they can reach their potential and learn without the burden of a treatable handicap going untreated. Why would we do less for a company with many employees that had a major learning disability? The first step to curing learning disabilities is to identify those present in your organization. Following are four of the most common learning disabilities in industrial business organizations. Anyone of these disabilities can cause a fatal outcome:

1. *External factors are to blame when things go wrong.* There is a tendency in all of us to find someone or something outside ourselves as the cause. For many American companies, the external blame has often been foreign competition, labor unions, government regulators, or even disloyal customers or distributors. The external enemy is not limited to pointing blame outside the organization. After blaming the weather, dumb competitors or past management, the blame may turn to the sales department for insufficient sales, to engineering for not enough new products, or to manufacturing for long lead times or inconsistent quality. An underperforming company situation is nearly always the result of both internal and external factors. The external causes make it difficult to accept the fact that the management is responsible for at least some and possibly most of the current situation.

2. *We're the best in everything.* Most companies underestimate the competition and overestimate themselves. This often fatal mind-set usually creates arrogance and complacency when humbleness and a sense of urgency is needed to improve. There is a fine line between being confident and being arrogant. When arrogance is masquerading as confidence, the organization is certainly not open to learning new ways. When any company believes it is the best, it will have great difficulty learning and becoming better. The following statements are clues that the organization believes it's the best:

   "Why should we compare or benchmark with competitors when we're the leader?"
   "Why should we investigate someone else's success or failure?"
   "How can we learn anything from a different industry than the one we lead in?"

   These common statements are heard in too many industrial companies. The statements underscore the defensive and denial mechanisms that inhibit industrial companies from learning from their own and other's experiences. These are the same companies that imagine they will automatically always be successful. However, even the most successful companies must periodically reinvent themselves. In reality, there are no best or world-class companies, only those that continually want to get better by experimenting and learning.

3. *Illusions from initiatives.* When performance declines, some executives give the impression that they know the root causes of the problem. Executives often focus on some big event or some theme-of-the-year slogan without understanding the pattern of events causing the decline in performance. Growing faster is often another illusion that masks the root causes of profit decline. For many simplistic managers, bigger and faster growth is always better, and working faster is better than a slower but more in-depth look at the systemic cause and effects. Big acquisitions are another way to become bigger and mask real problems. When these acquisitions are large, they can put the entire organization's survival at risk. If a company is preoccupied or dominated by a series of "rah-rah" initiatives, little or no learning will take place. Working fast today may result in working slower tomorrow. These managers do not realize that the best results may come from small, well-focused actions, not from large-scale initiatives, knee jerk reactions, or ill-conceived growth. Some Japanese companies have a saying that "you must work slower upfront in order to work faster later." This emphasis on up-front work helps get at the root causes and not treat the symptoms. With smart upfront work, the right areas to change will become more obvious.

4. *Close-minded top management.* A closed-minded top management does not tolerate the necessary "openness" and honesty necessary to change and improve an organization. A closed-minded CEO is bound to traditional ideas (especially his or hers) and usually lacks the capacity to continually challenge his or her own thinking. These so called leaders are the essence of authoritarianism. This learning deficiency is most prevalent in underperforming enterprises with previous histories of high performance. It has a considerable investment in existing products, facilities, and an entrenched set of rituals. The chairman, CEO, and top management team are apprehensive about the future and needed changes. They look to the past for solutions to all of today's challenges. These self-defeating executives systematically inhibit the organization's performance. They have too many connections to the company's historical past.

(Many boards of directors have the same closed-mindedness of the top management and CEOs they are supposed to evaluate. If the current chairman or CEO invited his or her pals to the board, they often come with the same deficiencies. When such directors feel uncertain or ignorant, they posture or kiss up to top management to protect themselves from the pain of appearing ignorant. The result is what psychologists have called skilled incompetence, where uninformed or ignorant people are incredibly proficient at playing a game of asking simple, nice questions, nodding and bobbing in meeting after meeting, and rubber stamping proposals when they should be asking the hard and big questions.)

These four common learning disabilities affect the way a company thinks, behaves, promotes people, and makes resource allocation decisions. Any one of these learning disabilities invariably results in lost business opportunities from existing and new customers, and the cost of these loses is usually great in terms of sales, profits, and jobs. These self-defeating characteristics may exist within a business group, division, or across the entire organization. An organization or any of its business units that ignores any one of these four learning disabilities is being dishonest to its stakeholders. No organization can rely on deceit to achieve long-term success; sooner or later the truth does come out, and when it does, the results aren't often pretty - the CEO is sacked, restructuring occurs, big write-offs are taken, divestitures are made, the company may be broken up, or a takeover might occur.

In contrast to those companies that are not learning organizations, there are the consistently high-performing ones committed to openness and learning. These companies see improved performance from individual and organizational learning that safely seeks the truth and cause and effect. The few companies that fit this model are always learning from their mistakes because it is a way that they implement continuous improvements.

Learning from Mistakes

As we shift to a knowledge-based and faster-moving environment, learning is a critical ingredient for continued success. *Nonstop learning is the foundation for continuous improvement.* Learning comes from formal training programs, coaching, mentoring, and from studying success and failures. A successful company is one that can learn effectively, especially from mistakes. A business unit that is reluctant to openly admit their mistakes is bound to resist most improvements. Many industrial companies are simply not learning organizations, and even fewer are able to objectively and safely learn from their failures. How do progressive companies handle business mistakes? When faced with failure, they recognize it, admit it, learn from it, and then move on. You don't drown by falling into water; you drown by staying under water. By refusing to stay under water and learning how to swim, you can become a great swimmer.

Tom Peters, the best-selling author, urges companies to celebrate failures, learn from them, and build on them. Peters said, "The essence of innovation is the pursuit of good intentions that turn into failure...and to be able to make mistakes and not get shot." The CEO of Cincinnati Machine (formerly Cincinnati Milacron), Kyle Seymour, told four of his business teams at one of our workshops:

> Why were our last two new products not as successful as we hoped? No one will be hurt from learning the causes and no finger pointing will occur. We're all here to learn together and it will help us improve our product and market development processes.

Let's now examine how great sport teams, Virgin Airlines, and 3M make "failures" an integral part of their learning processes.

How Sport Teams Learn

Winning sport teams, unlike most business teams, are very good at learning from their mistakes and identifying areas needing improvement. Before and after every athletic event, great sport teams analyze statistics, game films, competitive match ups, and game plans to learn where they need to focus and improve their capabilities. And, unlike many business teams, few excuses are accepted by athletic teams. Generally, most sport teams are better learning organizations and more performance driven than many business teams. College and professional sport teams have a low tolerance for losing coaches and losing teams.

When evaluating any coach, history looks at the win-loss record, but people tend to forget the losses if the wins are a lot greater. Any half-time discussion by a good coach and his team is about their mistakes - even if they are leading on the scoreboard. Regardless of whether a team wins or loses, everyone watches a game film the day after to see where they made mistakes and how they might have been avoided. Great coaches and athletes don't let failure scare or intimidate them. Mistakes make them learn and do better. Babe Ruth held two long-time baseball records - the greatest number of home runs and the greatest number of strikeouts. Failure can make managers, players, and teams better.

Case Study: Virgin Airlines

Richard Branson, founder of Virgin Airlines, always dreamed of owning an airline. Branson's market research showed that the transatlantic market was large enough to have a predominately business-class carrier at full coach fares. With significantly lower overhead than the high-fare carriers, he reasoned he could rapidly and profitably carve out a profitable niche. After reading about the demise of Laker Airways, whose concept he thought was sound but needing some refinement, Branson decided he would educate himself fast—from an airline pioneer, Freddie Laker, who started and closed Laker Airways. Laker ran low budget flights from London's Gatwick Airport to Newark, New Jersey.

Branson also learned that Laker bought too many planes too fast and incurred nearly $1 billion in debt. Laker not only bought a large fleet of planes, he bought them nearly all on borrowed money or debt. Each year, he had to first find the cash to repay the installments as well as the interest. With wafer-thin profit margins for the tourist class, he had to fly every plane at full capacity if he were to meet his debts, which he was never able to do. Laker bought all his new planes in U.S. dollars; repayment in strong British pounds added to his cycle of decay.

When Branson started, he leased a small handful of aircraft and, rather than only target the rock bottom tourist segment, he also offered first-class service at business-class prices. Branson's first plane, which still flies daily between Gatwick and Newark, is named "The Spirit of Freddie

Laker." Laker suggested to Branson that he not name the aircraft after him for image and super-stition reasons. Branson replied, "I want all our employees to remember and learn from your pio-neering efforts." Branson came to the United States to conduct intensive and "what if" inter-views with former employees of Peoples Express, another defunct discount airline. Branson learned that Peoples' weak management system and naïve pricing, without fully understanding their costs or how competitors could profitably retaliate, were their first mistakes. Peoples Express also lacked a frequent-flyer program. Branson concluded that there were two final caus-es for Peoples' demise: They grew too fast, and the $300 million acquisition of Frontier Airline was too much to absorb. In short, Branson learned from the mistakes of former competitors.

Case Study: 3M's Experimentation Culture

In 1953, a 3M-laboratory assistant who was working on the development of a fluorochemi-cal liquid coolant spilled a few drops on her tennis shoe. She tried to scrub the spots with soap and water, alcohol, and other solvents, but nothing worked. Suddenly, a flash of light came into her mind—if the chemical couldn't be removed with water, it made a good water repellant. If it was impervious to solvents, it could protect fabrics from stains. This insight led to the family of Scotchgard™ protectors now widely used on applications including clothing, carpets, furniture, wood, and leather.

Many industrial companies would have told the laboratory assistant to work on her original project and not to "waste time" on the possible new application of a fluorchemical coolant. Clearly defined business units and division charters in most companies do not allow people to consider applications or new products outside of their existing markets. These same companies stifle creativity and leverage very little technology into new markets. However, experimentation and new-market applications are a way of life throughout 3M. The culture appeals to imaginative and inquisitive people who share technology and information across the entire organization. Bootlegging is highly respectable at 3M; most other companies discourage or even penalize peo-ple for "thinking out of the box" about new products, new markets, and new applications. Management at 3M has a high tolerance for experimentation and risk taking. In encouraging risk taking, 3M's cultural advantage goes back to its visionary CEO, William McKnight, who stated more than 50 years ago, "Put fences around people and you'll get an organization of sheep." 3M takes new uses for technology seriously. Today, 3M is applying the latest technologies such as microreplication, adhesives, and fiber optics to a wide range of new applications.

Some of 3M's most famous products are the result of perseverance and mistakes; sandpaper, Post-it Notes™, and Scotchgard are examples. If a company has a 50 percent success rate with new products (which is good,) look at all the failed cases they can learn from. Those companies like 3M that experiment will sometimes fail, but the smarter ones learn from their failures. *If a company cannot safely analyze, discuss, and learn from its failures, it is bound to repeat them again and again.*

THE GROWTH DIAGNOSTIC

The 14-point growth diagnostic was designed to help audit any industrial company's growth capabilities. Precision is not the key to using this diagnostic; objectivity is. Experience shows that individuals should first make their own ratings. Then consensus (not average) ratings should be developed through cross-functional group discussions. The involvement of all business areas in rating these factors is very important. With the possible exception of a general manager, most individuals in an organization do not have the firsthand knowledge necessary to render an intel-ligent judgment on all fourteen factors. Even the general manager is often too far removed from certain areas of the business to really know how different areas are operating. Also, differing opinions and constructive arguments tend to get the entire group more deeply and objectively involved than any individual is likely to be on his or her own. The give-and-take discussion of rating each factor is a healthy exercise. Moreover, a better basis exists for improving low ratings when the determination is made by a group of cross-functional managers seeking a consensus on each factor rather than by an individual who could be viewed as simply having an ax to grind.

It doesn't make sense to improve on all the low ratings at once. The factors receiving the lowest ratings are not necessarily those needing improvement. Because of the time commitment and degree of change involved, most organizations can only digest corrective actions in three or at most, four areas at once. This means priorities must be set by a cross-functional team. Select and prioritize the three areas that your team feels need improvement. After identifying three of the fourteen areas for improvement, detailed improvement programs must be outlined for each of the three factors (see Exhibit 15-1).

Let's also examine the major underlying reasons for the weaker ratings on each of the fourteen factors and some of the comments made by workshop participants to describe the growth deficiencies in their company.

Exhibit 15-1

Market Driven Growth Diagnostic

Liabilities	-5	0	+5	Advantages	Consensus
1. Market facts about customer needs, trends and competition are nonexistent, unverified, or underutilized in planning and decision making.		‖‖‖‖‖‖‖‖‖‖		1. The value of market facts about customers' unmet needs, market trends, and competition is widely recognized as the foundation for all planning and decision making.	
2. Market segment definitions are too broad or based on an industry, products, technology, manufacturing, or customer sizes in each country and region.		‖‖‖‖‖‖‖‖‖‖		2. Market segments and key accounts are defined by common needs and prioritized as attack, counterattack, deemphasize, and withdraw in each country and region of the world.	
3. Side-by-side competitive comparisons are nonexistent, unverified, too broad, internal, or underutilized in decision making.		‖‖‖‖‖‖‖‖‖‖		3. Competitor analysis is done by segment, country, and region of the world and is used to develop product/market strategies.	
4. Accounting systems driven by GAAP and upward reporting rather than for management decision making.		‖‖‖‖‖‖‖‖‖‖		4. Net profitability is reported, shared, and reviewed regularly for each product line, customer, market segment, and distributor.	
5. Lower cost and productivity gains are unsupported, but competitor actions and results imply otherwise.		‖‖‖‖‖‖‖‖‖‖		5. Documented side-by-side comparisons show that all costs and productivity gains are in line with or lower than the best competitor's.	
6. Quality goals, product performance, and customer satisfaction measurements are nonexistent or talked about without programs for continual improvements.		‖‖‖‖‖‖‖‖‖‖		6. Superior quality is consistently demonstrated through global side-by-side comparisons of yield rates, product performance, delivery, services, and customer satisfaction.	
7. Machine efficiency and capacity utilization considerations dominate product line and customer mix decisions.		‖‖‖‖‖‖‖‖‖‖		7. Manufacturing achieves continuous productivity gains that lower costs and they seek a richer product and customer mix.	
8. Response and cycle times in many departments are lagging, and programs are not in place to improve response times and create a sense of urgency.		‖‖‖‖‖‖‖‖‖‖		8. Response and cycle times are equal or superior to the best competitors, and the organization relentlessly searches for more speed.	
9. Existing raw materials, know-how, and current technology suppress thinking about emerging market needs and new opportunities.		‖‖‖‖‖‖‖‖‖‖		9. People are willing to think beyond existing materials and technologies to serve current customer needs and new market segments.	
10. New products and services are too late, too costly, or not demonstrably better for target customer groups and are not a major source of sales and profits.		‖‖‖‖‖‖‖‖‖‖		10. New products and services are a major source of sales and profits and are developed by cross-functional teams focused on verified user needs, and benefits.	
11. Sales training is mostly product and feature driven, at odds with target market priorities, company profit goals, customer benefits, and competitive offerings.		‖‖‖‖‖‖‖‖‖‖		11. All direct and distributor sales training activities are focused to solve customer problems and communicate customer value to target markets and accounts.	
12. The organization is too structured around functions, wide families of products, large accounts, with too much bureaucracy and insufficient accountability.		‖‖‖‖‖‖‖‖‖‖		12. The organization is relatively flat, informal, and focused on small families of products or markets, and net profit responsibility is assigned for each major product, market, and key account.	
13. Planning is done sequentially by individuals and functions, and without necessary market focus, cross-functional integration, or team commitments.		‖‖‖‖‖‖‖‖‖‖		13. Cross-functional teams develop and implement business plans for each product, market, and key account to achieve sales and profit goals.	
14. Recognition and reward programs are not aligned to market priorities, to short- and long-term goals and individuals, business teams, and business unit performance.		‖‖‖‖‖‖‖‖‖‖		14. Recognition and reward programs honor both short- and long-term results and are aligned with market priorities that recognize individuals, business teams, and business unit performance.	

Factor 1: Market Fact

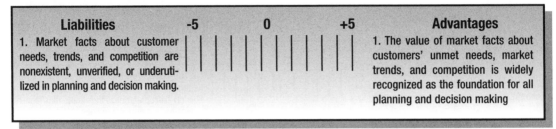

Many managers are unaware of the importance of market information about customers, market segments, and competition as a basis for all plans and decisions. Too few companies invest the time or effort required to obtain market facts. These same uninformed managers do not see the value of market information as key to selecting a focus in the business unit. With global markets and more rapidly changing customer requirements, the need for facts about customers and competition is greater than ever. Some typical comments from our workshops are given here:

- Our general managers and product managers don't believe that fact-based market information is key to product/market selection and don't budget any significant time or money to obtain such information, and they often waste big money without these vital facts.
- The value of marketing research is simply not appreciated by middle or top management, and market studies and verifications of customer needs are often dismissed in favor of gut feelings, hunches, or folklore.
- We need to know more about market trends, and our sales force needs to do a better job of gathering and sharing competitive intelligence.

Factor 2: Market Segment Definitions

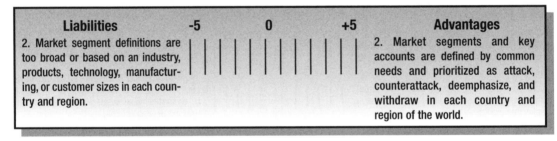

Market segmentation as a business practice has long been recognized and accepted in the consumer goods sector, but among industrial and high-tech manufacturers there has been no corresponding level of interest and rigor. However, the identification and selection of market segments is the most important strategic decision facing every industrial firm. Everything else follows this strategic decision. The following comments demonstrate this common weakness:

- We think too broadly about market segments and, as a result, miss the attractive opportunities our faster competitors capture.
- We think and act in terms of accounts—not in terms of target market segments. We equate a customer with a market segment.
- The value of our products and services vary greatly between different market segments, but we don't change the language, benefits received, or the prices charged to the respective segments and then customers.

Factor 3: Side-by-Side Competitive Comparisons

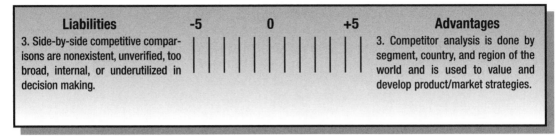

Liabilities	-5	0	+5	Advantages
3. Side-by-side competitive comparisons are nonexistent, unverified, too broad, internal, or underutilized in decision making.				3. Competitor analysis is done by segment, country, and region of the world and is used to value and develop product/market strategies.

Most managers are routinely required to make some kind of competitive statements in their planning process. However, it is usually a superficial listing of presumed strengths and weaknesses made with very little factual information, a reluctance to pinpoint fundamental advantages of competitors, and an exaggerated opinion of their company. Very few suppliers routinely do side-by-side comparisons of themselves and competitors on key dimensions. Here, again, are typical comments:

- We do broad-brush competitive analysis when it needs to be done by each application or market segment and in each region of the world.
- We need to compare ourselves against segment competitors on product performance, service, price, profitability, and other business factors in a war room.
- We need to learn more about the fastest-growing competitors in each market segment, not just the biggest or oldest players.

Factor 4: Accounting Systems and Net Profit

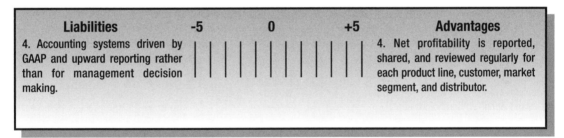

Liabilities	-5	0	+5	Advantages
4. Accounting systems driven by GAAP and upward reporting rather than for management decision making.				4. Net profitability is reported, shared, and reviewed regularly for each product line, customer, market segment, and distributor.

Many companies have incredibly inaccurate accounting information for decision making. Too many managers are still willing to settle for a profit report at the gross margin level or for profit-and-loss statements that relate to big families of products. They fail to realize that gross margins, at best, tell only half the story and that individual products within families often have significantly different cost-profit structures. When there are large pieces of shared costs that are not allocated, it is a sure clue that the supplier does not know its costs. Few companies know what it really costs to serve their key accounts. Typical comments include the following:

- We really don't work too closely with our controllers. We simply take the reports they give us as gospel. We have little confidence in the data they generate.
- Our controller says that he cannot accurately allocate the costs necessary to give me a true product-line profit-and-loss statement. We need to sit down with all the managers and match more of the shared costs to the products and customers.
- My overhead charge is calculated on a formula basis. I know it is way too high and the main reason my reported profit is so low.

Factor 5: Lower Cost and Productivity Gains

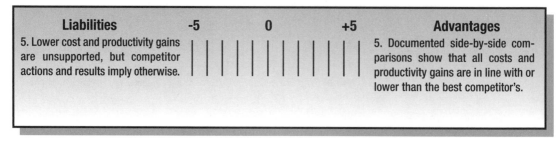

Liabilities	-5	0	+5	Advantages
5. Lower cost and productivity gains are unsupported, but competitor actions and results imply otherwise.				5. Documented side-by-side comparisons show that all costs and productivity gains are in line with or lower than the best competitor's.

Most managers too often make self-serving statements about being a lower-cost producer without having a factual basis for making this claim. It may sound good to stock analysts, but it is a highly suspect claim when margins are slim and competitors are selling the same product at a lower price. Many managers still don't know their own costs, and even fewer know their competitors' costs. Here are representative comments:

- We have always claimed to be the lower-cost producer, but some of our competitors have fewer management levels, less overhead, state-of-the-art manufacturing, and more sales and profit per employee.
- Because we know so little about our competitors' cost structures, especially the private and foreign ones, how can we really say that we are the low-cost supplier?
- We need to realize that without lower costs and sufficient gross margins we will not be able to sustain profitable top-line growth.

Factor 6: Quality Goals and Product Performance

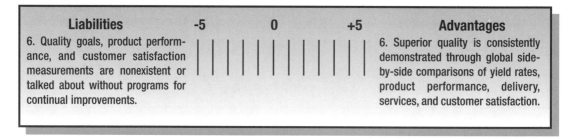

Liabilities	-5	0	+5	Advantages
6. Quality goals, product performance, and customer satisfaction measurements are nonexistent or talked about without programs for continual improvements.				6. Superior quality is consistently demonstrated through global side-by-side comparisons of yield rates, product performance, delivery, services, and customer satisfaction.

Every company I know talks a lot about quality and being a "world-class supplier." The fact is only a very few companies can clearly show that they do have superior quality or that they are "world class" in anything. Few companies identify sources of customer dissatisfaction and turn them into sources of satisfaction. Typical comments include the following:

- All the emphasis we have placed on quality has not shown up in results. We still have too much scrap and rework, too many customer complaints, high warranty costs, and too many competitors with equal or superior-performing products.
- We have talked a lot about quality, but our priorities have been on cost reductions, and our design engineers and manufacturing people rarely consider global quality standards.
- We forget that quality standards are a moving global target. Sure we have improved, but some of our competitors, especially foreign ones, have improved even faster, and we have slower delivery times.

Factor 7: Machine Efficiency and Capacity

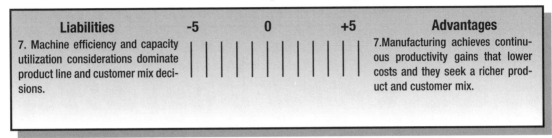

Liabilities	-5	0	+5	Advantages
7. Machine efficiency and capacity utilization considerations dominate product line and customer mix decisions.				7. Manufacturing achieves continuous productivity gains that lower costs and they seek a richer product and customer mix.

Many companies haphazardly add capacity, and most managers believe that too many manufacturing decisions are made independently and are often at odds with market facts, global capacity, and profit objectives. They are usually very reluctant to consider alternative approaches that would better serve customer needs and too quick to say something can't be done even though competitors are doing it. Here is what managers said:

- Our manufacturing investments and programs are not linked to the business plan, pricing strategy, needed customer lead times, or optimizing profit.
- Our manufacturing resists sourcing from Central Europe and Southeast Asia like the plague. They claim it doesn't make sense when we have open capacity. Yet our competitors are doing this and have a much lower cost as a result.
- Our manufacturing people just want to keep the plants filled and add more capacity when we could probably make more money with fewer products, fewer customers, and less production capacity.

Factor 8: Response and Cycle Times

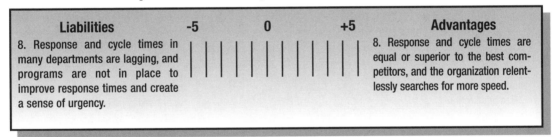

Liabilities	-5	0	+5	Advantages
8. Response and cycle times in many departments are lagging, and programs are not in place to improve response times and create a sense of urgency.				8. Response and cycle times are equal or superior to the best competitors, and the organization relentlessly searches for more speed.

Improvements have been made in manufacturing and delivery cycles, but not enough to catch up with many foreign and some smaller domestic competitors. Also, far too little time and attention has been directed toward improving response time in the service side of the business. It still takes too long to respond to customer questions or requests for special quotes, solve customer problems, and so on. Typical comments are listed here:

- Our setup and cycle times are still too long and unpredictable. We repeatedly miss promised dates because we can't ship to schedule and have no sense of urgency.
- Our response to customers' requests on specials takes three to five days. Our toughest competitor does this the same day.
- Our sales guys have claimed we lose a lot of profitable business because we don't respond to or solve problems quickly. Our best competitors respond with a heightned sense of urgency.

Factor 9: Existing Raw Materials, Know-How, and Current Technology

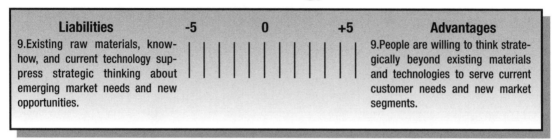

Liabilities	-5	0	+5	Advantages
9.Existing raw materials, know-how, and current technology suppress strategic thinking about emerging market needs and new opportunities.				9.People are willing to think strategically beyond existing materials and technologies to serve current customer needs and new market segments.

A deep-rooted commitment to existing technology, investments in special-purpose plant and equipment, and a general discomfort with the idea of moving into any completely new product or process combine to make most managers uneasy about even considering a departure from the status quo. Blindly sticking with existing products and technologies while these market changes occur, though, is a sure prescription for failure. The following comments from workshop participants indicate the types of problems that exist in this area:

- When a market segment begins to move to a different product form, new material, or new technology, we usually continue investing in yesterday's technology.
- Most of our senior management have backgrounds in yesterday's products and technologies. They give lip service to new technologies but won't seriously consider anything new.
- Our technical and salespeople are well schooled in our existing technology. Shifting to anything new would require a big change.

Factor 10. New Products and Services

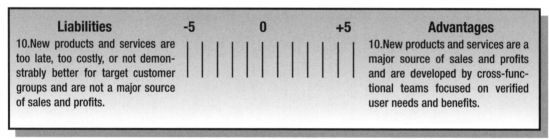

Liabilities	-5	0	+5	Advantages
10.New products and services are too late, too costly, or not demonstrably better for target customer groups and are not a major source of sales and profits.				10.New products and services are a major source of sales and profits and are developed by cross-functional teams focused on verified user needs and benefits.

New-product activities continue to be a contentious area largely because technical development groups are perceived as too independent in setting priorities and establishing their own pace. Both marketing and sales managers, who claim that the research and development group doesn't listen to them, hold this perception. R&D managers also have their complaints. They say manufacturing never meets new product cost targets, marketing never achieves their sales projections, and many salespeople lack the skill or aptitude to sell the new products:

- Our technical people are isolated from customers and marketing. They operate with no sense of urgency. We don't do post-launch reviews, and then learn.
- Our R&D people don't get close enough to customers—it is why they develop differentiated products that are not better in the customer's eyes.
- We can't take forever to develop new products. Life cycles are shrinking, and we have to get demonstrably better new products out much faster and launch them as if they were perishable fruit.

Factor 11. Sales Training for Solutions and Benefits

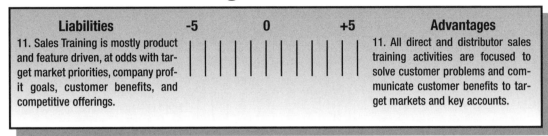

Liabilities	-5	0	+5	Advantages
11. Sales Training is mostly product and feature driven, at odds with target market priorities, company profit goals, customer benefits, and competitive offerings.				11. All direct and distributor sales training activities are focused to solve customer problems and communicate customer benefits to target markets and key accounts.

The problem in this area is that most sales training and sales promotion programs are product and feature driven. Markets have not been segmented, so there is no basis for designing sales programs that relate to specific customer benefits. These same companies rarely know the benefits of their products and services to their customers' customers. Thus, most sales training and promotion materials are tied to general product features and undocumented claims. Typical comments include these:

- We do product feature training with our factory and distribution people. We do little, if any, training on how to identify customer problems and how to document the tangible and intangible benefits of our products and services.
- Many of our sales representatives are in the comfort zone with their old accounts, and some are having difficulty with the increased complexity of our products and the customers' applications. We don't provide salespeople with any direction, selling tools, profit information, or incentives to improve the sales and profit of their accounts and territories.
- Our best competitors do problem solving and reference selling with a laptop computer. They also trust their salespeople with profit information and make them the account team leader.

Factor 12: The Organization Is Informal and Focused

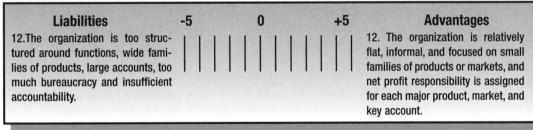

Liabilities	-5	0	+5	Advantages
12.The organization is too structured around functions, wide families of products, large accounts, too much bureaucracy and insufficient accountability.				12. The organization is relatively flat, informal, and focused on small families of products or markets, and net profit responsibility is assigned for each major product, market, and key account.

Many companies have done a reasonably good job of stripping away or cutting back staff groups and management layers that were obviously redundant, unneeded, or bottlenecks. However, it is apparent that a lot more work needs to be done. Far too many managers still complain about bureaucracy, interfunctional friction, and high overhead costs. Some representative comments are given here:

- We are still missing major opportunities because our decision-making and response time is too slow. Just look at all the longwinded meetings and lengthy memos that are a waste of time.
- All our cost-reduction savings last year were more than offset by increased overhead charges that provided no customer or shareowner value.

- Our managers are more loyal to their department than they are to the company or business unit. We just manage department silos and don't work well across functions to profitably serve customers.

Factor 13: Planning by Cross-Functional Business Teams

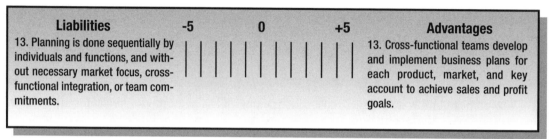

Liabilities	-5	0	+5	Advantages
13. Planning is done sequentially by individuals and functions, and without necessary market focus, cross-functional integration, or team commitments.				13. Cross-functional teams develop and implement business plans for each product, market, and key account to achieve sales and profit goals.

Most companies go through some type of formalized planning process. Planning schedules are published, planning meetings are held, planning forms and schedules are completed, and planning presentations are made. All this involves a great deal of work from many people, and there is an audible sigh of relief when the ritual is completed for another year. Unfortunately, in most companies all these efforts are long on form and frighteningly short on substance and implementation. Typical comments include the following:

- Our planning is a form-filling exercise for budgeting purposes with little cross-functional input and team buy-in.
- Department heads with baton-like hand-offs perform our planning. We are then given marching orders, and we wonder why implementation is weak or nonexistent.
- Our planning is still too top-down and around division activities as a whole. We need to do more bottom-up product/market planning for smaller pieces of business and then recognize and reward cross-functional teams for their results.

Factor 14: Recognition and Reward Programs

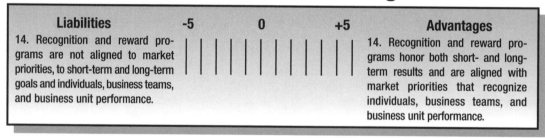

Liabilities	-5	0	+5	Advantages
14. Recognition and reward programs are not aligned to market priorities, to short-term and long-term goals and individuals, business teams, and business unit performance.				14. Recognition and reward programs honor both short- and long-term results and are aligned with market priorities that recognize individuals, business teams, and business unit performance.

Most managers are very critical of their incentive systems, claiming they are much too short-term oriented, usually paying off for quarterly or backward-looking annual performance. Others complain that the pay system resembles a nonprofit bureaucracy. Cross-functional teams are not accountable for results. There is no alignment with individuals, teams, or business unit performance. Frequent comments include the following:

- To make this concept work, we need both individual and business team incentives. Otherwise, team efforts will be subordinate to the functional or department interests.
- Our performance and pay systems recognize mediocrity and seniority. We need more variable pay based on goals, plans, and results.
- Accountability is inversely related to your organizational position in the

hierarchy-there is no reward for hustling or taking risks at the middle or lower levels.

Getting consensus agreement from give-and-take discussions on the ratings for each of the fourteen factors is only the starting point within each division or business unit and region of the world. Next comes the far more difficult task of determining how deficiencies can be corrected.

OVERCOMING DEFICIENCIES

Consensus agreement means that the division or business unit team has made a collective judgment that their business unit's performance on various factors is good or bad or needs improvement in certain areas. The profile they develop defines the problem areas and indicates the magnitude of improvement needed. If the ratings made by managers in our workshops are an indication of the norm, major improvements will be necessary in multiple areas.

General or business unit managers must lead their team in deciding which problems are most serious, what priorities should be established, and who should be assigned responsibility for corrective programs. Assuming strong general management leadership in this cross-functional team process, my experience suggests several guidelines that should be helpful to any management team seeking to improve their position:

1. There are no quick fixes to the cross-functional team's low ratings on any of the factors. Deficiencies will probably take many months to correct and will require fundamental departures from past management practices.
2. All areas of the diagnostic needing improvement cannot be addressed at once. Priorities must be set. Focus corrective actions on 3 of these 14 factors needing the most improvement. Develop action programs for improving each of the three areas with people responsible and with agreed to completion milestones.
3. It is better to assign improvement areas to small cross-functional teams rather than individuals. Doing so encourages a broader evaluation of the problems and helps avoid functionally biased solutions.
4. Team assignments must not be taken lightly. Each team should come up with concrete improvement programs that are acceptable to the entire management team and be held accountable for progress throughout implementation with firm milestones.
5. Don't look at the rating scale as a one-time tool. It should be institutionalized as part of the planning process and used repeatedly to measure performance and progress and to determine whether and where further improvements are needed.

The ultimate competitive advantage lies in an organization's capability to learn and to rapidly transform the learning into action. The market-driven growth diagnostic is also a way of identifying the best practices in each business unit and then spreading those practices throughout the organization. The ultimate purpose is to share ideas from other business units and to make the entire organization better. Hallmark companies do both internal and external benchmarking. Great improvement ideas can come from anyone and anywhere. The key is then getting people to understand what to do and how to mobilize their improvement efforts. Once you have everybody trying to "one-up" each other, the creativity and results are enormous.

ROLE OF TRAINING AND DEVELOPMENT

In most cases, accelerating profitable top-line growth requires a fundamental cultural change throughout the organization. As we all know, cultures don't change easily, and it is unlikely that many companies will be able to make the transition entirely on their own. The deficiencies that typically surface on the growth rating scale are deeply entrenched in the organization, and the attitudes of many people must be changed before meaningful improvements can be made. However, the task of overcoming the identified weaknesses usually requires cultural changes throughout the organization, first from top management commitment, and then from a high impact training program.

Top Management Commitment

It is hard to find a senior executive who does not believe that training is important. But when asked who should be actively involved in supporting and delivering training, already over-worked executives typically delegate the entire process to someone else, either because "they don't have the time" or because they believe training is "best left to a specialist" like those in HR who usually don't have a clue on what training is needed for profitable top-line growth. The delegation or abdication of training by senior executives is exactly the wrong thing to do. Management development is precisely what senior executives should be actively involved in. Andy Grove, chairman of Intel, and Jack Welch, chairman of GE, are two progressive executives who are very involved in their companies' management development programs. Do these great leaders know something that most CEOs and senior management don't know?

For any successful high-impact training program, top management must be totally committed to the program. Like the quality movement, top management has to be behind the training to make it happen. Senior managers in great companies realize that training is one of the few ways they have to really change the people or the culture. Every CEO, group president and general manager should consider training to be a lever for cultural improvement and any culture that is not improving is stagnant. Enlightened CEOs, are in fact, playing the role of chief learning officer by spending a significant amount of their time facilitating learning and building educational partnerships with the world's best training resources. As a good example, at the kickoff of each management development workshop for Unilever's industrial companies, their chairman, J. I. W. Anderson, stated at many of our workshops across the globe:

> You have no idea how little influence I have here. Management training is the only way we can continually move ourselves to the forefront of practice and results. With just one better decision, we will get the investment back from this workshop. If you think of this practical workshop as an expense, just try ignorance as an alternative.

To be a continuously outstanding business unit, a company must be open to changing anything, even some of the company's basic beliefs if they are out of alignment with the realities of today's employees, customers and global competition. Top or general managers who have tried to change a strong culture know that it is easy to talk about what should be done but far harder to get people to shed their inward-looking focus and historical approaches that no longer work. In companies I work with to improve their growth capabilities, there are often decades of old culture to change. Cross-functional teams must be involved in real issues at the workshop, and then they must immediately apply the better practices learned to support the old training point, "You must use it, or you will lose it."

There are six top management "musts" to make profitable top-line growth training successful:

1. Top management must see training as a way to maintain high performance over the long term and as a way to evolve, change, or continually improve the culture.
2. Top management must see profitable top-line growth as a general management or business unit responsibility and a cross-functional team process, not just limited to the sales and marketing people.

3. Top management must participate in the needs analysis and open the company up to an outside review of their management practices.

4. Top management must participate in an executive overview or, ideally, experience the entire workshop.

5. Top management must be part of the opening and especially the ending of each workshop session, where each cross-functional team's first-draft business plan, strategy and action programs for the company's product line, market segment, and key accounts are presented.

6. Top and general management must become partners with the workshop leader before and after the pilot session and during the entire training transformation process.

Top management must also be willing to create and maintain a working environment that will support and sustain the training. This is the acid test that any training must pass before it is rolled out to the masses. There is little or no point in teaching people new skills and approaches and then sending them back to an environment where it is nearly impossible to apply the training. I once worked with an industrial company that was sending its most promising managers to a weeklong program on global management. Top management wanted to evolve the organization to global business units. Yet the company still had a strong regional vice presidents organization, which resisted the concept of doing anything globally. Top management, had no follow-up to detect this huge discrepancy, and the program soon was viewed as a week of fun and relaxation.

Over many years I have developed and fine-tuned a proven management development process to accelerate profitable top-line growth in any industrial company. An overview of the management development process to accelerate growth is shown in Exhibit 15-2.

Exhibit 15-2

Management Development Overview

Stage 1 Pre-Work	Stage 2 4-5 Day Workshop	Stage 3 Interim Period (optional)	Stage 4 Follow-Up (optional)
▸ Company growth opportunities are identified and the corresponding cross-functional teams are established. ▸ Assigned readings and cross-functional team exercises based upon the needs analysis. ▸ Teams bring information about a growth opportunity to the workshop.	▸ Fundamental concepts and building blocks. ▸ 14-point growth diagnostic audit and three areas for improvement with action plans. ▸ First draft of the business plan for the company growth opportunity is presented to top management.	▸ Cross-functional team members gather additional information for the business plan. ▸ Cross-functional team meetings to finalize the business plan. ▸ Implementation of the three areas to improve from the 14-point growth diagnostic.	▸ Final adjustments to the business plan are presented by the team to top management for review. ▸ The team presents a progress report on the action programs for the three diagnostic areas being improved. ▸ Follow-up progress reviews

2 to 3 months ⟶

4 to 6 months ⟶

Great Role Models

Many corporations have created corporate universities that continually offer a range of in-house training programs to their employees. Some of these industrial companies include 3M,

Cabot, Dana, Dofasco, Dow, FedEx, General Electric, Intel, Milliken, and Parker Hannifin. As a percentage of sales, how much do great companies invest in management development? FedEx invests about 4 percent of sales on all types of training programs. Dofasco, the well-run Canadian steel maker, invests more than $17 million annually to develop the skills its people need. Dana Corporation and AlliedSignal (now Honeywell) both require every employee, including the CEO, to complete forty hours of training every year. Larry Bossidy, the former chairman of AlliedSignal (and a twenty-seven-year veteran of GE), believes it should be spending about 2 percent of sales on training year after year. A congressional study a few years ago found that the average U.S. worker at large firms spent 2.5 percent of his or her time on training compared with 8 to 10 percent among workers at German and Japanese firms. Intel invests more than $900 million on employee training. Andy Grove, chairman of Intel, teaches a course on preparing and delivering performance reviews. Grove argues that performance reviewers, which most managers do not pay sufficient attention to, are an excellent way to gain insights into the types of training and development your people need.

The granddaddy of all training programs (in terms of age and results) is General Electric's Crotonville, New York, campus. About 10,000 GE employees take at least one course at Crotonville each year. In many of the programs, participants attend in natural cross-functional business teams and are given action-learning assignments that directly pertain to their business unit. Throughout the difficult period in the 1980s and early 1990s when GE was downsizing (U.S. employment went from 300,000 to 180,000), the company kept investing in its Crotonville management development programs. GE spends more than $1 billion a year on its various training programs conducted at Crotonville and elsewhere. Having taught at Crotonville, I can say there is something unique about the fifty-acre complex. Other companies have corporate retreats that they own or send people to, but GE's approach is unique in two ways. First, every program, whether it is three days or three weeks in length, is intensive and competitive, and nearly everyone "speaks up" about current and proposed company practices. Second, the GE management development programs have always used forums as a place for the CEO and other senior top executives to mingle, ask questions, and to facilitate part of one session. Senior executives encourage and embrace the lively debates about what constitutes good management, and the search for better practices is always the outcome.

Corporate universities are a definite threat to traditional university business school programs. The growing relevance of in-house corporate universities, stresses active, not passive learning teams that work with the instructor on their real growth opportunities. More and more corporate universities have identified management experts who are able to develop and deliver high impact workshops for managers. Most of these experts have spent 20 or 30 years developing a global reputation with their practical industrial articles and books. The workshop leaders must be current, practical, dynamic, and have excellent executive workshop skills and references. Finally, astute companies don't accept hand-offs from the senior workshop leader to someone less qualified. The person who conducts the needs analysis is the same person who develops and presents the interactive workshop sessions.

Partnerships with Your Business Teams

If there is one race that every CEO must win, it is the race for skilled workers at all levels of the organization. In overwhelming numbers, chief executives single out the shortage of qualified personnel as a great barrier to profitable top-line growth. A company's ability to learn and innovate is a direct result of the company's capability to increase revenues, profits, and shareowner value. To launch new and better products, enter new markets and countries, improve operating efficiencies, and creating more value for customers requires the ability to learn. Without an ability to rapidly learn and adapt, a company's size and current market positions are irrelevant. It is refreshing to see a growing number of corporations realize that management development and training can have a significant effect on profitable top-line growth. These same companies know that to consistently grow the top line you need to maintain nonstop learning.

The truly great companies do not relegate employee development and training to discretionary budget items. When a business slow-up occurs, management development and training is not the first area for budget cuts. *These few companies realize that their competitive advantage is tied to the knowledge of their employees and they know that knowledge is not sustainable; it is temporary and you must keep investing in it.* Yet when the economy slows and times get tough, many companies invest less or stop training as a way to keep profits up. That's just dumb. People do become obsolete: They also need to grow. Can you imagine postponing maintenance on a jet aircraft for twelve months or never doing preventive maintenance in a plant? Great companies avoid this mistake. They recruit good people and keep making them better and, thus, more competitive.

There may never again be life-long job security in most companies. However, as long as a person is cost effectively adding value to the organization, job security will probably exist. Training is key to remaining a value-added employee. Today, anyone who wants to keep a job must be continually updated in that job and be prepared for wider responsibilities.

The old implied social contract—you work hard and we will give you a job for as long as you want—no longer exists. Job security no longer comes from "hanging around," but from maintaining current job-related skills. This shift signals a new psychological contract between employer and employee. Under the terms of this new contract, employers provide learning in place of job security.

As management knowledge and skills become antiquated at a faster rate, smart companies realize they have no choice but to invest more in training for their business teams. There are no quick fixes for continually developing and updating your people. Hiring bright or smart people is never enough. Advanced degrees from prestigious universities are never substitutes for nonstop learning and working smarter. There is no one more stupid than a bright person with little or no common sense, and the best industrial growth strategies make a lot of common sense; unfortunately they are not always commonly known or practiced.

In great industrial companies, top executives view themselves as personnel managers with the responsibility to place the right people in the right jobs at the right time and with the right skills. These few companies spend many days every month discussing their people, assessing their ability to be promoted, and determining what kinds of training they need. Bob Lurcott, president of Henkel Surface Technologies, says it well:

> All of our senior executives see themselves as talent scouts. They are constantly assessing people's needs and areas for improving their deficiencies. As a result of this nonstop work, we try very hard to have future managers ready for broader responsibilities. Every manager at Henkel knows that in order to continue our excellent record, we must have competent and highly skilled professionals in place and cadres of people in various stages of development all around the world. Our senior executives and general managers spend at least 20 percent of their time on questions of management readiness and development.

Unless more companies begin to view employees as Bob Lurcott at Henkel does, they will probably not remain competitive in the long term. The industrial world is not a steady state. User needs are changing more frequently. Global competitors are constantly on the prowl for your customers and employees. Markets fluctuate and technologies continue to change in even the most mature industrial markets. The longer any industrial manufacturer rests on its laurels, self- and public praise, and outdated management practices, the more likely it will be to fall behind and suffer all the negative consequences.

The workshop leader must team up with the CEO or COO to create the needed changes. Top management and people lower in the organization are typically very eager to embrace new ways to profitably grow the enterprise. However, sometimes the sources of resistance are general managers, and more often middle and department managers, who give lukewarm support or even sabotage the changes. The loss of power, respect, and ultimately their jobs is embedded in their initial resistance. Top management must change these people with training and coaching, or else they must eventually make personnel changes. Ken Burnes, the chairman and CEO of Cabot Corporation, a global specialty chemical company, said it well at each management workshop I conducted for his company around the world:

> "The purpose of this training investment is to increase the intellectual know-how and change the people. You will find this workshop interesting, challenging, practical and fun. However, if this training doesn't change all the people, we will then change some of the people."

SUMMARY

In many cases, becoming a high growth industrial company requires a fundamental cultural change throughout the organization. As we all know, cultures don't change easily, and it is unlikely that many companies will be able to make the transition entirely on their own. The deficiencies that typically surface on the diagnostic rating scale are deeply entrenched in the organization, and the attitudes of many people must be changed before meaningful improvements can be made. However, the task of overcoming the identified weaknesses usually requires learning throughout the organization. Open sharing across the enterprise is mandatory. Top management must realize that true change occurs by changing the people, first with intensive and practical in-house management training of natural cross-functional business teams, and if that doesn't work, by selectively changing some of the people who will not or cannot change. If top management has not created a culture conducive to non-stop learning, the top management must change itself or be replaced by leaders who create the environment for constant learning and improvement.

Clearly, reading about what it takes to create profitable top-line growth and actually doing what is necessary are two different things. I have shown how many great industrial companies achieve outstanding top-line results, even in depressed industries. There have been and always will be many opportunities for these very same great companies to fail during the life of this book. Ever-changing markets and technologies are capable of breaking any business organization if it is unprepared for change and has not developed the necessary mechanisms for anticipating and responding to change. Great industrial companies don't just react to the future; they create the future by constantly working smarter and plotting how they will achieve profitable top-line growth.

No company does everything well. Only by constant learning and training can any company secure its future. The hallmark industrial companies referred to in this book, realize that career long management learning is like rowing against the current in whitewater rapids. As soon as you stop, you will start going backward, and you may never catch up.

C

E

F

G

T

U